The Making and Unmaking of Francoist Kitsch Cinema

The Making and Unmaking of Francoist Kitsch Cinema

From *Raza* to *Pan's Labyrinth*

Alejandro Yarza

EDINBURGH
University Press

To my parents,
who faced the uglier side
of kitsch with courage
and dignity

Edinburgh University Press is one of the leading university presses in the UK. We publish academic books and journals in our selected subject areas across the humanities and social sciences, combining cutting-edge scholarship with high editorial and production values to produce academic works of lasting importance. For more information visit our website: edinburghuniversitypress.com

© Alejandro Yarza, 2018

Edinburgh University Press Ltd
The Tun—Holyrood Road
12 (2f) Jackson's Entry
Edinburgh EH8 8PJ

Typeset in Monotype Ehrhardt by
Servis Filmsetting Ltd, Stockport, Cheshire

A CIP record for this book is available from the British Library

ISBN 978 0 7486 9924 7 (hardback)
ISBN 978 0 7486 9923 0 (webready PDF)
ISBN 978 1 4744 2042 6 (epub)

The right of Alejandro Yarza to be identified as author of this work has been asserted in accordance with the Copyright, Designs and Patents Act 1988 and the Copyright and Related Rights Regulations 2003 (SI No. 2498).

Contents

List of Figures	vi
Acknowledgments	viii
Preface	xi
Introduction	1
1. The Petrified Tears of General Franco: Kitsch and Fascism in José Luis Sáenz de Heredia's *Raza*	23
2. *Romancero Marroquí* and the Francoist Kitsch Politics of Time	42
3. *Los últimos de Filipinas*: The Spatio-temporal Coordinates of Francoism	60
4. *Surcos*: Neorealism, Film Noir, and the Puppet Master	102
5. *Franco, ese hombre*: From Kitsch-Artist to Kitsch-Man	141
6. *Viridiana*: The World, the Flesh, and the Devil	179
7. *Balada triste de trompeta*: Of Ghosts and Clowns	203
8. Under the Sign of Saturn: The Labyrinth of Moral Choices in Francoist Spain	261
Works Cited	293
Index	311

Figures

P.1	*Blancanieves*, 2012	xii
P.2	*Blancanieves*, 2012	xiii
I.1	Carlos Sáenz de Tejada, 1940	6
I.2	Pedro Almodóvar as bullfighter	13
1.1	*Raza*, 1942	27
1.2	*Raza*, 1942	31
1.3	*Raza*, 1942	35
1.4	*Raza*, 1942	36
2.1	*Romancero marroquí*, 1939	49
2.2	*Romancero marroquí*, 1939	51
2.3	*Romancero marroquí*, 1939	53
2.4	*Romancero marroquí*, 1939	54
3.1	*Los últimos de Filipinas*, 1945	72
3.2	*Los últimos de Filipinas*, 1945	79
3.3	*Los últimos de Filipinas*, 1945	80
3.4	*Los últimos de Filipinas*, 1945	86
3.5	*Los últimos de Filipinas*, 1945	90
3.6	*Los últimos de Filipinas*, 1945	92
3.7	*Raza*, 1942	92
4.1	*Surcos*, 1951	110
4.2	*Surcos*, 1951	113
4.3	*Surcos*, 1951	115
4.4	*Surcos*, 1951	119
4.5	*Surcos*, 1951	125
4.6.	*Surcos*, 1951	126
4.7	*Surcos*, 1951	130
4.8	*Surcos*, 1951	131
4.9	*Surcos*, 1951	133
5.1	*Franco, ese hombre*, 1964	144
5.2	*Franco, ese hombre*, 1964	146
5.3	*Franco, ese hombre*, 1964	156
5.4	*Franco, ese hombre*, 1964	162
5.5	*Franco, ese hombre*, 1964	163

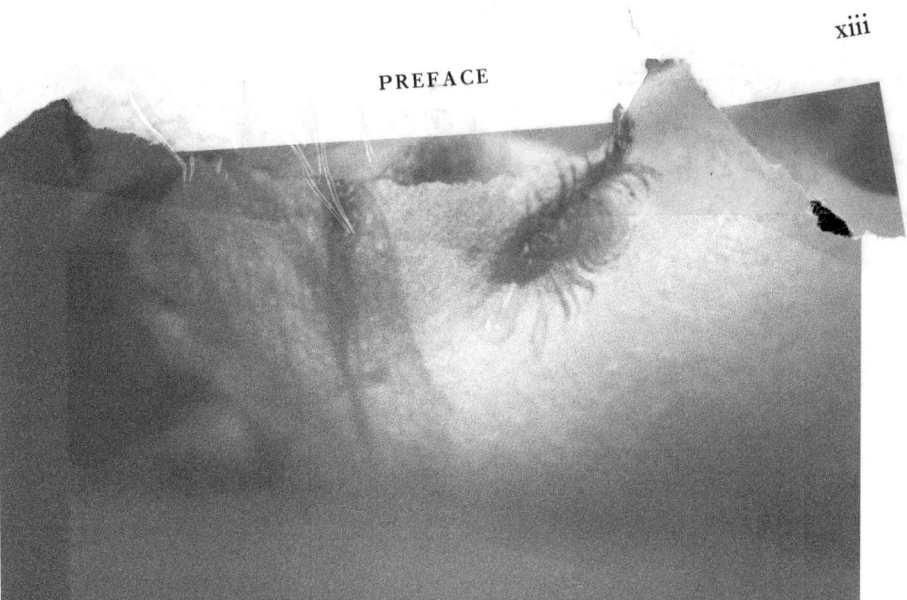

Figure P.2 *Blancanieves*, 2012

which they are rendered. They allow us to distinguish between the dulling effects of kitsch aesthetics (Encarna's tear) and the courageous solidarity shared with those who suffer (Carmencita's tear). I want to begin this study by calling attention to the lonely, single tear Carmencita sheds in the last scene of *Blancanieves*, a film that, through its allegorizing of bullfighting and of the persona of the innocent Carmencita, gets to the heart of Spanish kitsch and national identity.

Introduction

The side which things turn toward the dream is kitsch
—Walter Benjamin, *Selected Writings*

During his early life as an officer in the Spanish colonial army in Morocco, Francisco Franco was admired for his courage, which, oftentimes verging on reckless, assured him a rapid ascension of the military ladder.[1] Along with his bravery came extreme cruelty. Franco was feared by his soldiers—particularly once he became commander of the Spanish Foreign Legion in 1920—who knew he would not tolerate anything that in his mind amounted to insubordination, no matter how minor the perceived offense. Nevertheless, despite his unflinching sangfroid, and lack of compassion, Franco is reported to have cried often.

In his novel *The Unbearable Lightness of Being* (1984), Milan Kundera writes that, "Kitsch causes two tears to flow in quick succession. The first tear says: How nice to see children running on the grass! The second tear says: How nice to be moved, together with all mankind, by children running on the grass! It is the second tear that makes kitsch kitsch" (251). It is this second tear that provides the background for this study. The second tear, which flows from being moved together with all mankind—and in Franco's case also caused by a narcissistic identification with his self-appointed messianic role—implies both an initial separation from mankind as well as a longing to be reunited with it again. This longing to recover the original state of grace, to heal the wound opened up by human subjectivity—symbolically represented by the Fall—is the psychological subtext of kitsch. This is why Kundera defines kitsch, among other things, as the "categorical agreement with being" (251).

Since this desire emerges from the very nature of human subjectivity, Kundera concludes that the feeling induced by kitsch cannot depend on unique or unusual experiences, but "must be a kind the multitudes can share" (251). Kitsch, therefore, "must derive from the basic images people have engraved in their memories: the ungrateful daughter, the neglected father, children running on the grass, the motherland betrayed, first love" (251). In short, kitsch must derive from stock, prefabricated images, from clichés. When this yearning to recover the loss of a mythical state of grace transcends the level of fantasy and is brought down to the realm of politics, fascism is born. This is why, as Gillo Dorfles remarks, nothing "is more symptomatic of Kitsch than certain typical myths, such as the fascist and Nazi myths" (Dorfles 37).

Assuming a close, dialectical relationship between the aesthetic and political realms, this study examines the role of kitsch aesthetics in advancing Francoist totalitarian ideology and its subsequent undoing, which was already beginning during Franco's time. It explores the intersection between aesthetics and politics through the lens of kitsch and its relation to violence, and the silence that follows, in the context of European history.[2] More specifically, it engages the making and unmaking of Francoist kitsch aesthetics through the analysis of Spanish cinema by examining eight influential films ranging from 1938 to 2010: five Francoist films, and three oppositional films by critically acclaimed directors Luis Buñuel, Álex de la Iglesia and Guillermo del Toro who, by reimagining Francoist aesthetics' visual and narrative clichés, dismantled the fascist project.

In this study, the concept of kitsch is an important critical paradigm, which allows us to fully understand the ideological and aesthetic underpinnings of a significant number of Francoist films and their lasting effect on Spanish cinema and culture.[3] But it also helps explain Francoist and post-Francoist oppositional cinema, which itself dips into kitsch in order to overcome it. Throughout, kitsch is understood in terms of its fascist potential; what Saul Friedländer has called "uplifting kitsch," which he describes as being "rooted, symbol-centered, and emotionally linked to the values of a specific group" (27). This uplifting kitsch, which exploits mythical, cultural, and political patterns, has a clear mobilizing function: its emotionally coded and readily available messages are presented aesthetically and emotionally, eliciting from its audience an automatic and unreflective response.[4] This particular brand of kitsch, the kitsch of death, of destruction, the apocalyptic kitsch of "livid sk[ies] slashed by immense purple reflections, flames surging from cities, flocks and men fleeing toward the glowing horizon," which intoxicates with its romantic ideas of national belonging, is, as Friedländer remarks, the uplifting kitsch characteristic of fascism (2).

I understand Francoist kitsch to be an essential part of a politically eclectic discourse whose study brings together aesthetics, film theory, and the politics of fascist Spain. Drawing on conceptual work on fascism

Acknowledgments

Although writing is a solitary affair, it involves many people. I want to thank Georgetown University's Graduate School for the three summer research grants I received at the early stages of this project and, particularly, former Dean Gerald Mara for believing in it. I am most grateful to my colleagues in the Department of Spanish and Portuguese, and my Chair Gwen Kirkpatrick for her kind, unremitting support. I am also thankful to my former Chair, Alfonso Morales-Front, for his empathic support in the preliminary stages of this project. I am indebted to Bernie Cook, Caetlin Benson-Allot, Roberto Bocci, and the rest of my colleagues at the Film and Media Studies Program for providing a creative environment in which to think and write about film.

Special thanks to all my students throughout the years: their enthusiasm, intellectual honesty, and sharp critical comments have changed this study for the better. Without their frankness and contagious thirst for knowledge none of this would really be worth doing. Particular thanks to my former graduate students Eugenia Afinoguénova, Raquel Anido, Álvaro Baquero, Gabriela Copertari, Luis González, María José Navia, Trinidad Pardo-Ballester, Zaya Rustamova, and Bohumira Smidakova, who have enriched my intellectual life with their own and honored me with their friendship.

I am thankful to Carole Sargent, who with generosity and a steady hand helped me navigate the complicated waters of academic publishing. I wish to thank my research assistants Ashley Caja, Meagan Driver, and Porter O'Neill for their help and dedication. My warmest gratitude goes to Felipe Toro, Iván Espinosa, and Sophie Heller (a Vertovian "Council of Three") for their rigorous commitment to my project, their willingness to go beyond what is expected from them, their kindness, critical intelligence, and lively/wicked sense of humor. They brought rare joy to this solitary affair.

I also want to express my gratitude to my editor Gillian Leslie, and to Rebecca Mackenzie, Richard Strachan, Eddie Clark, Ian Brooke, and everyone else involved with the production of this book at Edinburgh University Press. This project could not have found a more caring and hospitable environment in which to come to fruition. I am forever grateful

5.6	*Franco, ese hombre*, 1964	170
6.1	*Viridiana*, 1961	184
6.2	*Viridiana*, 1961	185
6.3	*Viridiana*, 1961	186
6.4	*Viridiana*, 1961	187
6.5	*Viridiana*, 1961	192
6.6	*Viridiana*, 1961	194
6.7	*Viridiana*, 1961	197
6.8	*Viridiana*, 1961	198
7.1	*Balada triste de trompeta*, 2010	218
7.2	*Balada triste de trompeta*, 2010	222
7.3	*Balada triste de trompeta*, 2010	222
7.4	*Balada triste de trompeta*, 2010	229
7.5	*Balada triste de trompeta*, 2010	229
7.6	*Balada triste de trompeta*, 2010	238
7.7	*Balada triste de trompeta*, 2010	239
7.8	*Balada triste de trompeta*, 2010	241
7.9	*Balada triste de trompeta*, 2010	241
7.10	*Balada triste de trompeta*, 2010	242
7.11	*Balada triste de trompeta*, 2010	242
7.12	*Balada triste de trompeta*, 2010	244
7.13	*Balada triste de trompeta*, 2010	246
7.14	*Balada triste de trompeta*, 2010	248
7.15	*Balada triste de trompeta*, 2010	248
7.16	*Balada triste de trompeta*, 2010	251
8.1	*Pan's Labyrinth*, 2006	264
8.2	*Pan's Labyrinth*, 2006	267
8.3	*Pan's Labyrinth*, 2006	272
8.4	*Pan's Labyrinth*, 2006	275
8.5	*Pan's Labyrinth*, 2006	277
8.6	*Pan's Labyrinth*, 2006	277
8.7	*Pan's Labyrinth*, 2006	281
8.8	*Pan's Labyrinth*, 2006	283
8.9	*Pan's Labyrinth*, 2006	284

to Eva and Marta Yarza, the artistic wizards, for coming to the rescue and designing the final version of the cover. Thanks also to Raimundo Rubio for his artistic advice on the cover and his moral support and friendship. I am also grateful to Javier Herrera from the Filmoteca Española for providing valuable visual documentation. Many thanks, as well, to Changa Bell and Melissa Bruno for generously helping me with their technological expertise.

This book greatly benefited from the generous help of: Eugenia Afinoguénova, Celso Álvarez Cáccamo, Albert Andreu (kitsch enthusiast), Gabriela Copertari, Janis Jibrin, Luis González, Elena Herburger, Gastón Lillo, Karin Palmquist, Cathryn Teasley and Inés Yarza. I am indebted to all of them for their comments and suggestions at the different writing stages of the manuscript, and for their friendship and encouragement.

My deep gratitude goes to my brothers Javier, Juan José, and Joaquín, and my sister Ana, and to Marga García, Pilar Hilario, and Lola Fernández, and to my nieces and nephews, as well as to my extended Basque and Yugoslav families. And to Aksinja and Srećko Pesek I am thankful for their generosity and for opening their home to me and to this project. To Mary Froning I am most grateful for her uncanny wisdom and for just simply being there.

Additionally, thanks to the *Journal of Spanish Cultural Studies* (www.tandfonline.com) for granting me permission to include in Chapter 1 a revised version of my article "The Petrified Tears of General Franco: Kitsch and Fascism in Jose Luis Saenz de Heredia's *Raza*." And to Duke University Press for allowing me to include in Chapter 2 a revised version of "Romancero Marroquí and the Francoist Kitsch Politics of Time."

Special thanks to Lalitha Gopalan for reading and commenting on various chapters. Her relentless passion for film made the ups and downs of the writing process more bearable. I am also grateful to Carmela Ferradáns for revising several chapters and for her friendship and encouragement throughout the years. Ultimately, this project owes its existence, for better or for worse, to Alan Tansman who, several years ago, challenged me to embark on it. He never threw in the towel when others might have and graciously provided a safety net in which I could attempt a few conceptual pirouettes without the risk of being seriously hurt or, one hopes, publicly humiliated. To my amazement, he patiently edited countless versions of the manuscript and still remained a friend. I could not have asked for a more formidable yet irreverent intellectual guidance.

Finally, this project would not have been completed without the loving support of Sanja Pesek, who has humorously endured the darker side of writing. Her faith in me and in this project worked wonders. She tirelessly edited different versions of this study and steered me away from falling into treacherous conceptual holes. Without her luminous laughter, her willingness to discuss my half-baked ideas at any time and (almost) any place, her penetrating remarks and keen intelligence and, above all, her love, this project (and I) would have been irretrievably lost. *Volim te.*

Preface

In the climactic scene of *Blancanieves* [Snow White] (Berger, 2012), Carmencita, the young protagonist and a bullfighter who suffers from amnesia, faces Satanás, a mean, huge bull. Through a point of view shot which replicates that of the moment in which her father, a famous bullfighter, was severely gored, we see Satanás furiously running against Carmencita. At that precise moment—surrounded by the entire community gathered around the bullring—she begins to cry as flashes of her forgotten past suddenly rush through her mind. As tears fall profusely from her eyes, Satanás, a symbol of the evils of the Spanish past, stops in its tracks. Remembering now her father's instructions to never turn "your eyes away from the bull," Carmencita begins to fight with amazing grace, engaging in an intricate choreographic dance with the bull, a dance that suggests that only by directly confronting the past with courage can one co-exist with its devastating legacies.

To celebrate her bullfighting success, her evil stepmother, Encarna, gives Carmencita a poisoned apple as a gift. Encarna (Spanish for "incarnates") embodies the wicked, repressive historical forces that opportunistically took over Spain during Francoism. Because she is supposed to be in mourning for her husband's death, whom she in fact murdered, she is wearing a black veil and dress with a dark spot resembling a clown tear painted under her left eye (Fig. P.1). After some hesitation, Carmencita bites the apple and falls into a coma; this symbolizes the collective official amnesia suffered by Spain after the lost opportunity opened up by the brief political transitional moment, suggested by Carmencita's recovery of memory in front of the bull.

Unable to extract further profit from Carmencita as a matador, her unscrupulous agent decides to parade her in a freak show along with a troupe of dwarf bullfighter companions. For a fee, any spectator can kiss Carmencita/Blancanieves and witness first-hand the 'miracle' of her reawakening, which occurs when the agent activates a jack-in-the-box type of mechanism. In the last scene of the film we see Rafita, the nurturing dwarf who is in love with Carmencita, patiently brushing Carmencita's hair, applying lipstick to her mouth and perfume to her

Figure P.1 *Blancanieves*, 2012

body. He switches off the stage lights and lies down next to her in the see-through coffin in which she is on display. Before going to sleep, though, he leans over her and kisses her goodnight. At that very moment, the camera zooms in on Carmencita's right eye. After a brief second, a single tear slowly rolls down her face, and the film ends (Fig. P.2).

Reduced to a comatose state by her evil stepmother, Carmencita, the allegorical representation of Spain, appears to be moved by the tender care of her small companion. Carmencita's single tear represents the binding of a community through recognition of the kind, moral actions of the smallest of its members. While evil Encarna, in black attire with a tear painted on her cheek, pretends to go through the motions of mourning her famous husband's death, the good Carmencita, motionless, truly mourns the victims of Spain's evil past while waiting for the "miracle" of her reawakening to come.

By transporting the famous fairy tale to Spain in the early decades of the twentieth century, *Blancanieves* creates a pointed allegory about historical memory and the perils of forgetting the past. Carmencita's tear illustrates that although the past may never be mastered and cannot be ignored, we must act, for a rude moral awakening awaits us still. Her tear reminds us to remember.

Tears mean different things in this study, depending on the contexts in by thinkers such as Theodor Adorno, Walter Benjamin, Christopher Bollas, Mark Neocleous, and Susan Sontag, and studies on kitsch by Hermann Broch, Matei Calinescu, Gillo Dorfles, Umberto Eco, and Saul Friedländer, among others, I attempt to elucidate how Francoism appropriated the fetishistic nature of cinema and kitsch aesthetics, relying on its potential both to mobilize and hold ideological control over its audience and by extension over the Spanish citizenry more generally.

Drawing from recent scholarship as well as from more classic studies on the political and ideological nature of Francoism by Paul Preston, Michael Richards, and Ismael Saz Campos, among others, this study defines Francoism as a distinctive, politically, and aesthetically eclectic discourse that not only borrows extensively from fascist rhetoric and ideology—predominantly that of Italian fascism—but also incorporates the main themes and iconographic repertoire of traditional Spanish conservatism.[5] This happened with renewed intensity after the defeat of the Axis in 1945, when Francoist kitsch aesthetics began to draw on an existing repository of clichéd images of Spain originating in Europe's Romantic rediscovery of the country after Napoleon's exile to Elba in 1814, such as Prosper Mérimée's novel *Carmen* (1845) and Georges Bizet's subsequent opera (1875), the flamenco-inspired paintings of Édouard Manet and John Singer Sargent, and countless others. This notion of Spain as an exotic and rural country was also appropriated for political gain by Spain's hegemonic classes that sought to resist the reformist agenda of an enlightened elite. As we will see through the film *Surcos* (1951), for Spanish fascism, smallholding Castilian peasantry were still the authentic embodiment of *Hispanidad*.

This romantic kitsch image was perfectly encapsulated by Francoist Minister of Information and Tourism Manuel Fraga Iribarne's famous slogan "Spain is different," which in the 1960s was strategically used to attract tourists to Spain, cleverly combining the fetishism of the exotic with fetishism of the commodity. Carefully orchestrated by Franco's state-owned mass media, this kitsch image of Spain brought back to public consciousness an Orientalized notion of the nation—prevalent from the nineteenth century—that a more radical sector of Spanish fascists rejected. As we will see in Chapter 1, *Raza* (written by Franco under the pseudonym Jaime de Andrade) delineated the main characteristics of this Francoist kitsch aesthetic, whose extensive deployment of traditional Catholic iconography and religious themes markedly deviates from the more secular tenor of European fascism.

Like Spain's Orientalizing escapist reveries, kitsch is, as Broch has powerfully argued, an escapist lifeless "neurotic closed product" that smells, in Vladimir Nabokov's metaphor, like rotten conserved lobster (Broch 72).

Kitsch's lifeless fantasies fit perfectly with fascist politics' deadly fantasies and sinister contempt for human life. Since it communicates using "prefabricated expressions, which harden into clichés," kitsch tends toward the dogmatic influence of "what has already been" (Broch 72). It is precisely kitsch's hollowness that lends itself so well to it being co-opted by fascism. This is why, at a particular historical junction—arranging these "prefabricated expressions" around the "primitive syntax, of the constant beat of the drum"—kitsch became the ideal aesthetic of fascism (Broch 75).[6] And this is also why for Broch the producer of kitsch cannot be solely judged according to "aesthetic criteria; rather he should be judged as an ethically base being, a malefactor who profoundly desires evil" (Broch 75).

Nevertheless, contrary to Broch's somewhat dogmatic remarks, the potential for evil lurking inside the deceptive aesthetic system of kitsch is only a real threat when, as Kundera writes, a "single political movement corners power" (251). Only then, within "the realms of *totalitarian kitsch*," can it perform its deadly evil deed (251). Otherwise, kitsch is actually a needed lubricant of life; and, in fact, like fantasy, is necessary to sustain a "realistic" view of reality.[7] Kitsch, as a "guilty pleasure" is politically harmless and, as Kundera writes, "[a]s soon as kitsch is recognized for the lie it is, it moves into the context of non-kitsch, thus losing its authoritarian power and becoming as touching as any other human weakness" (248).[8]

Paradoxically, it is the radical renunciation of human weaknesses, typical of fascism, that in itself is the ultimate kitsch totalitarian attitude; an idea perfectly captured by Spanish avant-garde author Ramón Gómez de la Serna's startling phrase, "he is so 'cursi' [Spanish for kitsch] that doesn't want to be cursi" (41). In other words, it is the attempt to erase all human weakness from the picture that most characterizes the representation of reality typical of totalitarian, fascist kitsch, as exemplified by phrases such as "inasequible al desaliento" ("inaccessible to discouragement"). This phrase, coined by José Antonio Primo de Rivera, the founder of the Spanish political party known as the *Falange Española*, exemplified for Jorge Semprún the kitsch essence of the Falange's rhetoric.[9]

Anticipating by five decades Kundera's reflections on the subject, in his brilliant 1934 essay "Lo Cursi"—written two years before Franco's military uprising—de la Serna describes a new dangerously sentimental kitsch sensibility that was taking over Spain in the 1930s, which he differentiated from the reassuring and life-affirming kitsch aesthetic of the late nineteenth century.[10] It is worth pausing briefly over de la Serna's reflections on cursi aesthetics because they can help us better understand the historical context in which Francoist totalitarian kitsch emerged.

Against its normal usage of *cursi* as an adjective (or *cursilería* as a noun) describing the pretension and bad taste of the middle classes or the poor aesthetic value of an object, for de la Serna, *cursi* meant rather a feeling of well-being—of being at home with oneself and with one's beloved.[11] From his historical perspective, *cursi* signified the cozy and peaceful world view of the nineteenth-century urban middle classes which was quickly disappearing.[12] In 1934, *cursilería*, the bad-taste aesthetic wrapping of a nineteenth-century bourgeois lifestyle, offered de la Serna a protective shield against the turbulence caused by the sweeping historical changes that were rapidly transforming Spain at the time. It was this sense of total crisis, which did not seem to have a traditional solution, deeply felt by the European petty bourgeoisie of the 1930s, which, as Robert Paxton observes, provided the fuel for European fascism.[13]

For de la Serna, *Cursilería* is a nostalgic shield against the alienation and commodification of reality brought by capitalism in the twentieth century.[14] For him, the downfall of the modern world began at the very moment it triumphantly announced the dawn of a new era while ignoring the lessons of the past (23). As Giménez Caballero, the ideological founding father of Spanish fascism, put it, this attempt to create the world anew was ideally embodied in the "destructive and assertive hygienic enthusiasm" of the European younger generations which remade themselves after the defeatist bewilderment of the Great War (quoted in Saz 36). It was this "hygienic enthusiasm," exultantly praised by Giménez Caballero, that ultimately led to fascism and the concentration camps.[15] De la Serna chastizes this attempt to create a new world by destroying the old, as represented by Art Nouveau and good, harmless nineteenth-century kitsch: "a bad era is the one that destroys 'lo cursi,' that chases it away from its hideouts. An almost un-liveable era" (32).

However, next to this "good" *cursilería*, represented in part by Art Nouveau, de la Serna identifies a "bad" *cursilería*, a toxic kitsch that seems to prevail in Spain at the time he writes his essay: "we are surrounded by ... bad kitsch theater, by rhetorical phrases of the same style, etc" (27). This "bad" *cursilería* is redundant and "sugary" (26), and because it is overtly sentimental has a debilitating, narcotic effect, since "sentimentality coerces, anaesthetizes, paralyzes, overburdens, suppresses any flights of the spirit, and takes advantage of overwrought tenderness and the debilitating nature of softness" (27). Therefore, he concludes, bad *cursilería* "sterilizes life and impedes understanding" (28).

This "bad" *cursilería*, I argue, is the falsifying element necessary for the creation of totalitarian kitsch. It emerges, as de la Serna writes, "[i]n moments of great social worry ... taking advantage of the fact that people are vulnerable ..." (27). This overtly sentimental, "bad" *cursilería* takes hold of society surreptitiously then, when in dismaying social situations people are more vulnerable to ideological mystification. And lacking its own idiom it expresses itself with clichés that for de la Serna are suffocating "adenoids of the heart," and thus risks, as mentioned earlier, being co-opted for extraneous causes (27). In short, bad kitsch is not only ethically suffocating but politically dangerous.[16]

In the 1930s, and despite the glorification of straight, clear lines—politically and aesthetically—Spain, for de la Serna, is dominated by the overtly sentimental, deadening, and potentially dangerous attitudes of bad kitsch, which is the hidden ingredient in totalitarian/fascist kitsch.

Figure I.1 Carlos Sáenz de Tejada, 1940

For all the fascist talk of vitality and purity, it is this "debilitating, narcotic and overtly sentimental" bad kitsch of a petty bourgeoisie gone astray which is the *binding* force of fascism; as seen, for instance, in Carlos Sáenz de Tejada's 1940 painting "Traerán prendidas cinco rosas," depicting a Falangist militiaman raising to the sky Falange's famous symbol (Fig. I.1). It is thus not merely coincidental, as Broch points out, that besides his attraction for an apocalyptic, grandiose, Wagnerian kind of kitsch, Hitler was also a lover of a soft, "saccharine type" of kitsch that he found so moving; those silly postcards of pastel tones with little blond girls dressed as farmers (65). According to Gabriel Ashford, Franco regularly sent similar postcards of smiling little girls by the hundred when courting his first serious girlfriend (Ashford 149).

Reacting viscerally against the bad *cursilería* "in its simple evil manifestation" that is a sign of bad times, de la Serna wants to go back to the safe, sinuous, and protective world of the nineteenth century represented by the good kind (27). Good *cursilería* for him is not just aesthetically superior but also ethically superior because it aligns itself with life. Instead of rejecting human nature, as totalitarian kitsch does, good *cursilería* mimics "the complexity of the nervous system" (36). *Lo cursi* understands human nature so deeply that, for him, even "the composition of the blood" or "the soul" are fundamentally *cursi* (36).

In the Spanish context of 1934, however, his reflections on *cursi* ethics and aesthetics cannot be seen only as a reactionary petty bourgeois nostalgic longing for the erstwhile nineteenth-century cozy world, but a warning against things to come. He closes his essay by describing the liberal parliamentary political system as being *cursi* because, he seems to imply, only *cursi* politics, that care for real human beings, are successful politics (54); the same parliamentary system that European and Spanish Fascists alike, as well as their reactionary allies, wanted to destroy at the time. Even more tellingly, the embodiment of this *cursi* politics is the parliament building itself; "it is the most cursi thing in the world," with "its stenographers, its desks, its presidency, its cabinets and its bells" (54). This *cursi* parliamentary system—and what it represented—was the last bastion against the reactionary forces set to destroy it, which eventually saw their wish come true in the form of a military uprising originally planned by Generals Sanjurjo and Mola that eventually was controlled by Franco.[17]

Implicit in de la Serna's reflections is the fact that, despite their heralding of a new dawn, both fascism and the bad kitsch he fiercely denounced share a similar failed politics of time. Like kitsch, fascism is also a nostalgic reaction—a refuge—against the passing of time and the decay of the *aura* that for Benjamin was the defining feature of modernity. The fear of change—of the inevitability of permanent loss implied by the new modern teleological conception of history—with its disruption of cyclical notions of time is an important reason for fascism's emergence. And unlike the good kitsch that aligns itself with life because it genuinely expresses the temporal anguish of the human soul, as we will see in the second part of this study, bad, totalitarian kitsch does not. Instead it is co-opted by fascism to suppress it. Denying both real human needs and historical truth, totalitarian fascist kitsch aims to project into the future the illusion of an idyllic past.

Totalitarian kitsch thus combines fascism's politics of time with kitsch's politics of time, a politics of nostalgia that seeks refuge in an idealized, distorted past projected into the future and fused together in a timeless present. As we will see in Chapters 2 and 3 through the analysis of *Romancero marroquí* and *Los últimos de Filipinas*—set in Spanish-Morocco during the Spanish Civil War and the Philippines at the time of the Spanish-American War respectively—this notion of temporality is perfectly attuned to the concept of nation embraced by Francoist historiography. Both films, like Francoism itself, profess a notion of temporality that operates outside the homogenous time marked by clock and calendar and slips into an epic time, a mythic time of heroism that parallels the Francoist melancholic notions of history and nationhood.

Ultimately, the goal of fascist kitsch is to create illusions, to mimic the utopian goal of socialism only to homeopathically neutralize it. It provides the illusion of historical change but in reality brings society to an aesthetic standstill, and at its worst to self-annihilate. This fascist illusion of change—its smoke and mirrors—translates into what Alan Tansman has described, discussing modernist aesthetics in Japan, as "fascist moments," aesthetically cathartic epiphanies that when politically channeled create in turn a fascist mood favorable for the voluntary subjection of the citizens to the state (18). As Franco understood very well, this subjection of the citizens to the state is fascism's ultimate political goal: "[w]e need to sacrifice the 'self' to a unity that is the building block of our strength" (*Franco ha dicho* 109).

To accomplish this, fascist kitsch "[...] hallucinates empty spaces with an infinitely variegated assortment of beautiful appearances" (Calinescu 251). As we will see throughout the first three chapters of this study, kitsch lends its hallucinatory powers to fascism in order to fill these "empty spaces" with the seemingly "beautiful appearance" of death. It is precisely this juxtaposition of the apparent contradictory elements belonging to kitsch and to death—kitsch eliciting harmoniously idyllic sentiments, and death eliciting solitude and terror—in such a way that both are fused into one that for Friedländer constitutes the foundation of fascist aesthetics (3). Kitsch thus helps to neutralize the terror of death by presenting it as something idyllic and ultimately desirable (Friedländer 2). The beauty of death is represented as something worth dying for—as seen in the first three chapters in *Raza*, *Romancero marroquí* and *Los últimos de Filipinas*—a notion perfectly expressed by the slogan of "Viva la muerte" ("Long live Death") popularized by Franco's foreign legionnaires.

Finally, there is another important quality of kitsch particularly relevant for understanding Francoist totalitarian kitsch that provides fascism with the power that Phillip Lacoue-Labarth and Jean-Luc Nancy thought essential to the fascist myth (13–14). This is the mirroring quality of kitsch, that "highly considerate mirror" that sends back to the viewer a distorted but pleasing image of his own reality (Broch 49). This pleasing distortion of the truth typical of kitsch implies a close relationship between the kitsch-artist and the kitsch-man, as we will see in Chapter 5 through the analysis of *Franco, ese hombre*, a biopic documentary film glorifying the historical figure of Franco. Thus, aesthetically, morally, and ideologically, as Calinescu explains, "[t]he world of kitsch is a world of aesthetic make-believe and self-deception" (Calinescu 262).[18]

In the Francoist case, this can be seen most vividly in the medium of film. Since its inception, in the midst of the Spanish Civil War, Francoism took cinema seriously. As early as 1938 the *Departamento Nacional de Cinematografía* was created as part of the *Delegación Nacional de Prensa y Propaganda* (Alberich 53).[19] The *Departamento*'s task was to supervise cinema and to control all of the state's visual propaganda. Once the civil war ended in 1939, *falangista* radicals exerting a strong influence inside the *Departamento Nacional de Cinematografía* began to criticize the Spanish film industry for continuing to produce entertainment films that did not help in the construction of the new state (Alberich 53).

Although Spanish film production of the early 1940s did not by any means represent a unified ideological block, it was, however, carefully monitored by the Francoist regime through a mixed process of fiscal incentives, official awards, direct financial support, and direct intervention through state censorship. The *Departamento* championed film production within "clear genre patterns," among which *cine de cruzada* (civil war cinema), historical cinema, religious cinema, and folkloric musicals were clearly favored.[20] Among these, and especially in the eyes of the main Falangist ideologues, historical cinema was the preferred genre for disseminating the values of the new Spain, whose "glorious" imperial past was seen as a source of national pride that also provided moral guidance.

In the inaugural issue of "Primer Plano," the *Departamento*'s official journal, its first president, García Viñolas, penned an inflammatory editorial against the nearsighted and greedy policies of the Spanish film industry and in favor of creating a new type of cinema that would serve as an ideological vehicle for the creation of a new Spain: "Film as business has left its place to film as a vehicle for indoctrination ... cinema is the strongest weapon. It is not any longer about negotiating business deals but about combating ... in this war which as every war cannot be simply a mission of the private industry" (54).

After the scales of power tilted at the end of the Second World War in favor of the economic interests of the Spanish film industry, the *Falangista* hardliners were served a severe blow. The political downfall of Ramón Serrano Suñer—"el cuñadísimo" as he was referred to because he was Franco's brother-in-law—as the dictator's right arm marked the political shifting point. After Serrano Suñer's resignation, and the appointment of Carlos Fernández Cuenca to replace the more radical García Viñolas as director of the *Departamento*, "Primer Plano" changed its ideological orientation and began defending the interests of the Spanish film industry (Alberich 54). As Ferrán Alberich writes, "[from] 1942 one could read in 'Primer Plano' articles in defense of 'españoladas,' folkloric film and period pieces, which became the principal core of the Spanish film production during the 1940s" (54–5).[21]

Therefore, like its Italian counterpart under Benito Mussolini, for all its fascist bravado Spanish cinema during the early 1940s was also characterized by its escapism and social falsity, as seen, for instance, in the fact that 80 per cent of Cifesa's output—the most important Spanish film production company of the 1940s—was escapist comedies. Escapist comedies together with musicals and historical melodramas in fact made up the bulk of Spanish film production from the 1940s onwards.[22] Almost overwhelmingly, these comedies focused on social ascension and mistaken identity[23] and their action took place mainly in just one setting: the interior of an upper-class bourgeois mansion (124).[24] For Spanish film historian Félix Fanés, who has brilliantly studied Cifesa's film production during those years, the motif of mistaken identity fits perfectly with the split that Spanish society, and individuals, had to go through in order to cope with the country's bleak post-war reality (129).

Therefore, although this study argues that the power of Francoist totalitarian kitsch aesthetics and its ideological propaganda affected the lives of its consumers, it does not assume a direct influence between cultural representations and political affiliations. It understands Spanish audiences of the 1940s and '50s as neither passive, or easily "interpellated" subjects of ideology as per Althusser, nor as hypercritical reception theorists privately reading Francoist films against the grain to deconstruct their totalitarian ideology.

This study aims to show that, in fact, the most obvious Francoist ideological propaganda did not always necessarily hit its intended target, as I will demonstrate in Chapter 2 through the case of *Romancero marroquí*, an explicit Francoist propaganda film that mostly failed to connect with its intended audiences. Based on scant box-office records and press coverage, audiences, particularly in the first two decades of Francoism, tended to be more receptive to films—such as comedies, musicals, and historical melodramas—that indirectly communicated Francoist values (like the vastly successful Cifesa's fantasy comedies), rather than to explicitly didactic propaganda films. From this empirically observable phenomenon, I infer that the audience in Spain in the 1940s and '50s was somewhat critical (as illustrated by a rejection of overtly propagandistic films) yet simultaneously to a large extent passive (as illustrated by the popularity of Cifesa's comedies whose political message was nonetheless ultra-conservative and generally in line with Francoist nationalist ideology). In short, this study understands, in line with Lutz Koepnick's findings for Nazi Germany, that ideological hegemony is not successfully achieved by a complete subjugation of the population to the demands of totalitarian regimes, but rather by providing a seemingly free inner space that is not completely out of the reach of the reigning ideology (51–73).

Spanish audiences of the 1940s and '50s seem to have been much more inclined to embrace stories in which core Francoist Spanish traditional values were rendered under more palatable narrative forms, interspersed with bits of humor, music, character development, all cloaked in effective melodramatic form, as we will see in Chapter 3 through films such as *Los últimos de Filipinas* (or the box-office hit *Marcelino, pan y vino*), than they were to strict ideological propaganda films such as *Raza*, *¡Harka!*, or *¡A mí la legión!* And of course they were also seduced by the allure of popular Hollywood films once compulsory dubbing made them accessible after 1941.

It is in this context that kitsch aesthetics becomes an important indoctrinating tool for Francoism. When the audience flocked to movie theaters in order to momentarily escape from Spain's drab post-war reality, they entered a state of reverie, or fantasy, as if in a Freudian daydream, as Judith Mayne observes in *Cinema and Spectatorship*.[25] However, this state was not limited by the private sphere of dream-like fantasies, but, on the contrary, bled out into the political realm (79).[26] Kitsch aesthetics and its promise of an "easy catharsis," as Adorno famously put it—the temporary suspension of the traumatic core of social subjectivity—was the ideal form for inducing that state.

In this sense, Francoism's employment of kitsch aesthetics as a sentimental, escapist shield against trauma was ultimately politically effective. Kitsch's uncritical depiction of emotion is, then, crucial to understanding its ideological function in Francoist cinema. Kitsch, in this sense, aims at the creation of an artistic hypnosis in which emotions are not critically explored but stirred in order to fascinate and to hypnotically render its reactionary ideology to its audience. It is in a state of collective reverie, with their critical judgment severely impaired, that the spectators are potentially receptive to a film's mystifying ideology. Kitsch, then, functions as a pacifier of critical thought, rendering audiences to some extent more vulnerable to the workings of ideology, as de la Serna had warned. Lacking records of the audience's inner reaction to these films, however, we will never know for certain how effective cinema was as a medium of indoctrination in Franco's Spain.

I am aware that the category of kitsch in this study could become equally facilitating as constraining. It is precisely its usefulness as a conceptual category for understanding a vast array of Francoist cultural products, some of which—as we will see in Chapter 4 in the case of *Surcos*, a fascist film critical of Francoism—are apparently dissimilar to more orthodox films such as *Raza*, that could potentially become its constraining factor. I have tried my best not to succumb to its potentially reductive danger. I use kitsch as a critical paradigm to explain the political, ideological, and aesthetic make-up of Francoist ideology, not as a one size fits all interpretative methodology.[27]

This challenge becomes even greater in the second part of the study—on the unmaking of Francoist kitsch. This is particularly obvious in Chapter 6, devoted to Buñuel's *Viridiana*. Building from a previous essay on the film, this chapter does not attempt to reduce the richness and complexity of *Viridiana* to the realm of kitsch. Rather, it attempts to understand Buñuel's film as a metaphor that provides an acute visual and narrative representation of the rarefied elements that constituted Francoist kitsch ideology as a sublimated space suspended in a kitsch melancholy bubble lost in time and space. In the second part of this study, besides Buñuel's film, in Chapters 7 and 8 I examine two other films by Álex de la Iglesia and Guillermo del Toro—*Balada triste de trompeta* and *Pan's Labyrinth* respectively—two filmmakers of the post-transition generation, which, I argue, engage with what Norman Klein has called "digital Neo-Baroque" aesthetics to dismantle Francoist kitsch.

During the Spanish political transition to democracy, a number of important filmmakers and visual artists, marginalized at the time, reworked the Spanish iconic heritage of Francoist ideological discourse.[28] They were acutely aware of the ways in which Spain's own cultural legacy called out for revision and contextualization. The main objective of these artists was to liberate their cultural and artistic national heritage from forty years of a fascist ideological discourse that had largely appropriated traditional Spanish images for its own political agenda. For them, a key strategy in this process of cultural revision was the cultivation of a camp sensibility.[29] As camp artists they imbued old images with new meanings, looking back at the history of national icons in order to recycle a Francoist kitsch repertoire parodically, according to a set of aesthetic codes attuned to the tastes and social demands of the transition to democracy in the 1970s and early 1980s.

The political transition from Franco's dictatorship to democracy drastically altered Spain's cultural landscape. Ironically, when it finally arrived, the country's long-awaited integration with Europe caused a great deal of anxiety, particularly within intellectual and artistic circles. Beyond the well-known works of Velázquez, Goya, Gaudí, García Lorca, Dalí, Buñuel, Miró, or Picasso, what could contemporary Spain contribute artistically and culturally to the world after decades of relative isolation? How could a younger generation of Spanish artists fully embrace a toxic traditional Spanish popular culture tainted by forty years of Francoist rule? The clichéd images and sounds of Moorish-Andalusian Spain which served as the backdrop to the escapist reveries of European romantic imagination, as mentioned earlier, had been domestically internalized by Spanish reactionary ideologies and therefore tainted by the class interests they represented. During the 1960s, this iconographic repertoire of brave bullfighters, sprightly "tonadilleras," and sultry flamenco dancers constituted the staple representation of Spain in the shrewd rebranding campaign Francoism launched to attract European tourists. This repertoire, which was conveniently commodified, as we saw, under the famous slogan "Spain is different," had been stigmatized by the left as pure kitsch and derided for its Francoist leanings.

As I argued in my previous work on the cinema of Pedro Almodóvar, the camp aesthetic was the main strategy deployed by the Spanish artists during the political transition from the mid-1970s until the late 1980s to liberate this iconographic repertoire both from the ideological grip of the right and the disdain of the left. Resorting to irony as its main weapon, camp recycled Francoist kitsch, parodically mixing it with a wide range of styles from Western popular culture—from melodrama to pop art to punk aesthetics—imbuing it with new meanings. It was through this aesthetic cocktail, which filtered the artists' own personal styles through immediately recognizable Spanish motifs, that the most influential artists of the Spanish transition such as Almodóvar were able to contribute to the international artistic arena with their own voice instead of becoming mere imitators of foreign trends.

It is not my intention here to offer a rigorous analysis of this process of development of Spanish cultural identity during the transition —best seen in the first films of Almodóvar—which falls beyond the scope of the present study. For the purposes of this introduction, a brief analysis of a famous photograph of Almodóvar wearing a bullfighter's jacket should suffice to illustrate the cultural evolution of post-Franco Spain (Fig. I.2). The bullfighter was an emblematic figure of romantic Spain and, together with the legionnaire, represented the Francoist embodiment of courage and masculinity. In the photograph, however, Almodóvar subverts the bullfighter's traditional masculine image by wearing a *peineta*—the traditional Spanish female headwear connoting old-fashioned femininity, in his case defiantly tilted to the right. In the photograph he is grinning while holding a big cigar in his mouth, reminding us of Groucho Marx's ironic stance but—given that Almodóvar himself is a recognizable gay icon—the cigar also has obvious phallic connotations.

Figure I.2 Pedro Almodóvar as bullfighter

Almodóvar's cinema writ-large follows a

similar strategy: ironically juxtaposing old forms in a new postmodern context, they shed old meanings to be read anew. His first films recycled Francoist kitsch to reclaim traditional Spanish cinematic themes and popular characters, which had been largely ignored by high-minded critics suspicious of pop culture and by Spanish *auterist* filmmakers alike. Thus, in *Dark Habits*, for example, Almodóvar re-imagines Francoist religiosity—the subject of many successful Spanish films from *Marcelino, Pan y Vino* to *Sor Citroen* or *Balarrasa*—through the depiction of the convent's Mother Superior as an eccentric, bolero-loving, drug-using, lesbian nun. In *Matador*, the heroic bullfighter, the Francoist prototype of masculinity, becomes a serial killer actually terrified of women; and in *¿Qué he hecho yo para merecer esto!*, Gloria, a traditional, submissive, working-class housewife murders her abusive, fascist husband with a blow to the head (à la Hitchcock) with the bare bone of a Serrano ham. These Francoist popular characters and themes are not simply reclaimed but suffused with contemporary tastes, textures, and sensibilities. Almodóvar's earlier films, then, offered themselves to the spectator as spaces of inclusion, as negotiation arenas—as María's shrine in *Matador* or the convent itself in *Dark Habits*—opening themselves up to difference and heterogeneity while deconstructing traditional Spanish conservative ideologies.

In Chapters 7 and 8, as mentioned earlier, I focus on two filmmakers of the post-transitional generation: Álex de la Iglesia and Guillermo del Toro; the latter, a Mexican director who has made two central contributions to the growing body of films about early Francoism, *The Devil's Backbone* (2001) and *Pan's Labyrinth* (2006). Both had their directorial debut in 1993 with *Acción mutante*, a science-fiction satire, and *Cronos*, a horror/vampire movie, respectively. Belonging to a younger generation than that of Almodóvar, both partake of his campy sensibility and are influenced by pop culture, particularly comic books and horror movies, but both are also heavily indebted to the work of Luis Buñuel—Spanish film auteur par excellence. But more important for this study, both embody what Omar Calabrese, Severo Sarduy, Peter Wollen, Carlos Monsiváis, and Angela Ndalianis, among others, have called a neo-baroque aesthetic. Neo-baroque aesthetic is important for this study because, as we will see in *Balada triste de trompeta* and *Pan's Labyrinth*, it deepens camp aesthetic critique of Francoist kitsch by directly addressing, through its "mournful melancholy," Spain's confrontation with its criminal past.

De la Iglesia and several other Spanish filmmakers of his generation continued Almodóvar's recycling of popular Spanish themes and sensibilities. But, unlike Almodóvar, who relied heavily on pop art, film noir, and melodrama, they fully embraced a Spanish and Latin American Baroque aesthetic, characterized by its allegorical mode, melancholic nature, self-referentiality, and formal virtuosity; a Baroque sensibility filtered through popular genres: from sci-fi to horror to low-brow digital forms of contemporary entertainment, ranging from comic books to animation and video games.[30]

As we can see, for instance, in de la Iglesia's second feature film, *El día de la bestia*, a new cinematic sensibility creeps into Spanish film which, although still drawing from Almodóvar's camp re-writing of kitsch, can be more aptly characterized as neo-Baroque. Drawing from comic-book aesthetics but also from Cervantes' *Don Quixote* and the earlier picaresque novel, the film brings back the obsessive allegorical mode and mournful melancholic mood typical of Baroque aesthetics that Benjamin identified as characteristic of German Baroque drama, which, as he noted, was heavily influenced by the Baroque dramas of Calderón de la Barca (81).

In his classic study, *Culture of the Baroque: Analysis of a Historical Structure*, Spanish historian José Antonio Maravall identifies in the European Baroque of the seventeenth century the birth of mass culture and the incipient apparition of kitsch.[31] For Maravall, Baroque Europe was the first true society of the spectacle.[32] It was characterized by the attempt by both monarchy and church to engage in an early form of "cultural manufacturing," in order to strengthen the traditional values shaken by the religious, social, and economic crisis brought by the dramatic changes Europe underwent during the Renaissance (88).[33]

Building on Maravall's classic work, among others, film scholar Angela Ndalianis examines contemporary film and media through the category of a Baroque aesthetic. She argues that due to the radical changes brought about by modern technological innovations and economic development, "contemporary entertainment media reflect a dominant neo-baroque logic" (5). As she writes,

> the neo-baroque shares a baroque delight in spectacle and sensory experiences. Neo-baroque entertainments, however—which are the product of conglomerate entertainment industries, multimedia interest, and spectacle that is often reliant upon computer technology—present contemporary audiences with new baroque forms of expression that are aligned with late-twentieth- and early twenty-first-century concerns. The neo-baroque combines the visual, the auditory, and the textual in ways that parallel the dynamism of seventeenth-century baroque form, but that dynamism is expressed in the late twentieth and early twenty-first centuries in technologically and culturally different ways. (5)

Given the "baroque delight in spectacle and sensory experiences" so close to the sensibility of contemporary audiences, for the Spanish filmmakers represented in the last two chapters of this study, neo-Baroque aesthetics suited perfectly their desire not only to participate but also to contribute to the dissemination of mass culture.[34] The mass appeal of contemporary mainstream neo-Baroque as practiced by de la Iglesia and del Toro, however, has not lost its critical edge. On the contrary, as we will see, these two filmmakers manage to bring to the forefront the philosophical concerns of Baroque aesthetics: its epistemological skepticism and metafictional interrogations and more generally the probing relationship between truth and artistic representation.[35] And both managed to critically revisit the Francoist past to liberate it from ideological petrification, like Almodóvar had done through camp.

The neo-Baroque aesthetic in Spanish cinema continues camp's project of neutralizing kitsch but redirects it to delve more deeply into the allegorical modality characteristic both of the Baroque and also of Spanish anti-Francoist film. Furthermore, it also explores what, following David L. Eng and David Kazanjian, can be called a new "mournful Melancholia" (4). In doing so, de la Iglesia and del Toro upend the Francoist use of melancholia as a tool of political subjection, as Buñuel had previously done. They do this by using a neo-Baroque aesthetic different from the surrealist style privileged by their cinematic idol, which yields different ethical outcomes. Unlike the Francoist type, which wanted to re-create the past in the present, or Buñuel's deconstructive kind, neo-Baroque mournful melancholy proposes to mourn the past in the present to give proper acknowledgment to the suffering of the victims of Spain's traumatic past. As we will see in the analysis of de la Iglesia's *Balada triste de trompeta*, this happens through an incorporation of the specter from Shakespeare's *Hamlet*. And, in del Toro's *Pan's Labyrinth*, through a re-writing of kitsch-prone fairy tales and the re-casting of Goya's painting *Saturn Devouring his Sons* under a positive "mournful melancholy" light, as seen in Goya's famous etching *The Sleep of Reason Produces Monsters*.[36]

Notes

1. Because of his cold-blooded nature and "miraculous" survival after a near-fatal stomach bullet wound, Moroccan soldiers believed he was touched with "Baraka," the Arabic word for luck.
2. In so doing, it hopes to situate itself within the decades-long critical debate inaugurated by seminal works such as Saul Friedländer's *Reflections on Nazism: An Essay on Kitsch and Death*, and by Susan Sontag's essay "Fascinating Fascism," which were among the first to explore the links between fascist kitsch aesthetics and political violence.

3. While there are abundant studies on the cultural aspects of German and Italian fascism, there has been much less attention given to cultural variants of fascism in other Ibero-American contexts like those of Portugal, Brazil, Argentina, and Chile. This study hopes to join forces to fill that vacuum together with the few recent critical studies that undertake the study of fascist culture from a transatlantic perspective, such as Federico Finchelstein's *Transatlantic Fascism: Ideology, Violence, and the Sacred in Argentina and Italy, 1919–1945* (2013) and Patricia Vieira's *Portuguese Film, 1930–1960: The Staging of the New State Regime* (2013).
4. As Sianne Ngai writes, "precisely because the work of kitsch seems to 'address him only,' with an intimacy not unlike that of lyric address, the aesthetic subject does not perceive it from a contemplative distance 'like a bystander' but rather experiences or inhabits it like an atmosphere, one enveloping him like a coat ... or pulled over his head like a mask ..." (75).
5. Ismael Saz Campos has defined Francoism as a "régimen fascistizado," and as the "missing link between fascist dictatorships and authoritarian regimes" (90). For him, it combined characteristics of both types: "its fascist connotations explain its rigidity, its essential negation of liberal democracy, its constant resorting to repression, its willingness to be everlasting. Its non-fascist elements explain its versatility and capacity of adaptation, its longevity" (90).
6. Fascism and kitsch can both be seen as by-products of Romantic philosophical and aesthetic attitudes toward history and toward beauty. Philosophically, as Isaiah Berlin has shown, fascism has its roots in the anti-Enlightenment movement or, more precisely, in German Romanticism's response to a mechanistic vision of life derived from the Enlightenment (40). European fascism combined Romanticism's rebellion against the tyranny of reason with Nietzsche's exaltation of instinct and natural will and Bergson's vitalist critique of Western philosophy and his preference for intuition over reason. But, finally, it was through George Sorel's transformation of Marx's dialectical materialism into vibrant social myth—aided by kitsch aesthetics—that fascist ideology acquired its powerful mobilizing force (Neocleous 3).
7. As Slavoj Žižek pointed out, without a fantasy frame reality would be perceived as an "unreal nightmarish universe with no firm ontological foundation" (66).
8. As he writes, "[...] No matter how we scorn it, kitsch is an integral part of the human condition" (248). For Monica Kjellman-Chapin kitsch is, in fact, a "mechanism for coping with modernity" (37). In the words of C. E. Emmer, kitsch is a vehicle "to deal with the vicissitudes of modern life, to make it, in its implacability, inhabitable" (quoted in Kjellman-Chapin 37).
9. This is what Kundera's other definition of kitsch as "the absolute denial of shit" ultimately means, since "kitsch [and fascism, we may add] excludes everything from its purview which is essentially unacceptable in human existence" (248).

10. *Cursi* was first used in Spain at the end of the nineteenth century to refer to the bad taste of the middle class, and also to its sense of social inadequacy.
11. It is a feeling born when humans feel at ease with themselves and "with their beloved they want to create a microcosm out of their home to give shelter to peace, intimate torment and happiness" (12).
12. According to Nöel Valis, "the cultural marker we call *lo cursi*, has two significant moments in time when it will expand in meaning and usage. The first occurs in 1860s and 1870s and is centered on the Revolution of 1868, its aftereffects and the arrival of the Bourbon Restoration in early 1875. *Costumbrista* writers, satirists and realists like Galdós and Clarín will exploit this largely middle-class phenomenon as a sign of the times, a time of an uneasy transition from an ancien regime saving economy to an early version of commercialized, consumer interests and organizations. Middle-class desire to transcend one's origins, perceived as inadequate or as inauthentic, was capsulized in a telling phrase of *cursilería*, 'querer y no poder'" (Valis 328).
13. Victor Klemperer writes in *The Language of the Third Reich* about Hitler's middle-class support and antisemitism: "He never grew out of his initial childish and infantile attitude to the Jews. Herein lies a considerable part of his strength, because it unites him with the dullest section of the population, which, in the age of the machine, is plainly not made up of the industrial proletariat, nor does it consist exclusively of the peasantry, but rather derives from the concentrated masses of the petty bourgeoisie" (174).
14. As Alejandro Varderi observes, Gómez de la Serna sees the roots of kitsch in Baroque aesthetics (84).
15. This was an idea he borrowed from Mussolini, who, as Igor Golomstock explains, "took from Futurism the idea of war as 'the hygiene of the world' and remained true to it until his inglorious end" (245).
16. As Leopoldo Alas wrote, "Kitsch is always monstrous and malignant. It is enough to think about all these abject dwarfs who try to galvanize the foul entrails of the cadavers of old empires creating new monsters (fanaticism, Nazism, the movement) ... that were inevitably going to turn back on them, crushing them and adding them to the list of cadavers available" (10).
17. It does not come as a surprise, then, that an editorial vilifying intellectuals that appeared in April 1938 in *Arriba España*, a Francoist newspaper from Pamplona, recommended "the stupid clown Ramón Gómez de la Serna" to be purged from Espasa Calpe—the most important publishing house of the time—along with Descartes, Ortega y Gasset, Bertrand Russell, and Thomas Mann (Puértolas 51).
18. The kitsch-man is akin to the man of bad taste of Giorgio Agamben's definition, who "is not simply the one who, totally lacking the organ needed to be receptive to art, is blind to it or contemptuous of it: rather, the person of bad taste is the person ... who does not know how to identify the *point de perfection* of the work of art by distinguishing truth from falsehood" (17).

19. As Ignacio Prado puts it, "[t]he war machine was in sync with the mimetic desiring apparatus that constitutes cinema and makes up a mechanism of control and instruction that at the same time allows the public to avoid the dramatic reality that surrounds them" (102).
20. As Luis González wrote in *Fascismo, kitsch y cine histórico español*, "throughout the forties and at the beginning of the fifties a group of period films premiered that became the distinctive stamp of the production Company CIFESA (Compañía Industrial Film Español S.A.) and, by extension, of the film produced during the first phase of Francoism" (20). González's book covers some of Cifesa's most important productions, including *Agustina de Aragón* (Juan de Orduña, 1950), *Alba de América* (Juan de Orduña, 1951), *Amaya* (Luis Marquina, 1952), *La leona de Castilla* (Juan de Orduña, 1951), *Locura de amor* (Juan de Orduña, 1948), *Lola la piconera* (Luis Lucía,1951), and *La Princesa de los Ursinos* (Luis Lucía, 1947). As he writes, "Not all of the films produced under Francoism were in agreement with the ideological principles of the dictatorship, but, above all, they showed an enormous complicity with Franco's regime, in the sense that they backed up and extended with unequal intensity its political agenda and its social and spiritual values" (27).
21. As Barry Jordan and Rikki Morgan-Tamosunas write, "españoladas" "became the embodiment of escapism and the vehicle par excellence of the *mitología franquista* ... offering a seductive but false notion of Spanishness for both internal and external consumption" (106).
22. As Steve Marsh writes, "[i]t is both a commonplace and a falsehood ... that Spanish cinema of the early Francoist period comprised exclusively nation-building propaganda exercises in the form of rewritten history and religious epic. Of the more than five hundred films made in Spain between 1939 and 1951—the so called period of *autarky*—less than twenty conform to this particular caricature. The vast majority of Spain's filmic production of the period consists of popular comedies, melodramas, costume dramas that are often set in the 19th century, and musicals" (1–2).
23. According to Félix Fanés, "[t]his topic which already appeared in the group of films from 1939–1942, overwhelmingly dominates Cifesa's production from 1942 on" (125).
24. This *nacional-sindicalista* company, the most stable film production company in Spain, also achieved a more cohesive look than any other operating in Spain at the time. However, despite its Francoist ideology, Cifesa fashioned itself after the American studio system. Eighty per cent of Cifesa's production were comedies. In a typical Cifesa comedy, the main characters' objective was to ascend socially (Fanés 85).
25. For a full discussion on spectatorship and fantasy, see her chapter "Paradoxes of Spectatorship" (77–102).
26. Jacqueline Rose has also persuasively argued about the political uses of fantasy. As she writes, "[l]ong before psychoanalysis got the idea ... fantasy

has been where statehood takes hold and binds its subjects, and then, unequal to its own injunctions, lets slip just a little" (14).
27. As Steven Marsh writes, despite the official efforts of the "Nationalist victors ... of incorporating the bulk of the losing masses into their project" these attempts often failed. I am fully aware, as Marsh's Gramscian analysis of Spanish popular comedy in Spain has convincingly showed, that these failed efforts "opened up ideological spaces that enabled critical elements to work with relative freedom while, simultaneously, witnessing the appropriation of the cinematic legacy of the defeated Second Republic (1931–1939)" (2). That is, not even Cifesa's conservative comedies were free, as Sally Faulkner has also pointed out, from harboring oppositional tendencies (59).
28. Among the most notable are filmmakers such as Pedro Almodóvar, Bigas Luna, Ventura Pons, and Jaime Chávarri, as well as visual artists such as Ocaña, Pérez Villalta, Ceesepe, Nazario, Mariscal, and Las Costus.
29. See the introduction to Alejandro Yarza's *Un caníbal en Madrid: la sensibilidad camp y el reciclaje de la historia en el cine de Pedro Almodóvar* (1999), 15–34.
30. Alejandro Varderi examines the affiliations between Latino-American neo-Baroque aesthetics, as understood by Severo Sarduy, and Spanish postmodern cinema seen already in Pedro Almodóvar's films, which contain "elements of Latin American neobaroque and kitsch" (18).
31. Maravall readily admits that "the cultural commerce of kitsch in this incipient moment could never be the same as those that social researchers are concerned with today" (82). However, and despite the lack of "radio or widely circulated newspapers that the public could make use of," he maintains that in its germinal form kitsch "can already be discovered in the baroque" (82).
32. "The seventeenth century was an epoch of masses, undoubtedly the first in modern history, and the baroque was the first culture to make use of expedients to produce mass effects. This is attested to by the character of the theater, in its texts and scenario procedures; by the mechanized and external piety of post-Tridentine religion; by the politics of attraction and repression that the states began to use; by innovations in the warring arts. Might not printing, which since the mid-sixteenth century became the fundamental instrument of culture, also be considered the first known example of anything close to mass communication?" (102).
33. As he writes, "[w]hen in the seventeenth century ... the first productions appeared that were oriented toward a 'public' proper (or, more rigorously, to a public sociologically defined as such), kitsch was used as the effective expedient to shape types, form mentalities, and group masses together ideologically" (89).
In "The Neobaroque and Popular Culture," Carlos Monsiváis proposes the following definition of the neo-Baroque: "... we may understand neobaroque as the mise-en-scène of a sensibility composed of a thousand sensibilities, where elements related to the baroque are brought into the present: the fully realized profundity of darkness; horror vacui, or the fear of empty spaces; the

explosion of forms that delight in their own display; the re-creation of the human against a backdrop of organic Nature: the point of extreme tension that is synonymous with the creative act. And it is also always chaos, which in relation to this multifarious sensibility serves to reject the homogeneity and its false harmonies" (183).

34. In an influential study on the Spanish culture of the first decades after Franco's death, Cristina Moreiras-Menor coined the term "wounded culture" to refer to Spain's cultural representations as traversed by an affective crisis. In these representations, "[t]he present is always filtered ... by the presence of an almost faded spectral figure that shows itself in the interstices of the narratives, in its margins or folds, acting, intervening in the way the present is experienced" (16).

35. And as Timothy Murray writes, the digital Baroque "new screen arts" also play a role in the "paradigm shift away from the remnants of humanist visions of subjectivity and projection toward reflections on a baroque model of the folds of intersubjective and cross-cultural knowledge" (9).

36. All translations in the book are my own in collaboration with Sophie Heller. Ashley Caja translated the first draft of Chapter 6 from Spanish and edited a first draft of the manuscript.

CHAPTER 1

The Petrified Tears of General Franco: Kitsch and Fascism in José Luis Sáenz de Heredia's *Raza*

La Patria es quien borda con mano de Mujer—de madre, de novia—sobre el pecho . . . el yugo y el haz, las flechas simbólicas de nuestro emblema
—José Antonio Primo de Rivera, *Obras completas*

Francoism—like German and Italian fascism—produced its own particular brand of kitsch, whose ultimate goal was to attain cultural and ideological hegemony over post-Civil War Spain. Francoist ideologues had utilized religious and historical iconography (particularly that derived from the centuries-long struggle of Spain against Islam) as a main element in the creation of a kitsch scenario intended to replace more complex accounts of Spain's historical past. Francoism and kitsch aesthetics came together to constitute and project a false and picturesque image of Spain. This aesthetic, and its closeness to the realm of political power, is best exemplified in the 1941 film *Raza*, directed by José Luis Sáenz de Heredia and based on a script written by Francisco Franco himself.

The text—part film script, part play, part novel—was written by Franco under the pseudonym Jaime de Andrade toward the end of 1940 and the beginning of 1941, and was published in 1942 as *Raza: anecdotario para el guión de una película*. It has been characterized as little more than a melodramatic political pamphlet lacking the "most basic aesthetic or psychological foundation" (Prado 104). I would argue, however, that Franco's text is not simply a political pamphlet written in a melodramatic style, but—like the film—exemplifies the kind of totalitarian kitsch aesthetics that suited the Francoist attempt to rewrite Spanish history in order to establish ideological hegemony over post-war Spain. Though the film was meant to be the blueprint for Francoist cinematic aesthetics, honed to the highest standards of serious art, it became the template for Francoist kitsch.[1]

Raza was paradigmatic of a totalitarian kitsch aesthetic. By totalitarian kitsch aesthetic, I mean an aesthetic that, in Milan Kundera's words, erases "every display of individualism" as well as all doubt and irony (252). It is my contention that the film, like all totalitarian kitsch, restricted movement and produced a closing down of visual signifiers. It did this by creating a pseudo-poetic effect that sought the prestige derived from serious art in order to earn the spectator's respect and admiration. Such an effect was produced by the parasitic insertion of fragments taken out of prestigious artistic contexts. The film also mixed aesthetic and ethical categories—for Hermann Broch, the essence of kitsch—culminating in the fetishization of suffering and death (71).

Raza was conceived inside the *Palacio de El Pardo*, Franco's official residence, and was the brainchild of Franco himself. It was the biggest film production of its time, with a budget higher than that of other Spanish films of the period, and, unlike most of those other films, it was produced under the auspices of the newly created *Consejo de la Hispanidad*, an institution charged with propagating Spanish culture abroad, and whose director, Manuel Halcón, took part in the project as historical consultant (Alberich 55).[2]

Once the project got the green light, a director was chosen through a contest. Various Spanish directors were given the assignment of writing the first one hundred shots of the film. Finally, Franco himself selected José Luis Sáenz de Heredia, a first cousin of the founder of the main Spanish fascist party, *Falange Española*, and a former combatant during the Spanish Civil War, to direct what Román Gubern has called "Francoism's Potemkin" (98).[3] The screenplay, a close adaptation of Franco's text, was written by Sáenz de Heredia and Antonio Román. *Raza* was, then, from start to finish, a direct enterprise of the Francoist state. As Prado points out, only two other films, *Franco, ese hombre* (1964), a documentary about Franco made also by José Luis Sáenz de Heredia, which will be the focus of Chapter 5, and *Alba de América* [*Dawn of America*] (1951), a national epic about the Spanish Conquest, directed by Juan de Orduña, would ever be produced entirely by the Francoist state (103).

Given Franco's authorship of *Raza*'s original text and the film's state-sponsored production, the film should be considered an official attempt to justify the Spanish Civil War as a religious crusade of national liberation.[4] Francoism understood, to its advantage, the fetishistic nature of the cinematic apparatus, whose ultimate goal was to produce a submissive and unified cinematic subject who, by identifying with the camera's point of view, would identify with the state's ideology.[5] *Raza* wanted to set the historical record of the Spanish Civil War straight according to its own notion of that record. It also wanted to set straight its own genre—the *cine de cruzada*—throwing overboard, as it were, the excesses of melodramatic kitsch films that during this time threatened to sink that genre into oblivion.[6]

Raza traces the evolution of the Churruca family—Commander Pedro Churruca, his wife Isabel, and their four children, José, Pedro, Jaime, and Isabelita—from the late nineteenth century to the end of the Spanish Civil War in 1939. The first part of the film focuses on Commander Churruca's heroic death in the Spanish-American War. The second part follows the heroic exploits of his son José in the Spanish Civil War, but also the political "betrayal" of his brother, Pedro—who becomes a Republican parliamentarian—and the martyrdom of their younger brother Jaime, who is executed by the Republicans along with his fellow convent religious brothers.

In good kitsch fashion, the film incorporates various visual styles extracted from prestigious cinematic contexts, including the visual styles and narrative strategies of Soviet and American cinema and German expressionism, particularly in genres such as melodrama and war movies.[7] These references are taken out of their original artistic contexts and parasitically inserted into new ones where, as Gubern has shown, a mannered Francoist cinematographic academicism ultimately prevails (99).[8] The kitsch inserts, which in their original contexts had a specific structural function, are only used in *Raza* to create an effect, triggered by their mere association with the prestigious original contexts.[9] This parasitic insertion of fragments taken from other genuine contexts is precisely what, for Umberto Eco, defines kitsch (201).[10]

In order to show the workings of its kitsch fascist aesthetics, I will focus on two sequences from the film, referring in passing to crucial passages from Franco's script left out from the film. In the first sequence, Commander Churruca teaches his children a history lesson in the family garden. In the second, Jaime is executed on the beach. Both cases reveal a kitsch mixing of the aesthetic and ethical planes of imagined and real experience. The second sequence reveals the culmination of this aesthetic in the beautification of violence, and is a good example, as we will see, of the tension between movement and stillness that structures the movie and informs its kitsch aesthetic. I will also examine what I consider to be the most salient visual feature of *Raza*, namely, the use of non-diegetic shadows, which I argue cinematographically freeze the symbolic order.

Raza's major themes—guilt, punishment, redemption, and the beauty of death—are introduced early on in the narrative. They first occur in a scene where the father, Commander Churruca, walks with José, the chosen one, to his right, and Pedro to his left, as will be the case in almost every scene where the three are shown together. In this scene, the father answers his son Pedro's questions about a sailor who died on his father's ship during a storm. Pedro asks him if the reason why he chose that particular sailor to climb up the mast during the dangerous storm was because the sailor was morally bad. Commander Churruca answers him by saying, "All navy men are good. He who commits an error is assigned a punishment, endures it and is then purified" (Andrade 33). This moral universe of sin, punishment, and redemption, typical of Christianity but in its Francoist excess resembling the paranoid world view of Joseph de Maistre —according to Isaiah Berlin, the nineteenth-century progenitor of fascism—hovers over *Raza*, and is precisely the legacy that Commander Churruca wants to pass on to his children.[11] In its extreme form, this legacy calls for the activation of a fierce mental cleansing process as the only effective guard against mental contents that are regarded as contaminated. The idealization of this "process of purging itself of what it has contained," according to psychoanalyst Christopher Bollas, is precisely what characterizes the "Fascist state of mind" (203). It is only through this constant purging of the self that a new self can be born, empty of all mental content. This will be a self "... with no contact with others, with no past (which is severed), and with a future entirely of its own creation" (203). This notion of the self as a self-cleansing machine "with no contact with others, with no past," borne out of its constant purging, leads paradoxically to its own inevitable death. Politically, the logical result of this conception of the self is, as we will see in an analysis of the sequence of Jaime's death, its ultimate sacrifice to the cleansing machine of the totalitarian state. Only through its "beautiful" political death will the self, now purged of sin, achieve complete redemption. As Franco bluntly put it, "we need to sacrifice the 'self' to a unit that is the building block of our strength" (121).

This glamorizing of death is suggested by Pedro Churruca's answer to another question, put to him by his son José: "Father, is it true ... that navy men and soldiers get dressed up before they die?" (Andrade 33), to which Commander Churruca responds: "That's how it is. A navy man always gets dressed up for his biggest events. That's how he goes to his wedding. How could he not dress up for the most solemn day of his life, the day of his glorious death?[12] When it is one's turn to die, one dies with all of the arrogance, all the acceptance and with all of the splendor" (34).[13]

The themes of sin, punishment, redemption, and sacrificial death that occupy *Raza* converge during the climactic garden sequence. In this sequence, the whole family gathers in the garden for an afternoon picnic. The camera fades in from the previous shot of a church altar, where the family has been praying to the *Virgen de la Barca*, and to a thick bush of blossoming flowers surrounding the family garden, which connotes an idyllic family setting. Nature and mankind harmoniously blend with one another. While we hear Commander Churruca's voice beginning to tell his family the story of the glorious military past of the Spanish Navy, the camera starts panning to the right, letting the whole scene slowly unfold before our eyes. First, the camera shows Jaime's cradle, which, made of dark wood with a cross on top, foreshadows his innocent death years later when he is executed by Republican militia along with his convent religious brothers. The camera then keeps panning slowly toward Isabel, who, separated from the rest of her family by a dinner table, calmly knits while attentively listening to her husband's story. After a brief pause over Isabel, the camera continues to pan to the right, where it finally stops over the family group formed by Commander Churruca, dressed in his navy uniform, lovingly surrounded by his three children (once again, José on his right and Pedro on his left), with Isabelita seated close to him (Fig. 1.1). José asks his father the meaning of the word "Almogávar," which he has just uttered. His father explains that the *Almogávares* "were chosen warriors, the jewel of the Spanish race" (Andrade 28). The film now cuts to a close-up of a puzzled José, who, in turn, asks his father: "What, now there are no longer *Almogávares*?" His father solemnly answers: "When they are needed, they are always there. They just lose

Figure 1.1 *Raza*, 1942

their beautiful name. But *Almogávar* will always be the chosen soldier ..." (Andrade 29).

Like the shot of Jaime's cradle, José's close-up will also be retroactively charged with meaning, like everything else in this sequence. José, the new Santiago, will later in the film become an *Almogávar* during the Civil War, Spain's "chosen soldier." José will also transform himself into the *caudillo*, the medieval warrior-chief—and sobriquet of Franco—whose name he had unsuccessfully tried to carve in the Alcázar's walls in Franco's original screenplay.[14] In short, José will be the chosen soldier to bring back to Spain that lost reactionary paradise over which, as we will see, Pedro Churruca and his wife Isabel cry Milan Kundera's kitsch second tears, as mentioned in the Introduction.

The father ends this history lesson talking about their ancestor Cosme Damián Churruca, the Spanish admiral who died heroically in the battle of Trafalgar. The camera cuts now to a close-up of an oval portrait in profile of Cosme Damián Churruca. Looking at the portrait, Isabelita exclaims admiringly, "How young!," while her father explains to his children that their ancestor Churruca died at the age of forty-four (Andrade 30).

A long flashback takes us now to Trafalgar, where Churruca heroically died ordering "mount the flag, mount the flag." From Cosme Churruca's dying face the film cuts to a shot of the Spanish flag, which in turn dissolves into a close-up of Commander Pedro Churruca's face gazing at the flag. Not only are the two Churrucas visually linked by the Spanish flag: Cosme Damián Churruca's death at Trafalgar will be faithfully re-enacted in the Spanish-American War by Commander Pedro Churruca, who also dies heroically in battle on board his ship.

It is worth pausing here to glance back at Franco's script and examine the way in which the narrator describes the sinking of Churruca's ship, since this is the climactic moment in which the text's kitsch literary style causes meaning to close down. The script reads: "The boat is submerged rapidly, and in the immense whirlpool that forms, on the peak of the highest mast, the flag which Churruca ordered to be hung remains upright *as a symbol*" (54, emphasis added). The description immediately catches the reader's attention. Churruca has ordered the Spanish flag to be fixed to the highest point of the mast. But the narrator, anxious that even this most obvious symbol might be missed, guarantees that the reader will read the conventional symbol of the flag as a symbol: "the flag which Churruca ordered to be hung remains upright *as a symbol*."

Churruca's death, then, is the moment in which Franco's text comes to a complete semantic paralysis. As Eco explains, redundancy is one of the logical consequences of kitsch aesthetics, since the meanings of its symbols, which have already been depleted by their previous usages, need to be constantly reiterated (182). *Raza*'s kitsch literary style, then, breaks the syntagmatic linkage between signifiers, and the paradigmatic axis takes over and spins out of control, as it were. The end result is the unrelenting juxtaposition of signifiers in the same narrow linguistic space. Hence, flag and symbol appear in the same sentence. The fluidity of meaning is irreparably petrified.

To return to the film, this same petrification is visually rendered in the garden sequence, which ends with the father telling his children, while looking directly at José: "And that was the beautiful death of your great-grandfather" (Andrade 32). His son Pedro characteristically replies, "I don't understand how dying could be beautiful," to which Commander Churruca sanctimoniously retorts, "Duty is made all the more beautiful by the sacrifice it entails" (32).

This garden sequence becomes a sort of *tableau vivant*, in which the film's characters freeze into "types" stamped over the film's flat surface: little Jaime, the pure and innocent sacrificial lamb inside his black cradle; Isabel, the lonely Penelope knitting, separated from the rest, but attentively listening to her husband's voice; José, the future *Almogávar*, seated to his father's right, visually underscored by a close-up, his glorious future associated with the "magic" word "Almogávar," which ends Franco's text; Pedro, seated to his father's left, the fallen angel and political rebel for the duration of the film, until his final redemption by death; Isabelita, her obedient father's little daughter; and, finally, Commander Churruca himself, the Spanish military hero whose link to a Spanish heroic tradition is visually punctuated by three interlocking shots.

The garden sequence is a kitsch paradise that is a response to the terror of historical change. When this kind of kitsch paradise is brought into the realm of politics and becomes a political fantasy to be radically pursued in society, it transforms itself into the totalitarian kitsch that must erase—by a special act of binding—anything "from its purview which is essentially unacceptable in human existence" (Kundera 248).

It is instructive here to refer to a passage from Franco's script absent from the film, in which the entire Churruca family attends a traditional Galician *romería* where at sunset "a clear horizon allows contemplation of the marvelous spectacle of a discus of fire falling into the water" (Andrade 37). Men and women wearing traditional costumes form circles to sing and dance to the music of bagpipes. Suddenly, the narrator tells us, an individual, "a man or sometimes a woman, raises their voice above the group; they are accompanied by the chorus of the rest" (37). In this perfectly harmonious and idyllic place, illuminated by a big red solar disc —with its well-tuned chorus and under the protective mantle of the *Virgen de la Barca*— mankind recovers its lost state of grace and blends together with nature. Commander Churruca and his wife Isabel are now very close to dropping Kundera's kitsch second tear, which flows from being moved together with all mankind at the emotional sight—children running on the grass, etc. Deeply moved, Isabel exclaims, "With such beautiful lyrics those songs enter the soul" (38). She nostalgically confesses to her husband, "Pedro, how few times I've been able to find this beauty" (38). The chapter now comes to a close with the lyrics of a melancholic Galician song: "Oh my wounded heart!" (38). In this fleetingly idyllic moment, the song's wounded heart, as well as Isabel's and Pedro's, can momentarily heal, sutured by the perfect communion of mankind with nature and with itself.

In this late nineteenth-century Galician paradise everybody is submissive and happily accepts their social role. Undoubtedly, this is a kitsch paradise that offers an escape from the terror of historical change; terror that, as Matei Călinescu has pointed out, "kitsch attempts to assuage" (251). In order to assuage the terror of change, kitsch "hallucinates ... empty spaces with an infinitely variegated assortment of beautiful appearances" (252). In *Raza*, the "empty space" opened up in Franco's text by Pedro's and Isabel's yearning for their nearly lost Galician paradise is metaphorically filled with moral and political content; with irrationality and blind faith, with repentance, punishment, and the seemingly beautiful appearance of death; and it will be built, as we will see, upon Santiago "Matamoros's" foundational rock, opaque and ideologically impenetrable to the corrosion of subversive signifiers—a rock similar to the one that, with a monumental cross on top as its ship mast, was to be Franco's eternal resting place at The Valley of the Fallen.

It is in the garden sequence where *Raza*'s main themes come together, but it is in the shot of the close-up of Churruca's oval portrait, I would argue, where the mood of the entire sequence is visually condensed. In this close-up, the reflection of the garden flowers is projected over the portrait in the form of dark shadows, endowing the static profile of the ancestor Churruca with a delicate background movement, visually suggestive of the Spanish expression "to die in the flower of youth" (Fig. 1.2). The idyllic setting of the family scene is reflected, then, in the background of Churruca's portrait, and vice versa. The shadow of the flowers moving around the portrait, which signals the glorious death of the young navy hero, imbues now the whole scene with the scent of a fresh heroic death, inevitably evoking Commander Churruca's own words written by Franco himself in his script—"now it is the ocean that seems to scent the air" (38)—which, like Jaime's cradle, also connote the purity of death.

Figure 1.2 *Raza*, 1942

In its iconic flatness, Churruca's portrait has the same kind of visual to-be-looked-at-ness Laura Mulvey famously ascribed to the female image in classical Hollywood film. Visually rendered as a fetish, Mulvey argued, the female image has a halo of spectacularity around it that works against the cinematographic flow, bringing it to a momentary halt ("Visual Pleasure and Narrative Cinema" 203). In *Raza*, however, the diegetic flow will not be arrested by the fetishization of the female body, as in classical Hollywood cinema, but, as the alluring close-up of Churruca's oval mortuary portrait visually suggests, by the fetishization of death.

The close-up of Churruca's portrait is also a telling example of the film's extensive use of non-diegetic shadows that ultimately defines *Raza*'s visual style, arresting the narrative flow in moments of deadly fascist contemplation and thus closing down its visual signifiers. These non-diegetic shadows, I argue, are the visual equivalent of the kitsch literary style in Franco's text. In this sense, *Raza* provides a good illustration of the process described by Bollas as characterizing fascist states of mind: a special act of binding that purges the mind from contradictory views, an unrelenting breaking of the links between signifiers, and a filling of the gap previously occupied by the spellbinding diversity of the symbolic order with "material icons" (201). In *Raza*, Bollas's "material icon" is the Christian cross, surreptitiously brought into the film frame numerous times under the guise of a shadow.

Franco's script helps us better understand this process, and the important role played by the "material icon" of the cross in the film. In Franco's script, the process is set in motion by the first line of the text, and reaches its climax in the following episode in which the entire family pays a visit to the *Virgen de la Barca*. A few days after Commander Churruca returns from the Philippines, the entire family goes to the small town of Muxía to offer a prayer to "Our Lady of the Barge." All the members of the Churruca family are dressed in white and give money to the poor. They clearly stand out from the rest of the crowd dressed in traditional Galician costumes. Afterwards, they go to the seashore to see the famous *piedra de la barca*, a large stone that looks like an upside-down barge. This stone, I would argue, metaphorically embodies the freezing up of the text's symbolic order required by the kitsch fascist aesthetic. The stone (like the cross in the film) that occupies the emptied-out space of the narrative's *mind* is not an ordinary object, but precisely the "material icon" Bollas describes. The stone is particularly ideologically charged because it is believed to be the legendary barge St James used to come to Spain in order to convert its people from paganism to Christianity. As is well known, St James is referred to in Spain as Santiago "Matamoros," because, according to myth, he helped the Christian cause during the Spanish re-conquest by killing Moors with his sword while galloping on his white horse. As such, he was endlessly invoked in the Francoist expression "Santiago y cierra España," the infamous war cry meaning "Santiago and close, Spain!" Santiago's stone ship, the kernel of Francoist ideology, thus also signifies blind faith, and therefore is monolithically impenetrable to the corrosion of subversive signifiers.

The stone, then, signifies the opaque and impenetrable core of Francoist ideology, which is precisely the residue left by the special act of binding that, purging the mind from contradictory views, freezes up the symbolic order. To achieve such totality, Bollas argues, the mind performs a "special act of *binding*"—evoked in the etymology of the word *fascism*, we might add—by means of which it can purge itself from divergent, contradictory views (201). Once this is done, Bollas writes, "the mind ceases to be complex, achieving a simplicity held together initially by bindings around the signs of the ideology" (201). *Raza*'s kitsch literary style arrests movement, its clearly propagandistic ideological nature aiming, ultimately, at putting an end to the free sliding of signifiers. The ideological certainty achieved within the fascist mind by breaking the links between signifiers is precisely what the character of José Churruca, Franco's alter-ego, is meant to signify.[15]

In the film the ever-present cross is, like the stone, the image monolithically impenetrable to the corrosion of subversive signifiers. The cross appears sometimes through suggestion in the shape of a window or a door frame, like the one visible behind Isabel the first time she is shown on the screen. Or it appears inside a room in the form of heavy dark shadows projected (rather unconvincingly) by the sunlight cast upon the window frames. This type of cross appears to the right of José when, in a scene filled with biblical connotations, he announces to his mother the imminent arrival of his father from the Philippines. Another cross, very clearly shaped, shadows José's martyrdom as it is projected against his cell's wall and brought into focus by a traveling camera the night before his execution by the Republicans. The same kind of cross, a projected reflection of his cell's metal bars, is also shown in the shot of José receiving confession. Yet another cross appears diagonally to the left of a dangling phone right at the very moment of Jaime's arrest. Another, rather large one, appears in Pedro's office when, his faith now recovered, he finally converts to the "right" cause. Finally, a large cross hangs above José's and his girlfriend Marisol's shoulders when at the end of the war they can finally embrace.

On at least two different occasions—when Isabel talks to her son José in the above-mentioned scene, and when Pedro finally converts to the Francoist cause—the cross ceases to be just a mere shadow connoting the redemptive Christian values which suffuse the entire film, but actually enlarges the frame by adding to it, as it were, another spatial layer. In both scenes, Pedro and Isabel, acknowledging its existence, look directly at the virtual cross in the same way Commander Churruca looked at the Spanish flag in the garden sequence. During these fascistic blinding moments, all dialogue stops, and the two characters step out of character for a brief moment to speak to the cross in front of them. *Raza*'s visual "material icon" is, then, like St James's stone, also ideologically charged.

The climactic moment in which the cross appears to clearly signal the fetishization of death typical of totalitarian kitsch is Jaime's execution on the beach, for many film critics the most beautiful sequence of the entire film. It is also, I would argue, the moment in the film where the "confusion of the ethical with the aesthetic category" that for Broch, as we saw, is the essence of kitsch, becomes most transparent (71). It is precisely this deceptive nature of kitsch—the substitution of the aesthetic for the ethical—that allows it to perform that mixing of real and imagined planes of experience that, as Saul Friedländer points out, characterizes the fascist beautification of death (43)—its proffering of a beautiful "political" death, not an ethical one. As he explains, "not real death in its everyday horror and tragic banality, but a ritualized, stylized, and aestheticized death" (43).

At this point in our analysis it is important to recall Friedländer's crucial distinction between two different types of kitsch: "common kitsch," "which tends to universality," and "uplifting kitsch," which "is rooted, symbol-centered, and emotionally linked to the values of a specific group" ("Kitsch and the Apocalyptic Imagination" 203). This uplifting kitsch, which exploits "obvious mythical patterns" (203), has a clear mobilizing function: its emotionally coded and readily available message is presented aesthetically, not rationally, thus eliciting from its audience an automatic "unreflective ... emotional response," making that audience unaware of the ideology being imparted (203).

The sequence of Jaime's execution is a perfect example of Friedländer's uplifting kitsch, an apocalyptic kind of kitsch which, as we will see through Jaime's sacrificial death, taps into the source of religious emotion: death, resurrection, eternal life (205). It is also a perfect example of the intersection of Catholicism, melodramatic kitsch, and fascist discourse that Marsha Kinder deems so characteristic of Francoist film (72).[16] In this sequence, Jaime's convent is savagely ransacked by a group of militiamen who round up the monks and commit all sorts of sacrilegious acts: drinking from chalices, destroying relics and religious statues, etc. A desperate Jaime calls his brother Pedro on the phone to beg him to use his political influence to make sure that after they are all massacred the convent orphans will, at least, be taken care of. In the middle of the conversation, a militiaman comes and takes him forcefully away with the others. The phone receiver falls now from Jaime's hand and starts dangling against the wall. To the left of the phone receiver, a close-up shows a diagonal black cross projected over the white wall (Fig. 1.3). The cross, the symbol of blind faith that transcends human subjectivity and unites men into a community of believers, contrasts with the useless phone, the symbol of modernity and alienating human language that, contrary to blind faith, keeps men apart. It is significant that the entire sequence will be almost silent from now on, with the exception of a very short exchange among Republican soldiers and an absolving blessing by the Father Superior. Single, alienated human voices are replaced on the soundtrack by the unified voice of a male chorus.

The sequence is divided into a series of beautifully composed, extreme long shots of a column of monks who, escorted by Republican soldiers, march through a small wood to a nearby beach. There, the soldiers set up a machine gun, its mechanical nature contrasting with the spirituality sug-

Figure 1.3 *Raza*, 1942

gested by the monks walking in silence, the choral music of the soundtrack, and the shot of the seashore showing water and sand blending harmoniously. Next, we see a close-up of the sandals of the marching monks, whose footprints are marked tenuously on the wet sand only to be immediately washed away by the water, suggesting the immateriality of their bodies and the purity of their souls, their light walk contrasting heavily with the rugged faces and rude manners of the earthy militiamen. Their footprints blend perfectly with one another and with the sand and the water, their idyllic natural surroundings. After the Father Superior's blessing, punctuated by the rude spitting of a militiaman, the machine gun starts firing, killing all the monks. The film cuts to a close-up of the seashore, and then again to a close-up of an agonizing Jaime, on his back at the edge of the water with his right arm facing upwards (Fig. 1.4). The sequence finally ends with a shot of the shore, as a female chorus on the soundtrack sings a Hosanna. All now fades to black.

Formally, this sequence exemplifies better than any other in the film the fascist kitsch aesthetics characterized by the visual softness and false *Stimmung* that Lotte Eisner finds in Nazi costume period film (202).[17] The sequence of monks dying peacefully by the sea is also a perfect postcard of the totalitarian kitsch aesthetics Kundera describes, from which all

Figure 1.4 *Raza*, 1942

ugliness and vulgarity have been removed from sight. More precisely, all ugliness and vulgarity have been reassigned to the Republican forces, composed of rude, dirty, and bloodthirsty sacrilegious criminals.

The sequence, then, can also be characterized as a good example of the "fascist moment" described by Alan Tansman in his discussion of modern aesthetics in Japan (18). These fascist moments are aesthetically cathartic epiphanies susceptible to being politically channeled to create a politically fascist mood.[18] The fetishization of death that ultimately characterizes this sequence is formally achieved by rendering the monks' execution in a highly aestheticized manner: beautiful camera shots, sacred music, carefully chosen and highly stylized serene natural settings such as the forest, the beach, and the ocean. The sequence is narratively and visually constructed to extol martyrdom, particularly through Jaime's heroic, pure, and innocent death.

In this death, the bourgeois self dissolves, as is implied by the medium close-up shot of a clearly distinguishable agonizing Jaime. Here we see the political dissolution of the bourgeois self and the birth of the "forever empty" fascist self. The bourgeois self is gloriously dissolved, like a drop in the ocean, into the higher totality of the state. This dissolution occurs in a sacralizing of Jaime through his demise. As Georges Bataille writes, "after a violent death, what remains ... is the continuity of all existence with which the victim is now one" (22). In *Raza*'s representation of the totalitarian kitsch paradise, this continuity is preserved through the martyr Jaime's death.

It is no coincidence, then, that it is Jaime who told the convent orphans the story of the birth of Christ, in a scene immediately following his brother José's symbolic "resurrection" after being shot but not killed.[19] In that scene, José is narratively depicted by the film as the "savior" who comes to redeem Spain from evil and who ultimately will avenge his brother's death.[20] But since for José to be able to take revenge Jaime first must die, José's resurrection necessarily requires Jaime's death. This is visually rendered in the scene on the beach described above, in which Jaime's unified self spills onto the sand and dissolves slowly into nature in a beautifully composed shot, appropriately punctuated by the uplifting Hosanna of the soundtrack. The male chorus before the monks' execution becomes a children's chorus right after, suggesting both innocence and the fascist feminization of the self lured now into the masses and the feminine fetishization of death.

In Broch's estimation, this sequence would "work beautifully," but would not "work ethically," because Jaime's death is rendered aesthetically but not ethically. The film is doubly deceiving in the substitution of the two categories, since in portraying peaceful monks as innocent victims it manipulates the spectator into receiving a moral shock. Thus, the historical complexity behind the atrocities committed by both sides during the Spanish Civil War and the universality of suffering that any "good" work of art should explore—like Picasso's *Guernica* or Goya's *Desastres de la guerra* [*The Disasters of War*], for example—are replaced here by the historical cliché of evil anarchists and communists, bloodthirsty diabolical beasts performing heinous crimes—clichés used morally to justify the military uprising in the first place.

However, it is in the easily triggered sublime effect of the monks' footprints tenuously marked on the wet sand at the edge of the Mediterranean Sea that the sequence becomes quintessentially kitsch. *Raza*'s kitsch totalitarian political message is drawn precariously on the sand, and its contemplation suggests an intoxicating dissolution of the self. If effective, *Raza*'s message should also cause the film spectator's self to blur in the contemplation of Jaime's sacrificial death at the edge of the sea. Thus, *Raza*, anticipating Foucault's much-celebrated metaphor at the end of *The Order of Things* (1966), attempts to help the totalitarian political cause by trying to erase through kitsch the modern concept of man "like a face drawn in sand at the edge of the sea" (387)—as the beautiful shot of an agonizing Jaime with his right arm up evocatively suggests. The sequence might then be described as a visual metaphor of fascist ideology, which, despite fascism's endless talk of radical historical change, ultimately brings society to an aesthetic standstill, and, at its worst, to complete self-annihilation. Franco, the kitsch-artist, envisioned *Raza* as a perfect vehicle to satisfy Franco the kitsch-man, who ended up believing his own lie. As Paul Preston writes, "[a]t the first private showing of the completed film, Franco cried profusely. Over the next thirty years, he watched *Raza* many times" (418).

Notes

1. Interestingly, the original version of the film was lost until the mid-1990s, when a copy was found at the UFA laboratory in East Berlin.
2. *Raza* was shot in 109 days (from 5 August to 22 November 1941) in three different outdoor locations—Villagarcía, Barcelona, and Madrid. Fifty sets were built for interior shooting, five hundred costumes were made for period scenes, and one hundred more for the contemporary female characters (Crussells, *La Guerra Civil española* 207). In total, thirty-five principal actors, fifty secondary ones, and 1,500 extras performed in the film. Forty-five thousand meters of film stock were used to shoot "Francoism's Potemkin"—*el Potemkin del Franquismo*, as Román Gubern has called it (98).
3. As Gubern writes: "Sáenz de Heredia offered the political guarantee of being a first cousin of José Antonio Primo de Rivera and a former Francoist soldier, serving as second lieutenant of artillery. But even more, he offered the professional guarantee of having trained before the war in the production company Filmófono under Luis Buñuel, the most prestigious director of Republican film (who also freed him in 1936 from captivity at the hands of the socialist union, UGT, in Madrid which allowed him to reach the Francoist side)" (97).
4. In January 1942, Manuel Aznar, Franco's press secretary at the time, as well as historical and literary consultant for the project, said he expected the film *Raza* to accomplish the following goals: "I am certain that with the film *Raza*, cinema will victoriously begin a huge undertaking: that of voicing to the world the historical, religious, moral and social reasons behind the Gran Cruzada that began amongst cheers on July 18, 1936 and ended with laurel wreaths and clamors on April 1, 1939" (quoted in Alberich 55).
5. As Gubern notes, in order to accomplish this goal, two kinds of war film were being produced in Spain during the early 1940s. The first, what he calls *cine de cruzada*, was a series of films dealing directly with the Spanish Civil War; the second was a branch of militaristic films that, although exalting army life and war in general, were not set specifically during the Civil War (82). The *cine de cruzada* constitutes, then, its own genre. The other films Gubern groups together with *Raza* include *Frente de Madrid* [*Carmen fra i*

rossi] (Edgard Neville, 1939), *El crucero Baleares* (Enrique Del Campo, 1940), *Escuadrilla* (Antonio Román, 1941), *Porque te vi llorar* (Juan de Orduña, 1941), *Rojo y negro* (Carlos Arévalo, 1942), and *Boda en el infierno* (Antonio Román, 1942). Gubern also includes in the series *L'assedio dell'Alcazar* [*The Siege of the Alcazar*] (Augusto Genina, 1940), an Italian film that was the result of the film cooperation agreements between Mussolini's Italy and Franco's Spain (Gubern 82–3). The *cine de cruzada* ended abruptly in late 1942 due to the changes that occurred in the international political context (83).

6. The *cine de cruzada* seems to have had real problems maintaining its political aim of producing films ideologically attuned to what was the new, Francoist Spain. As Gubern has pointed out, one of the main problems with these films lies in the fact that they borrow extensively both narrative and visual strategies belonging to melodrama and romantic comedy (89). This was apparently one of the main reasons behind the decision to retire *El crucero Baleares* (1941) from commercial distribution. The film was also considered too frivolous for conveying the epic tragedy of the Francoist battleship sunk in 1938 by an enemy torpedo. Gubern also observes that two other 1941 releases belonging to this series, *Escuadrilla* and *Porque te vi llorar*, suffered immensely from poor quality and excessive melodramatic baggage (89–92).

7. Gubern has pointed out that *Raza* is influenced by the compositional style of Soviet cinema; for example, in the scenes at the harbor and on board the battleship, or in Jaime's execution sequence on the beach (99). This is not surprising since Soviet cinema was well known in Spain and widely exhibited during the 1930s, and, as Gubern also points out, it was highly regarded both by filmmakers on the left as well as on the right (99). In fact, in all political quarters it was considered as the best model for creating a specific national cinema.

8. As Gubern writes, "... nevertheless ... the style of the film appears to be dominated by the iconographic mannerism of the Francoist aesthetic, that is to say, the contemporary aesthetic of the triumphant illustrations of Carlos Sáenz de Tejada, of the Valley of the Fallen and of the official sculptures of Juan de Avalos" (99).

9. So, as Marsha Kinder lucidly points out, the dialectical way of thinking that lies behind Soviet montage is completely lost in *Raza*: "... in contrast to the dialectic interrogation of Eisenstein's montage, here [in *Raza*] the superimpositions and cross-dissolves help to construct a monolithic space in which images from the past, present, and future, and footage from newsreels and fiction, and fates of individuals and collectives are all united in a single diegetic space, creating a seamless idealized historical narrative that supposedly tells the universal truth of any people who refuse to perish ... when provoked by communism" (457).

10. Eco writes: "This is why I would like to define Kitsch in structural terms, as a styleme that has been abstracted from its original context and inserted into a context whose general structure does not possess the same characters of

homogeneity and necessity as the original's, while the result is proposed as a freshly created work capable of stimulating new experiences" (201).

11. As Eugenia Afinoguénova writes, "In the hands of the ideologues of early Francoism, the typical fascist myth of regeneration through a collective and individual purifying sacrifice that stands apart from Falange's ideology was transformed into a doctrine that exalted redemption as a necessary condition of the historic triumph of the community" (1).

12. The beauty of death as something worthy to die for is a notion perfectly expressed by the slogan *Viva la muerte* ("Long live death"), popularized by the Spanish legionnaires, or *novios de la muerte* ("lovers of death"), as they called themselves. In this context of glamorizing politically beautiful deaths, Franco's famous phrase *qué duro es morir* ("how difficult it is to die"), uttered during his prolonged agony, becomes highly ironic.

13. We are reminded here of both Susan Sontag's observation that "Fascist art glorifies surrender, it exalts mindlessness, it glamorizes death" (*Under the Sign of Saturn* 91), and of Saul Friedländer's comment that death is glamorized in fascist kitsch precisely to help neutralize the terror of death by presenting it as something idyllic and ultimately desirable (*Reflections of Nazism* 27).

14. As José proudly confesses, he was once nearly arrested when caught attempting to carve the name of his first real warden, who, as he explains to Luis, was not the king Alfonso VI but El Cid, into one of the Alcazar's walls. Clearly, this action is also meant to suggest Franco's own historical justification for usurping for himself, as Spain's new *caudillo*, the King's right: "I wanted to carve it there on that rock; but the captain came and kicked me out. He almost arrested me. He didn't understand me!" (Andrade 66).

15. For a reading of *Raza: anecdotario del guión de una película* as Franco's personal sublimation, see both Gubern's *Raza: un ensueño del general Franco* (1977) and Gonzalo Herralde's documentary *Raza: el espíritu de Franco* (1977).

16. In *Blood Cinema*, Marsha Kinder writes: "Only in Spain was Fascist ideology subordinated to and rewritten as traditional Catholic doctrine. Hence, Spain was the context that could take the greatest advantage of melodrama's drive to reinvest the secular world of the family with (what Brooks calls) 'the moral occult'—to create a 'domain of operative spiritual values' that would replace the 'Traditional Sacred' that was lost during the Enlightenment" (72).

17. For Eisner, this false *Stimmung* becomes the style typical of Nazi costume period films (202). She describes it as an "exaggeratedly sophisticated chiaroscuro," an "affected sfumato which blurs the outlines [and] becomes characteristic of what is known as the reactionary '*Ufastil*' in the late twenties" (202).

18. Japanese fascist aesthetic ideals were distilled in what Tansman calls "fascist moments," which, as he writes, are "images of self-obliteration evoked through the beauty of violence in the name of an idealized Japan anchored in

ancient myth and transcending the strictures of time. They conjure wholeness in images of perceptual blending where the individual merges with a higher totality" (18).
19. As Anne E. Hardcastle writes, "[p]resented as a sacrifice for a just cause, few scenes could engage the audience more sympathetically or depict more melodramatically the victimization of the protagonist than those of his heroic death" (5).
20. "The Spanish male subject of the 1930s and 1940s," as Cristina Moreiras-Menor points out, is, like José, "a mystical-rational subject who always places his life in the service of the ideological cause. Female subjects behave similarly. In *Raza*, Isabel and José's fiancée represent the pure woman (the Virgin Mary), ready at any moment to sacrifice herself for the cause and for her man" (127).

CHAPTER 2

Romancero Marroquí and the Francoist Kitsch Politics of Time

When the rose garden of victory finally flourishes, we will give its best flowers to you
—Francisco Franco, to the Moroccan delegation in April 1937

Romancero marroquí,[1] a documentary about the Spanish Protectorate of Morocco co-directed by Carlos Velo and Enrique Domínguez-Rodiño and shot in 1938, three years earlier than *Raza*, aimed to achieve ideological hegemony in torn, Civil War Spain by means of its totalitarian kitsch aesthetic. A film with a clear political intent, *Romancero* was officially sponsored by Franco's provisional government (Elena 123). While in traditional colonial representations the colony becomes an alluring, albeit inferior, Other to the colonizing Metropolis in need of progress and civilization, in *Romancero* Spanish-Moroccan society becomes a model to be imitated, a kitsch paradise opposing—like Francoism itself—modern materialism and the secular state. By presumably offering Moroccans a highly favorable portrait of themselves, the Spanish High Commission in Morocco aimed to pay homage to the Moroccans who had already enlisted in Franco's colonial army and hoped to procure a constant flow of new recruits. Still, *Romancero*'s creators wrongly presupposed a Moroccan audience that would positively respond to its kitschy message.

As it turned out, the idealized portrayal of the Spanish Protectorate offered by *Romancero* was rejected by high Moroccan officials, who objected to the film's depiction of Morocco as a picturesque yet backward country, and it was never dubbed into Arabic for its intended audience.[2] It is my contention, however, that by depicting Moroccan peasants through biblical religious iconography, *Romancero* also aimed to convince Catholic conservative Spaniards of the moral legitimacy of deploying forty thousand Muslim "infidel" soldiers on Spanish soil to fight for Franco's crusade against Republicans.

Romancero's failure to reach its intended audience—and its two-sided agenda—provides valuable insights into the question of how the state-planned attempts to secure consent from the Spanish citizenry seem ultimately to have failed. Through this "failure," the inner contradictions of Francoism were made clear: its lack of a unified social, political, and cultural agenda due to the vastly different political, economic, and ideological interests it tried to accommodate. In the cultural sphere, these contradictions were expressed most clearly in film legislation passed in 1941—such as compulsory dubbing—which almost single-handedly destroyed the Spanish film industry, seemingly undermining Franco's official cultural and political attempts to create a submissive Francoist subject.[3] However, the failure of the state-planned attempt to secure ideological consent from the Spanish citizenry through kitsch films like *Romancero*, or *Raza*, paradoxically also reveals the ideological strength of Francoism.

Fascist leadership in Europe and Asia attempted to establish hegemony by closely monitoring film legislation and imposing strict guidelines on ideological propaganda. Michael Baskett's exploration of intra-Axis cooperation on film legislation, however, reveals cracks and fissures in what to the eyes of the Western allies was supposedly a unified fascist aesthetic. Baskett's analysis of Arnold Fanck and Mansaku Itami's *The New Earth* [*Die Tochter des Samurai*] [新しき土] (1940)—a German-Japanese co-production about the Japanese colonization of Manchuria—for example, shows how the intra-Axis collaboration "did not lead to the successful creation of a collective 'fascist' identity" (213). Although the colonial film genre led to joint projects of this kind among axis film cultures, according to Baskett *The New Earth* ultimately failed with Japanese audiences precisely "because of the impossibility of Germans' understanding the Japanese experience of modernity" (228).

And still, I would argue, this failed attempt at creating a state-sponsored totalizing "fascist" cinema aesthetic based on a successful intra-Axis co-production policy did not amount to an ultimate failure of the various fascist states to achieve a high degree of ideological hegemony. In fact, as Lutz Koepnick has observed regarding the Nazi case, the German state attempted to impose ideological hegemony on its citizenry using a variety of cultural channels, thus implying a higher degree of laissez-faire governance than is normally assumed (51–73). This indicates that the cultural policies of the various national fascisms, as well as their attempts to reach out to one another, were weighed down by inner contradictions and substantial cultural differences right from the start. The Axis nations never formed the homogeneous political and cultural front that, as Baskett observes, Allied propagandists made them out to be (Baskett 230).[4]

Francoist film policy was even more contradictory and lackadaisical than that of its German, Italian, or Japanese counterparts, despite several grandiose but short-lived attempts to create a Francoist national cinema.[5] Much like the Imperial Japan described by Baskett, Franco's Spain lacked a cohesive film aesthetic, produced early film legislation plagued by apparent contradictions, and attempted to stimulate the production of a line of colonial films that ultimately failed to fully address their intended audiences.

In this sense, the case of Francoist film politics helps illuminate the hybrid and apparently contradictory ways in which fascist regimes attempted to secure ideological hegemony. *Romancero* was produced by Franco's *Alta Comisaría de España en Marruecos* and distributed by Hispania Tobis, one of the most important German film production companies of the Nazi era. *Romancero*'s own formal structure, which seems to burst at the seams, as well as the bizarre set of circumstances surrounding its production, ideally exemplifies Francoist ideological contradictions. According to the High Commissioner of the Spanish Protectorate in Morocco, Colonel Juan Beigbeder, under whose auspices the movie was produced, and who was primarily responsible for its narrative concept, *Romancero* should capture in documentary format "all the natural and artistic beauties of the area" (quoted in Madariaga 354), as well as its "regional traditions and costumes," while at the same time, "by means of its story line" pay homage to "the fervent participation of the Moroccan people in our glorious uprising" (quoted in Madariaga 354).

After a Falangist director declined the offer to direct the film due to a scheduling conflict, the job was offered to Carlos Velo, a relative of Beigbeder, despite his leftist, Marxist ideological leanings, by the film co-director Enrique Domínguez-Rodiño. Domínguez-Rodiño was a Falangist journalist who, having worked with him in Madrid for the same production company, was well aware of Velo's great reputation as a short feature documentary filmmaker.[6] As Velo explained in a 1996 interview, he accepted the commission because Beigbeder's conceit of narrating the life of a Moroccan peasant would give him the opportunity to make a Flaherty-style ethnographic documentary which was "an ideological terrain that I love" (Fernández 87).[7] The main character, Aalami, was played by a peasant from the Kabila of Beni Gorfet who had enlisted in Franco's colonial army and who, ironically, as Velo explained, "didn't want to go to war;" this was in fact the case for the majority of Moroccans who were enlisted to fight in Spain either by force or by circumstance (95). His devoted wife Fatma was played by a prostitute, because as film scholar Miguel Anxo Fernández explains, "their religion prevented women from being photographed" (88).

In a dramatic twist of events more typical of a political thriller than a film shooting, at the last minute Velo fled Morocco with his wife to go to

Paris, instead of going to Berlin to edit the last version of the film as he was required to do. *Romancero* was thus completed by German director Marcel Cleinow in the spring of 1939 under the close supervision of cinematographer Ricardo Torres (Fernández 91). The musical score was composed by Norbert Schultze, who would become world-famous as the author of the song "Lili Marlene", which he also composed in 1938. In the final version, the film's original ethnographic intent is thwarted by a heavy-handed Francoist ideological voice-over written and narrated by co-director Domínguez-Rodiño. As Velo stated years later, in its Falangist ideological depiction of Spanish-Morocco, the ethnographic approach he originally embraced, "with real characters speaking 'chleja,' an Arab-Moroccan dialect takes the backseat" (quoted in Fernández 91). The final result, according to Francoist film critic Fernández Cuenca, is thus "a beautiful vignette of African life, but also a truthful document of Spanishness" (quoted in Fernández 93). And against the veracity of the historical record, the official publicity of the film bombastically praised the film as "the most beautiful love letter from the New Spain to Morocco," which captures the "indescribable and beautiful Moroccan gesture which the strong men of this country made, at the beginning of our Glorious Movement, of leaving families, houses, and countryside behind in order to fight with valor and love" for Franco's cause (Fernández 93). Antonio Román—the celebrated director of *Los últimos de Filipinas* which will be the focus of the next chapter and for whom the true creator of *Romancero* was Dominguez-Rodiño—also praised the film both aesthetically and ideologically (Fernández 93). However, he noticed structural problems, found its footage too long and its "voice-over intrusive" (Fernández 95). He went as far as stating that the entire last sequence of Falangist militia youth doing military exercises in the city of Melilla lasting over fifteen minutes, although beautiful in itself, was completely out of place (Fernández 95).

The final version of the film was shown to Franco—who apparently was very satisfied with the results—in Burgos in July 1939 and commercially released in Spain on 17 July 1940, to commemorate the anniversary of the military uprising which had begun in Morocco (Fernández 84). Yet despite Franco's stamp of approval, the film did not run for more than a week in Spanish theaters.[8] Given its stunning imagery of Spanish-Morocco depicting an edenic, mythical Spanish Protectorate, *Romancero* became an image archive of sorts and was subsequently ransacked.[9] Several of its sequences were inserted, for instance, in *Harka*, a militarist pamphlet produced in 1941 which also takes place in Spanish-Morocco (Fernández 95).

Spanish-Morocco was for Francoism the kitschy, mythical place par excellence. It is where Francoism—that eclectic kitsch fascist ideology that established itself in Spain by means of a military uprising that began in Morocco—was born. For Francoism, Spanish-Morocco was not a geographical reality but a mental space, an ideological fantasy, "the cradle of the [Francoist] movement," as it was sometimes called (quoted in Casals Meseguer 214). This was the ideological fantasy that the final version of *Romancero* meant to signify and that was at the core of the Francoist kitsch politics of time.

One of the defining traits of early Francoism was a politics of time based on a notion of messianic time characterized by what Benedict Anderson, following Walter Benjamin, called "prefiguring and fulfillment" (24). *Romancero* is structured around this notion. The film is subdivided into four main segments: the first revolves around the family life of Aalami, a Moroccan peasant and the film's protagonist, in his native village around sowing time; the second focuses on Aalami's travels around Morocco in search for work; the third follows him to Spain, where he fights in Franco's colonial army; and the fourth depicts Aalami's return home from Spain in time for the harvest. Each segment prefigures and fulfills each other. Aalami first feels compelled to leave his village after receiving a sign while he is plowing his land, visually represented by the close-up of an ox's head underlined by a few musical chords on the soundtrack reminiscent of the music played at bullfights, which here is meant to underline the ancestral call Aalami receives back from Spain, his supposedly former fatherland.

He travels on foot around Morocco in search of work. The narrator's ethnographic excuse for photographing white mosques and villages, colorful markets and ritual weddings is nothing but a disguised pilgrimage to join Franco's higher cause. After a brief encounter with a Francoist messenger riding a white horse—an obvious reference to Santiago "Matamoros" (St James of Compostela), patron saint of Spain and the mythical Moor-slayer of the Spanish Reconquista—he finally stops his wandering at the recruitment office to join Franco's army; the strangeness of the visual reference to Santiago, "the Moor killer," in a Moorish land is appropriately punctuated by the camera radically breaking the imaginary 180 degree axis for the first and only time in the film. The importance of the moment is also underlined by the scene of another courier giving a message to a council of Moroccan elders, seated in front of a large tent, which the voice-over translates for us: "News has arrived that in Spain things have taken place," euphemistically referring to Franco's military uprising. Voicing unanimous accord, the tribal chieftain calmly reacts to the troubling news by simply uttering, "We will be with Franco and his friends," while glancing to the upper part of the frame. A following point of view shot reveals the peak of a mountain enveloped in clouds, visually translating the sublimity of Franco's uprising.

The representation of the sublime, fascist moment is followed by a fast-paced montage of ideologically charged images representing the preparations for the military uprising and its firm roots in Moroccan territory, described by the narrator as the "immortal cradle of the movement which saved Spain": Franco's aircraft; a diagonal extreme low-angle shot (à la Leni Riefenstahl) of Falangist militia giving the fascist salute to the Spanish flag waving in the wind; and finally the Falange's emblem of the yoke and the arrows, already seen in the opening credits superimposed on Moorish-style decorative artwork, coming alive by rapidly moving forward from the background to occupy the entire visual field. Its forward movement is enhanced by the increasingly excited, almost hysterical, patriotic recitation of the voice-over, which ends with a traditional "Long Live Spain" followed by the fascist war cry, "Arriba España."

It is at this point that the specular relationship of the two spaces—Morocco and Spain—is visually suggested by a cross-cutting scene, borrowing from Dovzhenko's cinematographic style, in which close-ups of Spanish types—only men, many in profile—counterpoint Moroccan ones. Besides the different headwear distinguishing Spaniards from Moroccans, and several long shots of a southern Spanish city later revealed to be Seville, which subtly emphasize Spain's superior civilization, both Spanish and Moroccan inhabitants are made to share a common cause: that of an ideal Spain, which as the narrator reminds us, "the majority of Spaniards, with endless bitterness, saw disappearing." The brotherhood shared by Moroccan and Spanish citizens is metaphorically conveyed by a take of the Giralda, the famous bell tower of Seville's cathedral, which originally served as minaret built by the Spanish Moors in the twelfth century. Given the fact that the Giralda underwent extensive renovations in Gothic and Renaissance architectonic style, to be adapted to its new function as bell tower to the Christian cathedral, it is here made to symbolize a perfect fusion between the two civilizations.

I should point out that the idea of using film politically to advance the interests of the Spanish state in Morocco, although revamped by Francoist ideologues at the beginning of the Spanish Civil War in 1936, had begun as early as 1909 at the onset of the military conflict in Spanish-Morocco. The Ministry of War enlisted cinema as part of its military effort against the hostile Moroccan tribes attacking Spanish positions in the city of Melilla. In requesting cinema's aid in this effort, the Ministry of War had a double objective: to help create a patriotic mood in Spain "against the waves of protest that the conflict produced in a wide sector of Spanish society," and to propagate Spain's *mission civilisatrice* in North Africa abroad (Martín Corrales 708). Thus, from the beginning, as Martín Corrales has suggested, "the movie camera aimed in the same direction as the Spanish rifles" (695).

As part of its recruitment effort, the Spanish Ministry of War supported and encouraged Spanish filmmakers to produce documentaries about the Spanish colonial army's fight against Moroccan tribes hostile to Spanish interests in Morocco. Even General Millán Astray, one of the most renowned Spanish generals of the time, used cinema as a medium to glamorize the Spanish Foreign Legion, the new military body he co-founded with General Franco in 1921. Franco himself was enthralled by the seductive power of cinema.[10] As a contemporary witness reported in 1924, he took the time amid enemy fire to personally film the withdrawal of Spanish troops from the Moroccan city of Xauen (Martín Corrales 696).

Pre-Francoist films had depicted Morocco and the Moors through a self-righteous colonial lens characteristic of all colonial film representation, which, as Bliss Cua Lim writes, frames "the other in terms of the primitive," the savage (22). But the films of 1937 through 1942 could be characterized, oddly enough, as José Manuel Domínguez Búrdalo has pointed out, as an attempt to replace old colonial clichés with a new, more positive view—albeit equally simplistic—of the Spanish Protectorate and its inhabitants (620). This was a radical move for Francoism, which had aligned itself ideologically with a Spanish ultra-Catholic and nationalist conservatism that had traditionally defined Spain's essence in radical opposition to the North African, Muslim other, seeing it as a heretical foreign intruder.

It is in this historical context of the Francoist shift in the film representation of Morocco that I would situate *Romancero marroquí*. *Romancero* attempted to stage a mythical representation of northern Morocco to persuade Moroccans to enlist in Franco's army; this representation in turn helped convince conservative Spaniards of the moral soundness of enlisting "Muslims" in Franco's "Christian crusade."

Because of *Romancero*'s double objective—convincing Moroccans to fight for Franco's cause, and justifying to Christian Spaniards the use of Muslim conscripts—it was a hybrid cultural product. In its visual idealization of the Moroccan lifestyle, it was influenced by Robert Flaherty's visually stunning documentaries—*Nanook of the North* (1922), *Moana* (1926), and *Man of Aran* (1934). The film portrays an organic community blending harmoniously with its environment—the Moroccan inhabitants from the Yebala area of the Spanish Protectorate—supposedly a spiritually unified community un-fractured by the alienating forces of modernity; in short, a typical colonial representation of the other as being anachronistically frozen in a mythical time.

With a painstaking eye for detail, *Romancero* tries to capture the "mythical" world of these Moroccan "natives" through a highly choreographed visual composition, beautiful cinematography, and an extensive cinematic repertoire in which dissolves and close-ups stand out. However, unlike Flaherty's documentaries, *Romancero* adds a voice-of-God-style commentary over the images of its Moroccan natives; it is the commentary's function to cue viewers into how to interpret the images. Trying to eliminate any possible ambiguity generated by the silent images themselves, this voice-over transformed an otherwise beautifully crafted film—albeit kitsch in its nostalgic idealization of Moroccan reality—into a perfect example of totalitarian kitsch aesthetics, with its ability to restrict meaning and close down visual signification. The tension generated by the friction between the visual images and the verbal commentary is paradoxically exemplified by exclusive visual means in the first shot of the film.

The opening still shot of the film joins the traditional Islamic decorative style in the background with "the yoke and the arrows," Falange's own visual icon, thus establishing a visual parallel between the Islamic tradition and the Francoist ideological cause (Fig. 2.1). Following this initial

Figure 2.1 *Romancero marroquí*, 1939

shot, a written text also informs us that *Romancero* was made "thinking of Franco," and "with deep love and respect towards our Muslim brothers," to whom, in fact, it wants to pay homage "for their virtues" and their "generous loyalty." The text describes the Moroccan people, as well as the film's hero, not as barbaric tribesmen, or as the heretic infidels of past traditional depictions, but as "noble and simple, brave and pure." Finally, it also reminds us that, like the protagonist, they took part in "our Crusade" voluntarily, guided by ancestral forces. The text ends with a poetic wish: "Let the blood ties that unite our two 'peoples' flourish in a luminous future for both."

Despite *Romancero*'s stated goal of paying homage to Moroccans helping in Franco's cause, the voice-over, narrated entirely in Spanish by Dominguez-Rodiño, the Falangist film co-director, betrays its intention to convince conservative Spaniards of the moral righteousness behind the decision to enlist Muslim soldiers—Spain's traditional enemies—in their "Christian" crusade against Republicans (*Romancero* did open, as mentioned earlier, however briefly, in every major provincial town in Franco's Spain).[11] It had to persuade conservative Spaniards that, unlike the old one, this new crusade was not launched to exterminate "pious" Muslim brothers but to eliminate Spanish Republicans now labeled traitors to the fatherland and thus unworthy of the term "Spaniard."[12]

Given its propagandistic and ideological agenda, it is no surprise that *Romancero* did not really attempt to seriously explore the cultural and ethnographic differences of Moroccans living under Spanish rule, as Velo had originally intended. On the contrary, and without ever abandoning the use of ethnographic cliché, it set out to reveal the deep similarities between Christian and Muslim "believers." Thus, in *Romancero*'s representation, northern Moroccans resemble much more the biblical images of Semitic tribesmen in white flowing robes tending to their flocks, plowing their land, or playing their musical instruments—images that filled the standard Spanish Catholic catechisms of the time—than they do the more realistic images that would correspond to the starker reality of a hungry and disease-ridden Spanish-Moroccan Protectorate in 1938 (Fig. 2.2).

Instead of envisioning a future in which the anachronistic Moroccan inhabitants "will one day be like us"—as for Cua Lim colonial film typically does—*Romancero* performs a temporal fusion between colony and metropolis (14).[13] Negating the linear conception of time and secular material progress embraced by the other European colonial powers such as France, Great Britain, and Germany—deemed rapacious by Franco—in the film the colony becomes a specular image of what the

Figure 2.2 *Romancero marroquí*, 1939

metropolis—Franco's New Spain—should become: an enchanted spiritual space—the spiritual reservoir of the Western world, as Franco liked to call it—living outside the empty, homogenous time of the other European nations where, as Lorraine Daston and Katherine Park observe, "Enlightenment, and the marvelous were no longer compatible" (quoted in Cua Lim 23).

For Francoism, Spanish-Morocco was thus an edenic, kitschy, mythical place. It was a lost object which, as the narrator reminds us when describing the "sacred and mysterious" Moroccan city of Xauen, was founded by Andalusian Moors and seems "as if it had been transported from Ronda's mountain ranges [in Spain] to the Magreb's ones." As this description suggests, Spanish-Morocco is presented as a geographical appendix of the metropolis still enjoying the sacred and mysterious qualities Spain once embodied itself before it lost its essence emulating foreign, progressive ideals.[14] In short, in the film Morocco is not a geographical reality but a mental space, an ideological fantasy that was at the core of the Francoist kitsch politics of time.

To return to the film's protagonist's travels from Morocco to Spain: his has been a pilgrimage in search of a destiny that has already been determined for him. His fighting in Spain—where he receives three wounds—fulfills this predetermined "destiny." Finally, his return home in time for the harvest not only brings the narrative to a close but also implies that even nature itself rewards his courage for fighting for the right cause with a bountiful crop.

Romancero's narrative thus "moves" cyclically, revolving around agricultural events inextricably tied to the religious, the political, and the transcendental. Time is contained within an organic community of believers and never spills out into the empty, homogenous time of history, the linear historical time of the modern nation. This circular, ahistorical, Francoist temporality, around which *Romancero*'s narrative is built, is what Mark Neocleous sees at the heart of fascism, as a "reactionary modernism," which can also be said to characterize all forms of kitsch (73). At the heart of the power of fascist kitsch is its hallucinatory power, its "compulsion to escape from abstract sameness," to use Adorno's phrase, from the empty homogenous time of modernity (quoted in Călinescu 228). Kitsch, like Francoism, promised a refuge against the passing of time, against the decay of the aura that Benjamin saw at the center of modernity. This fear of change and, ultimately, of the inevitability of death implied by the modern teleological conception of history, accounts for the emergence of kitsch as refuge, as "home"—as the Spanish avant-garde writer Gómez de la Serna calls it—looking into the ideologically reconstructed past, not into the future, as we saw in the Introduction (12).

Yet this notion of kitsch only goes so far in explaining the film's political aesthetic. To fully understand *Romancero*'s attempt to persuade Moroccans to join Franco's army, it is important to recall Saul Friedländer's crucial distinction, which we already encountered in Chapter 1, between two different types of kitsch: "common kitsch," "which tends to universality," and "uplifting kitsch," which "is rooted, symbol-centered, and emotionally linked to the values of a specific group" ("Kitsch and the Apocalyptic Imagination" 203). This uplifting kitsch, which exploits "obvious mythical patterns" (203), has a clear mobilizing function: its emotionally coded and readily available message is presented aesthetically, not rationally, thus eliciting from its audience an automatic "unreflective ... emotional response," making that audience unaware of the ideology being imparted (203). It is the harnessing of the power of kitsch for political purposes that Francoism shared with German, Italian, and Japanese fascism.

Romancero's narrative, whose explicit goal was military mobilization, to make Francoist soldiers out of starving Moroccan peasants by promising them the "best roses watered with the generous blood of our people united in one ideal," is carefully constructed around this notion of uplifting kitsch; appealing to Moroccan "tribal" emotion in order to mobilize. *Romancero* attempts to link the pristine natural landscape of the Moroccan

Rif to the traditional values of its inhabitants. It pre-packages its own political message as a closed ideological system, which, to be made more effective, it renders aesthetically, producing that "confusion of the ethical with the aesthetic category" that for Broch is the essence of kitsch (71).

The first section of the film introduces us to the harsh natural environment of Spanish-Morocco and directly into the land of the mythical patterns of uplifting kitsch. The various shots of giant cacti, and the mosque's white tower with the muezzin calling to prayer, combine with shots of arid mountains and ocean waters through a chain of dissolves (Fig. 2.3). These establishing shots visually conflate the natural and the spiritual in a series of "organically" linked shots—with hardly any visible cuts—rendered in that "curative imagery of unity" that for Kenneth Burke was so characteristic of fascism (177). Immediately after these shots, the camera gives us a long panoramic shot of Aalami's village, followed by a long panning take accenting the immaculate pure white dwelling against whose walls a few rural implements idly rest. The palm roof is metaphorically linked to the tree branches surrounding the small house, suggesting nature and civilization blending harmoniously (Fig. 2.4). The camera comes finally to rest with a medium shot on two pairs of traditional Moroccan slippers in front of the house—metonymically indicating the people resting inside.

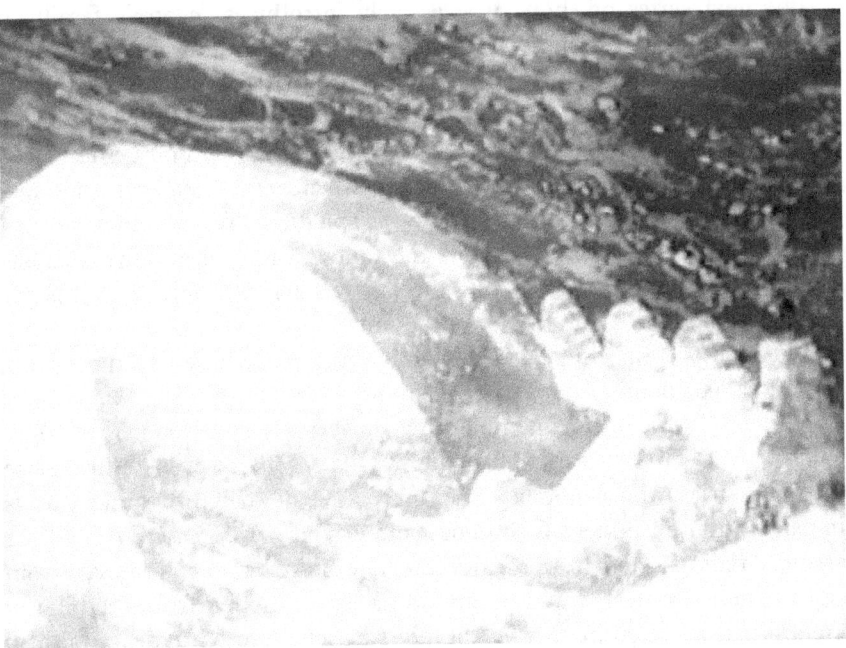

Figure 2.3 *Romancero marroquí*, 1939

Figure 2.4 *Romancero marroquí*, 1939

The next series of shots progressively introduces Aalami's family: a crying baby in the cradle; his eldest son, Ahmed, waking up and immediately transforming his blanket into a *chilaba* (robe), leaving the house moments later with his mother Fatima; and finally, a shot of Aalami himself tightening his turban around his head. At this point, the voice-over, guiding the viewer on how to see the scene, makes its first utterance connecting the natural, the social, and the spiritual: "the Muezzin's voice, extending itself through mountains and valleys, the skies and the seas, has called to life. Morocco wakes up, the day has arrived, and the fields get flooded with light."

These first shots, then, visually follow the pattern set by films such as Walter Ruttman's *Berlin, Symphony of a Great City* [*Die Sinfonie der Großstadt*] (1927), or the opening of Dziga Vertov's *The Man with a Movie Camera* [Человек с киноаппаратом] (1929). However, unlike those documentaries, whose opening shots emphasize new rhythms and patterns in celebration of modern technology and city life, in *Romancero* anything artificial that distracts from the organic flow of life has been removed from sight. The voice-over draws on an old narrative model, from the biblical Genesis, in an attempt to give the phrase "let there be light" a faithful visual representation. Therefore, from the very beginning *Romancero* frames an unfamiliar Moroccan reality for the Spanish audience within the parameters of an immediately familiar narrative structure—a structure that stands outside linear historical time.

This paternalistic and conservative representation of Morocco reveals Franco's own paternalistic conception of the metropolis. In this temporal merger between colony and metropolis, Morocco is perfectly self-contained, living harmoniously in its spiritual daily existence. Contributing to this idyllic picture is the caring, protective hand of the metropolis as evinced in the scenes in which the protagonist's wife's son becomes ill. After his mother has tried all the local remedies to cure her child to no avail, she finally goes to the Spanish infirmary to get effective treatment. In exchange for Franco's protective care, Morocco opens to Franco its precious mines to help him with the war effort. The role of the Protectorate is not to modernize Morocco or intrude upon its ancestral traditions but to ensure that its inhabitants—aided by Spanish medicine whenever necessary—can go on living their meaningful cyclical lives undisturbed.

It is in this kitschy visual idealization of a pre-modern way of life—a self-sustaining moral ecosystem minimally intruded upon by modernity in the form of medical assistance or industrial mining, so Franco can wage his war against modernity—that the Spanish-Morocco depicted in *Romancero* becomes the ideal embodiment of the "scattered fragment" of the aura, to use Celeste Olalquiaga's term, that Franco hoped to restore and bring back to Spain by his new crusade of Reconquista (95). In this kind of Francoist kitsch, the "empty space" opened up by the flattening out of a distinct geographical and cultural reality and its replacement by a historical cliché is metaphorically filled with moral and political content: with irrationality and blind faith and the seemingly seductive appearance of death. *Romancero* was, after all, a cry for war, an attempt to persuade young Moroccans to die for Franco's cause.

The militarization of Morocco is made obvious at the end of the film, which drastically changes its visual tone and mood, losing part of its exotic mystique and shot in a more realist style with sharper edges. These final scenes depict the naval and infantry military exercises of Falangist youth in the North African Spanish city of Melilla, geographically belonging to Morocco. They show young fascist cadets—the future of Franco's New Spain—receiving military training to ensure that neither Morocco nor Spain will ever succumb to foreign, secular, modernizing influences. The presence of the fascist youth in North Africa also acts as a counterbalance to that of the Moor soldiers in the Iberian Peninsula during the Civil War.

Romancero ultimately failed to connect with its Moroccan target audience. Ironically, and much like the rejection of Fanck and Itami's *The New*

Earth by Japanese critics because it failed to come to terms with Japan's modernity, high Moroccan officials ultimately rejected the film because it depicted northern Morocco as a poor, pre-modern, backward place (Elena 124). *Romancero* had a very limited distribution within the Spanish Protectorate; in fact, it was never released with its soundtrack dubbed into Arabic. It also had a very short run in Spain. *Romancero* was supposed to be the beginning of a soon to be abandoned new line of "Africanist cinema" that would help advance Spain's colonial expansion in Africa.

Romancero's difficulty in successfully addressing its intended audience, however, allows us a precious glimpse into the inner ideological contradictions that plagued Francoism right from the start—contradictions that are highly visible in the cultural and political arena in apparently self-defeating Francoist film legislation. In helping its own cause, Franco's regime could have created screen quotas or prohibited the import of foreign, ideologically suspect films; instead, as early as 1941, and under the excuse of preserving Spain's imperial language from foreign contamination, it passed legislation enforcing compulsory dubbing and ruled that only producers of Spanish films could import foreign films (Triana-Toribio 53). This legislation single-handedly struck a powerful blow to the Spanish film industry, from which it would never fully recover. As expected, Spanish audiences flocked to Hollywood films dubbed into Spanish and, after the Second World War, widely available in Spanish theaters (53). Such legislative measures undermined the efforts of the more genuine fascist elements within Franco's regime. As a result, their attempt to conduct a uniform process of ideological interpellation never really worked, though its effects were certainly not negligible.

It has often been said that because Francoism was an "ersatz" form of fascism from the start, formed by competing political interests, it was able to outlast other purer forms of fascism. Francoism was a perfect example of Ernesto Laclau's "empty signifier," which can be filled with all kinds of contradictory content, and, as such, it perfectly fitted Ortega y Gasset's well-known definition: "fascism ... is A and not A" (106). In reality, Francoism, like Japanese fascism, was A, B, and C. Ultimately, Francoism, as seen in its film legislation, was an arrangement that suited all concerned: "the regime got its films, the producers massive profits and the public the Hollywood films they liked" (Bosch and Del Rincón, quoted in Triana-Toribio 53). But perhaps in the end what the regime really needed was not its propaganda films, whose effect on audiences is at best dubious, but the Hollywood films Spanish audiences loved to watch. In the end, then, I would argue that Francoism, though lacking a systematic and cohesive cultural politics, was able to secure ideological consent less through centralized, grandiose projects such as *Raza* or *Romancero* than through the popularity of American films and sentimental comedies. It might be argued that in this diffuse mode of securing consent, Francoist Spain shared much with Nazi Germany, fascist Italy and Imperial Japan.

Francoism practiced above all a very successful politics of survival. It is not purely coincidental, after all, that while Mussolini was executed by Italian partisans and his body hung upside down in Loreto Square, and Hitler killed himself in a bunker, and Japan was transformed by its American conquerors into a democratic, neo-liberal state, Franco died in bed at the age of eighty-two, softly uttering the words, "How hard it is to die." He was buried with all the honors of a head of state.

Notes

1. I thank Javier Herrera of Filmoteca Nacional Española for his generosity in providing me with a copy of this film.
2. As Alberto Elena explains, upon the viewing of an unfinished, earlier version of the film, "Unidad Marroquí," the weekly Spanish-language supplement of *Al-Wahda al-Maghribya*, the newspaper of the Nationalist *Partido de la Unidad Marroquí*, published a vitriolic attack on the film (*Romancero* 41). The article criticized the documentary for its attempt "to capture the sad and painful side of our country" (*Romancero* 41). The review categorically rejected the film as "anti-Moroccan propaganda aimed against the honor and dignity of our country" (*Romancero* 41). Also, by the time the film was completed the Civil War had ended and it was never commercially released in the Spanish Protectorate, its propagandistic import completely diminished by the altered historical context (*Romancero* 59).
3. As Nuria Triana-Toribio has observed, "[d]irect legislation such as screen quotas or a prohibition to import could have 'imposed' Spanish films on audiences, if making national productions more attractive by other means failed. Instead, from the very first legislation, the government ruled in a manner conflicting with its purported nationalist ideology" (53). For her, "economic reasons such as the willingness to make cinema subsidize itself, the need to obtain strong foreign currencies and to 'favour the economic interests of some monopolistic sectors supporting the regime' (Estivill 1999: 678), help just to interpret the contradictory nature of two decrees passed in 1941: compulsory dubbing (27 April) and the ruling that only producers of Spanish films could import foreign films (28 October)" (53).
4. Although Franco's Spain did not have any official ties with wartime Japan's film industry, as early as 1938 it did collaborate in a variety of film projects with German and Italian production companies, resulting in five feature films made in less than two years through the Spanish-German joint venture Hispano-Film-Produktion, and in the shooting in 1940 of *L'assedio*

dell'Alcazar [*The Siege of the Alcazar*], the film by the renowned Italian fascist director Augusto Genina about the siege of the Alcazar of Toledo by Republican forces during the Spanish Civil War. The five films produced by Hispano-Film-Produktion were *El barbero de Sevilla* (Benito Perojo, 1938); *Mariquilla Terremoto* (Benito Perojo, 1938); *Suspiros de España* [*Sighs of Spain*] (Benito Perojo, 1938); *Carmen (la de Triana)* (Florián Rey, 1939); and *La canción de Aixa* (Florián Rey, 1939).

5. In fact, as Ruth Ben-Ghiat writes, the Italian *Direzione Generale di Cinematografia* itself "inspired by Goebbels's Reich Film Chamber ... would serve as the model for the *Dirección General de Teatro y Cine* in Franco's Spain" (89).
6. The bizarre occurrence of Velo's participation in such a Francoist project was not lost on Falangist film critic Félix Martialay, who, in an obituary he wrote for the Falangist *El Alcázar* entitled "Velo, un cineasta muy peculiar" ("Velo, a Very Peculiar Director") observed, "And he did not explain why, quite magically, a political fugitive was commissioned to make a documentary about Morocco" (Fernández 87).
7. As Velo recounted, the mood around the shooting was bitter: "Paniagua and myself were the only Republicans. The sound engineer was a 'falangista' and, thus, there was a great tension among us" (Fernández 86).
8. According to Alberto Elena, the film was released on 18 July 1939 at the *Palacio de la Música* movie theater and lasted for less than a week (until the 24th), being replaced by the American *Private Number* (Roy del Ruth, 1936) with Loretta Young and Robert Taylor (*Romancero* 78). The film was re-released for an entire week "at the end of August at the Salamanca and Monumental film theaters but soon afterwards disappeared from circulation" (*Romancero* 75).
9. With the title of *Dern Stern von Tetuan* and undergoing substantial editing changes, the film was released in Berlin in November 1939. As Alberto Elena writes, "the film would end up serving the German authorities as a cornerstone of their pro-Arab and anticolonial propaganda (meaning anti-French and anti-British) in the roar of the famous 'battle of the radio waves' and in the context of their great aspirations on the world stage" (*La llamada* 47).
10. Francoism took the political potential of cinema seriously. As early as 1938, still in the midst of the Spanish Civil War, the *Departamento Nacional de Cinematografía* was created both to supervise "nationalist" cinema and to control the state's visual propaganda (Alberich 53).
11. In fact, very satisfied with its outcome, Franco himself gave *Romancero marroquí* the green light. Its Spanish release was set for 17 July, the third anniversary of Franco's uprising against the Republic (Elena 123).
12. In Dionisio Viscarri's words, "The I and the Other got fused and confused ... The Moors were now 'the good guys' ... Morocco was now that which was necessary to retain and Spain what needed to be conquered" (75).

13. As she explains, in this colonial temporal scenario, the metropolis becomes a universal Ur-clock, as it were, assuring that the future will reap the same benefits for everyone: "the achievement of progress, secular disenchantment, and rationality" (14). In other words, as she concludes, "the primitive will one day be like the modern observer," their future "extrapolated from 'our' past" (14).
14. Alberto Elena observes that "[t]he descriptions of Tetuán, Larache and above all Xauen underlined the common history and the harmonious relationship between Moorish and Spanish elements, thus anticipating the rhetoric which later characterized the Spanish colonial documentary during Francoism" (*Romancero* 69).

CHAPTER 3

Los últimos de Filipinas: The Spatio-temporal Coordinates of Francoism

The moon shone down on everything with that simplicity and serenity which no other light possesses

—Franz Kafka, *The Trial*

The religious character that was one centrally defining quality of Francoist cinema was envisioned as early as 1935 by Ernesto Giménez Caballero, Franco's future first director of propaganda. In *El cine y la cultura humana*, he wrote, "[c]inema has found its scientific path: its commercial and spectacular expansion: its political function. But there still remains a last and decisive step: to be on God's side. Will this be the spiritual mission of Spain regarding cinema?" (33).

Director Antonio Román's 1945 film *Los últimos de Filipinas* [*Last Stand in the Philippines*]—hereafter *Los últimos*—is exemplary of the kind of Spanish cinema Giménez Caballero envisaged. The film focuses on the fierce resistance of a besieged Spanish garrison inside a church. Set in 1898, against the general backdrop of the Spanish-American War and the ensuing loss of the remnants of the Spanish Empire, *Los últimos* represents Francoist cinema's attempt "to be on God's side." It tries to redeem a humiliating loss by recapturing through violence the Catholic "spiritual essence" that, for conservative Spanish intellectual Ramiro de Maeztu, was the truth of *Hispanidad*.

As *Raza* did a few years earlier, *Los últimos* portrayed *Hispanidad* by reinterpreting one of the bleakest episodes of Spanish history according to Francoist notions of heroism and redemptive violence. The film was a vehicle through which these Francoist notions could be effectively expressed.

Like *Raza*, Román's film offered a perfect vignette of Spanish heroism, in this case enacted by a group of Spanish soldiers who, trapped inside an isolated church in the Philippines, were willing to sacrifice their lives in defense of one of Spain's last colonies.[1] And as in *Romancero marroquí*—whose highly stylized visual representation of Spanish-Morocco was symptomatic of Francoist kitsch aesthetics and ideology—the film's portrayal of a besieged colonial church standing defiantly against a Tagalog rebellion in the small town of Baler transformed the colonial reality of the Philippines into a political myth that condensed Francoist kitsch ideology to perfection.

The plot of *Los últimos* follows the heroic exploits of its two main characters: Captain Enrique Las Morenas, the garrison commander who dies during the siege, and Lieutenant Saturnino Martín Cerezo, who assumes command after his captain's death and whose memoir serves as the basis for the film.[2] The plot also follows the struggles of a few secondary characters: Dr Vigil, the garrison doctor; Fray Cándido, the garrison chaplain; and Juan Chamizo, a soldier who falls in love with Tala, a local Filipino woman who sings in the village tavern.[3]

The loss of the Philippines, Cuba, and Puerto Rico in 1898 stirred a vigorous public debate in Spain. The importance of Román's film cannot be fully grasped without understanding this debate and the ramifications of the loss. "El desastre del 98," as the US defeat of Spain in the Spanish-American War was commonly called, opened the gates for what historian Raymond Carr has called a "flood of self-examination" around the notion of Spanish decadence (224). The most pressing questions of the day were, "Why, at the moment when other Europeans were building empires, had Spain lost hers? Was Spain a decadent nation, or did it have ... powers within itself to stage a national recovery?" (Carr 224). In Carr's words, "[t]his complex of pessimism and optimism coalesced into what was called regenerationism," a nationwide intellectual movement that emerged around the figure of Joaquín Costa, an influential Spanish lawyer and politician whose main goal was to identify possible causes and promote desirable solutions to end the country's decline (224).[4] Despite its obvious dramatic historical consequences, however, the events of 1898 operated more as a symbolic matrix stirring public debate than as a real indicator of Spain's standing in the world (Loureiro 67).[5]

Symbolically, "El desastre" had a tremendous impact on Spanish society, and the subsequent "regeneracionista" discourse became pervasive among the Spanish intelligentsia, lasting, in one form or another, almost without interruption until 1936, the year of Franco's military uprising. In fact, the most radical form of regenerationism became the ideological fuel for justifying Franco's military coup d'état against the Spanish Second Republic. Disillusioned by the failure to overcome the serious challenges facing the country, in 1902 Joaquín Costa had famously called for an "iron surgeon" to restore Spain's health (115).[6] This call would be answered two decades later, first somewhat tentatively by General Miguel Primo de Rivera—who connived with the Spanish monarch to become the dictator of Spain from 1923 until 1930—and then in 1936 by General Franco, who would rule Spain for the next forty years. In fact, Franco would become the "loving" but ruthless father with a "stone where the heart is," as prophesied by Spanish writer Ángel Ganivet, an early member of the *Generación del 98* (54).

In typical *regeneracionista* fashion, Lieutenant Martín Cerezo, the author of the widely read memoir upon which *Los últimos* was based,[7] felt compelled to narrate the story of the siege of Baler precisely because it proved that Spanish military virtue abroad had not decayed despite the colonial mishandling of Spanish politicians at home. He believed that remembering this heroic deed would boost Spain's morale:

> Living yet in my soul, as though of yesterday, those eleven months of anguish that we suffered in the church of Baler, I believe I owe to my country the story of the happenings within those four walls, the last remnants of its dominion in the Philippines ... A small detachment of soldiers there proved that our military virtues have not decayed. It is well to record it, if it be only to reanimate that saving faith of which we so sorely stand in need. (Martín Cerezo 4)

According to the Lieutenant's memoir, the siege of Baler began well before the actual siege ever took place, due to the Spanish government's neglect of the military post, which had left the garrison to cope entirely on its own. As he bitterly wrote, "... the fact is, and it is well to point out, that from the 12th of February, 1898, the day of our arrival at Baler, until the 2[n]d of June, 1899, the day of our memorable capitulation, we received, as I have said before, not one cent, not one biscuit, not one cartridge" (17).

United States Army Major F. L. Dodds translated the memoir into English in 1909 as *Under the Red and Gold: Being Notes and Recollections of the Siege of Baler*, and it soon became recommended reading in several American military academies because the conduct of the besieged Spanish garrison exemplified the ideals of military courage. As Dodds wrote in his introduction, "[t]he story is one of patient endurance, of bitter suffering from hunger, disease, and wounds, of death bravely met, of heroic deeds, and of sublime devotion to the flag under which those men were serving" (5).

In the introductory remarks to his translation, Dodds appropriately describes the space in which the story unfolds as "a siege space," isolated and cut off from its immediate surroundings (5). In stark contrast to the idyllic Moroccan environment portrayed in *Romancero marroquí*, his description of the severity of the natural environment and the bleak isolation of the town of Baler highlights the adversity of the circumstances the Spanish garrison faced: it was "... a desolate and lonely spot, with stern mountain walls enclosing it upon the landward side, the vast Pacific spread before it, and an exposed and dangerous coast stretching away to north and south" (5). Soon after the Spanish garrison arrived in Baler, the Tagalog insurrection reached such a level of intensity that the Spanish were forced to take refuge inside the town church. In retrospect, the Lieutenant described this critical occasion as "... a moment always agonizing, in which the voice of honor rises impelling the consummation of the sacrifice, and when death is probable, imminent, without other glory than that of our own consciences" (Martín Cerezo 23). Five months into the siege, the situation was dire:

> The constant fire of the enemy, at times furiously general and sustained, as though they were trying to suddenly annihilate us, to blot us out; and at other times slow and deliberate, as though they desired only to remind us of the extremity we had reached; the increasing casualties; the appearance of disease, the symptoms of which were very alarming; the annoying affliction of letters, warnings, and counsel; treason which never sleeps; and the melancholy situation of the Mother Country, which was becoming more and more clear to our eyes—make up the picture ... of the [first] seventy-two days of the siege ... (Dodds 35)

Due to a lack of proper nourishment and adequately hygienic conditions, the situation would soon reach hellish proportions, made worse by a fatal outbreak of beriberi. The Lieutenant conveys with detached accuracy the increasingly desperate conditions inside the church, and his account is worth quoting at length to get a measure of the unspeakable horror the garrison endured:

> The disease which now attacked us is a terrible one, not only in its termination, but also on account of the steady advance it makes as it goes on devouring, so to speak, and annihilating its victim. It is called beri-beri. It begins its invasions through the lower extremities, which it swells and renders useless, covering them with loathsome tumefactions. The attack is preceded by excessive debility and convulsive tremblings. It goes on rising and rising until, when in its development it reaches certain organs, it produces death with frightful sufferings. (41)[8]

Yet despite these desperate circumstances, the Lieutenant found two powerful reasons to persevere: "a *flag* to defend while there was a cartridge left, and a *sacred depository*, that of the remains of our dead comrades, to guard against profanation by the enemy. It was possible for us to resist, and we resisted" (54, emphasis added).[9]

Given the symbolic importance of 1898, the exceptionally courageous conduct of the Spanish garrison at Baler, and the detailed account of the Lieutenant's unflinching love of flag and country, it is not surprising that this single historical event resonated so deeply both with Francoist officials and with Spaniards in general.[10] It also comes as no surprise that the dramatization of this heroic deed destined *Los últimos* to become the most successful of all of the earlier films of Francoism, including state-sponsored super-productions like *Raza*.[11] Nor is it surprising that Román's film was particularly careful to erase any trace of the bitter criticism the Lieutenant's memoir directed against the Spanish government for mishandling its colonies, given that the film was produced in the historical context of Franco's triumphant vision of Spain during the 1940s and was meant to advance the Francoist cause both domestically and abroad (Kinder 133).[12]

The siege of Baler exemplified to perfection the metaphor of siege that was part and parcel of Francoist ideology at the time, when the condition of the country and its citizens, also under siege, closely resembled those of the Spanish soldiers in Baler in 1898. The siege, as Francoist history textbooks tirelessly repeated, was the foundational moment when the Spanish national character was fully revealed.[13] Franco himself viewed Spanish history as a long series of sieges wherein "Spaniards" displayed unimaginable courage and heroic dignity, particularly in defeat.[14]

In Francoist historiography, the siege metaphor was a particularly important ideological tool because it allowed "a reinterpretation of the country's recent violence [the military uprising against the Republican government] against itself as the product of the attack of an evil and external force, thus legitimating the violence as self-defense" (Triana-Toribio 49). The siege metaphor also perfectly encapsulates the ideal Francoist self, the self "under siege" that is obsessively vigilant against any perceived source of contamination. This Francoist self has cut all ties with the outside world in order to carve out an empty space where it can project its own political utopia.

In the following pages I will examine the film's spatio-temporal coordinates, which, drawing from Francoism itself, are firmly rooted in political and ideological clichés assuring the film's critical acclaim. I argue that *Los últimos*'s kitsch aesthetic offered a distorted representation of the siege of Baler, despite having been inspired by the historical event (treated realistically in the Lieutenant's memoir) and despite the Francoist obsession with the notion of the siege, central both to its historiography and its political rhetoric.

A realistic representation of time and space under siege—such as the one offered in the Lieutenant's memoir and in several other international siege films—would, presumably, help the film bring back the bourgeois decadent self to its own truer temporal reality, because it would be a true representation of time and space under siege. For Henri Bergson, whose philosophical vitalism was a major inspiration for fascist ideologues, portraying temporality accurately was art's main role in rescuing the self from deadening layers of abstraction.[15] As he wrote, through the formal arrangement of his art, the true artist allows us to "put aside for an instant the veil which we interposed between our consciousness and ourselves. He has brought us back into our own presence" (134).[16] According to this rhetoric, an accurate artistic rendering of the intensity and immediacy of the subjective experience of time and space under siege would liberate the self from abstraction.

The irony of the movie is that its kitsch aesthetics betrayed this liberating proclamation. *Los últimos* does not try to capture the reality of the siege, the disintegration of the sense of reality caused by the siege's slowing down of time, and by its abstracting of space. For, ironically, a faithful depiction of time and space, and the horrors of life under siege would have only helped to undermine the main political goal of Francoist ideology: securing consent from the Spanish citizenry. An accurate representation of time and space under siege would, rather, have encapsulated the deadly isolation and destructive madness of the fascist state of mind, as evidenced by, for instance, Werner Herzog's *Aguirre, the Wrath of God* (1982), an unorthodox siege film about the infamous Spanish conquistador.

A wide range of aesthetic, political, and ideological factors contributed to the unconvincing and kitschy representation of the siege itself and of the Philippines in *Los últimos*. As visually suggested by the layout of the natives' sleepy bamboo huts, which seem to obediently embrace the Spanish church at the beginning of the film, the film's representation was far more attuned to the Francoist political and ideological agenda than to the veracity of the historical record or the Lieutenant's account of the siege. Right from the start, Román's choice of settings contributed to the film's unconvincing representation of its subject matter, since it relied heavily on obviously artificial sets. Given the precariousness of the Spanish film industry in the 1940s, this aesthetic choice rendered the film unable to convincingly represent reality under siege, resulting inevitably in its fake, unrealistic look.[17] While Román's decision to film in the studio followed standard practice in the Spanish film industry, it was also due to his belief that battle scenes could only achieve their visual dramatic splendor when shot inside. This choice of studio settings makes visible a layer of the ideological, kitsch interpretation of the historical event that would otherwise be occluded if it had been shot on location.[18]

The film's convincing portrayal of the siege and its character development were also marred by bombastic dialogue. Although its dialogue is far subtler than that of *Raza*—even daringly resorting to comic relief as a means of dramatic construction— *Los últimos* still relies on dialogue culled from Francoism's narrow repertoire of ideological clichés as its main source of meaning. Notwithstanding some moments of well-wrought humor in the exchanges between the Spanish soldiers—particularly in scenes involving the garrison's cook, a traditional stock character derived from Spanish *sainete*—most of the dialogue between the Lieutenant, the Captain, Dr Vigil and Fray Cándido lacks any humor and aspires to be morally edifying. The main exchanges among these characters revolve almost exclusively around traditional Francoist themes: military courage, obedience, religious zeal, personal sacrifice, heroic death, and the fatherland.[19] This bombastic dialogue reaches its peak in a scene in which Captain Las Morenas, after being informed that a soldier has been killed by cannon fire, stares messianically into empty space, as the main characters of Francoist cinema often do, and says, "It must have been arranged from above. Without God's permission, death doesn't kill anyone."

The film's shooting style also contributed to its unconvincing cinematic representation of the state of siege. Román was an eclectic filmmaker, artistically ambitious and conversant with the various styles of world cinema. To the extent that he wanted *Los últimos* to be faithful to the Francoist rhetoric of self-regeneration, he could have benefitted from a cinematographic style more akin to that of Orson Welles's *Citizen Kane* (1941) or from the Italian neorealism Román admired: a style of deep focus, long takes, and minimal montage, which would have captured the continuum of the reality of the besieged. Instead, *Los últimos* followed a tight film script that, by Román's own account, was made up of 595 shots. In a film with a running time of ninety minutes, this reveals a radical disregard for long takes that, as exemplified by Welles's and the Italian neorealist films, would have captured more accurately the continuum of reality under siege.

This combination of cheap studio settings, bombastic dialogue, and a much too conventional editing style resulted in a false representation of the siege that, deeply entrenched in Francoist ideology, veiled reality through symbolic form, achieving the opposite of what Bergson argued art should do. Instead, it substituted Francoist symbolic cliché for reality and thus potentially alienated the self even further, rendering it lost in a Francoist rhetoric of stasis, which, as we will see, blends time and space into a melancholic space suspended like the town of Baler in a timeless vacuum.

To explore the ideological consequences of this betrayal, I will closely examine four scenes from *Los últimos*: the film's opening establishing shot, which shows the idyllic town of Baler through a point of view shot of a military courier arriving at the site; the above-mentioned scene of the Lieutenant and the Captain staring at the church building, portrayed both as sacred refuge and sacrificial altar; the farewell scene between the characters Tala and Juan Chamizo, set in the midst of the Philippine jungle; and, finally, the close-up of the Lieutenant that brings the film to an end. Each scene illustrates a different facet of Francoist ideology as expressed through its kitsch aesthetics: its melancholic longing for a lost Empire; its glamorization of death; its substitution of history with nostalgic clichés; its emptying out of the psychological contents of the modern self; and its aesthetic cheapness. All together, these create the Francoist theme of the sacrifice of the self (under siege) to the glory of the totalitarian state as the true embodiment of the Spanish nation "rooted in an a-temporal principle of permanence" (quoted in Herzberger 22).

Before pursuing this analysis, however, it is important to situate Román's film both within the domestic and international film contexts, and within the proper historical context of 1940s Spain, in order to elucidate the full implications of the siege metaphor and of the political dimension of the film's Francoist totalitarian kitsch aesthetic.

Los últimos received a prestigious award from the *Sindicato Nacional del Espectáculo* (the official artists' union), and was declared a film of national interest by the *Departamento Nacional de Cinematografía*,[20] the main official channel for regulating the Spanish film industry. Through characteristic Francoist rhetoric, Adriano del Valle—director of the influential Falangist cinema journal *Primer Plano*—described *Los últimos* as "the most genuine anatomy of our race, the most glorious thread of our lost colonial empire, when the heart of Spain extended itself in the far East to the church of Baler, and in the Caribbean Sea to Cuba's manigua" (quoted in Elena 197).[21] For contemporary Spanish film historians such as Alberto Elena, Román's film stands out from the early Francoist film corpus typically characterized as worthless propaganda. As he writes, "*Los últimos de Filipinas* was destined to become not only the most famous and celebrated patriotic film of the 1940s, but also the best of them all" (197).[22]

The best of them all, perhaps, because the Spanish garrison under siege, fighting inside a church for eleven months even after the signing of the 1898 Treaty of Paris officially ended the Spanish-American War, became, as we saw, a perfect metaphor for a Spain suspended, like the garrison itself, in a historical limbo during the 1940s, after the defeat of the Axis in 1945 turned the country into an international pariah state.

Los últimos was filmed and shown in an extremely delicate international political context that threatened to undermine the very existence of Franco's regime. The apparently contradictory double message of *Los últimos*—conciliatory for international audiences (as Spain was now courting politically the United States, which is not only never named as an enemy in the film, but is depicted as a rescuer of the Spanish under siege); and also dutifully defiant for Spanish audiences—makes perfect sense in this context, which Marsha Kinder has referred to as the "defascistization" of the Franco regime (34).[23] On the one hand stood a defiant Spain isolated from the rest of the world, a "rogue state" under siege without representation in any major international institution. On the other hand, an integrationist Spain determined to secure the international recognition that was vital to its survival. Despite its defiant political posturing, the nation was taking the necessary steps toward reconciliation with the Allies.[24] As Marsha Kinder and Roland Tolentino have both observed, *Los últimos* can be seen as an attempt to negotiate these two poles: by portraying the heroic defense of the isolated Spanish garrison under foreign attack, it struck a pose of political defiance for the domestic market while, by erasing any "expressions of hostility toward the United States"—its principal enemy in that war—it simultaneously signaled its willingness for reconciliation with the US (Kinder 141).[25]

Los últimos thus offered Francoism a useful political metaphor (internationally as well as domestically) in the midst of a complex international situation.[26] It also embodied the Francoist ideological edifice, a political utopia that was grounded in a kitsch politics of time and space.

The creation of the image of that political utopia had the backing of the regime itself. *Los últimos* is an important example of the historical film genre, but it is also a major representative of the colonial film, a genre particularly cherished by Franco.[27] Spanish colonial films were typically set in a foreign land that, in most cases, formerly belonged to the Spanish Empire.[28] They were characterized by nationalistic overtones and religious fervor, and they enjoyed ample representation in Spanish film production of the 1940s and 1950s, experiencing a steep decline during the 1960s.[29]

Finally, and most importantly, the film belonged to the genre of the siege film,[30] which often intersected with the colonial genre, and was ideally suited to conveying the precarious political situation of Francoism after the Second World War. In the hostile international political environments of the second half of the 1940s and the early 1950s, a number of

Spanish films that depicted a fatherland under siege were produced.[31] Román's film was the most successful of the lot.

In attempting to re-create life under siege, Román was directly influenced by two movies that explored to the fullest the dramatic possibilities provided by the physical limitations of enclosed spaces: Hitchcock's *Lifeboat* (1944) and Tay Garnett's *Bataan* (1943), a successful Hollywood production starring Robert Taylor about an American patrol lost in the Philippine jungle. In fact, *Los últimos* closely follows *Bataan*'s cinematographic structure, from the title credits superimposed on a map of the Philippines onward (Santaolalla 55). But, while both *Lifeboat* and *Bataan* successfully convey the claustrophobia and the slowing down of time as sensed by both the spectator and the characters—which in the case of *Bataan* includes the psychological breakdown of the American soldiers under duress—*Los últimos* negates this experience.

As visually suggested by the layout of the natives' sleepy bamboo huts surrounding the Spanish church in the establishing shot, mentioned earlier, the clichéd cinematic style of *Los últimos*—deeply entrenched in Francoist ideology—stifled the film's potential for a fuller, realistic representation of the siege: namely, the slow and excruciating process of physical and mental decay endured by the besieged, whose sense of reality disintegrated under the slowing down of time and increased compression of space.

For the besieged, who eagerly await its arrival or its passing, time slows down its invisible flow and ceases to be the measurable background of unfolding events, becoming instead the focal point of their attention. During a siege, time becomes almost tangible, revealing its true substance, the *stuff it is made of*, as it were.[32] In a siege, the physical limits imposed by the line of defense also cause space to disintegrate. Every inch of ground that requires protection from the enemy's attack becomes instantly dematerialized, made to metonymically represent the whole of the nation. During the course of a siege, then, time no longer refers to a concrete historical reality, causing that reality to disintegrate, and space no longer signals a concrete geographical reality, instead disintegrating into an abstraction.

But in Román's film, this disintegration of reality is shown to us superficially and statically, exclusively by means of its narrative plot and not by proper cinematic means. The passing of time is simply indicated by a series of inserts, functioning almost as intertitles. For instance, soon after the Spanish soldiers take refuge inside the church, a series of scenes shows us how they prepare for the siege and endure the first rebel attacks. Then the camera cuts to a shot of the church tower with the Spanish flag hoisted on top. A voice-over informs us that "four months have already passed under this flag—four months of siege during which those living under the flag feel happy because they know they are there to fulfill their duty." A few scenes later, while the Lieutenant dictates the death report of Captain Las Morenas to Dr Vigil, we are told that five months have passed since the beginning of the siege.[33]

These few temporal markers—slices of space that interrupt the flow of time—simulate time's passing, but beyond their insertion there is little attempt to grasp cinematically the halting of time: the here and now of the state of siege. The painful "awareness of time" is implied, but never re-created, as illustrated by a conversation between a very somber Lieutenant Martín Cerezo and Dr Vigil. When the doctor tries to cheer up the Lieutenant by reminding him that at least they are still alive, he replies, "The dead don't know what it means to be waiting, and waiting to see time go by."

The portrayal of the disintegration of space is equally unconvincing. Again, it is implied but not visually shown, lacking the disorienting force of such films as *Paths of Glory* (1957) or *Gallipoli* (1981), which convey the all-engulfing horror of First World War trench warfare. It simply conveys allegorically the religious essence of the Spanish nation. The "consecrated" space within the thick walls of the church of Baler—where the Spanish soldiers fight for their colony against Tagalog rebels—all too obviously represents the sacredness of the Spanish nation for which every true Spaniard is willing to die. After all, the overlapping of military and religious spaces is the defining trait of Francoist ideology, whose ideal hero is evoked by the popular Francoist image of the soldier-monk who, as Spanish historian Teresa González Aja has remarked, was a "compound of austerity, spirit of sacrifice, and impassiveness when faced with bloodshed..." (75).

Contrasting the film to the memoir it was based on is instructive here. In the Lieutenant's memoirs, the collapse of time and space resulting from perceptual disorientation produced by the siege reaches its climax in an episode that depicts with convincing accuracy the slowing down of time and the constraints of space under siege. This episode is conveniently excluded from the film, perhaps because the Lieutenant and the rest of the Spanish soldiers are unheroically shown to suffer from a temporary lapse of reason. In the memoir, we are told that a Spanish officer arrives at Baler and lets the Lieutenant know that a steamer boat will come to shore to take the Spanish soldiers to Manila. Upon sighting the steamer on the bay, the Lieutenant seems to finally come to his senses for a brief moment. However, shortly after, he concludes that the steamer is not real, but only a figment of his imagination, with its apparent reality being the result of "being deceived first by optical illusion" (Martín Cerezo 118). Once the steamer has been dismissed as a mere optical illusion, the Lieutenant decides the boat is simply a decoy, an ingenious visual trick deployed by the enemy to fool him. He writes in his memoir:

> ... in the obsession that dominated us, we concluded certainly that all this was a comedy, and that the alleged steamer was nothing but a lighter theatrically dressed up, and rigged for the purpose of mocking us. So true was this that some of the soldiers were betting that the funnel was made of *nipa*, and others were sure that they could see those who were towing the contrivance. (119)

The Lieutenant's maddening obsession, which led him to "being deceived... by an optical illusion," is the end result the film painstakingly attempts to avoid: the accurate portrayal of the horrifying reality of the siege. This is because the sensual chaotic existence of the state of siege, its invigorating madness—the temporary liberation of the self from the straitjacketing of abstract reason to which, as we saw, fascism continually paid lip service—is in fundamental contradiction of the totalitarian social policies that fascist propaganda hoped to help bring forward. Unlike the Lieutenant's memoir, Román's film, suffused in kitsch aesthetics, does not capture the specificity of the sensual, chaotic existence of the state of siege, as the memoir does at its best moments, precisely because kitsch aesthetics impose the uniformity of the commonplace upon reality and upon the self.

In *Los últimos*, this commonplace is an ideological fantasy space created by the spatio-temporal coordinates of Francoist kitsch: a mythical, messianic concept of time flowing outside the realm of history (suggesting the transcendental mission of Spain), and a mythic concept of space overflowing any real geographical boundary (accommodating Francoist notions of Empire). As illustrated by the siege of Baler, for Francoism time and space were not created by the secular coordinates underlying the emergence of the modern nation. And as we observed in the case of *Romancero marroquí*, (kitsch) religious coordinates helped Francoism justify its military uprising against the Republic and its modernizing agenda.

In the introduction to his translation of the Lieutenant's memoir, Dodds sets up the story that follows by first describing the small church with thick white walls at the center of Baler where the action will take place:

> Its oldest and most substantial building, the universal hallmark of Spanish conquest, is its church. It is a rude stone edifice, gaunt and bare and neglected; yet this desolate sanctuary is the shrine of the noblest epic of Spanish sovereignty in those ill-starred

islands. For within the shelter of its walls a company of Spanish soldiers, starving, forgotten, yet unconquerable, withstood a siege of eleven long months, under circumstances of suffering and heroism, during the last days of the Spanish and the early days of the American dominion in the Philippines. (5)

This small church of Baler will also be the dominant structure in the film, providing the visual architectural frame against which the plot of *Los últimos* unfolds. In the film, the church is both a religious colonial building in the sleepy town of Baler and a Francoist ideological edifice suspended in time and space—like Don Jaime's house in Luis Buñuel's *Viridiana* (1961), as we will see in a later chapter—as is visually suggested by the first establishing shot.[34] This establishing shot shows a Spanish military courier galloping furiously, having just barely escaped a Tagalog ambush. At dusk, the soldier reaches a hill from which he can see the town below, and he smiles with relief at the idyllic picture.[35] This point of view shot reveals a tiny village illuminated by a full moon and separated from the sea by a narrow winding river (Fig. 3.1). The shot is composed in such a way that the village seems to rest at the bottom half of the frame, while the upper half is occupied by a gleaming sea reminiscent of the sky. The church dominates the small town, made up of a few rows of rustic huts with palm roofs. In its postcard-like composition and its moonlit nocturnal charm, this shot evokes a romantic, melancholy beauty, a nostalgic vision of a self-contained town suspended in time and space. This idealized shot—with the Spanish church at the center of the town—brought home for the Spanish audiences of the 1940s a clichéd, melancholy representation of Spain's long-gone colony.

Figure 3.1 *Los últimos de Filipinas*, 1945

Román's film embodied this Francoist kitsch melancholy aesthetic that had fully emerged during Spain's post-war political isolation. After all, the tenuous link with the outside world forged by a Spain under siege in the mid-1940s allowed Francoism to fill the vacuum with its own, religiously inflected, political fantasy, its *nacional-catolicismo* (an orderly space with the church at its center), as the point of view establishing shot of the military courier blissfully contemplating the town below him evocatively suggests. As we saw earlier, this was a melancholy political vision attuned to the concept of the nation embraced by Francoist historiography. Francoist melancholy became, as Alberto Medina observes, a powerful political tool, whose function was to bring an idealized past back into the present to be projected into the future (33).

Resulting in a coalescing of past, present, and future, Francoist melancholia revels in the isolation of the besieged and thus overturns the normal balance between *identity* and *relations* that, for Marc Augé, lies at the core of all spatial arrangements, and also of history (37). As illustrated by *Los últimos*, identity—understood now as sameness—gained the upper hand over difference and historical change, and solely presided over the "closed space of the group withdrawn into itself" (47); in this case, a group of Spanish soldiers that, like the country itself, has cut ties with the outside world and lives in a self-imposed siege several months after the real siege has ended.

In *Los últimos*, the establishing shot—a shot usually shown to establish the film's spatial and temporal coordinates—is rendered from the point of view of a dying man. The courier will not be so lucky the second time around; he is shot dead while attempting to deliver an important message from the Lieutenant to Manila. This man also happens to be the only link between this idyllic nocturnal vision and the outside world. From the outset, the film introduces us to a ghostly, melancholic world lost in time and space: a world shown to us precisely through a point of view shot of the Spanish soldier, which hints at the pure subjective existence of the melancholy object. However, in *Los últimos* the subjective existence of the object should not be understood as being generated by the purely private sphere of dream-like fantasies. On the contrary, it is tightly linked to the political realm.

As mentioned earlier, the siege metaphor perfectly encapsulates the ideal fascist self, which can be described as a self *under siege*, obsessively vigilant against mental contents that are regarded as contaminated. The idealization of this "process of purging itself of what it has contained" is, as we saw in earlier chapters, according to psychoanalyst Christopher Bollas, precisely what characterizes the fascist mind (203). As Bollas explains, it is only through the constant purging of the self *under siege* that a new fascist self can be born, emptied of all mental content. This newly born fascist self emerges precisely from its radical separation from a contaminating *prosaic* reality; a self "with no contact with others, with no past (which is severed), and with a future entirely of its own creation" (203). As in the case of *Raza*, whose screenplay was revised in part by Román, it is only through this constant purging of the self *under siege* that a new self can be born empty of all mental content. In its Francoist version, this is an empty self for whom blind obedience to the greater cause is the only legitimate content, as illustrated by *Los últimos*'s portrayal of the Lieutenant, who, unlike in the much fuller representation in his own memoir, is depicted in the film as a military automaton who follows orders until the unreasonable end.

However, instead of a radical fascist self "with no past (which is severed), and with a future entirely of its own creation," the Francoist self could be more accurately described—as *Los últimos*'s establishing shot strongly suggests—as a melancholic self through which a nostalgically distorted past has been projected into the future and fused together in a timeless present. This Francoist self attempts to glance directly at the world, but the resulting image is deflected by Francoist kitsch aesthetics, as suggested by the nostalgic postcard vision of the town of Baler, made even more unattainable by its depiction of the sea as sky.

As the voice-over explicitly states, the courier's arrival in Baler is meant to emphasize the heroic isolation of the Spanish garrison, and to signal the importance of their cause at a time when the purity of the fatherland began to be eroded by the evils of modernity, as the news the courier brings with him promptly reveals. Upon his arrival at the Spanish military post, the courier delivers letters and packages from Spain. Since he has just returned from Madrid, his fellow soldiers surround him, eager to hear the news from the fatherland. The courier brags that he went by electric streetcar to a bullfight, and, when asked if streetcars are dangerous, he quickly replies, "Each time it derails, fifteen or twenty people die." Shocked by his answer, a soldier says, "I prefer mules." The courier complains that the bulls are thinner than they used to be, and when asked about a recently arrived cinematographer to Spain, he matter of factly declares, "Nothing. Moving portraits. A train arriving. People walking in the street." A frustrated soldier finally interrupts the courier's narrative and declares bitterly, "Such foolishness! Now tell us something worthwhile." Not surprisingly, the news brought from the fatherland to the isolated military post of Baler highlights the deterioration of traditional Spanish ways and the threat posed by foreign inventions: the diminishing of the bullfighters' heroic exploits by the thinning of the bulls; the arrival of dangerous foreign new trends symbolized by the perils of Madrid's newly acquired electric streetcars; and the banality of the moving pictures (ironically conveyed by one).

The courier dies while attempting to deliver a message to Manila. His failed attempt to deliver his message to the outside world reminds us of the psychoanalytic insight that the melancholic self, like Francoism itself, never reaches its destination, its true object of desire, since, as Freud explained, the irretrievable loss of the object (in *Los últimos*'s case the loss of the Spanish Empire and of the Spanish traditional way of life) is precisely what causes the desire for it in the first place ("Mourning and Melancholia" 245). In other words, the Francoist object of desire as characterized in *Los últimos* was a narcissistic attachment to an unattainably interiorized ideal of the nation that only existed in opposition to historical reality, transcending all limitation of time and space. As we saw in the sequence immediately following the establishing shot, the garrison's courier does not come from the outside to infuse the Spanish garrison with the energy of the external world but, on the contrary, to seal off its space from the pernicious influences of the outside world, as represented by the "bad news" he delivers about the modernization of the country.

Though the isolated, melancholic self never reaches its destination, since its object of desire is already lost *within*, the letter (in this case the film's ideological message) usually does. The courier gets killed by the insurgents before reaching Manila, but his message does finally reach home. For the movie's domestic audience, the message is simply the belief that the isolation of Franco's Spain under siege is at best a blessed state of affairs; and at worst the result of a conspiracy of the world powers against a heroic nation, "the Judeo-Masonic-leftist-conspiracy," which Franco never tired of uncovering. As suggested by the idyllic and self-enveloping nostalgic quality of the establishing point of view shot of *Los últimos*, with the church at its center, the Francoist self under siege has cut all ties with the world around it in order to carve out an empty space in which to project its own political utopia. Matei Călinescu points out that this is precisely one of the key features of kitsch: its power to hallucinate "empty spaces with an infinitely variegated assortment of 'beautiful' appearances" as a response to the terror of change (252).[36] Román's decision to film in the studio gave him complete freedom to "hallucinate" this kitsch empty space.

Therefore, as the establishing shot of *Los últimos* powerfully illustrates through its idealized depiction of Spain's former colony, Francoist political utopia was best expressed by kitsch. It is worth recalling that this establishing point of view shot is also a still shot that immediately follows a fast-paced action sequence showing the courier galloping at full speed to avoid insurgent sniper fire. The film thus begins chaotically, in media res, to quickly re-establish order. From the outset the establishing shot secures the meaning of the image of Baler, with the church at its center: a safe haven for the soldier, and also, through the soldier's point of view shot, for the spectator.

In this context of a Spain under siege, isolated from the world and existing in a historical vacuum, it is only too fitting that the only piece of evidence that finally convinces the Lieutenant to accept that the war has ended is a newspaper brought to him from the outside by a Spanish officer. Only after Dr Vigil picks it up and reads out loud a column listing the new destinations of some Spanish officers in Spain, among whom a close friend of the Lieutenant is mentioned, does the Lieutenant finally let reality in. After every possible available means has been used to convince him that the armistice has been signed, only a newspaper, the tool par excellence of modern nation-building, can wake the garrison from its pre-modern nationalistic slumber. In this way, the film suggests that Spain, defeated yet pragmatic and proud like the courageous garrison in Baler, must ready itself to end its autarchic phase and join the new world order.

Until then, the Spanish garrison denies the authenticity of the proofs brought from the outside world, thereby extricating itself from historical developments, and keeps on fighting for several months in a historical vacuum. The film's temporal narrative builds upon a vicious circularity in which every attempt to convince the commander that the war has ended is met with his incredulity, born out of the fierce obstinacy of the siege mentality. For several months after the signing of the treaty of Paris, the Spanish garrison lives in a temporal loop, in a sort of time bubble existing outside historical time, until the Lieutenant finally comes to his senses. This notion of temporality is perfectly attuned to the concept of nation embraced by Francoist historiography. Thus, the film, like Francoism, professes a notion of temporality that operates outside of the homogenous time marked by clock and calendar and slips into an epic time, a mythic time of heroism that parallels the Francoist melancholy notions of history and nationhood.

Francoist notions of time, embodied by the temporal ahistoricity of *Los últimos*, thus abstract time from its possible flow in either direction: from the past–future linear time of empirical science and modernity, but also from the future–past direction of human freedom. For Francoist historiography time stands still, suspended like the church of Baler in an eternal present. Rafael Sánchez Mazas, one of the most important ideologues of the Falange, used the Falange's iconic symbol—the yoke and the bundle of arrows, which after the Civil War branded every street corner and every official building in Franco's new Spain—as a metaphor to define this Francoist temporality: "... time of the bundle and time of the yoke: perfect balance between the Pastoral and the Epic; divine key, supreme key of History made of the patience of the yoke and the impetus of the arrow: ideal government that Plato called divine" (7). This Francoist "divine" and "supreme" key of history is perfectly balanced "between the Pastoral and the Epic," and is made of "the patience of the yoke," symbolizing the slow-moving and harmonious traditional agrarian past of the Pastoral with "the impetus of the arrow," pointing towards the heroism of the Epic.

The film's ahistorical temporality embodies the mythic time of the Pastoral and the Epic, and thus condenses to perfection the very idea of nation extolled by Francoist historiography. The Francoist concept of the nation—a far cry from Benedict Anderson's famous definition of the modern secular nation as an imagined community—rested on the influential ideas of Marcelino Menéndez Pelayo, the nineteenth-century ultra-conservative polymath for whom, as Palacio Atard states, "the nation is not a historic, temporal, and contingent entity in the whole of its purity, but rather ... is rooted in an a-temporal principle of permanence" (quoted in Herzerberg 9).[37] The church of Baler exemplifies this transcendent Francoist concept of nation. With the Spanish flag on top, the Spanish soldiers fight their epic battle inside. Shown throughout the film with low-angled shots to emphasize its importance, the church is defiantly erected in the pastoral setting of Spain's backward Philippine colony far away from modernization and progress. Moreover, as suggested by the film's mise-en-scène of the establishing shot discussed above, with its imposing church building at its center, the spatial arrangement favored by Franco's Spain is the one represented by the "flag" and "the sacred depository," also described in the Lieutenant's own account of the siege: the flag on top of the church of Baler, which too obviously represents the country and emphasizes group identity, and the "remains of dead comrades" buried in the church backyard whom the Lieutenant wanted "to protect from profanation" (Martín Cerezo 54). In short, the preferred spatial arrangement favored by Franco's Spain—and by the film—was that of medieval times when, as Marc Augé observes, "the church, surrounded by the cemetery, lay at the very centre of active social life" (53). This is an arrangement emphasized throughout the film by many shots of the church building and of the Lieutenant's frequent visits to its graveyard: Francoist Nationalist religious sentiment accompanied by death and the idea of eternal resurrection was, after all, part and parcel of the film's fascist uplifting kitsch aesthetic intended to mobilize Spaniards to fight for the Francoist cause.

As suggested by the stillness of the establishing shot described above, and the many frontal shots of the church facade, the dynamic notion of space implicit in the Lieutenant's memoir in Román's film is transformed into a static notion of space, a theatrical space that demands obedient visual contemplation. This static, kitsch notion of space solicits spectatorial passivity and ideological compliance, and thus serves as a perfect visual backdrop for Francoist ideology.

As we will see with the help of a few examples taken from Franco's early official photographs, the film portrays the church as a sacred refuge for the Spaniards under siege. However, as revealed by the scene in which the Lieutenant and his Captain first become aware of the rebel attack and look at the church building as their only possible salvation, the church also becomes a "living" character that incites them to die for Franco's cause, which conjures a fetishistic scenario whose ambiguity and disruptive political potential is brought under control by the film's kitsch aesthetics.

The church described in the Lieutenant's memoir is a dynamic space, a space for transformation and renewal. In fact, a major point of narrative interest in his text is his description of the constant transformation of the church in order to secure its adequate sanitation and guarantee its proper defense. Although the Lieutenant's detailed account of these efforts provides a dynamic notion of space that is attuned to fascism's obsessive attempts to isolate the self from contamination and is also ideally suited for cinema, in Román's film the church is no longer represented as a dynamic space. On the contrary, the church is now a static space: a sacred shelter for the Spanish soldiers under siege. As the establishing shot indicates, *Los últimos* conforms to the type of cinema that for Benjamin "reproduced the static frame of the painting or proscenium" (Wollen 201). This is an essentially "theatrical" cinema that "demand[s] detached visual contemplation" (Wollen 201). Fray Cándido makes explicit this protective function of the church's space to Captain Las Morenas when he answers his plea for help: "the protection of the Lord accompanies those who seek refuge in his house," to which the Captain replies: "I'll try to leave everything exactly as it was ...," emphasizing the idea that the church is a protective mantle, not a space to inhabit and transform. The role of the church as enveloping space is emphasized further by a shot of its main door being shut off, not to be reopened until the very end of the film.

The protective and immutable character of the church is visually suggested throughout the film by subsequent shots in which the precariousness of the village dwellings contrasts with the solidity of the church, and also by shots of a devastating fire that devours the Philippine huts but causes no harm to the Spanish church. The shift in the spatial representation of the church from the dynamic space of the memoir to the static space of the film reveals the ultra-religious conservative nature of Francoism; throughout its existence, and particularly from the Axis defeat in 1945 to the mid-1960s, Francoism actively sought the Church's protective blessings as its principal mode of achieving political and social legitimacy within Spanish society and internationally.

The role of the church as an immutable structure that keeps the Spaniards safe from harm is visually suggested early on in the film, in a scene in which Captain Las Morenas and the Lieutenant realize the true danger of the Philippine rebellion and decide that the only viable solution for survival is to seek refuge inside the church. At this very moment, as if struck by a sudden revelation, the two men look up to a point out-of-field in the direction where the church stands (Fig. 3.2).[38] This shot of the two Spanish officers looking up is immediately followed by a low-angle reverse shot of the church facade accompanied by sudden dramatic musical chords (Fig. 3.3). The abrupt use of the soundtrack, underlined by the close-up, in this shot is reminiscent of that in *Romancero marroquí* in which Aalami's historical destiny—enlisting in Franco's colonial army—is finally revealed to him. In this low-angle reverse shot the church building becomes a "living" character that looks back imposingly at the two men.

Figure 3.2 *Los últimos de Filipinas*, 1945

Figure 3.3 *Los últimos de Filipinas*, 1945

This initial impression is almost immediately reinforced by another shot in which Captain Las Morenas and the Lieutenant are shown from behind and framed against the formidable background of the church. The shot concludes with Captain Las Morenas exiting the frame, leaving the Lieutenant alone and standing on the left looking up at the church before he too exits the frame.

Unlike in the classical Hollywood cinema analyzed by suture theorists, where the absent visual field opened by a shot is immediately contained by a reverse shot, this low-angle reverse shot of the church attempts to give back the terrifying gaze of the big Other itself: in this case the fascist injunction to sacrifice one's life for one's country, as represented by the imposing church building "looking down" upon the two figures; a church building that until now has only suggested protection from danger.

In fact, the low-angle reverse shot of the church's facade echoes the visual structure of a series of images of Franco circulated in a documentary produced in 1939 by Cifesa, the most important production company in Franco's Spain. The documentary, titled *Ya viene el cortejo*, employed footage mostly taken from the first grandiose public commemoration of Franco's victory in the Spanish Civil War as a visual background to Rubén Darío's poem "Marcha triunfal," recited as a voice-over. At the end of the poem, a blow-up of Franco's head as he casts a defiant look appears in the sky. Franco's gaze, as Rafael Tranche has pointed out, "half arrogant half defying ... seems to interpellate us *to situate himself above all witnesses*" (87, emphasis added). This image neatly condenses the nature of Franco's regime. Franco's head is at the center with a church bell tower to his right and fighter planes up in the sky: that is, the church and the military, the two main pillars of Franco's regime, sustain the dictator's gaze, which, like the shot of the church, incites viewers to sacrifice themselves for his cause.

However, in addition to the severe and authoritarian images of Franco, there were also other kinds of images of him, in which he appears nurturing and smiling. This was the sort of image favored by Giménez Caballero, Franco's first head of propaganda, who wanted to disseminate them across the country in order to differentiate Franco's official portraits from Benito Mussolini's or Adolph Hitler's. As he wrote,

> Here, where passions have exploded in blood, where every Spaniard fights his own shadow, where the soul of the people was and is troubled and everything is wrath, war and struggle, only this supreme smile of peace and love, that is Franco, will be able *to sooth him, calm him down, and heal his wounds.* Franco's smile is like the virgin's mantle thrown over the sinners. *It has maternal and paternal tenderness at the same time.* (Giménez Caballero, *España y Franco* 54, emphasis added)

In short, Giménez Caballero wanted these blow-up heads of Franco's early official portraits endowed with the same thaumaturgic powers old monarchs were believed to possess in their subjects' imaginations: the power both to soothe the troubled soul of the Spaniards and to "heal their wounds." The Francoist subject was prompted officially, then, to establish a fetishistic relationship with the head of state.[39]

As Franco's early official propaganda carefully portrayed him fetishistically in his dual role as terrible father and nurturing mother, in the reverse shot of the church described above the image of the church building also suggests simultaneously the coercive Other—the fascist injunction to sacrifice oneself for one's country—and the benign protective other—the walls that literally keep the Spaniards safe from harm.[40] The church, like the head shot of Franco, defiantly "looks down" upon the two characters, encouraging them to fight for their country, but it also offers itself up as a sacred shelter for the besieged Spaniards. In this sense, the church in this shot can be read on the one hand, as all fetishes can, as the "substitute for meanings ... that cannot be faced," representing the castrating father's fascist injunction to die (Brooks 57). Yet also, on the other hand, it can be read as the protective enveloping mother, the "Santa-madre-iglesia" as the Catholic Church was affectionately known. In short, the shot of the church is both "maternal and paternal ... at the same time," like Giménez Caballero wanted the head shots of Franco to be. However, in its structural ambivalence of belief and disbelief—of disavowing the lack while knowing all too well—fetishism opens up a tension, a potentially disruptive effect against blind faith and dogmatic belief, which Francoism brought under control by means of its kitsch aesthetics.

This fetishistic relationship of knowing all too well but believing nonetheless is, as Christian Metz explained, characteristic of film spectatorship (72)—its suspension of disbelief—and is suggested in the last moment of the shot reverse series when the Lieutenant walks toward the church and strikes a pose of visual contemplation. In this shot, the church at the right of the frame forms a triangle whose apex converges on the Lieutenant's body to the left. For a brief moment, this shot positions the Lieutenant as a film spectator who looks at the *screen* where the events in which he will be the main protagonist will soon unfold. As in the case of the shot of the church, which suggests both the castrating father and enveloping mother, in this shot the Lieutenant is split in two: for a brief moment, he is both protagonist and spectator of his own story. What the Lieutenant now contemplates is both his fullness and his loss. He embraces the illusory safety provided by the church facade, the fetish that covers up the lack but that, at the same time, inevitably points toward it, as Freud explained (152). Precisely because of his contradictory vision of maternal castration (the knowing but not knowing), the fetishist, like the Lieutenant in this brief shot, fails in his attempt to detach himself completely from the original traumatic event, as Laura Mulvey observes, and thus "continues to refer back to the moment in time … which [he] is witness [of], to [his] own historical dimension" ("Some Thoughts" 11).

For a split second, the Lieutenant is simultaneously in and outside of his own story; in other words, as the fetishist, he is not yet completely detached from the original traumatic event (the siege in his case), and thus, as Mulvey remarks, is still aware of his "own historical dimension." Unlike the fetishist, however, who is structurally bound to keep the ambivalence alive, the Lieutenant, prompted by his leader's gaze, is forced to do otherwise and becomes his true opposite: the blind and dogmatic believer. He becomes the perfect Francoist subject who, like his leader, attempts to situate "himself above all witnesses," all above his former self. After all, it is he, not Captain Las Morenas, who is the true protagonist of the story and the only character who really fully answers the fascist injunction to sacrifice. This shot allows the spectator to briefly catch a rare glimpse at the cinematic representation of reflective self-consciousness in the film. This is a rare moment in the film when Franco's message is not forced upon the spectator but allowed to simmer. Once the decision to sacrifice the self for Franco's cause has finally been made, the door of reflective self-distance shuts completely and, unlike that of the church, never opens again. In fact, as we will see in the last section of this chapter, the Lieutenant stops being a human character altogether, to become an embodiment of Franco's ideal of courage and heroism: the very object of audience emulation prompted by the movie.

Unlike the camp aesthetic sensibility of many artists of the Spanish political transition, such as Pedro Almodóvar, whose main goal was to dismantle this Francoist kitsch by keeping the fetishistic tension alive, Francoist kitsch in *Los últimos* wants the subject to be blind, unaware of the original traumatic event and thus completely detached from "his own historical dimension." In order to accomplish this, the film shows only one side of the fetishistic scenario—the politically useful heroic death—while suppressing the other—the castrating reality of that death. The film's kitsch portrayal of a besieged colonial church where a group of ill-equipped, sick, and hungry Spanish soldiers stand defiantly against a Tagalog rebellion in the small town of Baler transforms the stark colonial reality of the Philippines described in the Lieutenant's memoir into glamorous political myth. As Dodds writes in his introduction, the memoir is a story of "death bravely met, of heroic deeds, and of sublime devotion to the flag under which those men were serving" (5). The film's representation of the siege provides an accurate visual translation of Dodds's words but neglects to show its darker side. It is worth recalling that, as the Lieutenant bitterly informs us in his memoir, the metropolis in fact neglected the garrison entirely from the start; even before the siege began, it received "not one cent, not one biscuit, not one cartridge" (Martín Cerezo 17). In *Los últimos* the reality of the fascist injunction to sacrifice oneself for one's country—a senseless sacrifice at that, since the war was already over—is thus concealed, mediated through kitsch powers of catharsis.

In this sense, *Los últimos* vividly illustrates what Adorno called kitsch's "parody of catharsis," which is central to its potential political effectiveness (Calinescu 241). As we saw in *Romancero marroquí*, here too, kitsch's one-sided manipulative representation emotionally codes the fascist political message and presents it aesthetically, not rationally, thus eliciting from its audience an automatic "unreflective emotional response" (Kulka 26), making spectators unaware of the ideology being imparted on them. This pseudo-cathartic power makes kitsch the perfect aesthetic expression of fascism's ideological fantasy, as it helps fascism accomplish its goal of letting its myth blind the masses.[41] Kitsch is after all an aesthetic suturing device that tries to disavow the subject's traumatic past, erasing his/her role as witness to his/her own moment in time. In the case of *Los últimos*, the kitsch aesthetic helps sever the link between the Spaniards and their own traumatic past.

Los últimos's kitsch aesthetic gains its full force in the jungle farewell scene between the Spanish soldier Juan Chamizo and his love interest Tala, the Tagalog woman who sings at the village tavern. The figure of the woman is central to the siege film and critical for understanding *Los últimos*'s fascist aesthetic. In these films it is common to see a woman with strong emotional ties to the male protagonist forced to leave the premises or simply left behind. Often a farewell scene in which the couple embraces takes place in an idyllic pastoral setting that contrasts with the purely arbitrary and abstract limits of the site under siege. This pastoral setting typically suggests fertility, emotional grounding, and the deep communal roots that the besieged willingly sacrifice themselves to defend. However, neither the pastoral setting nor the female character in *Los últimos* evokes these associations, but instead they become the kitsch, orientalizing backdrop against which Spain's dark colonial legacy in the Philippines (and every other ex-colony) is recast in a completely different, favorable light. It allows the film to be about a new kind of founding father.

The substitution of historical reality with nostalgic cliché is one of the main functions of kitsch (Calinescu 239). In this sense, *Los últimos*'s farewell scene—set in the heart of an obviously fake Philippine jungle—not only provides us with a good example of Francoist kitsch, but also offers a precious glimpse at the intersection of kitsch aesthetics and fascist ideology.[42]

It is worth pausing here for a brief comparison to *Raza*'s garden sequence, which, as we saw in Chapter 1, also takes place in a pastoral setting: the Churruca family garden. This comparison will elucidate the different meanings Francoism assigned to the fatherland and to its colonial territories. Produced four years earlier, *Raza*'s themes of sin, punishment, redemption, and sacrificial death converged in the film's garden sequence. In it, the father teaches his children a history lesson in a "kitsch paradise" in which nature and mankind harmoniously blend with one another. Unlike *Raza*'s garden sequence, whose idyllic natural setting signified the glorious Spanish past—the scattered fragment of the aura that Franco felt compelled to restore—*Los últimos*'s farewell love scene depicts a colonial space that should be kept at a proper distance. This was not the sacred space of the fatherland, but an *orientalized* space that Spain dominated in order to prove its masculine prowess among European nations.

Raza's garden sequence represented a lost paradise whose recovery would allow the Spanish family to heal, safe from social unrest and political trauma. Although set around 1898, the sequence's main subtext was the future event of the Spanish Civil War. Shot in 1941, the primary goal of *Raza* was to retroactively provide ideological justification and political legitimacy to Franco's 1936 uprising. Produced in 1945 and set in 1898, *Los últimos* wanted to offer both isolated Spaniards and the surrounding hostile world a perfect vignette of *Hispanidad* drawn from one of the most celebrated episodes of Spain's illustrious colonial past. The subtext of its pastoral farewell scene was Spain's supposedly altruistic relationship with its Philippine colony, a subtext buried under the guise of the conventional love scene between Juan, a generic Spanish soldier, and Tala, the local villager: an irrelevant but relaxing narrative pause before the real dramatic action begins.

The sequence begins with a close-up of Juan's hands using his army knife to carve his and Tala's names in a tree trunk. As we see Juan's hands moving, we suddenly hear Tala's voice asking him, "What are the women in your country like?" Juan stops carving and replies, "I hardly remember them." Tala presses the issue, asking "Not even one?" and the camera slowly pans to the left to pause briefly over Juan, who reassuringly answers, "Not even one." Continuously panning to the left, the camera finally reveals to us the location of the scene, an idyllic and secluded area bursting with tropical vegetation outside the village. The camera then stops briefly to give us a long shot of Tala, slowly beginning to zoom in on her. She sits in a hammock hanging from a tree, surrounded by vegetation. By emphasizing how Tala blends harmoniously with the luscious landscape of the Philippine jungle, the composition of the shot constructs the woman as a visual allegory of the Spanish colony.

The apparent banality of this love sequence comes into sharper focus when seen through the colonial lens. The farewell scene attempts to transform Spain's exploitative colonial domination of the Philippines into a spiritual love affair between the metropolis and its colony, free from the vulgarity of material profit, which Francoism had always accused other world powers of pursuing. However, this scene also reveals the darker fantasies of the metropolis that the film is supposed to hide, through its portrayal of its two protagonists, with Juan, as his plain rank and common Spanish name indicate, representing ordinary Spaniards, and Tala, the pretty native allegorical woman, representing the Philippines.

In the scene, Tala is anxious about the possibility of losing Juan. He tries to console her by reassuring her that she will be as happy as she was before they met when he is sent to another post. An emotionally distressed Tala then reveals to him: "Nothing mattered to me this much. I swam in the river, ran along the beach. Before your arrival, I didn't realize how lonely I was or how big the forest was." Juan informs her that he will likely be sent back to Spain soon, and Tala nervously asks him why he does not take her with him. Deflecting her question, Juan tells her that after he is gone her life will go on as it did before. And when Tala melodramatically utters, "I will never get over you," Juan calmly replies, "But Tala, this is your land. Your people are here." Finally, Tala confesses her unremitting love for him: "I don't care about my people nor do I care for anyone but you. I was born here and I've always lived here and loved all this, the village, the river. I love it almost as much as my own life. But I love you more. I love you much more than I do my own life." Disarmed by Tala's devotion, Juan whispers her name in her ear and gently pushes her against the tree trunk he was carving minutes before. Leaning against the tree and about to embrace, Tala takes the headscarf Juan just gave her and asks him, "How do you wear it in Spain? In case someone takes me there." She places the scarf on her head like a Spanish woman would. Then, Juan gently pulls down the scarf before they fuse in a passionate kiss that gets interrupted by an army bugle calling the soldiers to their posts (Fig. 3.4).

In a characteristic Francoist reversal of historical truth, the neglectful and unbalanced power relation between colonized and colonizer, represented by Tala and Juan, is now transformed into a scene of gallantry, an almost spiritual exchange between two lovers, which, when read allegorically, shows that Spain has nothing material to gain. This spiritual relationship between Spain and its colony, free from the stain of material profit, is clearly expressed in an exchange between Dr Vigil and Fray Cándido during a Christmas Eve truce. The Lieutenant asks a guard if the enemy has opened fire yet, to which the guard replies, "No, sir. They are celebrating Christmas Eve." Witnessing this exchange, Dr Vigil adds, "This is the work of Fray Cándido," to which Fray Cándido modestly

Figure 3.4 *Los últimos de Filipinas*, 1945

replies, "Do not exaggerate the importance of a poor missionary. It is the work of Spain, a work of centuries. And if some day we have to leave this island, our faith and our language will remain here."

Indeed, the entire film can be seen as a portrayal of how Spain lost one of her last important colonies courageously, with dignity in defeat. But it also intends to suggest that, unlike other colonial powers, Spain's interest in the Philippines was solely altruistic. It only wanted to bequeath the right faith and the proper language to its lost natives. This was the overarching (and proselytizing) role de Maeztu assigned to *Hispanidad*: "Hispanics are ... all the peoples owing their civilization or their being to the Hispanic peoples of the [Iberian] peninsula. Hispanidad is the concept that embraces them all" (34). Appropriately, a grateful Tala, about to lose her unselfish master, confesses her eternal love and adoration to him, her desire to be *his* forever.

This colonial subtext plays out mainly through the characters' dialogue and through the use of a particular prop: namely, the typical Spanish headscarf Juan ordered from Manila as a gift for Tala, brought to him by the garrison's postman. It is revealed to us subtly, almost imperceptibly, conveyed by Tala's putting on of the scarf in the proper Spanish manner while pretending not to know how, and by Juan's pulling it down gently before he passionately kisses her. As implied by the scene's dialogue, Tala's prelapsarian existence comes to an end when she falls in love with Juan. Her former native life, which she now imagines unfolding in complete accord with nature—swimming in the river, running along the beach—is interrupted. As she reveals to Juan, "Before your arrival I didn't realize how lonely I was or quite how big the forest was." Thus, the colonial encounter, represented by her falling in love with Juan, signals the end of innocence and, for Tala, the beginning of subjective awareness and the fear and loneliness it brings with it. But it also signals Tala's ascent to personhood and civilization, clearly expressed by her desire to leave the Philippine landscape behind and move to metropolitan Spain, the "civilized" country that she heard so much about from her teacher Lucio, whose name is clearly reminiscent of the Spanish word *luz*, meaning "light", and obviously connotes enlightenment. In asking Juan to show her how to wear the scarf in the Spanish style, even though she already knows, Tala communicates her desire to be "baptized" as a Spanish woman. As she explains, "It is important to me that you are the one who tells me how to do it."

Yet Juan's desire for Tala derives from the fact that she is not a "civilized" Spanish woman, but a pretty native colonial girl, and he has no intention of bringing her home. Now, Juan's earlier response to Tala's remark that he will surely forget her like he has already forgotten all his Spanish women acquires its proper meaning: "It is different, Tala. You're different." This meaning is not lost on Tala: "Different. Am I so much worse than they are?" For Juan, Tala is "much worse than they are." Thus, despite the fact that she wants to become a true Spanish woman, placing her scarf properly on her head, and follow Juan to Spain, Juan is only interested in taking off the scarf and lying with her in the luscious Philippine jungle.

In Tala's eyes, the headscarf, the sign of her desire to become a true Spanish woman, acquires the magical properties of what W. J. T. Mitchell has called the "bad object" of imperialism.[43] In this sequence, the traditional Spanish headscarf—the colonizer's gift, not an object belonging to the colonized—is appropriated by the latter and endowed with the magical properties traditionally assigned to the fetishes of their own creation. Therefore, it is precisely the colonizer's own gift, not the made-up fetish of the colonized, that the colonizer now has to disavow. The headscarf Tala has converted into a fetish signifies the allure of civilization in the native's mind.

In its conventional orientalization of female sexuality, this scene betrays *Los últimos*'s pretense to a higher civilizing purpose. Tala wants to "become a Spaniard" and go to Spain with Juan. Juan wants Tala as a mistress while he is stationed in the Philippines. In fact, in the jungle sequence Juan becomes a "Don Juan" who is interested in seducing the native girl, not in "civilizing" her. Ironically, his behavior echoes Spain's rapacious and neglectful conduct in the Philippines, where the colonizer's three hundred years of rule did not amount to the creation of a substantial legacy of any kind, not even a linguistic one.

This colonial subtext is clearly implied early on in the movie when Tala tells another Spanish soldier, a friend of Juan who is also in love with her, about the day she met Juan for the first time. She admits that she fell in love with Juan because the first time he laid eyes on her he immediately went to embrace her after throwing his backpack violently to Tala's boss, Moisés, the Filipino tavern keeper, whom the film depicts as a two-faced traitor; and who in fact is actively involved in the rebellion. As Tala's account reveals, the colonial subject only surrenders her will and begins to love her colonial master through a direct and forceful encounter.

Unlike in other siege films, in *Los últimos* the pastoral scene does not take place in a piece of land symbolizing home, fertility, emotional grounding, and deep communal roots. Instead, it takes place in the colonial space of the Philippine jungle, a kitsch paradise devoid of historical substance and filled with nature. And it is not a farewell between the male protagonist and his future wife—which is also an allegory of the fatherland—but an erotic colonial fantasy interlude, prelude to the siege, from which, as we saw, the fatherland is conveniently excluded.

Unlike in more canonical siege films, then, it is not the alien, eroticized Philippine jungle but rather the church building itself that signifies Spain's emotional grounding and the deep communal roots that the Spaniards willingly die to defend. The church represents a national and sacred space, like the garden in *Raza*, from which the colonial subject is ultimately excluded. The devoted Tala is arrested by her own countrymen for trying to help her beloved Juan. The farewell sequence begins with a shot of the lovers' names, Tala and Juan, fused together, inscribed into the tree trunk. At its end, Juan fittingly runs away from Tala, followed by a shot of the distraught woman screaming his name. Ultimately she is silenced by the sound of the army bugle, the commanding army's voice thus drowning Tala's desperate plea for love.

The original song composed for the movie, "Yo te diré," which became an instant hit on Spanish radio and was replayed well into the 1960s, can be best understood in this colonial subtext. Fitting with the film's colonial theme, the song is a habanera, a nineteenth-century musical style that originated in Cuba and has a characteristic nostalgic air, brought to Spain by sailors and subsequently exported to the Philippines. The song was written by the film's screenwriter, who considered it to be the "film's engine," and was composed by the Hungarian Jorge Halpern. Sung by Tala twice in the film, its lyrics are the words of a fearful woman who begs her lover not to abandon her: "Each time the wind blows/and takes away a flower/I think you'll never come back/my love don't ever abandon me at dusk/the moon rises late and I could get lost." Read in light of the colonial subtext, the lyrics of this love song can be interpreted as the colony's heartfelt plea to the metropolis—Tala's plea to Juan—not to be abandoned. In fact, the song makes this plea overtly explicit: "I'll tell you/why my song/calls you incessantly/I miss your laughter/I miss your kisses/I miss your waking up/my blood pulsating/my life begging/that you don't go away any more."

Tala performs this song for the first time at the tavern in a smoke-filled scene reminiscent of films such as *Casablanca* (1942) and *To Have and Have Not* (1944), in which musical numbers are also an integral part of the film's narrative. The song's haunting melody, enhanced by the slow strumming of guitar chords and by Tala's alluring voice and emotional delivery, charges the scene with a distinctive mood of longing. This longing is mirrored back by various shots of the mesmerized faces of the soldiers who listen to Tala's voice transfixed as if it were that of a mythological siren.

Tala agrees to sing the famous song once more when she is imprisoned by the insurgents, because she is tricked into thinking that Juan himself has requested that she do so. In fact, Moisés, who is aware of Tala's erotic hold over the Spanish soldiers, tells his superiors to put Tala's alluring voice to good use in reminding the Spaniards "of the existence of women." As suggested by a tracking shot that shows her inside her cell as she approaches the window to sing to her beloved Spaniard, Tala is now a prisoner of her own people, the Filipino insurgents who are trying to recover sovereignty over their own land. She hugs the cell bars as she begins to sing. The camera pulls away slowly. Her high-pitched voice resonates throughout the village, floating freely around the external space. Unlike the camera, which is free, Tala is not. She is a caged bird, as this shot of her hugging the cell bars visually suggests (Fig. 3.5). Her song floods the diegetic space of the film and causes the Spanish soldiers to emerge from their posts to listen to her. Her singing connotes the seductive allure of the colony, whose hypnotic sway over the Spanish soldiers is used by the insurgents as a psychological weapon to demoralize their oppressors. Nonetheless, Tala is oblivious that she is being used as a psychological weapon, and remains completely devoted to the metropolis; she is not a threatening siren for the Spaniards, but a faithful mistress who loves her lover more than her own life. In fact, when the Spanish garrison finally leaves its post, Tala, who is waiting outside, approaches Juan, takes him by the arm and proceeds to march by his side. The film depicts, then, a Philippines that is at core

Figure 3.5 *Los últimos de Filipinas*, 1945

faithfully devoted to its colonial master despite having been liberated by the insurgents.

This is a kitsch, ahistorical, nostalgic representation of the ex-colony. The reality of an unwanted Spain that was defeated and expelled from her former colony is now masked by the historical cliché of a Philippines that, despite all historical evidence against it, is still secretly in love with the metropolis. Kitsch and fascism blend to make the film about a different kind of benevolent founding father.

Kitsch's ability to hypostasize reality by labeling it according to simple categories—seen above in the nostalgic representation of the ex-colony as exotic, romantic Other—has also the potential to reduce the complexities of the self to a label representing a concept: in *Los últimos*'s case, the cliché Francoist concept of heroism. This is a process best exemplified by the close-up of the Lieutenant which brings the film to an end.

Upon realizing his mistake in failing to accept that the war is over, Lieutenant Martín Cerezo informs his men that the siege has finally ended. Soon after, the church gate is opened and the Spaniards march out in military formation. Ceremoniously flanking the Spanish column, the Filipino army salutes them with the respect due to a defeated but heroic enemy. Next the camera cuts to a close-up of the Lieutenant, who solemnly leads the column. This sustained close-up of the Lieutenant, which lasts for a couple of minutes, will bring the film to a close. As we watch his face on the screen, we also hear the worrying thoughts inside his head that echo the warning issued by the last Spanish envoy: "You will be thrown out of the army. You will be put on trial. You are a rebel." However, the voice in his head is immediately contradicted by a series of superimposed images: a front page of a Spanish newspaper heralding the Spanish garrison's heroic exploits, and a Spanish crowd cheering the soldiers. These superimposed images are followed by another front page announcing that the Lieutenant has received the "Laureate Cross of St Ferdinand," the highest military honor a Spanish soldier can receive, which was also awarded to Franco himself immediately following the end of the Spanish Civil War. The film comes to an end with a close-up of the Lieutenant's face superimposed on the image of the Laureate Cross, while a voice-over utters these final words: "Once again Lieutenant Martín Cerezo heard the news too late. In Spain he was already a hero" (Fig. 3.6). Given their complementary function, it is worth discussing this final shot together with the close-up of Marisol that brings *Raza* to an end (Fig. 3.7). These close-ups function to cover up the brutal reality of the Francoist injunction to die.

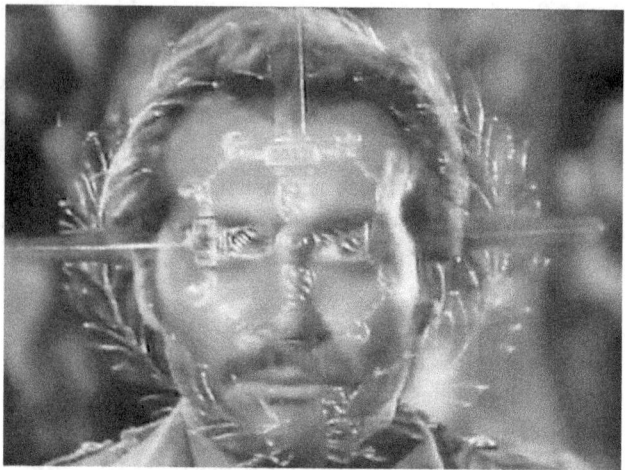

Figure 3.6 *Los últimos de Filipinas*, 1945

Figure 3.7 *Raza*, 1942

The close-up of Marisol sets off a final series of shots: a medium shot of Isabel Churruca's son declaring to his mother, "How beautiful! What is this called?" in reference to Franco's spectacular *Desfile de la Victoria*, the celebratory military parade at the end of the Spanish Civil War; another medium shot of his mother who tearfully replies, "This is called *Raza*, my son," a long back shot of Franco reviewing his troops from the tribune; and, finally, a brief montage that reminds the audience of the personal suffering and sacrifice of the fallen heroes through a series of superimpositions showing most of the major and minor characters of the film. This brief montage and the film as a whole end with a close-up of the Spanish flag waving in the wind. The series, then, begins with Marisol's face lost in thought and wonder, smiling enigmatically like the sphinx, and ends with the Spanish flag, the symbol of the traditional "Spanish" values in defense of which Franco waged a "cleansing" war against the Republic.

In *Cinema 1* (1983), Gilles Deleuze explains that every close-up of a human face leans towards two distinctive poles. One pole is the reflecting face that, like Marisol's, is lost in thought, in wonder. The reflecting face "expresses a pure Quality ... a 'something' common to several objects of different kinds," and in it the outline of the face contains its features (Deleuze 90). The other pole is the intensive face which, like the Lieutenant's, seems to feel something and "expresses a pure Power ... defined by a series which carries us from one quality to another" (Deleuze 90). Griffith's facial close-ups, "in which everything is organized [as in Marisol's face] for the pure and soft outline of a feminine face ... ," belong to the first pole (Deleuze 89). Eisenstein's close-ups, in which "the traits of faceity" seem to be "escaping the outline," belong to the second (Deleuze 89).[44]

At first sight, both Lieutenant Martín Cerezo's final close-up in *Los últimos* and Marisol's close-up at the end of *Raza* would appear to fall neatly into one of Deleuze's two categories. But they seem to belong to neither. They do not possess Griffith's reflective intensive quality or Eisenstein's extensive power. And, unlike Von Sternberg's close-ups, that for Deleuze seem to defy easy characterization, they do not have the ability to traverse or invert the given polarities. In fact, as mentioned earlier, these close-ups could be more aptly characterized as labels referring to a concept.

Like the headshot of Franco and the facade of the church building, the close-ups of the smiling Marisol and the somber Lieutenant show human faces in order to cover up meanings that cannot be faced. These faces are not real faces, which reflect astonishment like Griffith's or express desire like Eisenstein's, but only visual masks used to soften the blow, to cover up the brutal injunction to sacrifice oneself for Franco's cause. In this sense, the two close-ups are on opposite but complementary poles of what Franco's official portraiture was intended to represent: on the one hand, that of the Lieutenant indicates the "loving but ruthless father with a stone where the heart is," and, on the other, that of Marisol suggests the nurturing, smiling mother that Giménez Caballero also wanted posters of Franco to portray.

Marisol's close-up opens a final series of shots that culminates with a shot of the Spanish flag waving up in the air. From the smiling Marisol to the Spanish flag, this final series is intended to remind us of the personal sacrifice, often ending in death, true Spaniards should endure for their fatherland. An enchanted Marisol, with her face slightly turned sideways, gazes obliquely to the beautiful, out-of-field spectacle that conjures up for Isabel's son the equivalent "beautiful" feeling he has no name for; a feeling his mother will ultimately call *raza*. In this Francoist context, the term *raza* represents *Hispanidad* and the spirit of sacrifice and violence it entails. The soft-focused Griffith-style close-up of Marisol, the image projected on the screen when Isabel's son asks his question, provides that "beautiful" feeling with its visual equivalent in the form of a beautiful feminine face. As the scene suggests, the spirit of *Hispanidad* is "passed" from mother to son, and is visually condensed between Marisol's enigmatic smile at the beginning and the Spanish flag at the end. In this sense, and despite her sphinx-like enigmatic smile, Marisol's face, the allegorical visual representation of the brutally repressive spirit of *Hispanidad*, resembles not so much a sphinx but a harpy, a mythological creature whose upper half is that of a nurturing woman but whose lower half holds the claws of a bird of prey.[45] In *Los últimos*, the Lieutenant's close-up functions in a similar way. Isolated on the screen, it leaves behind any traces of spatio-temporal coordinates of the town of Baler, as all close-ups do (Dalle Vacche 120). Like Marisol's, the Lieutenant's face is also transformed from a person into a "feeling thing," an empty signifying vessel upon which anything can be projected.[46]

Despite the inner turmoil expressed by the voice inside his head, the Lieutenant's face at the end of *Los últimos* is not a human face. It is a symbol made of human flesh, behind which lies another symbol: the "Laureate Cross of St Ferdinand," the military award given to the national heroes who are willing to risk their lives in defense of their fatherland, which, as indicated on screen beneath his face, symbolizes heroism and military courage.[47] Marisol's face and the Lieutenant's, then, are both masks without a face; a female mask and a male mask, one representing the nation, the other the heroism required for its defense. These two close-ups are not images of individuals; instead, they are images representing linguistic labels which point toward fixed referents: nationhood and Francoist heroism.

Devoid of the desire and astonishment that for Deleuze infuse life into faces, the Francoist close-up of the face—a transparent mask without hidden human meanings—is a synecdoche that visually condenses the film's ideological fantasy. In this sense, the film itself becomes an appendix to the close-up, a kitsch-fetish that, like Franco's propaganda posters, encourages Spaniards to die while covering up that injunction.[48]

Veiled by kitsch in this way, in *Los últimos* the self's temporal historical nature is distorted, represented as a clear outline shadowed by the contours of normative categories: Francoist concepts of nationhood and heroism. Unlike genuine art, which, as mentioned earlier, for Bergson, encourages us "to put aside for an instant the veil which we interposed between our consciousness and ourselves," these kitsch films do the opposite: they prompt us never to lift that veil.

Notes

1. As Spanish scholar José Colmeiro writes, "[i]n search of the psychological complicity of the viewer, the film settles into the affective field of nostalgia, subsumed in that feeling of melancholy produced by a period from the past from the awareness of its irretrievability ("Nostalgia colonial" 296–7).
2. Lieutenant Martín Cerezo's personal account of the siege of Baler was titled *La pérdida de Filipinas*, published in 1904.
3. While *Los últimos*'s storyline broadly follows the Lieutenant's memoirs, director Antonio Román and his co-writers Enrique Llovet and Pedro de Juan made use of other sources for the final script: Llovet's radio script *Los héroes de Baler*, as well as Enrique Alfonso Barcones and Rafael Sánchez Campoy's award-winning film script *El fuerte de Baler*, which was included due to official political pressure. Román's final script also incorporated "suggestions" from external sources: mainly from Captain Las Morenas's highly influential son, an aviation colonel, and the state's official religious adviser. The main thrust of these suggestions was to alter the memoir's depiction of a few minor characters in order to either enhance their overall importance, as in the case of the Captain or the priest Fray Cándido, or to make them conform to ultra-conservative Francoist religious values, as in the case of Dr Vigil.
4. "'Regenerationism,'" writes Carr, "was neither novel in content nor coherent. Joaquín Costa (1846–1911), son of an Aragonese peasant and a self-educated polymath who became the prophet of regenerationism, had long meditated on the historical roots of Spanish backwardness. Regeneration would sweep away *caciquismo*—a term of universal condemnation which he coined—and allow the 'live forces' of society to enter political life" (224).
5. As Angel Loureiro writes, "[i]n spite of the repeated characterization of the outcome of the Spanish American War as a 'national disaster' ('el desastre del 98'), such expression points to nothing more than the reiteration of the topical view regarding Spain's decline that had been bandied about well before 1898" (67). In fact, the Spanish economy grew more rapidly during the following decades than it had in previous ones.
6. However, as Loureiro rightly observes, the concern with the notion of Spain's decadence was not new among Spanish intellectuals or their European counterparts, who were acutely aware "that Spain's history ran a course

that went from an early peak in the fifteenth or early sixteenth centuries to a period of extended decline [that] can be traced to at least the beginning of the seventeenth century" (66).
7. In fact, Lieutenant Martín Cerezo, then in his nineties, was present for much of the shooting to make sure the film stayed faithful to his account of the story. He died just a few months before the film's release.
8. In actuality, a large percentage of the Spanish soldiers were so sick during most of the siege that, according to Lieutenant Cerezo, the sentinels had to be carried out on stretchers by their healthier peers, only to be left at their posts with barely enough strength to hold their rifles. Ultimately, as food rations spoiled and diminished, hunger and utter despair began to set in.
9. Alberto Medina has called this emphasis on the protection of the dead a "rhetoric of historical debt," which, for him, was characteristic of Francoism and thought of as a mere fulfillment of moral duty to the dead (34). As Medina remembers, for Francoists, "our work is the mandate of our dead" (quoted in Medina 34).
10. In fact, a new version of the film was released in 2016 titled *1898. Los últimos de Filipinas*, to great critical acclaim.
11. A press article at the time of the film's release chronicles the enthusiastic reception received by the film: "in the past three weeks since its release, the projection of the film has been interrupted with warm applause and long cheers several times a day, and at the end a clamorous and long ovation always erupts" (quoted in Coira 106).
12. As José Colmeiro writes, "thus in accordance with its exemplary and moralizing purpose the hierarchical latent tension between Captain Las Morenas and Lieutenant Martin Cerezo is suppressed in the film and the open rift between the Spanish military and religious groups in the Philippines is sublimated ... ; the skepticism of demoralized garrison Dr Vigil is substituted by faith in providence, thanks to the intervention of the priest ... conveniently assuring itself of the ideological blessing of the regime, the film recognizes in the initial credits the work of the literary adviser ... of the military adviser ... and of the religious adviser who were all responsible for the Falangist Catholic dogma to be properly maintained in this epic film" ("Nostalgia Colonial" 296).
13. Its preferred chronology was as follows: Hannibal's siege of the city of Sagunto at the end of the third century BC, which would ignite the Second Punic War; the long and brutal Roman siege of the city of Numancia in 133 BC; the siege of the small Asturian mountain village of Covadonga in AD 773, where Iberian Christians won the first battle against the occupying Moors; the defense of the city of Tarifa against the siege of the Moors in AD 1296, which was the origin of the endlessly repeated story of Guzmán el Bueno, who, rather than surrender the city, let his enemies execute his own son; and, finally, the siege of the Alcazar of Toledo, which took place during the Spanish Civil War from 21 July to 27 September 1936.

14. During the course of the Spanish Civil War, he even diverted a military operation that, according to many military analysts, could have considerably shortened the span of the Civil War with one definitive blow to the city of Madrid, in order to rescue a large group of Nationalists who took refuge from the Republicans inside the Alcazar of Toledo. Carefully calibrating the propagandistic value for his cause that this episode could internationally bring, he postponed the Nationalist attack on Madrid, giving the Spanish capital precious time to adequately prepare for its defense. As early as 1940, the episode would be immortalized in the film *L'assedio dell'Alcazar* [*The Siege of the Alcazar*], directed by fascist Italian director Augusto Genina, as the result of film cooperation agreements between Mussolini's Italy and Franco's Spain.
15. For Bergson's influence in Spain, see the introduction to Benjamin Fraser's *Encounters with Bergson(ism) in Spain*, pp. 11–34.
16. Bergson himself was famously dismissive of the potential of cinematic representation (Flaxman 88). Nevertheless, due to its potential for transferring the continuum of reality to the screen, cinema is in fact ideally suited for carrying out Bergson's project of recovery of the self through time. Rather than creating a formal arrangement through which the symbol might *reveal* reality instead of *substituting* for it, however, Román's film does exactly the opposite: it depicts reality through the symbol, as for Tomas Kulka all kitsch aesthetic does (79).
17. The sets and overall aesthetics of the film were compromised by the harsh economic conditions of Spain during the 1940s, when film stock was hard to obtain and often of poor or uneven quality. Román was even forced to shoot at dawn due to the fact that the electrical voltage during the day was not strong enough for the operation of bright studio lights (Diez Puertas 75).
18. This unintentionally fake look could have been easily avoided had Román decided to shoot on location, like Rossellini did in 1946 for *Paisà*, which, despite being shot under similarly precarious circumstances, achieved a convincingly real look in its last episode about the fate of besieged Italian partisans after the end of the war.
19. In this sense, the few exchanges that take place between Dr Vigil and Fray Cándido are particularly interesting. Absent from the memoir, they were written in solely to allow the audience to witness the process of Dr Vigil's conversion from a "cold-fact" scientist at the beginning of the film to a fervent believer in "that place beyond the stars" by the film's end.
20. The denomination "film of national interest" was awarded to films "that highlight the 'racial values' or contain 'lessons of our moral and political principles.' Such a classification guarantees, among other things, a release date in the best time of the year, as well as it guarantees that the distributor be obliged to keep showing it in the movies, as long as it fills 50 per cent of the cinema's capacity" (Diez Puertas 92).
21. In equally bombastic rhetoric, Del Valle characterized the film by stating that "the heart of the homeland affected [Román's] beats, the pulse of

its blood, its feeling, in an electrocardiogram of a movie" (quoted in Coira 106).

22. As Elena writes: "[t]he movie's director, Antonio Román, a veteran movie critic with five movies under his belt in spite of his recent debut with another warlike film, *Escuadrilla* (1941), was interested in the topic of the heroes of Baler after reading Enrique Llovet's radio script by the same name. This would be the basis for the script of *Last Stand in the Philippines*, reinforced by the material coming from 'El fuerte de Baler,' a script by Enrique Alfonso Barcones and Rafael Sánchez Campoy about the same topic, which had recently been award the title of best script by the *Sindicato Nacional del Espectáculo*" (197).

23. As Kinder writes, following historian Stanley Payne, "the defascistization of Spain began as soon as it became clear that Hitler and Mussolini were going to lose World War II: 'Franco had to develop an alternate political theory and tactic, unveiling his new scheme of a corporative *Rechtsstaat* "organic democracy" based on Catholic doctrine by the time that the war ended in 1945'" (Kinder 34–5).

24. In *Arte e ideología del Franquismo,* Ángel Llorente observes that, just after the defeat of the Axis, Francoism began a new phase that would last until 1951. As he writes, this new phase begins with: "the proclamation of the Code of the Spanish on July 17, 1945, which was a mere statement of principles. In October 1945, the Referendum law was proclaimed, and on July 27, 1947, the Succession Law to the function of Head of State was approved by the referendum. This law restored the monarchy as a form of State. The new government implied changes derived from the defeat of the Axis powers, in favor of the Catholics from the A.C.N.P., and continued the displacement of the Falange" (112).

25. On the one hand, as Tolentino remarks, "[t]he troop's isolation in the Philippines is analogous to the isolation of the Francoist regime from other nations. The value of defending the empire to death is the latent hegemonic nationalist call" (141). On the other hand, Kinder writes that the film does not, however, contain "expressions of hostility toward the United States, even though Spain lost the Philippines while fighting against this country; for, in the post-World War II context in which the film was made, Franco hoped that the United States would help Spain break out of its political isolation with dignity" (153).

26. As Román's biographer points out, in this delicate international political context it was not purely coincidental that the film's trailer highlighted a phrase uttered by Captain Las Morenas to resonate with Spanish audiences; he says, as the Spanish flag is raised to the top of the church of Baler, "It is not a challenge, it is simply to let it be known that we are here." This phrase was reminiscent of the one Franco himself would utter in a 1946 speech to a delegation of Falangist Civil War ex-combatants, in which he addressed the hostile international environment the country was facing, letting the world

know "that we exist, that we are not dead and that our flag waves in the winds" (quoted in Coira 108).
27. As a main example of the genre, *Los últimos de Filipinas* is often grouped with two other colonial films set in the final years of Spanish rule in Cuba: *Bambú* [*Bamboo*] (José Luis Sáenz de Heredia, 1945) and *Héroes del 95* [*Heroes of '95*] (Raúl Alfonso, 1946).
28. As Spanish critic Isabel Santaolalla writes, "... these stories— and among them those set in Spain's former overseas colonies—were often seasoned with nostalgia, and designed to sublimate what, after all, were narratives of defeat and loss" (52).
29. Most of these films are set in North Africa, including titles such as *Las últimas banderas* (Luis Marquina, 1954), *La canción de Aixa* (Florián Rey, 1939), *¡Harka!* (C. Arévalo, 1941), *Alhucemas* (José López Rubio, 1948), *La llamada de África* (César Fernández Ardavín, 1952), *La corona negra* [*Black Crown*] (Luis Saslavsky, 1951), *¡Ahí va otro recluta!* (Ramón Fernández, 1960), and *Novios de la muerte* (Rafael Gil, 1975). Within the colonial genre, a smaller group of films, set in places such as Guinea, *Misión Blanca* (Juan de Orduña, 1946); sub-Saharan Africa, *Cristo Negro* (Ramón Torrado, 1963); India, *La mies es mucha* (José Luis Sáenz de Heredia, 1948); Indochina, *Una cruz en el infierno* [*Flame Over Vietnam*] (José María Elorrieta, 1956); and the Philippines, *Aquellas palabras* (Luis Arroyo, 1949) (*Diccionario del cine español*, 242–3), was commonly referred to as the *Cine de misioneros* ('Missionary cinema') for its religious themes.
30. The most notable titles of siege films include epics such as *Cabiria* (Giovanni Pastrone, 1914), *El Cid* (Anthony Mann, 1961), and *Ran* (Akira Kurosawa, 1985); colonial movies such as *Beau Geste* (William Wellman, 1939)— Franco's favorite film of all time—and *Zulu* (Cy Endfield, 1964); westerns such as *They Died with Their Boots On* (Raoul Walsh, 1941), *High Noon* (Fred Zinnemann, 1952), and *The Alamo* (John Wayne, 1960); dramas such as *Dog Day Afternoon* (Sidney Lumet, 1975) and *Straw Dogs* (Sam Peckinpah, 1971); and political thrillers such as *La battaglia di Algeri* [*The Battle of Algiers*] (Gillo Pontecorvo, 1966) and *État de siège* [*State of Siege*] (Costa-Gavras, 1972), among many others.
31. As Spanish film scholar Luis González wrote, these films "re-enact situations in which the fatherland is besieged and in danger of succumbing to foreign forces" (*Fascismo, kitsch y cine histórico español* 178). These series include films such as *La princesa de los Ursinos* (1947), *El santuario no se rinde* (Arturo Ruiz Castillo, 1949), *Lola la piconera* (1951), *Agustina de Aragón* (1951), *La leona de Castilla* (1951), and *Los últimos de Filipinas*, among others.
32. For Arthur Koestler, time is the fundamental problem of anyone living under extreme conditions: "... in unnatural, confined, hermetically sealed conditions; in sanatoria, in the colonies" (292). Reflecting on his own experience in solitary confinement in a Francoist prison cell during the Spanish Civil War, he wrote, "increasing awareness of time slows down its pace, complete

awareness of time would bring it to a standstill. Only in death does the present become reality; time freezes—he who succeeds in experiencing 'pure time' experiences nothingness" (324). Along similar lines, Frank Kermode wrote that "without the sense of passing time, one is virtually ceasing to live; one loses 'contact with reality'" (160).

33. Soon after, another insert shot—of the front page of a Spanish newspaper announcing the signing of the armistice ending the Spanish-American War—informs us of the date, 10 December 1898, while the voice-over bombastically remarks, "The end of the war had arrived for everybody except for a handful of brave soldiers who were not aware the war had ended and who *did not want* to be aware of it."

34. In *Paris Hollywood: Writings on Film* (2002), Peter Wollen writes, "[a]rchitecture in film is never just itself. It is always a simulacrum of somewhere else, a symbolic representation of some other place" (199).

35. In his *Los últimos de Filipinas* (1954), which the film script follows closely, Enrique Llovet depicts the moment like this: "From the highest point one could make out a dark village, of humble shacks, tended to sweetly by the ocean and, as a silhouette, separated almost from the earth, by the dark border of the river. The river harmonized with the rock from the church, standing upright, and the horseman turned around and smiled in the face of the familiar vision" (6).

36. Peter Pelzer indicates that this terror is caused by the perception of universal chaos and disorder that results from glancing melancholically at the world: "Utopia[, then,] as remedy for melancholy[,] must be the contrary of it" (6). When the melancholic glance is cast by a fascist eye, utopia must be a "call for complete order" (6).

37. In fact, for Menéndez Pelayo, Spain transcends historical contingency to become a principle of permanence, and, above all, an instrument of the divine, as seen in his famous definition of the country as, "hammer of heretics, light of Trent, sword of Rome, cradle of San Ignatius..." (quoted in Payne 101).

38. Santos Zunzunegui writes that in this moment the church building, "possessor of the attributes of the church is thus invested with those of the military barracks offering a good small scale model in which one could conceive of certain ideology, during the Francoist state of the mid-forties" (20).

39. Peter Brooks defines classic fetishism precisely as "the investment of accessory and ancillary objects—objects metonymically associated with the body—with desire" (56). If not necessarily ancillary objects, Franco's early propaganda head shots do function as "hypersignificant accessories," as all fetishes do for Brooks. The "hypersignificant accessory" "means far beyond itself, ... means more than meaning itself, in that the fetish, in classic psychoanalytic doctrine, is a substitute for meanings—such as 'castration'—that cannot be faced" (57).

40. Freud observed that the fetish, as a sign that replaces the lost object, has a double role of negation and representation. Functioning as a mask, it covers emptiness and loss, but as a sign it inevitably signifies that loss. Fetishism

can be thus understood as a narrative fabricated by the subject in order to assuage his anxiety, negotiate his loss, and negate the castrating power of the father (152).

41. As Hermann Broch so pointedly remarked, and as seen in *Los últimos*'s political eulogizing of death, kitsch keeps you dreaming, unlike authentic art that "dazzles you until it blinds you and then gives you back your sight" (67).
42. As Mark Neocleous remarked, one of fascism's main traits is precisely the filling of the void left by its betrayal of history with nature: in this case, with the fake Philippine jungle (79).
43. "Bad objects," Mitchell writes, "are generally seen as worthless or disgusting from the imperial perspective, but are understood to be of great and no doubt excessive value to the colonial Other" (158).
44. For Deleuze, however, these two poles are not so rigidly drawn and can be easily traversed, as in the case of Von Sternberg's facial close-ups, whose gradating shades, which go from transparency to pure whiteness, are not only confined to "pure quality and its reflecting aspect" but are also aware of "power and intensities" (Deleuze 94).
45. For Franco Moretti the harpy is the mythological creature which encapsulates to perfection the dual workings of ideology (41).
46. This transformative quality of the close-up is precisely what, according to Deleuze, Jean Epstein meant when he said: "this face of a fleeing coward, as soon as we see it in close-up, we see cowardice in person, the 'feeling-thing', the entity" (Deleuze 96).
47. Thus, as Zunzunegui points out, "Anyone could assign a proper name, contemporary to the production of the film, to the inexpressive and calculating face that hides itself behind the mask of the 'the last one of Baler'" (23).
48. The same lack of depth that characterizes *Los últimos*'s final close-up can also be seen in the very treatment of Franco's face in Francoist propaganda. As Rafael Tranche writes, "the construction of his image ... was above all a common place (where every cliché about the thaumaturgic dimension of his power could be reiterated), a mask without a face in which, if held up close, the illusions of grandeur of his regime were hardly reflected" (95).

CHAPTER 4

Surcos: Neorealism, Film Noir, and the Puppet Master

Cinema is the art of the index; it is an attempt to make art out of a footprint
—Lev Manovich, *The Language of New Media*

Raza, Romancero marroquí, and *Los últimos de Filipinas,* as we saw in previous chapters, attempted to advance the Francoist political agenda by resorting to a bombastic film style representative of totalitarian kitsch aesthetics. In its unwavering depiction of the stark conditions of Madrid's working-class tenements at the beginning of the 1950s, José Antonio Nieves Conde's *Surcos* [*Furrows*] (1951) substantially deviated from this earlier triumphalist Francoist cinema.[1] Although there is general consensus about the film's ultra-conservative political message—like the directors Sáenz de Heredia and Antonio Román, Nieves Conde was a Falangist combatant in the Spanish Civil War—for most Spanish film scholars *Surcos* is the film that single-handedly revolutionized Spanish cinema by introducing the spirit of Italian neorealism[2] and the bleak vision of film noir.[3]

In the first in-depth analysis of *Surcos,* Marsha Kinder characterizes *Surcos* more precisely as a formal hybrid that mixes neorealist cinematic conventions with those of Hollywood, particularly the stylistic conventions of film noir and melodrama.[4] Given the multitude of institutional checkpoints firmly in place that made direct criticism of Franco's regime virtually impossible, Kinder argues, *Surcos* resorted to an indirect, formally hybrid approach to deliver a powerful critique of Francoism, in which political issues were displaced either onto the domestic sphere of the family through melodrama or onto the "other scene of fiction" through the stylistic conventions of film noir (40).

Contrary to the predominant understanding of *Surcos* as a legitimate neorealist noir project, I will argue that the film's re-appropriation of Italian neorealism and film noir is brought into sharper focus when seen through the lens of kitsch aesthetics. This lens brings to the fore the internal tension between the film's progressive neorealist and noir aesthetics—the former characterized by its humanist emancipatory message, the latter by its holding up a dark mirror to social realities—and its Falangist, right-wing message of the moral collapse of Spanish values under modern, corrupting urban pressure. While exposing Franco's triumphalist lies with acrid determination through its seemingly honest cinematic neorealist noir representation, Nieves Conde's film creates a new set of lies. *Surcos* is a kitsch film that, resorting to critically acclaimed prestigious cinematic styles, encapsulates Spanish fascist ideology even more efficiently than previous Francoist films did.

Surcos was produced at the height of Italian neorealism's influence in Spain—although its director always denied having seen any of its titles—but also at a time when American film noir cast its long shadow over European cinema in general.[5] The film borrows extensively from these two critically acclaimed film styles to advance its fascist ideological agenda. *Surcos*'s use of culturally prestigious film references to propagate a reactionary ideology contrary to these cinematic styles transforms Nieves Conde's film into a quintessential kitsch product. This deceptive form of messaging is the poisonous heart of the political danger of kitsch, which Hermann Broch described in appropriate moral terms as the "element of evil in the value system of art" (63). As *Surcos*'s positive critical reception perfectly illustrates, kitsch becomes more insidious the more it appears to be what it is not.

Surcos narrates the tragic experience of the Pérez family, small-holding Castilian peasants who leave their village for Madrid in search of a better life. In the Spanish capital, they move in with relatives in a working-class tenement in the neighborhood of Lavapiés—Madrid's famous "vertical slum"—and immediately begin a desperate search for work. The lures and temptations of Madrid—a city represented in the film as corrupt and mostly populated by a brutish crowd lacking in human solidarity—take hold of most of the family, with the exception of two of its members: the father, Manuel, and his youngest son, Manolo. Urban pressures, as well as the city's alluring promise of easy money, rapidly disrupt familial harmony and almost instantly upend the centuries-long hierarchy of the traditional peasant Castilian family. In this ruthless, Hobbesian urban order, the father loses his power to his wife and his oldest son Pepe, who, having already spent several months in Madrid serving in the military, is more "savvy" about the modern ways of the big city than the rest of the family. Pepe angrily reminds them of this fact soon after their arrival in Madrid in a comment that foreshadows his own fate at the end of the film: "If it weren't for me you'd rot to death digging into the ground."

The film's main focus is the moral collapse of three members of the Pérez family: the mother, whose name is never revealed, Pepe, the above-mentioned eldest son, and Tonia, his sister who, seduced by the city's tempting glamour, decides to pursue a singing career and becomes the lover of Don Roque, a ruthless racketeer known as "El Chamberlain," who is also Pepe's boss and *Surcos*'s almighty villain. The moral collapse is linked to the dissipation of the traditional patriarchal family structure, as revealed by the father's "loss" of masculinity. After a series of failed attempts at finding suitable "man's" work, he ends up at home wearing an apron, peeling potatoes, and washing pots. This narrative of moral collapse is redeemed through the struggles of the kind-hearted youngest son, Manolo. He is fired from his job as a delivery boy for having been robbed while working but falls in love with Rosario—a puppeteer's daughter—with whom he finds domestic bliss on the outskirts of Madrid. Manolo's happy fate is the only glimpse of hope in this dark moral tale of fatalism.

Despite its neorealist appearance, with its predominance of real urban settings and its focus on the rhythms and textures of the everyday life of a working-class family, *Surcos* is divorced from the progressive spirit of neorealism and from its message of human emancipation. And despite the noir look and feel of the subplot revolving around the underworld criminal activities of Don Roque —the film's omnipotent villain— in the bar and garage scenes, where most of the smuggling takes place, *Surcos* is also detached from noir's unrelenting questioning of conventional morality.[6] As mentioned earlier, the film resorts to the borrowing of innovative prestigious artistic styles, as kitsch typically does: not only neorealism and film noir, both in vogue at the time, but also Soviet montage, and, as we will see in a brief comparative analysis of one of its scenes, the critically acclaimed stylistic traits of Orson Welles's *Citizen Kane*, through which its kitsch fascist message is successfully smuggled.

Surcos's ultra-conservative ideological make-up is fairly evident. Mark Allinson, among many others, understands the movie as a "reactionary demonisation of the metropolis" (83), while film historian John Hopewell categorically describes it as a "Falangist thesis drama" (quoted in Kinder 40). To be sure, *Surcos* is an ultra-conservative, fascist film. After all, the screenwriters and the director himself were staunch Falangists. However, it is also simultaneously and paradoxically the first truly oppositional Spanish film, which shed light on the everyday reality of Franco's Spain, its rampant corruption, and its failed promises of a better life.

It is through its use of noir aesthetics—the noir visual mood the film cloaks itself in—rather than its supposedly neorealist traits, I argue, that the film injects some life into what is overall a predictably fascist, kitsch ideological message. The film's noir aesthetic reaches its climax in one of *Surcos*'s final sequences, in which Don Roque drags Pepe's body along a dirt road before finally dumping it over the railroad tracks in front of an oncoming train. As we will see through an analysis of this sequence, Pepe's feet, dragged along the ground, leave their imprint in the soil in the form of long marks that, highlighted by the camerawork and dramatic low-key lighting, are reminiscent of the agricultural furrows—the very "surcos" of the film's title—that provide the opening and closing shots of the film.[7] I will thus propose that it is not the film's supposedly neorealist features but, as this sequence reveals, its noir aesthetic with its unbridled movement between light and shadow, its wisecracks, and the harsh, slang-inflected dialogue associated with it that at times seems to subvert its own kitsch aesthetic, undermining this otherwise rigid "Falangist thesis drama."

Due to its daring cinematic approach and harsh critique of Francoist failed policies, *Surcos* caused a scandal within official Spanish political circles. Its focus on the corrupting influence of the black market, and its innovative cinematic style, shot mainly on location and resorting to natural sound whenever possible—a rarity in Spanish film production even decades later—had no precedent in Spanish cinema since 1940. The film's release resulted in the forced resignation of José María García Escudero, Franco's under-secretary of cinema.[8]

A firm believer in the need to reinvigorate Spanish cinema through the production of films like *Surcos* that dealt with relevant contemporary issues, García Escudero used his considerable influence to promote the film, which he defined as "the first glance at reality in a cinema of papier-maché" (quoted in Vernon 328). He went so far as to grant *Surcos* the highly desired category of "special interest" at the expense of *Alba de América* [*Dawn of America*] (1951), a "papier-maché" Francoist bio-epic of Christopher Columbus, strongly favored by Franco's right-hand Admiral Carrero Blanco and by the dictator himself. He also courageously defended *Surcos* as an "artistically and morally exceptional film" (quoted in Zumalde Arregui 295), against the accusations of the ecclesiastical representative of the Censorship junta, Father Antonio Garau Planas, who rejected it as "pure immorality, deserving only of being officially banned" (quoted in Zumalde Arregui 295).

Ironically, the idea behind the film originated in the same political circles that came to reject it once it was completed (Cortés Salinas 87). Initially, *Surcos* was supposed to be a propaganda film whose aim was to call attention to the problem of the massive migration from rural areas to Spain's major cities, which at the beginning of the 1950s was depopulating the Spanish countryside and straining Spain's precarious urban infrastructure, contributing to the rapid creation of depressed slums, particularly in large cities like Madrid or Barcelona (87).[9] The film was based on a series of articles about the exodus affecting rural Spain written by renowned Falangist writer Eugenio Montes. Natividad Zaro and Gonzalo Torrente Ballester, both Falangists —the latter would two decades later become one of Spain's best and most influential experimental novelists— were assigned the task of turning this series of articles into a coherent film script.[10]

The tension between the film's progressive aesthetics and its reactionary content is not only detectable in its formal mixing of neorealism and film noir, but is also seen in its use of puppet theater, a popular form of entertainment often characterized by its biting social satire and progressive politics, as seen, for example, in Guignol, the famous French puppet character. Puppet theater, as we will see, is the dramatic form that most clearly brings home the film's fascist message. Manuel —the fallen patriarch— reclaims his lost authority precisely by beating his wife and his daughter into submission, "re-enacting" a scene from the puppet show that Rosario's father performs to entertain Manolo and Rosario. In it, in a supposedly humorous fashion, a male puppet beats his wife to a pulp until her head becomes detached from her body. From the tiny stage of the puppet theater, traditional Spanish values rapidly expand to take over *Surcos*'s entire cinematic space. In fact, the puppet show operated by Rosario's father reinforces the brutally misogynist traditional Spanish values that the film encapsulates by making sexist violence, for example, more palatable when displayed through a seemingly innocent children's spectacle.

In order to examine how *Surcos* smuggles its fascist ideology by means of a deceptive kitsch recycling of prestigious cinematic styles—and the narrative conventions of puppet theater—in the following pages I will examine several scenes from the film, each mimicking a cinematic style which is referenced in an opportunistic fashion: the family's arrival in Madrid and of Manolo's arrival at Rosario's neighborhood, both shot in neorealist style; the scene inside Rosario's home, which borrows *Citizen Kane*'s trademark compositional style; the scene of Don Roque buying stolen property in his garage, which is shot in characteristic noir fashion, as are the rest of the scenes portraying Don Roque's criminal underworld; the montage sequence of Manuel's collapse at his first day of work at the factory, which recycles the conventions of Soviet montage; the street fair scenes, in which puppet theater first appears to advance *Surcos*'s reactionary ideology; and, finally, the sequence of Pepe's body being dumped onto the railroad tracks in which noir's signature visual style returns to bring the film to a close. These scenes will illustrate how the film's totalitarian kitsch aesthetic builds from the structural tension between the film's fascist ideology and its formal appropriation of the stylistic cinematic conventions of neorealism, film noir, Orson Welles's cinema, Soviet montage, and the narrative conventions of puppet theater.

Surcos opens with a visual pattern similar to that of *Los últimos de Filipinas*, accentuating the contrast between movement and stillness. The first shot of the credits superimposed on the image of a cultivated lot of land where a wheat plant stands straight on the right edge of the frame is immediately followed by another shot in which the film's title, *Surcos*, the Spanish word for "furrows," appears written across the screen over the orderly furrows of the cultivated field. Then a match-cut takes us to what seems to be a point of view shot of railway tracks, reminiscent of the furrows of the previous shot, taken from the front of a locomotive as it crosses the barren Castilian landscape at full speed towards the Spanish capital. A few seconds into the shot, a quotation from one of Eugenio Montes's articles on immigration appears on the screen, jarringly obstructing the view from the train:

> The city's appeal reaches the most remote villages, inviting the peasants to leave their lots behind with the promise of easy wealth. These peasants, tempted by the city, are not prepared to resist. They have lost their farms and lack the sophistication of urban civilization. They are *rootless trees*, *slum splinters* that life destroys and corrupts. This constitutes the most painful problem of our time. (Emphasis added)

This beginning shot from a moving vehicle reminds us not only of *Los últimos de Filipinas* but also of the famous opening shot of Roberto Rossellini's *Viaggio in Italia* [*Journey to Italy*] (1954), in which the protagonists' car roars through the Italian landscape. However, *Viaggio in Italia* opens frantically in media res and closes with a famous crane shot which allows an almost imperceptible glimpse of the camera operator's own shadow as it hovers over the cinematic space, subtly revealing cinema's dramatic artifice. *Surcos*, whose dynamic opening immediately follows a still shot of a wheat field ripe for harvest, closes with a shot of a similar field, thus bringing the film statically to a close. If Rossellini's film's subtle glimpse of the camera at the end hints at the artificial nature of cinematic representation, *Surcos* points to the dehumanizing nature of technology and mechanical inventions, like the train itself, and the evil urban settings from which they originate.

Throughout the film, technology will be sharply contrasted with organic growth, morally degraded urban life with pre-modern rural innocence, and materialist, selfish norms with family values and the communal spirit derived from them. *Surcos* sets up from the beginning a clearly contrasting pattern between rural stasis and urban speed, between the organic and the mechanical, between the Spanishness of the Castilian peasant and the alienation of the city dweller.

Since its first frightening arrival at the station in the Lumière brothers' famous short, the train has been a staple feature in cinematic representation.[11] In *Surcos*, the train signifies the dark illusory nature of fantasy and dream, which in the film are dangerous and immoral categories associated with the city's allure and false promises. It is a menace, a conveyor of death and moral degradation, which delivers the Pérez family directly into the belly of the beast: the corrupt city of Madrid. Moreover, as we will see, the train returns at the end to finish off its lethal job as it runs over Pepe's corpse. The initial shot of the train will be retroactively transformed in the spectator's mind at the end of the film into a sinister weapon whose main function is to carry Spanish peasants to their final destination, where they will become "slum splinters that life shatters and corrupts," as Eugenio Montes warns us from the outset.

As suggested by the match-cut described above, shot from the point of view of the locomotive itself, the organic nature of the furrows is contrasted with the cold steel straight lines formed by the railroad tracks. In the initial shots of the train sequence, a winding country road to the right of the train also serves as contrast to the steely abstract lines of the railroad tracks. These two divergent roads—the bending dirt country road and the train's straight iron path—hint at two divergent kinds of consciousness: a pre-modern consciousness praised by the film and an industrial consciousness denigrated by it that, as in *Los últimos de Filipinas*, is also paradoxically conveyed by the modern medium of film.

Surcos extols pre-modern consciousness by depicting the train as a disruptive menace. It is not a coincidence that the above-mentioned point of view shot does not belong to any of the members of the Pérez family, who, being in a train for the first time, might have been looking out through the train's windows. It is also not a coincidence that it is not a point of view shot of the train conductor either. Instead, the initial scene that puts *Surcos*'s dramatic engine in motion belongs to the train itself, the "projectile" that carries those "rootless trees" to the Spanish capital. In *Surcos*, the peasants who uproot themselves in search of an easier material life are dehumanized by modernity to become commodities—mere parcels—to be expediently delivered to their destination.[12]

This contrast between the natural and the artificial, between the village and the urban center, will later be allegorized in the differences between

Manuel, the authentic but endangered Spanish patriarch, and the strong yet immoral and inauthentic Don Roque, an evil, "foreign" patriarch, as suggested by his moniker "Chamberlain" and his hat and umbrella, the foreign attire that he wears as if it were a costume. Thus, by exploring the fate of the Pérez family in the sprawling Spanish capital, as its generic patronymic suggests, *Surcos* explores none other than the denigration of Spanishness in Spain's brave new urban world.[13]

In its Manichean treatment of location, the common characterization of *Surcos* as a neorealist film can easily be dismissed right from the start. I will argue, however, that *Surcos*'s defining characteristic is its opportunistic use of neorealist cinematic traits to promote an ideology that is alien to it. As we will see next, in *Surcos* the neorealist image-fact that for André Bazin was a "fragment of concrete reality in itself multiple and full of ambiguity" ("An Aesthetic of Reality" 37), becomes a fact-image upon which a preconceived view of reality is built into its mise-en-scène to communicate its ideological point.

After the train stops in the station, which, unlike in the oblique dynamic composition of the Lumierès' train arrival, is rendered from an almost flat angle that focuses mostly on the family and only minimally on the surrounding context, the Pérez family takes the subway to reach its final destination. The subway scene is an early example of why *Surcos* is divorced from the spirit of Italian neorealism, and its "subtlety and suppleness of movement within . . . cluttered spaces" (38). In this scene, shot from a high angle in a stuffed subway car, the family is engulfed in a hostile crowd that harasses them by poking fun at their peasant origins. Other passengers verbally humiliate them as ignorant hillbillies while asking one another sarcastic questions such as "Where are they hiding their mattresses?" as if the family were not even present. The scene comes to an end with the crowd bursting into laughter as a chicken attempts to escape from the basket carried by the mother. The mere absurdity of the image of a chicken struggling to escape from its basket inside a subway car mimics the oddity and absurdity of the Pérez family itself, encaged in an urban oppressive environment they do not fully understand.

The subway scene reduces "the naturalness of the behavior of everyone," which for Bazin was one of neorealism's trademarks, to mere authorial choreography (38). The crowd is simply there to underline the film's frequently repeated message—city people are cold-hearted, ruthless, morally degraded, and lacking in human solidarity. Thus, for all its admirable attempts at cinematic verisimilitude, in *Surcos* real locations lose any sense of randomness and become instead a tightly controlled environment through which to simulate the appearance of chaotic random spontaneity. This places *Surcos* at odds with Italian neorealist aesthetics from the outset.

The same deceiving impulse we observed in the subway scene is repeated when the Pérez family arrives at its final destination, a tenement building where they finally settle. This sequence follows the ascent of the family from street level to the third-floor apartment they will share with their relatives. The sequence is visually structured to emphasize confinement and lack of freedom through multiple shots of the family seen through the cast-iron bars of the railings and through the visual and acoustic chaos that dominates the tenement, predominantly inhabited by scores of bickering women and unruly children. The cacophonous soundtrack creates an aural space that highlights sordidness and absence of proper human interaction, as we hear neighbors nastily arguing with each other. When the family finally reaches their floor, the camera pauses briefly on a group of urban urchins dressed like adults. Sitting on the floor, smoking and playing cards, they are framed by metal-bar railings that suggest them being imprisoned in their degrading urban environment (Fig. 4.1). As they lay eyes on the family, one of the children asks the others, "Why are these hillbillies coming?" to which another child from

Figure 4.1 *Surcos*, 1951

the gang boorishly replies, "Don't you see you stupid, they are coming to sell their chickens to the racketeer," referring to Pili's—the distant cousin who invited Pepe to come to Madrid—own mother. These children, with their transgressive moral behavior and adult insensitivity, are portrayed as devoid of innocence and reduced to witnessing their own degraded moral landscape.

The narrative climax of the tenement scene takes place right after Pepe rings the bell to their relatives' apartment. After he briefly introduces his family to Pili, who dismissively looks them up and down as if they were damaged goods, a few children from the gang quietly approach the mother from behind, open her basket and throw a chicken down to the patio. Predictably enough, this action causes instant mayhem in the patio below as the children begin chasing the chicken, trying to capture it. By depicting them as hungry scavengers rather than as innocent children having fun, this bird's-eye view shot dehumanizes the urban youth. This scene is typical of the representation of crowd behavior throughout the movie: unruly, selfish crowds living a nasty, brutish, and short Hobbesian existence; and this is a representation completely foreign to the dignifying treatment of crowds in Italian neorealist film.[14]

The episode in which the youngest son, Manolo, wanders around Madrid's outskirts, running away from his family after they utterly humiliate him for being fired, is where *Surcos* reminds us more closely of Italian neorealism, particularly of Rossellini's films such as *Paisà* [*Paisan*] (1946) and *Germania Anno Zero* [*Germany Year Zero*] (1948). But it is through its similarity that its radical difference from neorealism becomes more readily apparent. The first part of *Surcos* is suffused in gloom and fatalism. The second part of the film, inaugurated by this episode, begins to delineate a redeeming kitsch space that stands completely opposite to the spirit of neorealism. Manolo's wandering around the outskirts of Madrid showcases the failure of Franco's promise to regenerate the nation by highlighting the crisis of unemployment in Spain in its depiction of neighborhoods populated by men sitting around military barracks, idly waiting for the soldiers to provide them with a free lunch. This urban landscape, with its share of houses in ruins, reminds us of similar scenes in *Germania Anno Zero*, in which the child protagonist and his older brother similarly stroll through the rubble of deserted streets against the barren cityscape of post-war Berlin. But unlike the existential crisis of the child protagonist in *Germania Anno Zero*, which ends in suicide, Manolo's existential crisis—amid this urban decay of unemployed masses—signals the beginning of the phallic reconstitution of traditional Spanish values.

Manolo finds shelter in a roofless house amid the ruins and proceeds to wash and hang dry his white shirt. While he stands in line to get some free lunch from the soldiers, a group of street urchins who are playing in the street steal his shirt, attach it to a wood stick as if it were a flag, and march down the road right in front of the military barracks, parodying a surrendering Republican army column. This is a poignant scene that perhaps also hints at the surrendering of Francoist military prowess; as we see Spanish soldiers reduced to running a soup kitchen to feed the hungry citizens, we are reminded of the failure of Franco's victorious army to create a true fascist Spain more than a decade after the Spanish Civil War had ended. Manolo loses his spot in the soup line as he chases the children to retrieve his shirt. Upon his return to the line, he realizes that the soup has run out. On top of that, a couple of unsympathetic soldiers answer his desperate plea for food by shutting the gate right in front of his nose. Manolo's wandering through the city now acquires a truly dramatic tone. He is fighting for his survival in the overwhelming Spanish capital.

This episode introduces for the first time an entirely new cinematic space located in the outskirts of Madrid, a hopeful and harmonious kitsch space filled with light where houses are painted white. This is a space *in-between*, located at a proper distance between city and country. This new episode opens with a wide shot of the sky in which the upper part of a very tall chimney looms large to the right of the frame. The shot features the same swelling dramatic music chords that we heard in the beginning of the film, which serve as its main musical leitmotif. The camera then tilts downward to reveal the rest of the tall structure and the new space surrounding it, mainly composed of whitewashed, humble dwellings. A long shot follows Manolo, who is walking amid children forming harmonious circles, peacefully holding hands and singing happily, a stark contrast to the previous scenes in which children are represented as an unruly thieving bunch. Utterly exhausted, Manolo enters this new space barely able to walk, but keeps going as if he were a shipwreck survivor trying to reach safety on shore. The new environment looks modest with its humble dwellings and unpaved roads. Still, unlike in the shady working-class tenements of the opening scenes, there is no room for moral misery here. Manolo, like the shipwrecked Ulysses stumbling upon Nausicaa and her father King Alcinous on the island of Sheria, stumbles onto Rosario and her father.[15] To emphasize the redemptive, orderly nature of this new space, we witness Rosario's father painting a short pole in front of his house white, which replicates at a smaller, domestic scale the big phallic tower that protectively watches over the entire neighborhood.[16] Rosario and her father recognize the exhausted Manolo, and after a series of intercalated jerky jump-cuts between Manolo and Rosario that awkwardly suggest Manolo's faint mental state and their immediate emotional connection, he finally collapses onto the floor. His fall is accompanied by the same musical motif used in the scene when Manolo's father faints at the factory, which we will analyze later. But if the earlier scene, as we will see, suggests a fall from grace, the latter suggests a fall into grace. Manolo's fall is visually punctuated by a close-up of his peasant espadrilles as they slide against the ground, foreshadowing the tragic fate of his brother Pepe at the end of the film (Fig. 4.2). Manolo's fall symbolizes the end of his old urban life and the beginning of a new moral one that will advance the rural moral order. Unlike the scene toward the end of the movie in which the dragging of Pepe's feet on the ground reminds us of his tragic fate due to his moral degradation, here the marks left on the ground by Manolo's peasant espadrilles—the traditional Spanish peasant footwear—seem to point to the opposite: Manolo has finally secured his footing; he is in touch with *real moral* ground for the first time since his arrival in the big city.

As this analysis has hopefully shown, *Surcos*'s neorealism is in fact a ruse. Nieves Conde's film cannot be more removed from the neorealist spirit in Bazin's sense of neorealism: a cinema "whose unit of cinematic

Figure 4.2 *Surcos*, 1951

narrative is not the shot" but, as in Rossellini's *Paisà*, the image-fact, which, as mentioned earlier, is a "fragment of concrete reality in itself multiple and full of ambiguity" (37).

The film's apparent neorealist traits are just the logical result of the visual depiction of its chosen subject matter—the life of poor peasants living in the big city in a working-class neighborhood. Undeniably, this is represented with rare verisimilitude for a Francoist film of the period, as demonstrated by its shooting on location, the use of real sound, and the care shown with even the smallest detail of its mise-en-scène, including having the actors wear clothes previously worn by the real people they are supposed to represent. In these ways, *Surcos* borrows stylistic traits from neorealism but rejects its humanist, progressive spirit and its ambiguous cinematic representation. *Surcos*'s fascist manner of seeing things could not be more removed from that of Italian neorealism, despite the neorealist trimmings with which the film embellishes its discourse as a way of seeking artistic credibility.

The following scene inside the house, when Rosario serves Manolo a nourishing meal and asks her father to hire him as an assistant in the puppet theater, is a perfect example of *Surcos*'s recycling of culturally prestigious cinematic references to smuggle its reactionary, fascist message. It is visually structured like the famous boarding house sequence from Orson Welles's *Citizen Kane*, in which Mr Thatcher, representing the bank, visits Kane's parents to sign the agreement that will take little Charlie away from them.

Both *Citizen Kane* and *Surcos* share a similar underlying theme of loss due to the pressures of modernity.[17] Like Welles's film, *Surcos* also juggles the idea of myth, in its case that of *Hispanidad*, politics, and the collective psyche. While both films take diametrically opposing ideological stances in exploring their overlapping themes, they also cross the same path of kitsch. Unlike *Citizen Kane*, which explores the fissures and cracks of the human psyche and its political ramifications, *Surcos* offers an unattainable kitsch solution to the personal and the political.

The scene inside Rosario's house has a startling structural resemblance to that from *Citizen Kane*. Here we also have three adults in the room and, in this case, a group of children playing innocently outside the house, framed by a window in an almost identical manner (Fig. 4.3). Its meaning, however, is vastly different, and its formal execution reveals its kitsch aesthetics. In *Surcos*, the child whose fate is being discussed is Manolo, who, unlike little Charles in *Citizen Kane*, is already inside the house. Manolo is not about to be sent away for adoption but, on the

Figure 4.3 *Surcos*, 1951

contrary, he is being metaphorically adopted by Rosario and her father, the puppeteer; after all, his own mother refused to help him pay the amount his boss demanded to cover the losses of the stolen goods.

The tension in the boarding house sequence of *Citizen Kane* is built around the dramatic irony between three distinctive visual planes—two inside the house where Kane's future is being discussed, and one outside where the little boy plays, poignantly framed by a window. In *Surcos*, like in all kitsch, where symbols weakened by cliché need to keep reinforcing themselves through constant repetition, the different visual planes—the interior and the exterior—do not create dramatic tension but on the contrary only serve to reinforce each other. The harmonious circle of kids singing and holding hands seen outside the window does not offer a visual counterpoint to the scene inside, but only echoes the harmonious circle being formed inside, where Manolo finally finds shelter from the cruel urban reality outside.

While *Citizen Kane* explores kitsch to reveal the populist, fascist dangers of reclaiming the lost garden—symbolized by Kane's lost childhood cabin in the woods—*Surcos* revels in this reclaiming. In both films the lost garden ultimately points to the experience of loss faced by immigrants: in *Citizen Kane*, as Mulvey remarked, to the American experience (the quintessential immigrant experience), inextricably bound to a lost world left behind; in *Surcos*, to the rural exodus from the Spanish countryside to the cities that shook the country during the 1950s, upending centuries of a traditional Spanish way of life.

But unlike *Citizen Kane*, which exposes the personal and political dangers of actively pursuing a return to the past, *Surcos* presents Manolo's return to the edenic womb—in his case a paternal womb, as it were—as a viable alternative. In fact, inside Rosario's house he finds a safe haven where he can live a moral life protected from the outside dangers.[18] In Rosario, Manolo finds a future wife and mother of his children, because, as she tells his father the first time Manolo introduces her to him, "We loved each other as God ordered." But even more importantly, through Rosario he finds the father figure he has lost, his own puppet master.

Surcos's scene is suffused with similar Oedipal dynamics to *Citizen Kane*.[19] Like Kane, Manolo is expelled from Eden—the Castilian countryside—when economic circumstances force him to move with his family to Madrid. He relives the trauma of separation once again when, humiliated by his own mother, he decides to run away from his family to prove to them that he can fend for himself. Like Charles's, Manolo's Oedipal scenario is also polarized between two father figures. His own father, who is poor, uneducated, and brutally misogynistic, despite his soft, kind-hearted appearance, and Rosario's father, a widower, who, assuming as many roles in the Oedipal scenario as he does in his puppetry, represents the maternal and the paternal alike—the imaginary and the symbolic—the unmediated personal bonds of familial love but also the abstract symbolic systems of law and money. And, more importantly, he also represents a successful incarnation of Spanish misogynous traditional values, a perfect synthesis of the paternal and the maternal, which, as we saw in the previous chapter, Franco's early propaganda posters also strived to achieve. In short, Manolo's future father-in-law, whose proper name we never learn, embodies in the film the Law-of-the-Father, from which the Pérez family has strayed because of their migration to the city; this is a law he lays bare in all its fascist brutality through his graceful puppets.

In *Surcos*, unlike in Welles's film, it is the father figure then who represents the imaginary plenitude associated with rural Spain, and its moral and ideological rigidity, to which the figure of the mother takes second place. In *Surcos*, Manolo's mother is depicted as morally corrupt because, following her ambitious son Pepe, she has freed herself from her husband's moral leash, unlike Charles's mother, who sacrifices her own happiness for his son's future. Having being exposed to city life, she has also embraced the cold-hearted rationality characteristic of the symbolic—while completely lacking in maternal affection—as represented by her material ambition and efficiency with money, which in the film connotes moral wanting; her ease with money is made perfectly clear in a scene in which she aggressively drills her husband about the prices of the smuggled goods of his own basket.

While *Citizen Kane* is a narrative labyrinth without a center, as Borges once called it, *Surcos*, on the contrary, narrates the downfall of the Pérez family and Manolo's redemption in a linear omniscient narrative style that glosses over difference while aspiring to final truths. *Surcos* is not a narrative labyrinth, but it does portray a maze-like, urban space where peasant newcomers get morally lost. At its center lurks the evil Don Roque, who, like the mythological Minotaur—and Captain Vidal in Guillermo del Toro's *Pan's Labyrinth* (2006), as we will see in the last chapter—devours his innocent victims over time.

A similar dissonance between style and content seen in *Surcos*'s ersatz use of neorealist aesthetics and of the prestigious stylistic traits of *Citizen Kane* also arises in the film's appropriation of film noir aesthetics: low-key lighting, nocturnal scenes, smoke-filled high and low angle shots, and the use of various framing devices that tinge the images with an air of fatalism and despair, as well as a widespread use of wisecracks and the slang dialect traditionally associated with film noir. This was an aesthetic particularly deployed in *Surcos*'s subplot surrounding Don Roque's criminal activities in Madrid's black market. However, as we saw in *Surcos*'s disregard for the image-fact, which for Bazin was central to neorealism, in the film, as Rob Stone observes, "the essential psychosexual turmoil [of noir] is missing and the moral ambiguity of noir is excised; for 'film noir' is characterized by a certain anxiety over the existence and definition of masculinity and normality" (193). To be sure, *Surcos* exhibits, as we will see shortly, a great deal of anxiety about the crisis of traditional concepts of masculinity that take place when morally good country people go to the evil city. But the film is characterized by its black-and-white moral righteousness, which stands in stark contrast to film noir's relentless questioning of conventional morality.

In describing the important influence of film noir in Franco's Spain, Stone paradoxically observes that film noir did not explicitly appear in Spain until after the death of General Franco (185). The moral ambiguity associated with film noir was simply not acceptable in a society dominated by "rigid catholic doctrine," and the private detective and the femme fatale, two main ingredients of the genre, were not welcome in a police state deemed infallible in law enforcement, which closely monitored female sexuality (185). Nonetheless, Stone concludes that film noir in Spain "was never more insidious and, even by its absence, was never more relevant" (185). He argues, following Paul Schrader's famous argument, that in Spain noir was not defined by its conventional settings or dramatic conflict, but rather by the "more subtle qualities of tone and mood" (quoted in Stone 191). As he reminds us, it is precisely noir's realism that for Schrader was "key to the tone and mood" (quoted in Stone 191).

It was through the realism of film noir—not through its fake neorealist aesthetic—that *Surcos* indeed offered a major critique of Franco's regime, which was displaced in the "other scene" of fiction of Kinder's words (40). It presented the stark reality of a Spanish capital controlled by unscrupulous racketeers, who use and abuse dispensable *paletos* who were desperately trying to make it in the big city. It was through the more subtle qualities of tone and mood that the powerful element of realism identified by most critics, regardless of their ideological leanings, sneaks back in through the back door. Its ruthless depiction of everyday life in Francoist Spain was a drastic rebuttal of the previous idealized versions of Spanishness proposed by the Francoist kitsch films of the 1940s.

In *Surcos*, this realist noir aesthetic gravitates around the bar owned by Don Roque that serves as a front for money laundering and a base for his illegal operations. The bar, filled with the usual suspects Don Roque hires for his clandestine activities—mostly the nighttime theft of sacks of goods from trucks coming from the provinces to Madrid—is the epicenter of the film's moral corruption. This is a space manipulated at will by Don Roque, comfortably seated in his office while stacking up the illegal profits in his safe. The office and the garage, where Don Roque keeps the station wagon Pepe drives for him during the illegal operations, are the main stages for the various scenes in which Don Roque displays his phallic prowess, controlling Madrid's underworld while ominously smoking his cigar and handling wads of dirty money. These scenes are crafted using a conventional noir visual repertoire of high and low angles, low-key lighting and various kinds of expressionistic framing devices (windows, doors, iron gates, etc.), and are often enveloped in clouds of cigarette smoke. In these scenes, the camerawork not only shows us Don Roque's corrupt underworld but also highlights money's inherent sordidness, its vulgar corrupting materiality. This happens particularly in a scene in which Don Roque counts the bills used to pay off a crook for selling a batch of stolen watches. We watch him handling the worn-out bills in a manner that deliberately emphasizes their dirty, contaminated nature, which starkly contrasts with the pure, spiritual moral fabric of Manuel's rural values of backbreaking labor[20] (Fig. 4.4).

Figure 4.4 *Surcos*, 1951

The crisis of masculinity typical of canonic noir films such as *Out of the Past* (1947) or *The Killers* (1946), in which the protagonist exhibits a pathological passivity despite all his strength and wit as he is finally devoured by the femme fatale, is dramatized in *Surcos* as a duel between two different modes of masculinity: the Spanish traditional rural model, characterized by its Catholic moral righteousness and rigid misogyny, represented by Manuel, and a new urban model, selfishly immoral, profit-seeking and exploitative, epitomized by Don Roque, "El Chamberlain," the ruthless racketeer, who, as mentioned earlier, is paradoxically feminized as suggested by his admittedly costume-like, "ornamental" wearing of a hat and carrying of an umbrella. In short, a masculine rural Spain engulfed by an accessorized, feminine, labyrinth-like, and perverse urban one.

Surcos borrowed both film noir's and Italian neorealism's concern with the unveiling of social truths mentioned by George J. Becker and represented a similar phenomenon of disenchantment identified by Carl Richardson—for whom film noir was the artistic expression of a disenchanted left—but only in reverse. It materialized the artistic liberation of a sector of Falange (Hedillista), which was profoundly disillusioned with the results of Franco's construction of a new Spain.[21] In this sense, it meant a big departure from the triumphalist, bombastic kind of kitsch film prominent during the 1940s that we saw in the previous chapters. But, unlike Italian neorealism or American film noir, it was not the result of a historical liberating change—the fall of fascism, the post-war hangover—but of the further consolidation of Franco's regime. *Surcos*'s intention was precisely to express a fascist disenchantment with Francoism's pragmatic status quo, which for Nieves Conde and other staunch Falangists had betrayed the fascist revolution. Like film noir or Italian neorealism, *Surcos* concerns itself with the unveiling of social truth, but unlike those two film styles it further mystifies social truth, veiling the real causes of Spain's social and economic stagnation during the autarchic period of the Francoist regime. Instead of providing a lucid analysis of the troubles of Franco's Spain, it offers, as we will see, a reactionary account that blames society's ills on the abandonment of the traditional Spanish rural values associated with fascist notions of *Hispanidad*, which the Castilian peasantry truly embodied.[22]

The first part of the film deals with Manuel's progressive loss of authority and control over his own family in a new urban environment he no longer understands. Manuel's loss is Don Roque's gain, as he—a classic mighty noir villain—not only exploits and ultimately kills Pepe, the oldest son, but also takes Tonia as a lover by pretending to help her launch a singing career that he simultaneously cynically helps to sabotage. Throughout, *Surcos* endows Don Roque with indestructible phallic power. He overpowers anyone who dares challenge him, either by his wit or by his sheer physical prowess. His phallic mastery of Madrid's underworld reaches its climax in a scene toward the end of the film in which, after confessing to Pepe that he gave him a job only to gain access to his sister Tonia, Don Roque hands his own knife to an armless Pepe only to knock him down by force seconds later while making fun of his hillbilly ways.

Don Roque's hardened core—epitomized even in his own name reminiscent of the Spanish word for rock, *roca*—and phallic power heavily contrast with Manuel's softer, empathic core. After being unable to find a "man's job" in the city, Manuel's wife forces him to carry a basket around his neck and sell candy and cigarettes in the streets. Predictably enough, good-hearted Manuel, lacking the basic skills for surviving in a black market environment, fails to make any profit. In a well-known scene, after reluctantly giving a few kids free candy, Manuel is surrounded by a flock of children who, as in Hitchcock's *The Birds* (1963), appear suddenly out of nowhere in growing numbers to ominously chant, "We want candy, we want candy." This scene is rendered in a high angle shot with Manuel at its center surrounded by the children, who, like in the scene with the chickens discussed earlier, look more like hungry birds than cute, innocent children. The commotion soon catches the attention of a police officer, who fines Manuel after he naively offers him some of his illegal cigarettes.

His failure as a street vendor—punctuated by several sudden musical chords which constitute the film's leitmotif for such moments—signifies Manuel's first ominous fall from grace and the beginning of his forced feminization. Upon returning home, Manuel's wife treats him harshly as she hands him an apron and orders him to peel potatoes. In a shot in which Manuel is seated with a barred window behind him—continuing the visual leitmotif of city imprisonment introduced at the beginning of the film—his wife hovers over him while yelling mercilessly. From this moment on, the father will remain symbolically castrated until he receives a letter from the employment agency with a job offer to work in a factory. After his daughter Tonia reads the letter aloud to him, an allusion to his illiteracy that emphasizes further his childlike innocence, a terribly excited Manuel takes off his apron and resentfully tells his wife, "I got a man's job, you see. Put this on and take your place in the kitchen."

The much-celebrated scene in which Manuel shows up for his first day at the new job in the factory is one of the dramatic climaxes of the film and depicts the pinnacle of Manuel's social castration. This scene, shot in a Soviet-style montage, is also a perfect example of *Surcos*'s kitsch eclectic borrowing of prestigious cinematic styles to smuggle its reactionary content. It opportunistically uses Soviet-style montage, paradoxically, to denigrate factory work and the revolutionary role of the proletariat often depicted in Spanish communist propaganda during the Civil War. Upon showing up at the steel mill, where workers operating heavy machinery are molding various pieces of steel into shape, the foreman dismissively greets him, hands him a worker's jumpsuit, and provides him with a wheelbarrow. From the moment Manuel sets foot inside the factory, the soundtrack pounds the spectator with a cacophony of industrial sounds. Shot on location, the scene's mise-en-scène and an agile montage decisively convey the impression of unbearable heat emanating from the furnaces and the hectic pace of industrial work with which Manuel can hardly keep up.

Manuel is seen helping other workers operate a big sledgehammer whose powerful blows gradually mold into shape a white-hot piece of metal. Manuel's expression grows increasingly anxious as an alternate Soviet-style montage cuts from a close-up of his face to the piece of metal at a gradually accelerating pace. The piece of metal being brutally pounded into shape metaphorically conveys city life's brutal demands on rural Manuel. Every blow of the sledgehammer on the piece of metal is dramatically paired with a close-up of Manuel's face, showing his growing distress at his experience at the factory. The elongated piece of metal being twisted and turned by the powerful sledgehammer has obvious phallic connotations that point to Manuel's social castration. Finally, after a series of back and forth rapid cross-cuts between close-ups of Manuel and the twisted metal bar, he gets dizzy and faints to the same musical theme we heard at the opening of the film, which signals a fall from grace. Manuel is now not only a "slum splinter" but also a "fallen tree," as badly battered as the piece of hot metal. Once again, like in the train sequence at the beginning of the film, modern technology, with its abstract precision and rapid movements, dramatically contrasts with the slow, harmonious rhythms of rural life. Stemming from organic growth, these are the rhythms that Manuel is accustomed to and that the film romanticizes. As the foreman tells Manuel with annoyance right after he comes to his senses, "I'm sorry. Here we do not sow or harvest. This is a factory. Not a field left fallow." In typical kitsch fashion, the Soviet-style montage chosen for the whole sequence further vilifies technology and factory work by associating it with bolshevism and Soviet glorification of the proletariat, while at the same time profiting from the cultural cinematic prestige of Soviet cinema among Spanish filmmakers and selective audiences alike.

Manuel's attempt to land a "man's job" ironically delivers the final blow to his masculinity. Upon returning home, Manuel will obediently assume his submissive place in the household, again wearing an apron and doing domestic chores while being constantly harassed by his wife. Manuel's masculine collapse coincides with the peak of the power of Don Roque, who not only hires Pepe for his dangerous clandestine nocturnal operations, but also takes Tonia as his lover. It is at this point that *Surcos*'s bleak noir atmosphere and harsh language hold up a dark mirror to the polished Francoist image offered by official political propaganda and the type of bombastic films we saw in previous chapters.

However, the fatalism that is otherwise pervasive throughout *Surcos* is kitschily redeemed by the traditional redemptive fascist message that emanates from the tiny stage of the puppet theater to ultimately gain the ideological upper hand. Puppetry in *Surcos* becomes the main vehicle by which to transmit the film's fascist values. The puppet theater's traditional misogynist Spanish values, contemplated by Rosario and Manolo, who are as transfixed as enchanted children, offer a powerful ideological antidote to the progressive values associated with film noir and the contemporary fad of neorealist films, to which the film self-referentially alludes.[23]

The puppet theater first appears in a scene in which young Manolo becomes distracted from his job as a delivery boy by the noise of a carnival street fair. This is a scene in which the audience is subtly reminded of those Spanish traditional values endangered by modern city life through the spectacle of bullfighting. A long establishing shot brings us into a crowded street fair with the standard array of barrack attractions. A following medium-long shot zooms in on a street puppet theater show to the left of the frame, and upon its tiny stage a bullfight is re-enacted to a resounding accompaniment of *olés* cheered by the crowd, mostly composed of children. Excited by the spectacle, Manolo leaves his delivery basket on the ground and becomes immersed in the puppet show. The camera cuts to another medium-long shot which brings the puppet show a bit closer and also gives us a first glimpse of a smiling Rosario, the puppeteer's daughter, with whom Manolo eventually settles down in the outskirts of Madrid. Manolo is now framed in a medium shot in which we also see a suspicious character who, standing behind him, is eyeing his basket filled with goods.

In this medium shot, Manolo smiles boyishly as he watches the bullfight being performed by the puppet theater. Seconds later, he notices Rosario for the first time as she goes around asking for donations from the crowd, and turns his head toward her. The camera cuts to a medium close-up of Manolo looking at Rosario with the exact same boyish smile he had earlier when he was looking at the puppets. He puts some money on Rosario's tray and she thanks him with a big smile. She immediately notices the crook behind Manolo snatching something from the basket and warns him that he is being robbed. As Manolo begins to chase the thief, the camera cuts to a close-up of the puppet theater stage from which the puppets have completely vanished. Instead, on the stage, we now see—rather comically—the head of Rosario's father, who emerges from his puppeteer's hideout to watch the commotion. Finally, Manolo catches a man whom he mistakes for the thief and a fight ensues, while the crowd simply circles around them as if it were a boxing ring (as it happens more than once throughout the movie) and does nothing to separate them. Seconds later the police come to put an end to the scuffle.

In this scene, the spectacularization of the female image—characterized, as Mulvey has shown, by her looked-at-ness in contrast to her male counterparts—is almost literal, since Manolo's gaze substitutes Rosario's face for the bullfight spectacle of the puppet theater, which the camera conflates into one ("Visual Pleasure" 203). But the moment of contemplation that "freezes the flow of action" is not "erotic" in the usual way, but rather suggests Manolo's close identification with the notion of Spanishness the film propagates; this is an erotic contemplation *of* Spanishness, as it were, which also arrests the spectators' look, thus preventing us "from achieving any distance from the image in front of him" (209).

In an inversion of the Kuleshov effect, in which the same identical close-up of a character seems to convey a different range of emotions according to the shot that comes immediately before or after it, here the two completely different objects of Manolo's gaze—a bullfight puppet show and Rosario's face—seemingly elicit the same emotion in him. His boyishly innocent expression in the two different shots of his face—one looking at the show, the other looking at Rosario—is identical and seems to convey an emotion resulting from the combination of both objects of his gaze: Rosario's face and bullfighting.

The interchangeability of the two close-ups of Manolo suggests that he projects onto Rosario's face the spectacle of bullfighting, the Spanish national celebration par excellence. In the film, we will soon learn, Rosario—the puppeteer's daughter—comes to symbolize the traditional Spanish woman who counter-poses the other female characters deemed immoral in the film: she is a blonde, virginal, God-fearing woman. She is thus the exact opposite of the noir femme fatale. And as her own name suggests—Rosario, meaning the Rosary—she embodies that communal religious ritual, the communal prayer of the Rosary, that the Pérez family was engaged in early on in the film when they were embarrassingly *caught* by Pepe and Pili in a high angle point of view shot that made them seem vulnerable and out of place; a *paleto* family lost in the big city clinging to their reassuring old religious habits. Eventually, Rosario will become Manolo's fiancée, and thus the broken communal link, represented by the interrupted Rosary, will be restored. This is a broken link that the circular design of the traditional bullring also hints at restoring.

Like Rosario's face, turned into a fetish by Manolo's gaze, bullfighting—Spain's national feast—being performed by the puppet show also becomes a fetish; in this case signifying a traditional, authentic, and courageous Spanish way of life, which, acting as antidote for the ills of modernity, has the capacity to mend the broken bonds of society. At the center of the spectacle is the matador, who seeks fame and glory, unlike the bourgeois businessmen and racketeers obsessed with accumulating material wealth. The matador is the authentic Spanish hero who, by defying death every afternoon, leads an aesthetically dangerous life, the only kind of life that Spanish fascists thought worth living.

Bullfighting as a fetish does not veil sexual castration, as for Freud all fetish does, but in this case the social anxiety produced by the moral perils of modernity, its secular/vulgar materiality, which corrupts Spanish elites and transforms peasants into robotic, soulless proletarians, as we saw in the factory sequence described above. In short, bullfighting counteracts a conflictive modernity that turns Spanish values upside down. It is only through the channeling of authentic Spanish values that, according to the film, Spaniards will recover their original state of grace.

Since puppets remain motionless without their puppeteer's will, this sequence also introduces us to their puppet master. The puppeteer—Rosario's father—exemplifies the Spanish traditional patriarchal model, metonymically suggested in the film by a shot of his head—the head of the family—which occupies center stage (Fig. 4.5). Aided by the morally edifying fables (disguised as children's entertainment) regularly on display on the stage where bullfighting, Spain's national celebration, was just performed, *Surcos*'s Spanish traditional values—threatened by city life—will finally be restored.[24]

The only chance for Manolo's redemption in this brave new world will be for him to find solace within the puppeteer's family by marrying Rosario. Manolo's running away from his own home after having lost his job not only paradoxically propels his own redemption, his return to an original state of grace, but plunges us straight into the land of kitsch. After endlessly wandering around the streets of Madrid in search of a better life, as we saw, he ends up by mere chance at the doorstep of Rosario's house where, after collapsing from hunger and exhaustion, he will be nursed back to health and given a second chance in life.

Figure 4.5 *Surcos*, 1951

The scene inside Rosario's house, staged, as we saw, like *Citizen Kane*'s boarding house sequence, also reveals, albeit unwittingly, the misogynist role of puppet theater. In this scene, the puppeteer, who is prompted by Rosario to hire Manolo as an assistant, illustrates how easy it is to operate the little theatre: "The curtain rises and the show begins," he says, and immediately proceeds to put on a show. The next shot frames Manolo against the background of a wall where the puppeteer has various puppet heads on a shelf, unconsciously suggesting that Manolo is also a puppet with his own part to play. The improvised show is a short sketch in which a housewife complains that her husband has squandered his two-week salary without bringing anything home. The husband appears, informing the audience that his father told him that he had a "powerful argument to persuade women." He leaves the stage only to return with a big stick and proceeds to hit his wife on the head. After each blow, he asks her if she is convinced that he is right yet. The wife confesses she is getting there, until the final blow decapitates her, prompting the husband's laughter.

The camera cuts from the stage to a medium close-up of Manolo and Rosario, both smiling like children, enchanted by the violent sexist sketch (Fig. 4.6). Both now have an expression similar to the one Manolo had

Figure 4.6 *Surcos*, 1951

back at the street fair. Like in the fair scene, when Manolo was transfixed watching the bullfight puppet show, Rosario and he are caught in an erotic contemplation of Spanish patriarchal values, which arrests the spectators and prevents them from "achieving any distance from the image" before them. After the brutal beating, humorously rendered by the puppets, the husband confesses to the audience, "This is the best argument that one can use to deal with women," as he gradually goes down until vanishing completely from the stage. At this point, the father's head emerges and takes center stage, like he did the first time we saw the puppet theater—reinforcing the first impression that he is the head of the family and the originator of his brainchild puppet moral tales—to warn Rosario that since Manolo will stay with them, she should stay with a neighbor to avoid staining their moral reputation.

Kitsch's uncritical description of emotion, as exemplified by Manolo and Rosario's transfixed gaze, is crucial to understanding its ideological function in *Surcos*. In *Surcos*, emotions are not critically explored but stirred in order to fascinate—in its literal etymological sense of *fascinum*, referring to the phallus—to hypnotically render its sexist, fascist ideology to its audience. It is in a state of collective reverie, with their critical judgment severely impaired, that, supposedly, the spectators are to be more receptive to the film's mystifying ideology.

Rosario's father's humorous moral lessons and benevolent disposition also suggest the ideal role model of a respectable Spanish patriarch, stern but full of understanding and compassion; he is the kind of patriarch Manuel himself used to be back in the village and will become once again at the end of the film. Both of these good, down-to-earth, kind-hearted Spanish patriarchs contrast with evil, frivolous, calculating foreign ones, as represented by Don Roque, whose very moniker "Chamberlain," and the umbrella and hat he admittedly uses "as ornaments," connote an Anglo-Saxon feminized immoral influence; because, as Mussolini once said, "a man carrying an umbrella does not know the moral significance of War."

The scenes that take place inside the puppeteer's and his daughter Rosario's house have their own temporality set apart from the rest of the film. Manolo's fall at the beginning of the sequence is framed, as we saw, by a few jump-cuts which can be interpreted as an awkward attempt to insinuate a temporal discontinuity with the rest of the film's narrative. Moreover, the precise location of this space-in-between where Manolo arrives after a painful odyssey around Madrid's outskirts is never fully disclosed to us; this is a space no outside character other than Manolo will ever set foot in. In short, *Surcos*'s space-in-between is a harmonious, kitsch space whose location is not geographical but ideological.

Surcos's kitsch space-in-between the country and the city is watched over by the tall, vertical structure that hovers over the entire neighborhood, suggesting a reconstitution of masculinity, as highlighted by the establishing shot that opens the above-mentioned sequence. Contrary to the corrupt city controlled by Don Roque, this is a moral space suffused with Spanish traditional values under the watchful eye of the puppeteer, a righteous Spanish patriarch. Like all kitsch, which, as Olalquiaga reminds us, is "a time capsule with a two-way ticket to the realm of myth—the collective or individual land of dreams," this space-in-between is also a time capsule to a mythical irretrievable past (28). In that "land of dreams" the consumer of kitsch momentarily gains access to an illusion of completeness, to "a universe devoid of past and future, a moment whose sheer intensity is to a large degree predicated on its very inexistence" (29). But unlike typical commercial kitsch, whose products are a "virtual image, existing in the impossibility of fully being" (28), *Surcos*'s fascist kitsch aesthetic is instead a one-way ticket back to the land where "reigns an illusion of completeness" (28).

The space-in-between Manolo has *chosen* is a moral community, a "collective or individual land of dreams," representing the reality of the myth of *Hispanidad* which, according to its fascist message, had been betrayed by Franco's failed revolution. Not coincidentally, Manuel's recovery of his masculinity is prompted by a visit from Manolo and Rosario, and the puppet master's values that they now embody. The mise-en-scène of the medium shot where the father opens the door—completely taken by surprise by his son's visit—is carefully shot to emphasize those traditional values. Visually, father and son are separated by a framed photograph on the wall that shows a traditional Spanish couple, a stern man with a moustache and a woman with a traditional headscarf. The affectionate smile when Manuel first sees his son is immediately replaced by a stern frown upon seeing the unknown Rosario standing behind. Angrily the father asks his son, "Who is that?" "Her name is Rosario," Manolo replies, and she quickly interrupts him to add, "Manolo works and lives with my father. Of course, we love each other, but like God demands." Rosario's impromptu phrase puts a smile back on the face of Manolo's father. The stern man in the photo behind him is now hidden, visually substituted by the big head of a smiling Manuel next to the woman. Manuel is on his way to regaining his lost masculinity. Manolo and Rosario have come to help him reclaim his position as the head of his family, as the photograph behind him suggests. They ask Manuel to go with them to the theater to watch his daughter Tonia sing, and, when he declines, arguing he has a lot of dishes to wash, Rosario immediately steps up and offers "to clean up everything in a flash" while helping Manuel untie his apron. Traditional Spanish values are reconstituted once and for all.

But Manuel's full reconstitution of his masculinity will take place a little later, after he witnesses the humiliation inflicted upon his daughter Tonia in a singing contest when a few hooligans sabotage her performance, having been paid by Don Roque—who tries to manipulate and control Tonia's career like Kane does with his lover Susan. Manuel's reconstitution as a traditional Spanish man is visually suggested by his movements, which resemble those of a puppet—unlike in *Citizen Kane*, where Kane visually resembles a puppet in a couple of scenes that suggest his lack of control over his actions. A high angle shot frames Manuel, Manolo, and Rosario around the kitchen table waiting for the mother to arrive. Manolo stands behind Manuel and pats his back trying to console his father, who for the first time has realized that his daughter Tonia is Don Roque's lover. His wife soon enters the house and asks if Tonia has arrived, seemingly worried. The camera cuts to a medium shot of Manuel who, with a stern expression—like the man in the photograph—raises his head and proceeds to slowly stand up, in a deliberately menacing manner. A following shot frames Manuel obliquely to the left and his wife to the right. His face is dramatically lit to emphasize his regained self-confidence. Visibly scared, the mother begins to retreat. Manuel moves forward, holds her by her lapel, and proceeds to slap her, resembling the character of the puppet show in the aforementioned scene. His actions and body movements almost replicate those of a puppet. After slapping her repeatedly, he finally throws her onto the bed and calls her a "viper," an insult that obviously echoes Eve's transgression at the Garden of Eden causing humankind's Fall from Grace.

The camera now shifts position to cross cinema's 180-degree taboo imaginary line. The camera's shift not only suggests the dramatic and sudden turnover in power relations, but also frames husband and wife from the back of the small alcove bed. The curtains hanging from each side of the alcove clearly simulate the stage of Rosario's father's puppet theater (Fig.4.7). From this new angle, which frames the couple as if they were on a stage, we see Manuel running toward the door. The audience knows he is now going after Tonia in order to bring her home. As this shot indicates, Spain's ultra-conservative values sponsored by the puppeteer are propelled from the puppet stage into reality.

Figure 4.7 *Surcos*, 1951

The scene in which Manuel finally confronts Tonia at her lover's nest, signaling Manuel's complete reconstitution as the family patriarch, is also staged to resemble a puppet theater. It begins with a shot of Tonia dressed exactly like Don Roque's ex-lover—with a silk robe and hair bandana—and smoking through a long cigarette holder. She is standing next to a big radio set, on top of which rests a female doll wearing traditional Flamenco garb, emphasizing by contrast Tonia's newly acquired, frivolous cosmopolitan clothing style. On each side of the radio set rest two dolls, a male and a female, dressed in traditional rural clothing. As Tonia turns the radio on and a song begins to play, she picks up the female doll, which holds an *ovillo de espigas*, and begins to gently sway to the music.

This little dance poignantly reminds us of the contrast between the former Tonia, an innocent country girl resembling the doll she holds in her hands, and the new Tonia, a kept, frivolous, and corrupt woman, "dolled up" like her former employer. Tonia puts down the doll and picks up a nylon stocking, a precious item in Spain's black market that she was seen secretly admiring at the beginning of the film, suggesting her newly achieved status but also indicating her moral decline. The doorbell rings, and a smiling Tonia goes to open the door. A medium close-up now frames her father, who wears his old peasant attire from the beginning

Figure 4.8 *Surcos*, 1951

of the film. He stares menacingly at a scared Tonia, who slowly begins to retreat, mimicking her mother's movements in the previous scene. The father walks toward her and a medium shot of Tonia frames her paralyzed by fear against the back wall that is covered in striking modern wallpaper, highlighting once again her alienation from her original natural environment (Fig. 4.8). Next to her hangs a framed photograph of Rita Hayworth posing as a pin-up girl. The camera zooms onto Tonia who, increasingly anxious, begins to scream. Her father grabs her like he did his wife moments earlier and throws her to the center of the room. A medium shot shows both at either side of the frame. Like in the previous scene, the spatial positions are reversed once again, indicating the dramatic turn of events. The father is shown on the right side of the frame—underlining his regained rightful place—with his daughter on the left. He begins to beat Tonia, again replicating the movements of a puppet, like he had done while beating his wife. After a series of blows, he orders, "Put on your clothes and come with me." He then walks toward the wall where Rita Hayworth's photograph hangs and begins to cry while burying his head against the wall. He might have regained his patriarchal position, but he knows perfectly well that his actions are too little too late: Tonia is already a fallen woman resembling the picture of the pin-up woman on the wall.²⁵ Therefore, in *Surcos*, although the reactionary message conveyed by puppet theater ultimately gains the ideological upper hand, the triumphalist mood of earlier Francoist cinema is tarnished by the melodramatic moral downfall of most of its characters.

The characters' moral downfall is exemplarily displayed in the long sequence of Pepe's death, in which, I argue, the noir aesthetic returns at the end to chink the film's kitsch armor, bringing the film momentarily back to a contemporary reality. This sequence brings back the film's indexical nature and thus re-establishes the connection of the film's narrative to its own historical temporality, disrupting, however briefly, *Surcos*'s ideological *locus amoenus*.²⁶

Mulvey's exploration of the indexical nature of film, whose photographic images are always of "something specific and unique" (*Death 24x a Second* 10), is useful for a reading of this sequence, characterized by a beautifully crafted mise-en-scène that seems to highlight cinematic representation at its purest. Pepe is badly wounded in a night raid when a security officer discovers him robbing sacks from a moving truck. Upon returning to Don Roque's garage, where he also shares a room with Pili on the upper floor, he encounters Pili's ex-lover, el Mellao, who has come to win her back. A fight between the two men ensues, which is depicted in a realistic noir tradition without resorting to the puppet theater style of the scenes previously described. After exchanging a few blows, el Mellao hits Pepe on the head with a monkey wrench, leaving him fatally wounded. Pili flees the scene and el Mellao runs after her at the precise moment that Don Roque enters the premises.

Don Roque ignores Pepe's repeated pleas for help as he coldly replies, "I already warned you that if anything went wrong I'd wash my hands of it." He is framed by the car window in a classical noir visual composition. Pepe eventually loses consciousness, and Don Roque, putting on his leather gloves, proceeds to upload Pepe's body onto the back of the station wagon in a high angle shot with no soundtrack in the background, just silence. Two long nocturnal shots follow the car to its final destination. A close medium shot shows an inert Pepe in the back of the van with the handle of Don Roque's umbrella—indicating his phallic prowess—menacingly hovering over him. The van approaches the railroad tracks and finally stops near a bridge over them. Don Roque opens the back and proceeds to pull Pepe's body out of the car. Pepe's feet, being dragged, make two parallel tracks on the ground, visually reminiscent of the furrows of the film's title (Fig. 4.9). They are intensely lit, although there is no apparent diegetic source of light in this shot. After dragging him for a while, Don Roque

Figure 4.9 *Surcos*, 1951

throws Pepe's body onto the railway tracks below. He ominously lights a cigarette and we soon hear the sound of an oncoming train we never get to see, like in *Citizen Kane*'s boarding house scene. Rapidly approaching, the train blows its whistle as the smoke from its locomotive gradually clouds the entire frame. Don Roque becomes completely surrounded by smoke until he vanishes in the fog, in a final attempt to metaphorically convey his diabolical nature.

As mentioned earlier, the marks left by Pepe's inert limbs on the ground can be characterized as indexical signs because, as in Peirce's classification, they establish an existential relation with their referent, as a footprint does with the foot that makes it. This long, silent sequence—the most purely cinematic and noir of the whole film—arguably brings the index— pre-digital cinema's constitutive sign—to the fore, linking inextricably together reality, history, and death, as for Mulvey all indexes do. The indexical marks in the sequence of Pepe's death, anchored in reality itself, bring back momentarily the film narrative to its own historical dimension.

The indexical marks left by Pepe's heels are material traces of the *real*, which not only reference Pepe's lifeless body, fixing "a real image of reality across time," (*Death 24x a Second* 10) but also inscribe on the soil the film's own title that appeared written across the screen in the opening shot superimposed on a wheat field's furrows. Pepe's death scene thus visually translates the title's linguistic sign into an indexical sign at the end of the film to give Pepe's own opening statement, "If it weren't for me you'd rot to death digging into the ground," a tragic, ironic twist. Pepe's attempt to escape working the fields of his childhood is metaphorically exposed—in purely visual terms—as vain, since he now becomes a human plow himself, which, rotting to death, is "digging into the ground." In *Surcos*, then, the cinematic index returns literally from the dead to briefly disrupt the film's own static Falangist kitsch ideological message, but is soon contained by its metaphorical function—its "ambiguous status as a real thing ... easily betrayed" by its secondary symbolic meaning expressing Pepe's inescapable fate.[27]

As we saw in the previous chapters, kitsch necessarily deals with stock images, since one of its defining characteristics is a labeling function that hypostasizes reality by substituting the generality of the cliché for the contingencies of reality. To do this successfully, it needs to "overwhelm" and "betray"—to denaturalize—the cinematic sign; it needs to suppress its anchoring in reality. But unlike the Francoist cinema examined in previous chapters, as illustrated by the noir sequence just analyzed, *Surcos* exposes, however fleetingly, the film's indexical nature to expose Spain's historical trauma. Yet, simultaneously, it covers up the trauma through heavy-handed visual metaphors and ideologically suturing scenes such as those of Rosario and Manolo in their newly found kitsch home. In this sense, *Surcos* performs a double maneuver. It exposes Franco's triumphalist lies with acrid determination through a seemingly honest cinematic representation, while at the same time it creates a new set of lies, thus overwhelming the film's indexical nature with Fascist ideology. Still, the noir aesthetic undeniably leaves its imprint on the film's surface, just as Pepe's dragged limp body leaves traces on the ground. It is precisely due to its more noir realistic moments that *Surcos* has gained its critically acclaimed reputation.

In the end, the film cleverly appropriates for its own kitsch aesthetic what Paul de Man called the "proliferating and disruptive power of figural language," betraying cinema's indexical nature by hijacking its potential realism for its mystifying ideological cause (30). The last shot of Don Roque disappearing in the smoke dissolves into a beautiful tracking shot of a cemetery where Pepe's funeral is being held. The camera slowly tracks to the left through a series of crosses before finally pausing over Pepe's grave, where a priest delivers a final blessing in the presence of the entire family. The funereal tracking shot echoes the earlier shot of the train, also moving from right to left, that comes to finish Pepe off; a train that surely brings many other *paletos*, like the Pérez family, to Madrid in search of a better life. At the end of the shot, the camera frames Rosario and Manolo to the right and the rest of them to the left, which indicates the irretrievable moral gulf that separates them. As the gravediggers begin throwing spades of soil onto the grave, Manuel, who is standing next to his wife and his daughter Tonia (both wearing traditional headscarves), grabs a handful of soil, smells it, and extends his arm solemnly exclaiming, "We have to go back [to the village]," to which the mother replies, "But the people will laugh at us," and Tonia adds, "What a shame." Unflinchingly, Manuel says, "Shame or not, we have to go back." A medium shot of Pepe's grave being filled with soil dissolves into a long shot of the furrows of a field. Finally, the camera cuts from the furrows in this shot to a long shot of a pristine Castilian landscape, which, although similar to the opening shot, also displays a big swath of the Castilian sky with the words *the end* written across it.

The two final climatic events of the movie—Pepe's death and his funeral—point to the return to the earth—both literally and figuratively—putting a tragic end to the Pérez family's urban adventures. Paraphrasing Peter Brooks, Mulvey reminds us that "when the drive of the narrative ends literally with death, the metonymic structure of narrative, its causal links, changes to the register of metaphor. Death marks the end but also the point 'beyond narratability'" (*Death 24x a Second* 79). In *Surcos*, Pepe's death and the return of the family to their village also signify a "point beyond narratability," opening the film to the register of metaphor, as exemplified in the visual vanishing of Don Roque, the handling of Pepe's dead body, and in the metaphorical injunction to return to the "earth." The "causal links" of the narrative's metonymic structure that advance the plot and its chronological temporality are now finally broken. Pepe's death—and the family's return to the village—opens up the film to the register of metaphor.

Unhinged from the historicity of metonymical linking, this register is more adequate to deliver the film's fascist kitsch message of recapturing politically a lost state of grace. Appropriately, the film closes with a static shot of a Castilian landscape that dramatically contrasts with the point of view shot of the train roaring through a similar landscape at the opening. The strenuous struggle of the Pérez family in Madrid ends in the death of one of its members and the return to a lethargic but moral existence in the countryside where the remaining members of the family will try to regain their lost state of grace.

Pepe's death sequence ends, as we saw, with a shot filled with smoke in which Don Roque vanishes into the corrupt urban labyrinth he ruthlessly controls. Pepe's funeral sequence ends with a still shot of the perfect Castilian landscape. The capricious nature of smoke—its whimsical, "feminine" unpredictability—helps to emphasize the solidity and dependability of the Spanish rural landscape in the last shot, its "masculine" ahistorical permanence.

As Paul de Man writes of the metaphorical nature of language, "tropes are not just travelers, they tend to be smugglers and probably smugglers of stolen goods at that" (19). *Surcos*'s fascist kitsch aesthetic relies on metaphor's tendency to assimilate or erase difference, and it builds around prestigious cinematic referents (and puppet theater) to smuggle its stolen goods. Despite its appearance of neorealist attention to detail and brief noir moments of honest representation, the film mystifies the complexity of reality, conflating as it does its critical and ideological agendas. It thus follows in the footsteps of its Francoist cinema predecessors by betraying historical reality anew. While Don Roque successfully smuggles his stolen goods into the capital, Nieves Conde's film smuggles in its fascist ideology.

Notes

1. Spanish film scholar Luis Mariano González writes that *Surcos* "premiered in Barcelona on October 26, 1951 and two weeks later, on November 12, in Madrid. According to the National Film Library, the film was poorly received as the audience barely reached one thousand spectators, and the box office earnings merely amounted to around one thousand Euros in today's currency" ("Francoist Spaces" 221).
2. Mark Allinson, for instance, characterizes it as "Spain's first truly neorealist film (and arguably its best)," despite its reactionary ideology (83). For Marvin D'Lugo, *Surcos* is a "powerful expression of Spanish neorealism" which, "[t]hough marred by its melodramatic plotting ... nonetheless reveals a powerful realist image of Spanish urban life, never before shown so vividly in Spanish film" (182). José María García Escudero, Franco's highly regarded undersecretary of cinema and the film's main official supporter, declared that *Surcos* is proof that "we should have discovered neorealism, since we were better endowed for it than Italians themselves by our ethical sense of life" (quoted in Camporesi 50). For renowned Spanish film director Mario Camus, *Surcos* was "a crucial film" since it contained within it the seeds of the future New Spanish cinema ("De Salamanca a ninguna parte"). And according to prominent Spanish writer Carmen Martín Gaite, "for the first time our cinema moved away from its pretentious settings in order to let the camera register everyday life in the streets" (80).
3. For other film critics, however, *Surcos* was not representative of neorealism or film noir, but is rather better placed within the naturalist tendencies of

the Spanish literary tradition of Miguel de Cervantes, Benito Pérez Galdós, and Pío Baroja, among others. Thus, in his discussion of the influence of the Italian neorealist film week celebrated in Madrid in 1951, Bernard P. E. Bentley concludes: "[i]t may be more accurate to attribute this fresher and more realistic expression of Spanish cinema to a natural progression made by filmmakers, whose original impulses will have been stimulated and reaffirmed by exposure to Neorealism. The new aesthetic can also be linked to the prior development of the Spanish post-war novel. It is notable that whilst acknowledging the literary precedents, Nieves Conde denied any Neorealist influence" (131).

4. According to Kinder, the film uses "the neorealist conventions to document the immediate socio-economic reality of Spain … and [the] noir [conventions] to construct the 'other scene' of fiction onto which the harsher political critique could be displaced …" (40).
5. As Sally Faulkner writes, "[m]uch critical work has examined the affiliation of *Furrows* to Neorealist 'social problems' cinema. It is perhaps too tidy to note the increasing availability of Neorealist films through cinema clubs and film weeks in Spain … then link it to the birth of a Neorealist Spanish cinema. Nieves Conde denies having seen any of the films … though critics have noted the extensive influence of documentary techniques in general, and the inspiration of key scenes of Roberto Rossellini's *Paisá* (1946) and *Europa 51* (1951) in particular. More nuanced is Marsha Kinder's analysis … of *Furrows* as a 'Falangist Neorealist' hybrid of Hollywood melodrama and Neorealism … in which the leftist politics of the Italian movement are paradoxically redeployed, in the Spanish context, for the Falangist end of criticizing urban life" (66).
6. As Nathan E. Richardson writes, "[by] setting a criminal as the film's lone bourgeois character, *Surcos* could be said to displace economic and social contradictions onto Manichean moral oppositions, glossing over issues of class conflict in favor of city/country and family/society strife" (46).
7. These marks could be described as indexes since they share an existential contiguity with their marker (a footprint points to the foot that made it). As we will see through an analysis of the sequence at the end of this chapter, they bring to the fore the index, pre-digital cinema's constitutive sign, thus linking together—as for Laura Mulvey the index sign does—history, reality, and death, bringing the subject to his own historical dimension.
8. As Luis González writes, "The polemic generated by this decision forced García Escudero to resign (he would return to office in 1962) and in some ways opened a new stage in the history of Spanish cinematography during Franco's dictatorship" ("Francoist Spaces" 221).
9. In *La España vacía: viaje por un país que nunca fue*, Sergio del Molino refers to this process as "The Great Trauma." As he explains, "[b]etween 1950 and 1970 the exodus took place. Even though, since the end of the nineteenth-century the emigration from the countryside to the city (and

from the Peninsula to Latin America) was constant, in those two decades, millions of people made the trip. The capital cities collapsed and the building contractors were not able to handle the demand for cheap blocks of houses in the periphery, that also filled up with shanty towns. In a very short amount of time the countryside was abandoned. Thousands of villages disappeared and other thousands became home to the elderly without any economic assistance or without the most basic services" (28).

10. As Luis González explains, Nieves Conde, Montes, Zaro, and Torrente-Ballester all "shared a progressive distancing from Franco's regime and their subscription to what has been called 'Left Fascism' because of its position against the dictatorship and in favor of the vindication of the original agenda of Spanish Fascism and its national-syndicalist revolution" ("Francoist Spaces" 222).

11. For Lynne Kirby, the train is "... a metaphor in the Greek sense of the word: movement, the conveyance of meaning. Like film's illusion of movement, the experience of the railroad is based on a fundamental paradox: simultaneous motion and stillness. In both cases, passengers sit still as they rush through space and time, whether physically and visually, as in the train, or merely visually, as in the cinema" (2).

12. The bending road strays from the straight iron path set by the train in which, to paraphrase Wolfgang Schivelbusch in *Railway Journey*, the seated passenger ceases to be a traveler and becomes a mere parcel (54).

13. As Michael Richards wrote in *A Time of Silence* (1998), the "eulogising of the Spanish peasantry as the mass embodiment of immortal religious and racial virtues ..." was precisely one of the main ingredients of the Francoist notion of *Hispanidad* (16).

14. In fact, as Luis González observes, *Surcos* portrayed the Spanish capital as "dominated by ... the threatening masses against which Ortega y Gasset (whose texts have been essential readings for the Spanish fascist intellectuals) had warned" ("Francoist Spaces" 223–4).

15. Classical subtexts were characteristic of Francoist film.

16. Rossellini's *Paisà* also has such a space-in-between, but, as Noa Steimatsky shows, this space in the outskirts of Naples, the Mergellina Caves, "Part primeval habitation, part catacomb, part ruin, ... is a place so wretched and elemental, bereft of anything but the most basic definition of 'shelter'... that the MP—who has come there to retrieve his stolen boots ...—falls silent, drops the boots, and retreats in his jeep kicking up a cloud of dust" (42).

17. Orson Welles's film, as Mulvey writes, goes "[q]uite beyond Bazin's conception of the 'democratic' nature of deep focus" usually associated with Welles's style to juggle with "American myth, politics and the collective psyche" (*Citizen Kane* 32).

18. Kane's, like Hearst's, fervent advocacy of American isolationism (and anti-Roosevelt's New Deal politics) also resonates with the Spanish fascist isolationist politics proclaimed by *Surcos*, where evil has a definite foreign air,

as suggested by the Chamberlain's moniker and attire. As Mulvey writes regarding Welles's film, "The film's dominant allegorical image is surely that of isolation from the world within the self-constructed 'womb/tomb' of Xanadu" (*Citizen Kane* 12). *Citizen Kane* thus exposes Kane's deep plunge into the suffocating world of kitsch.

19. The log cabin scene at the beginning of *Citizen Kane* represents, as Mulvey observes, the end of Charles's Lacanian imaginary plenitude, the severing of the unmediated bond with his mother. This is a pre-Oedipal moment whose threshold Charles will never be able to successfully cross. In Mulvey's reading, the scene inside the log cabin "polarises Kane's split father figures on each side of these symbolic systems": Mr Kane "represents poverty, failure and ignorance," and Mr Thatcher, "wealth, success and education" (*Citizen Kane* 64).

20. In the film, rural values seem to be inspired by the Bible verse, "In the sweat of thy face shalt thou eat bread, till thou return unto the ground" (Genesis 3:19), which in the Bible is immediately followed by "for out of it wast thou taken: for dust thou *art*, and unto dust shalt thou return" (Genesis 3:19). This second verse points out precisely to the fate the movie has in store for Pepe's transgression of the first.

21. As Sergio del Molino explains, "the falangists behind *Surcos* believed that the regime had succumbed to all which they fought against, that it had made Spain into another liberal country with its capitalist miseries and moral decadence. This was a recurrent accusation amongst many members of the Old Guard, who felt that they had participated in the War for nothing, and that all of the evils against which they had fought continued to triumph" (58–9).

22. For Isolina Ballesteros, "unlike the other neorealist products which had been produced by the generation of independent and anti-Francoist directors (Berlanga, Bardem, Patino, Ferreri, Mariscal), *Surcos* lacks a social analysis of the problems of the proletariat and blames the fracturing of the family union on the corrupting influence of individualism and the desire for social mobility" (250).

23. Neorealist films are even mentioned in the movie itself, despite the fact that Nieves Conde denies having ever seeing any of them, in an oft-quoted scene in which "El Chamberlain" explains to his lover that these new fashionable films depict "social problems, local folk." Upon returning from watching one of them, the lover complains, "What a bore that movie was … I don't understand why they enjoy so much exposing all this misery. The life of millionaires is so beautiful!"

24. Rossellini's *Paisà*, a movie often cited as a source of *Surcos*'s neorealist style, though Nieves Conde has denied ever seeing it, also prominently featured a marionette show which, unlike the one in *Surcos*, is in line with neorealism's progressive aesthetics. In a famous scene, a black American GI stationed in Naples during the Second World War attends a puppet show completely

inebriated. The show re-enacts a fight between two knights, a black Muslim and a white Christian. Offended by the character's stereotypical representation (the good white Christian knight versus the evil black Muslim one), the soldier runs toward the puppet stage in order to interrupt the performance and beat up the puppeteers.
25. Rita Hayworth, originally Margarita Rita Cansino, was of Spanish descent and was married to Orson Welles. Primarily because of her role as Gilda, she became the poster girl for indecency and immorality—and the Spanish Church's bête noire.
26. As Mulvey remarks, photography's indexical nature, which registers the marks of light, and the unconscious, which registers the traces of repressed memories, "[b]oth have the attributes of the indexical sign, the mark of trauma or the mark of light, and both need to be deciphered retrospectively across delayed time" (*Death 24x a Second* 9).
27. Pepe's inescapable fate was also intimated in an earlier scene in which, upon returning to Don Roque's garage after a night raid, he quickly proceeds to close the garage door and the main gate to hide inside safely. In this scene, Pepe's actions are framed from a back window. The word *surcos*—furrows—is written in a barely visible graffiti against the opposite wall, a subtle mise-en-scène sleight of hand in an otherwise often heavy-handed film. No matter how hard he tries to hide, there is no escape from the furrows he desperately sought to leave behind.

CHAPTER 5

Franco, ese hombre:
From Kitsch-Artist to Kitsch-Man

Franco is a sphinx but he has no secret
—Pedro Sáinz Rodríguez, Franco's first Minister of Education

To commemorate twenty-five years of Franco's regime, *Raza*'s director, José Luis Sáenz de Heredia, made a documentary in 1964 about Franco titled *Franco, ese hombre*. As we saw in Chapter 1, Franco's screenplay for *Raza* was a narcissistic fantasy in which the dictator created an alter-ego for the silver screen—the character of José Churruca—in order to project himself as the ideal hero Spain needed to save the country. Made twenty-two years later, *Franco, ese hombre* attempts to render the elderly, historical Franco as such a hero and, in doing so, rewrites Spanish history according to Francoist ideological and political clichés.

As its title suggests, Sáenz de Heredia made the film to bring Franco closer to the average Spaniard by revealing his human side. In this chapter, I will argue that *Franco, ese hombre* betrays Sáenz de Heredia's proclaimed intention. Instead of bringing Franco closer to us, it creates a myth out of the man. The mythologizing of Franco as Spain's savior relies upon the ideological fabrication of historical truth, which transforms the documentary into a kitsch fiction masquerading as a document of truth. To accomplish this, it resorts to the formal traits of standard documentary, what Carl R. Plantinga has called the "formal voice documentary," featuring voice-over, archival footage, still photographs, interviews with expert witnesses, etc. (110).

A critical strategy used to create a fictional portrait of Franco as a mythical character, father figure, and moral compass of the nation is the interaction between what Michel Chion termed the *acousmêtre*—the 'acousmatic,' invisible presence of the voice-over (21)—and the silent images of Franco culled from archival footage. I will return to this toward the end of the chapter. However, the documentary's successful creation of the myth of Franco as a major global historical figure—compared by the voice-over to Napoleon as the youngest general in Europe—is shattered in the final scene by the appearance of Franco himself—the *real* man. In this last scene of the film, in which Franco is interviewed by Sáenz de Heredia, Franco looks awkwardly off-camera as he answers the director's questions while reading banal answers from cue cards written for him by José Sánchez Silva, the documentary's co-screenwriter. The content of Franco's voice—the master's voice—does not here originate from the dictator himself. Incapable of transcending the totalitarian system he created, Franco the dictator, the sole source of authority and meaning, thus becomes Franco the dictated, a dummy spoken for by its real ventriloquist master: the clichéd, right-wing ideological core of Spanish conservatism that supported Franco's military uprising, which was initiated much earlier than he became the "chosen" one. In this scene, Franco performs both roles—that of heroic protagonist of Spanish history and that of its ideal spectator, watching inside the film theater of his official residence the documentary of his own exploits. A purveyor of kitsch, as we saw in Chapter 1, Franco is also a kitsch-man, who believes his own lies and is therefore the ideal consumer of kitsch aesthetics. Through Franco's point of view, the viewers/citizens thereby also become kitsch consumers.

This last effort to bring Franco closer to the audience backfires, however, setting in motion a triple process of disintegration: of the myth, of the human being behind, and, finally, of the overall fascist sublimating impulse to transcend corrupting bodily matter. Instead, this closing scene exposes Francoism for what it really is: a cacophony of clichéd narratives and kitsch utterances, which—by definition—come from elsewhere, ventriloquized, like the content of the cue cards read by Franco.

Originally, *Franco, ese hombre* was supposed to be a short propaganda film sponsored by the *Ministerio de Información y Turismo* as part of the twenty-five-year peace campaign featured prominently on Spanish news media, which included a barely nascent state-owned Spanish Television. Sáenz de Heredia, *Raza*'s director and first cousin of Falange founder José Antonio Primo de Rivera, a director of enormous clout in official circles, proposed to expand the project to a full-length documentary feature instead. His proposal was accepted and he received funds from the *Ministerio* to produce the film. As he recounts:

> I suggested that it would be called *Franco, ese hombre*, well aware that it was not a good title so it would be clear that it was not supposed to be a political film but a film that would stress the humanity of its main character. I spent ten months working with

my moviola and absolutely nobody saw the film until it was finished. There was no interference of any kind. (Quoted in Crussells, *Las brigadas internacionales* ... 307)

In line with what Adorno claimed to be the psychological basis of fascist propaganda, the stated goal of the film was thus to expose Franco's humanity to ordinary Spaniards so that they could feel closer to him ("Freudian Theory and the Pattern of Fascist Propaganda" 124). Despite its director's admitted claims, however, *Franco, ese hombre* is a political film whose goal was to extol the figure of Franco, to make a myth out of the man, and to perform a clean break with Spain's traumatic past. The documentary follows Franco's meteoric military career from his early start in Morocco as a colonial officer, focusing particularly on his self-appointed messianic role to rescue Spain from the illusory threat of a Stalinist takeover. It portrays him as founding father and national savior against the background of a fictionalized and tumultuous twentieth-century Spanish history. In so doing, Franco is seen not only as a brave military hero but also as a wise and efficient statesman who steered his nation with a steady hand out of a chaotic social and political abyss into the new world order. *Franco, ese hombre*'s mythologizing of Franco falsifies Spanish history and paradoxically undermines Franco's humanity, the proclaimed goal of its director. The falsification of history is achieved by presenting Spanish history as if it were a memory flashback, an intimate recollection of Franco himself.

The fusion between the historical and the personal is done at the very opening of the documentary. As in a fiction film, the opening of a documentary also provides a context, a frame from which the subsequent images are meant to be interpreted. *Franco, ese hombre* opens with a series of still photographs while the credits (white on a red background) roll on the left edge of the frame. The soundtrack of a playful theme inflected with military chords provides the musical accompaniment to the images. Aiming at identifying with the audience, these opening images, and the accompanying music, seek to capture the two sides of the historical figure, the leisurely family man and the military hero, the private and the public: Franco playing with his granddaughter, holding a baptized baby, fishing, playing cards with friends, hunting, greeting a bullfighter, handing a tournament cup to a soccer player—bullfighting and soccer being the staple bread and circuses of his regime—painting *en plein air*, greeting Belgian monarchs Balduino and Fabiola, greeting General Eisenhower, and on board his yacht *Azor*. The series ends with a still image of Franco seated at his official desk wearing a military uniform, pen in hand, signing official documents. It opens with an image of Franco the man relaxing with his granddaughter and closes with another of Generalissimo Franco in his official capacity as supreme commander, the law-creating pen substituting now for his *caudillo* warring sword, which nonetheless he used with the same lethal dexterity.

The first still photograph, in plain clothes with the yachtsman's cap, connotes leisure, and the last, in full military regalia, supreme power; both kinds of attire are carefully chosen to represent the two facets of Franco's persona, the personal and the political (Fig. 5.1). Stressing the figure of

Figure 5.1 (upper and lower) *Franco, ese hombre*, 1964

Franco as family man—as the Father of the nation—the documentary's opening resembles a family album documenting the established rituals of the life of a large Spanish family—baptisms, birthdays, weddings, first communions, holiday family gatherings—interspersed with the official ceremonies of the country—greetings to presidents and monarchs, award-giving ceremonies, etc. The ending of the film gives us Franco inside his official private movie theater watching the documentary, reinforcing for the viewer the idea of Franco as a family man watching the home movies of his family's precious moments that he was also fond of shooting.

These alternations of the official images of Franco the statesman with the images of Franco the man, relaxing with his family or engrossed in his beloved hobbies, suggests that the personal and the political are inextricably bound together in *Franco, ese hombre*. The events marking the official calendar of his country are seamlessly woven into the events of his private life. This mixing of the public and the private in Franco's life is the documentary's main strategy of seeking identification with the viewer and of falsifying Spanish history. Spain's traumatic history is represented not as an objective historical circumstance encompassing and suffered by all Spaniards, but as Franco's own memory flashback—his nostalgic historical fantasy. In this personal flashback, which begins early on while he presides over the military parade in 1964—appropriately characterized by the voice-over as an "album of memories'"— the emergence of Franco the historical figure is consubstantially linked with Spain's need to be rescued.

According to this narrative, Franco developed his sense of self completely in synch with the needs of his beloved fatherland. Since early childhood, we are told, he learned to be the ever-vigilant warrior, the savior awaited by all Spaniards, regardless of their political affiliation, to rescue Spain from the political and social chaos brought about by the Second Republic. The very first image we see as the film credits begin to roll is a close-up of a photograph of Franco playing with his granddaughter. This first image unwittingly reveals the ideological character of Franco's regime. It shows an elderly Franco (he was seventy-two at the time of the production) in civilian clothes wearing a yacht captain's cap, extending his two arms toward his granddaughter with his fists closed, as if hiding something in one of them, so she can make a choice. In the photograph, which is first presented in an extreme close-up of the fists before the camera zooms out to show it entirely, her eyes are closed while she tries to decide which hand contains the hidden treasure (Fig. 5.2). This is a perfect visual metaphor of the political nature of Francoism. Franco gives his granddaughter an apparent choice. But this is a choice that she cannot make by *seeing* and thus comparing what to choose; she has to choose *blindly* as her eyes wide

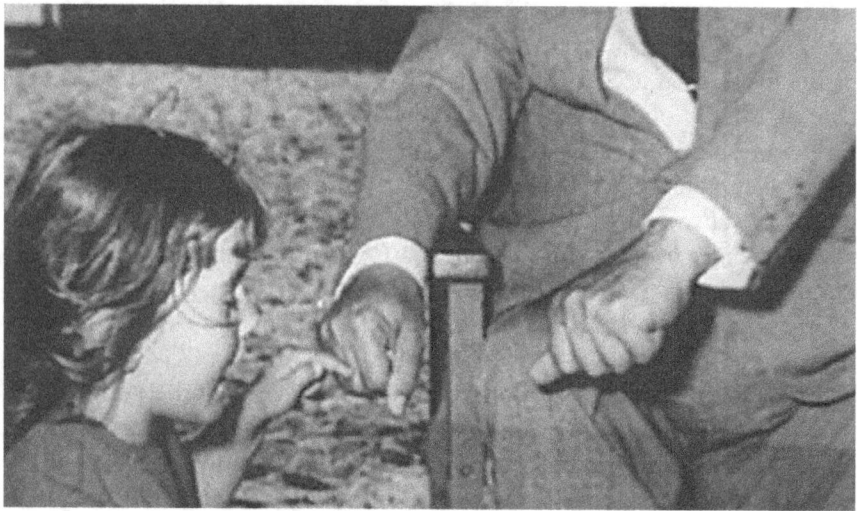

Figure 5.2 *Franco, ese hombre, 1964*

shut appropriately seem to suggest. As in this innocent game, the real political choice of Spaniards does not matter. It is just a matter of trust, of blind faith. The rest of the documentary stresses the historical figure of Franco as benevolent and trustworthy *pater familias*, whom Spaniards, as Franco's own granddaughter, can trust with equally blind faith. Only then might they be rewarded with the hidden treasure.

The documentary is structured in a way that reinforces the idea that the personal and the political—Franco the historical figure and Franco the man—are one and the same, consubstantial, like Father and Son in the Christian gospels that greatly influenced Francoist propaganda. After the series of still shots, the first moving image is an establishing panoramic shot of Madrid at sunrise. It is the day of the military parade celebrating Spain's "25 years of peace." As the voice-over solemnly announces, "above the city a daily miracle is occurring. The sun rises. As in the first day of creation it rises slowly, in silence and humility, as if pretending not to call attention to the greatness of its own spectacle." The day of the military parade is thus a repetition of the day of God's creation, and thus no less miraculous. The military parade itself is also a repetition of the 1939 "Desfile de la Victoria," the first military parade celebrating Franco's victory in the Civil War, "our glorious crusade" as Franco usually called it, which created a "new dawn" for Spain. In contrast to the humility of the sunrise, the military parade is arrogant and bombastic, calling attention to its overpowering greatness, to its "shining sea of rifles and bayonets," as the voice-over poetically describes it.

Like *Romancero marroquí*, *Franco, ese hombre* utilizes the traditional metaphor of the day's dawn—the biblical "let there be light"—to convey the idea of a New Spain. This metaphor was pervasive in Spanish fascist and Francoist rhetoric, already manifest in the well-known lyrics of *Cara al sol*, the Falangist anthem: "Onwards, squadrons to victory that a new day dawns in Spain!" The voice-over reminds us, with a sudden shift in inflection to a more dramatic tone that will become characteristic throughout the film, that the city of Madrid "knew a traumatic past which is already forgotten, long buried in 25 years of peace." Thanks to Franco's victory, we are supposed to infer, a new dawn emerged in Spain, casting a healing light over its dark, traumatic past.

This is a cosmic, organic opening befitting fascist ideology, which resonates with Franco's new political arrangement; his euphemistically nonsensical term *democracia orgánica del estado*. Francoist Spain was to be politically organized as a harmonious living organism that binds all citizens, regardless of class, into one, like soldiers and war machinery in the military parade. Soldiers march together as a well-oiled machine, and the voice-over observes that they even "drink water to prevent a possible future thirst," as if they were engines being filled with coolant so as not to overheat. This reification of human beings goes hand in hand with an anthropomorphizing of war machines, which are now described, as in the case of the tanks, as "still sleepy war machines" that have just awoken to the day and have proceeded to "take their first morning shower near the fish market," referring to the venue where the peace exhibit is being housed.

In typical fascist fashion, the voice-over depicts military parades as cathartic spectacles that best showcase the martial discipline and virtues of a country and its people. The voice-over explains, "Military parades are eternal spectacles that affect all of us, producing a purifying shiver," as the camera cuts to shots of a parading battalion of the Spanish Foreign Legion, where Franco began his military career in the Moroccan Wars of the 1920s. Something in military parades, the narrator adds, "speaks to our hearts in a happy and straightforward manner that cleanses the soul because it prompts us to become better." Changing the inflection slightly to a more intimate tone, he now muses that this particular military parade "speaks the same language with a different accent." The military parade marking twenty-five years of peace celebrates a different kind of victory, "more difficult than an armed victory, a *total* victory in which there is no pain of the defeated, where there is only joy for everybody." From the *total* war of fascist rhetoric, which, as Mark Neocleous writes, "brings to their highest tension all human energies and puts the stamp of nobility upon the peoples who have the courage to meet it" (16), the military parade we are about to see celebrates the "more difficult" victory of peace. The 1964 military parade is not only cathartic for the soul, as all displays of military prowess were for fascists, but is supposed to transmit joy to everyone, embracing all Spaniards regardless of their status as victors or losers of the Civil War.

To visually underline this idea, the camera shifts from the parading soldiers to a series of shots of the onlookers. The tense calm that precedes Franco's arrival to the tribune is now abruptly interrupted by an army bugle that "runs through the crowds as if it were a shiver," with the voice-over repeating for the second time the word "shiver" in order to emphasize that the spectacle is indelibly registered in the nervous system of the crowd, at the most primordial level of their being. As we hear the chords of the national anthem we see an aerial shot of Franco's car, which was in fact a gift from Hitler, though this fact was not widely known. The aerial shot of the car approaching the tribune is reminiscent of the Führer's descent from above in Leni Riefenstahl's *Triumph des Willens* [*Triumph of the Will*] (1935). This bird's-eye view shot also connotes the idea of Franco as heavenly creature, as God's sent messiah, while suggesting—since he is already on the ground—that his descent to earth already took place twenty-five years ago. Spaniards, we are told, salute their leader with immense gratitude because they know that "in him resides together with the glory of the past and the industry and peace of the present the sovereign key of the future."[1] Historical time collapses as past, present, and future coalesce in a primordial bundle like fascism's own etymology of binding together separate things—like the soldiers and their weapons, like all Spaniards, "fraternally joined together like God demands" in Franco's messianic presence.

As the camera cuts to a medium shot of an elderly Franco saluting his troops from the tribune, the focus shifts from the spectacle and the masses to the presiding Franco himself, the true protagonist of the historical events to follow. The voice-over hints at Franco's psychological state as he watches his troops march. It speculates that Franco, whose eyes "were consecrated since he was a child with unique concentration, only in Spain," might not be able to see the spectacle in front of him. In the act of reviewing his troops, the narrator says, his vision has probably gone inward, lost in nostalgic reverie, and in the midst of this "shining sea of rifles and bayonets ... [he has] begun to reminisce about that corner of our Galicia, his maritime El Ferrol, where God wanted him to be born." This focalized narration style tinges the historical lesson about to be delivered—from the time he was born until 1964—with the emotional coloring of Franco's own nostalgic historical fantasy, his personal recollection of the events. In *Franco, ese hombre*, history is not interpreted from a critical distance, intellectually, and thus devoid of emotion. It is rather culled from the repository of Franco's own memory, suffused with his own spiritual yearning for the well-being of his fatherland. What thus follows is to be understood as Franco's own recollections—his own "album of memories"—of his fateful intervention in Spain's historical affairs in order to rectify its wrongdoings. Franco's internalizing of historical circumstance fills that history with true spiritual meaning, substituting nostalgic cliché for historical reality, which, as mentioned earlier, is one of the main characteristics of kitsch.

As the voice-over reminds us with a cliché that betrays its manipulative, kitsch notion of history, Franco was "that man that has forged twenty-five years of peace with his steely spirit in the anvil of his life." Franco thus becomes, like in some fascist political version of the Holy Trinity, simultaneously the smith, the anvil, and the saving sword—a transcendent image of Franco described not only as the smith in charge of the forge but also as the weapon and the tool that made it possible; it is an image of Franco perfectly attuned to the previous one that described him as a temporal vessel, already containing within himself the past, the present, and the future of the nation. In short, Franco is depicted as a self-sustaining divine figure, both cause and effect of its own being.

The establishing shot which initiates the long historical flashback is filled with a melancholy mood emanating from the Galician bagpipe music of the soundtrack, almost identical to the one used by Sáenz de Heredia in the opening scenes of *Raza*, and brings us back in time to 1892 and the city of El Ferrol: the time and the place of Franco's birth. The rest of the "history" lesson will be framed by what is carefully construed as Franco's messianic birth. He was born, the voice-over reminds us, in turbulent times, as the camera cuts to newspaper headlines of the day of his birth highlighting the bleak state of the nation: anarchist bombings, general strikes, parliamentary corruption, and an overwhelming sense of lawlessness, among many other ailments draining the spirit of the nation.

The voice-over is that of Spanish actor Angel Picazo, a successful theater and film actor who specialized in the role of a ladies' man and who was known for his good looks and velvety voice.[2] Through a dramatic delivery style that alternates strong assertions with mellifluous, seductive whispering, the voice-over guides the spectator through a wealth of archival footage largely composed of newsreels, newspaper headlines, and old photographs. The documentary also made use of original footage, including material from the 1964 military parade shown at the beginning of the film presided over by Franco; the scene showing its own director addressing the audience from inside the film lab; and two interviews with "expert" witnesses. It also resorts to various kinds of maps for didactic purposes.

The history lesson that comprises most of the documentary is framed by the idea of a messianic Franco who rescues Spain from the atheist and communist claws of Stalinism. Spain, we are asked to believe, was in peril of becoming a major historical shipwreck until Franco came to the rescue. The first part of this revisionist historical summary covers the period from Franco's birth in 1892 until the military uprising in 1936, and its goal is to justify Franco's coup against Spain's Second Republic. The second part, which begins after Sáenz de Heredia's first appearance to personally tell his audience he will not show footage of the Spanish Civil War, and immediately following his personal interview with military historian Manuel Aznar, focuses on Franco the statesman, who, in defiance of UN condemnation and a crippling economic embargo, was able to consolidate his totalitarian regime and bring Spain back, as a legitimate member of the world of nations, into the new global political order. This second part ends with the arrival of the Western diplomatic delegations to Spain—which had left the country in 1948—and the critical visit of General Eisenhower in 1953, which brought international legitimacy to Franco's regime. Through a mixture of gravely distorted historical content dramatically delivered by Picazo's voice-over, and a manipulative use of standard documentary evidentiary editing, Franco is represented to the world no longer as a fascist leader, a friend of Hitler and Mussolini whose framed portraits he kept on his desk until the fall of the Axis, but as European champion of anticommunism who prevented the Stalinist takeover of Western Europe.

The history lesson begins, as mentioned earlier, with Franco's personal flashback while he is presiding over the military parade. In didactic fashion, the camera cuts to Franco's birthplace, and immediately to a map of imperial Spain at the height of its glory, which opportunistically includes Portugal and Brazil.[3] Using rudimentary animation, the map shows the gradual shrinking of the once-vast Empire as the narrator muses, "[a]ll the stones crumbled down from this Empire that once knew no sunsets." The Spanish imperial decadence, we are told, reached its peak at the turn of the nineteenth century, coinciding with Franco's early childhood. The voice-over laments that, in 1898, "[t]he pathetic symphony that had started three centuries before played its two final chords: Cuba and the Philippines." Shifting now into the role of an omniscient narrator so we can have access to Franco's own psyche, the voice-over tells us that Franco was aware from early childhood that Spain needed rescuing: "his infant consciousness was forged by the idea that Spain was sick and depressed and that nothing would be better than to learn how to defend it." His concern from infancy about the ill-fared status of his beloved nation predetermined his future as *caudillo*, the savior of his country. Franco the child was truly a father to the man.

The documentary carefully conveys Franco's personal involvement as the savior in Spanish history. It is a fictional account of history, an escapist fantasy lacking any historical rigor. The narration is filled with misleading information ranging from vague, inaccurate statements to blatant lies. In fact, *Franco ese hombre* shows a complete disregard for historical truth: the demagogical statements of the voice-over are visually backed up— particularly those covering the Republican years— with images of street crowds, police charges, workers' strikes, targeted political assassinations, portraits of Joseph Stalin and other 'revolutionary' leftist figures, religious buildings sacked by mobs, all taken out of their proper context.[4] The depiction of modern Spanish history and particularly of the Republican years is one of utter political and social unrest.

The first part, covering the time period up to the Civil War in 1936, pays special attention to Franco's African years during the 1920s, which Franco himself admitted were instrumental in his military and ideological formation. As Franco's official biographer Joaquin Arrarás wrote, "The call of Africa echoed in his soul ... ensnaring him within its deadly grip" (quoted in Ashford 41), despite the fact that "he never mastered Arabic, or showed the slightest interest, or empathy with, the traditions or customs of the [Moroccan] tribesman" (Ashford 41). The documentary pays tribute to Franco the brave warrior, but makes it very clear that he was not just a courageous officer but also an able commander ready to undertake complicated logistical operations, as in the section devoted to the establishment of the Spanish Foreign Legion.[5] Downplaying the romantic exoticism that typically surrounded the affairs of the Spanish Foreign Legion, the documentary highlights Franco's gargantuan role in creating the Legion's infrastructure in Morocco. His role is admiringly described as an "authentic governmental task." In a few months Franco brings "sewerage, electricity, schools, recreational areas, even farms with livestock that not only provided quality food supplies to the legionnaires but also yielded economic profit to be reinvested in future improvements," while the camera shows us footage of animal farms, construction sites, and modern-looking well-equipped military facilities.

With the surrender of Abd el-krim in Alhucemas in 1925 as a result of a French and Spanish joint military effort, we are then told, the Moroccan resistance is finally crushed and Morocco *pacified*. In the bombastic and flowery language characteristic of Francoist rhetoric—borrowing heavily from what Jorge Semprún has called *cursilería falangista*, and also from the Nazi persistent imagery of "blood and soil"—the voice-over poetically describes Morocco as "a deep-seated resonance, as an eternal fraternal link, as a telluric impregnation that transcends the blood."[6] This description has a visual counterpart in the black-and-white images of a cemetery that gradually turn into color images, as if the dead of the past and the dead of the present could communicate in "an eternal fraternal link" through Moroccan consecrated cemetery soil seeped in the blood of the fallen.[7]

The same visual and narrative structure of bombastic narration, underlined by misleading footage taken mostly out of context, used to portray Franco's African years and his loyal service to the Bourbon King, is used as a template for the portrayal of Franco during the Republican years from 1931 to 1936. Beginning with the episode when he stubbornly refuses to raise the Republican flag in the military academy he commands until receiving confirming orders from his superiors, Franco is portrayed as a vigilant watchdog, as the faithful Spanish warrior, a guarantor of decency, legality, and truth; Franco will always be there to defend the interests of the fatherland when needed.

As recounted in *Franco, ese hombre*, the balance of the first years (1931–3) of the Republic was appalling: Spain plunges into social, political, and economic chaos while communism spreads rampant throughout the country where political meetings are held "under the honorary presidency of Stalin, Molotov, etc.," as the camera manipulatively cuts to a giant poster of Stalin to underline the words of the voice-over. The country, we are told, is almost paralyzed by "endless strikes, university closings and suppression of newspapers." The government, we are supposed to infer, even resorts to mass imprisonment, being unable to provide work to half a million unemployed workers. And worst of all, as suggested by Picazo's mournful vocal delivery, Spain has ceased to be a Catholic country, as the Republican government bans "the cross ... from schools," while the camera cuts to a shot of crucifixes hanging upside down.

Given this bleak panorama of social chaos and political turmoil, we are informed that even those who initially voted for the Second Republic are apparently dismayed about these disturbing developments. This chaotic picture of the Republican years is thus the perfect justification for the rise of proto-fascist parties like the CEDA of Gil Robles and the 1933 *Falange Española*, Spain's leading fascist party. The Falange is here de-politicized, not described as a far-right political party but as a "movement" "that defines man as carrier of eternal values and that proclaims the fatherland as indissoluble entity;" words underlined by the chords of "Cara al sol," Falange's infamous anthem.

In this version of history, the Franco-led coup of 1936 against a democratically elected government is depicted as a legitimate power struggle to defend the constitutional monarchy whose rights had actually been usurped by the Second Republic. Despite historical evidence suggesting otherwise, the narrator muses in an ironic tone that the Spanish pro-Republican parties had obtained a majority of votes only in Spain's major cities, but the final tally revealed that the monarchists had actually won the 1931 elections. Regrettably, "once the wick was set on fire ... It was already too late" to reverse the electoral verdict because the crowds had taken to the streets, "climbing on top of streetcars waving the Republican flag." Republicans dismantled the monarchy, we are told, because it was too weak to make legality prevail. This distortion of the historical record served the purpose of exonerating Franco and his generals of the charge of treason, since they came to power by means of a military uprising against a democratically elected government. For Francoist historiography, it was the Second Republic that usurped the legitimate rule of the Spanish Bourbon monarchy under the guise of a phony electoral victory. Franco's coup d'état was just a way to amend this grave historical injustice—one of Spain's wrong historical turns—as corroborated by the fact that Franco chose the young prince Juan Carlos, a Bourbon heir, as his legitimate successor.[8] Thus, instead of being a traitor who usurped the Second Republic's constitutional order, Franco becomes a savior who helped restore the Spanish monarchy to its rightful heir.

In a tragic repetition of the events of April 1931, after two years of a right-wing Republican government, the narrator explains, the Popular Front wins the general election in February 1936 and "without waiting for the final vote count, the Republican conservative government is overwhelmed by the red waves that begin putting in practice Moscow's orders," just as Spanish fascist leader José Antonio had warned.[9] The film characterizes the Popular Front as a mere front for the takeover of Spain that "Marxism was meticulously planning this time," so as not to repeat previous mistakes. The documentary goes as far as stating that documents discussed by the London *Times* indicated that Stalin was planning a revolutionary coup "for a "Soviet takeover of Spain ... set to coincide with the International Workers' Olympics" taking place in Barcelona in July 1936.[10]

In March 1936, in the midst of this red apocalypse, a group of policemen kidnap and assassinate foremost Spanish ultra-conservative monarchist politician José Calvo Sotelo in an apparent reprisal for right-wing militants' assassination of a Republican police lieutenant. As the voice-over reminds us, just few days before his death, Calvo Sotelo gave a speech in parliament that ended with these prophetic words: "You can take my life but that's all you can do." Upon hearing the news, Franco is said to have exclaimed, "This is the signal." As the narrator concludes, "Calvo Sotelo's corpse is what enabled the military uprising to anticipate the communist plan to take over Spain and begin the dictatorship of the proletariat." In July 1936, aided by Hitler and Mussolini, Franco brings the colonial army from Africa to the Peninsula. What Franco and the other rebellious generals intended as a brief coup d'état to depose the Republic results in a war of attrition lasting three years. These are the years that the documentary chooses to skip over, for reasons explained by director Sáenz de Heredia in his first appearance on camera to address his audience, which we will examine next.

For John Grierson, often considered the father of the non-fiction film genre, documentary is "a means of propaganda, a 'bully pulpit' through which the masses could be educated about their complex industrial society" (Plantinga 172). In that sense, *Franco, ese hombre* does not differentiate itself from canonical titles of the genre such as *Night-mail* (1936), *The City* (1939), *The Plow that Broke the Plains* (1936), *Power and the Land* (1940), or *The River* (1938). All these documentaries try to educate their audiences on a wide range of issues, and to persuade them that the perspective shown is in fact the right one. Documentaries, naturally, are not simply neutral recordings of the real and, despite their vast differences, they all resort to various narrative and stylistic cinematic conventions—voice-over, selected camera angles, film editing, carefully composed soundtracks—to create the ideal cinematic mood which might help persuade the spectator that the given perspective on reality is the correct one. Therefore, for Plantinga, "what makes a film nonfiction is not a presumed lack of manipulation of the real, but its assertion that its states of affairs are true in the actual world" (215).

What differentiates *Franco, ese hombre* from most non-fiction films is not any formal traits, but the fact that, as we saw in the previous section, its states of affairs are not true in the actual world, but are a pure ideological fabrication. The historical world projected in Sáenz de Heredia's film is, as we just saw, a fantasy designed to justify, relativize, and normalize the dark legacy of Francoism. In that sense, *Franco, ese hombre* is a false documentary; it is a kitsch, escapist fiction film disguised as a non-fiction film. To pass itself off as one, it resorts to almost every trick of the trade in the non-fiction film genre to persuade its spectators of its historical veracity: voice-over, archival footage, the summoning of expert witnesses, and even, as we will see next, a sophisticated from of self-reflexivity.

As the appearance of director Sáenz de Heredia to address his audience, and the visual *mise-en-abîme* of Franco himself watching the documentary of his own exploits at the end of the documentary, reveals, despite aspiring to be a traditional expository documentary, *Franco, ese hombre* also resorts to the traits of what Bill Nichols has called "reflexive mode" (34). The reflexive mode tends to weaken epistemic authority in favor of empathy, solidarity, insight, or epistemological reflection. In *Franco, ese hombre*, I argue, quite to the contrary, the reflexive mode does not function to weaken epistemic authority, thus puncturing tightly constructed ideological world views, but to convince the audience that it is watching a documentary, an authentic re-interpretation of history, not a fabrication of it. In short, resorting to traits of the reflexive mode, *Franco, ese hombre* cleverly turns this most radical documentary mode on its head to paradoxically authenticate its ultra-right-wing dogmatic world view.

Director Sáenz de Heredia appears three times in the documentary, thus calling attention to the medium itself: the first time inside a film lab to address his audience; the second time, as we saw, to interview Spanish Civil War expert Manuel Aznar—Spain's ambassador to the UN and grandfather of José María Aznar, Spain's former president (2000–8)—inside the Spanish pavilion of the 1964 New York World Fair; and, finally, he appears once more at the end of the film to personally conduct the aforementioned brief interview with Franco, who is watching the final cut of the documentary inside the private film theater of his official residence.

Here, I focus only on his first appearance, when the director breaks the fourth wall to address the audience, because it best illustrates how the reflexive mode does not function in *Franco, ese hombre* to weaken epistemic authority, but quite to the contrary to convince the audience we are watching a documentary, an authentic reinterpretation of history, not a highly distorted fabrication of it. Sáenz de Heredia first appears on screen interrupting the flow of archival footage to address the spectator directly from a film lab, surrounded by shelves containing piles of film reels, and a moviola (Fig. 5.3). The director's appearance inevitably brings attention to the film's apparatus itself. This appearance occurs in the middle of the historical summary at the precise moment, as we saw, that the documentary is about to cover the period of the Spanish Civil War. After a few images of Franco sitting at his desk and giving speeches, the camera cuts to a still shot of Franco discussing military strategy with his generals. The camera zooms out and we now realize that we are not on a battlefield but inside a film laboratory. Looking straight into the camera, Sáenz de

Figure 5.3 *Franco, ese hombre,* 1964

Heredia begins to speak. He informs us that the film reels surrounding him contain live footage shot during the Civil War, adding that to the "disappointment of many we will not show them to you," since, as he explains, such a "transcendental event exceeds the scope and the intentions" of the documentary.

Unlike in self-reflexive documentaries, here the sole purpose of self-reflexivity, I argue, is to make a clean cut with Spain's traumatic historical past. The scene inside the film lab calls attention to the cinematic apparatus but does not prod "the viewer to a heightened form of consciousness" about documentary representation or question cinematic referential verisimilitude (128). The director's appearance in the modern environs of the film lab simply signals a historical break. In *Franco, ese hombre*, we are led to believe, Spain's traumatic past, redeemed by the coming of Franco as a messiah, no longer has a direct grip on the present. It has been successfully contained and stored away in the film reels whose content will not be projected. Spain's traumatic past—"long buried after Franco's twenty-five years of peace," as the narrator reminded us at the beginning of the film—is now only accessible in its archival format. Sáenz de Heredia ends his brief speech by stating that in Spain there was a war in the midst of two "irrefutable justifications": the chaos of 1936 and the promising reality of 1964. Reaching for the goal of a better Spain, he reminds us, a "million Spaniards gave their lives on both sides." He concludes his intervention by adding, "We want to remember this period of our history ... serenely in what in our opinion is the most appropriate environment and one that best synthesizes this Spain that has become possible thanks to that unavoidable experience"— the 1964 New York World Fair.[11] And for that effect he goes to New York to conduct the interview with Manuel Aznar we will examine later.

These interruptions of the flow of images thus do not function here as they do in reflexive documentaries. They do not shed light on non-fiction film narrative conventions or question the referential illusion of cinematic representation. Their narrative purpose is to hide Spain's traumatic historical past from the audience's memory. The modern-looking surroundings of the film lab, from where Sáenz de Heredia addresses the audience, function as a marker of modernity signaling the new era that emerged after Franco's victory in the Civil War. Spain's traumatic past, which Franco as messiah came to redeem, is successfully contained and conveniently stored away inside those film cans holding the precious archival footage.

The footage that, we are told, fills the film cans surrounding Sáenz de Heredia certifies the Civil War was real. It functions as archeological—indexical—evidence of the traumatic event, and yet Sáenz de Heredia's refusal to verbally engage with it keeps the evidence buried, unexposed to the present. The archival footage in *Franco, ese hombre*, I argue, connotes "authenticity," giving Sáenz de Heredia credibility as a true historian with direct access to the raw material of the past. It also gives him an aura of benevolent impartiality, since his decision to keep the trauma of the Civil War buried, hidden away from plain sight from the modern-day Spanish citizen—a percentage of whom had surely belonged themselves or their siblings to the defeated Republican side—could be understood as a reconciliatory gesture. Obviously, this is a manipulative strategy designed to enhance Sáenz de Heredia's credibility as an impartial historian, when in reality he was a Francoist militant filmmaker.

Unlike in truly reflexive documentaries, thus, this opportunistic use of a self-reflexive strategy reminds its audience, at the crucial moment when the documentary deals with the Spanish Civil War, that the film we are watching is by association also a truthful document of history, as it unfolded in its true, unadulterated form, as the piles of film cans implicitly suggest. The scene of director Sáenz de Heredia alone in a room surrounded by true archival historical footage makes him the custodian of historical truth. It paradoxically authenticates the true rendering of that history with his decision not to show the precious material. Thus, *Franco, ese hombre* cleverly turns the reflexive documentary mode on its head. Here the reflexive mode serves to strengthen epistemic authority and to render as a truthful state of affairs a blatant ideological rendering of that truth.

Sáenz de Heredia's brief appearance to address his audience cannily prepares the ground for the much shorter second part of the historical summary, which resumes right after his interview with military expert Manuel Aznar, immediately following his address to the audience. The Civil War years are thus simply skimmed over. Its traumatic core is now safely hidden away from plain sight so as not to spoil the modern, happier historical present. The second part of the history lesson can now draw a straight temporal line from the end of the Civil War in 1939—the Spanish traumatic event par excellence—to the stable, peaceful, and prosperous modern Spain of the 1960s, which, we are led to conclude, was made possible by Franco's victory. The camera cuts to a scene of jubilant crowds—which prominently features fascist salutes—celebrating the Francoist victory and the subsequent overthrow of the Second Republic. We are informed that although the war has ended an even more difficult war has just begun: that of the reconstruction of "a mutilated and exhausted fatherland without economic reserves because our gold had been exiled to Russia and Mexico..."

In a delicate balancing act between not being able to blatantly deny Franco's collaboration with the Axis during the Second World War and the propagandistic need in 1964 (when the documentary was shot) to conceal that role, the narrator sponsors the view that Franco's Spain was in fact a victim of the Second World War. In this new version of history, Franco's Spain was the nation that most fiercely defended the traditional values of the Western world, as already proven by its victory over the Stalinist threat posed by the Second Republic, but it was still punished by the same world it fought to defend. The voice-over quickly passes over the events of the Second World War, depicting Spain's role as strictly neutral, although it admits its deep admiration for Hitler's war machine which "in an incredibly short span of time trampled over Europe to take Paris, its most precious goal."[12] Above all, the documentary attempts to present Franco himself—first and foremost—as a fierce anti-communist. Thus, as the narrator observes with resignation, when Germany capitulates and the "Allied troops enter Berlin victoriously communism sits at the victor's table." Spain, the narrator concludes, cannot expect anything good from the Potsdam conference since "one of its main voices belongs to the one defeated in Spain in 1939," referring, of course, to Stalin.

The delicate balance the documentary has to strike between distancing itself from its fascist past and the need to vindicate its anti-Republican historical role is seen most acutely in the retelling of the meeting between Franco and Hitler in Hendaye in October 1940. The meeting's main purpose was to discuss the possibility of Spain's entering the war as part of the Axis. There is ample historiographical consensus that although

Franco and Foreign Affairs Minister Serrano Suñer did not think Spain was militarily ready to join the war, Franco was willing to do so in exchange for help from Germany and large swaths of African territory, particularly French-Morocco and Oran, where Spain could re-create the glory of its imperial past. Yet Hitler was not interested in pursuing this deal. The meeting ended with his infamous pronouncement, "I would rather have four teeth extracted than talk with Franco again," which the voice-over repeats without qualms as proof that Franco's strategy of warding off Hitler's plans for Spain to join the Axis had been successful. Instead of revealing how ideologically close Franco was to Nazi Germany during this period, the meeting is reinterpreted as evidence of Franco's political astuteness, for Franco had cunningly asked for the moon knowing that Hitler would not acquiesce to his demands, providing him with a perfect excuse not to participate in the war.

According to this propagandistic version of the past, Spain was the only Western, Christian nation that fought to impede the spread of communism in Europe. Instead of recognizing this and rewarding Spain for its heroic role in the Second World War, the Western powers selfishly decided to punish her with a brutal international isolationist policy. The crucial point not to be missed here is that the rest of the European nations, with the exception of Portugal, had secularized themselves to the point of betraying their Christian heritage. This was the standard Francoist reading of Spain's role in the world, as the true champion of Western, Christian values: Spain as the "spiritual reservoir of the Western world," a phrase Franco liked to repeat as if it were his political mantra. Spain, we are told, was completely alone in the task of national reconstruction because most nations were diplomatically hostile to the country and had closed down their embassies. In short, Spain itself was now under siege, much like the Spanish garrison fighting inside a church in the Philippines in 1898, as seen in Chapter 3.

But for Francoism, the narrator dramatically explains, the siege is the moment of truth in which the country's new collective identity can be forged. Therefore, in 1946, as they had previously done during the sieges of Sagunto, Numancia, Zaragoza, and El Alcázar de Toledo, Spaniards, "hurt by foreign influence," take to the streets to support their fearless leader. The camera cuts to a panoramic view of a completely packed Plaza de Oriente in "which 600,000 white handkerchiefs are waved in the air." This is the only time we hear Franco's own voice during the historical summary, who from the balcony of his palace harangues the multitudes, "We respect and do not interfere with the private affairs of other nations. Therefore, we have the right to be respected and to be left in peace."

But the truth is finally vindicated, the narrator reminds us, when the ambassadors return to Spain in 1953. They "were different, but the man who welcomed them was the same." The camera cuts now to the present time, to Franco saluting from the tribune the day of the military parade, just where we left him at the beginning of the historical flashback. History has come full circle. Franco is now described in another example of "Falangist Kitsch" as, "A man of integrity, of rectilinear life welded to a reason of being that always ends up being right. A man sincerely human, who has never played at being a demi-god, who does not know the word fatigue, who is, as José Antonio demanded of leaders, 'unavailable to despondency.'" With the parading of the civil guard, the narrator informs us, "the album of memories" is closed. This is an image which reminds us that the historical overview was made available to us through Franco's own recollections. It was a summary of history retrieved from Franco's inner self, sanctified as it were by the dictator's conscience. After having been allowed to access its contents, the narrator explains, Spaniards are now closer to their leader. When Franco steps down the tribune, we will be able to go beyond "the rigid trappings of a Head of State" to see "the man we now know, the one with whom we have shared risks and adventures, the man, who because we have accompanied him in his entire journey and have almost felt him breathe, is now much closer to us."

Adding to the voice-over's sycophantic praise that Franco was the messiah Spain needed to redeem its traumatic past, the documentary resorts to interviews with expert witnesses to further enhance the myth of Franco, following the model inaugurated in the late 1950s by the American series *The Twentieth Century*, narrated by Walter Cronkite. Through these interviews, Franco is presented as demigod, as the chosen one, as the messiah, who *inexplicably* guides his troops to victory, like El Cid—the medieval warlord whose title *caudillo* Franco opportunistically appropriated—did when, according to legend, his dead body was hoisted onto his galloping horse in a charge against the Moors.[13]

The first is an interview—which takes place early in the film during the recounting of Franco's Moroccan years —with Dr Blasco-Salas, the military surgeon and army colonel who treated Franco's almost fatal gunshot wound sustained when he was attempting to take a rebel Moroccan position in June 1916. The second is an interview with Manuel Aznar, the Spanish ambassador to the UN, shown toward the middle of the film, right after Sáenz de Heredia's appearance to address his audience inside a film lab. Both interviews serve the purpose of enhancing the myth of Franco by attributing him messianic, supernatural characteristics; and they are staged in modern, rational-looking settings—a doctor's office, and an architecturally functionalist lounge inside the Spanish pavilion at the 1964 New York World Fair—to help deliver its irrational content.

The first interview takes place in the office of Dr Blasco-Salas, where the doctor, dressed in a white robe, sits at his desk pretending to work. An unidentifiable voice (not spoken by the voice-over or by Sáenz de Heredia) abruptly interrupts the doctor to ask him about the famous episode when Franco was gravely wounded. After uttering that the "combat was too violent," the doctor recounts how Franco fell to the ground after being shot in the stomach, ironically undermining the more heroic account of the voice-over, which had previously stated that Franco had continued fighting despite having been shot until the Spanish soldiers took the *Loma de las trincheras* from the Moroccan "rebels."

The interviewer presses the doctor to further elaborate on the nature and the gravity of Franco's wound—a wound that had been previously described by Dr Blasco-Salas as well as by other medical doctors as being "miraculous." To properly answer the question, the doctor gets up from his desk to fetch the X-ray of Franco's wound, although it is highly questionable whether X-ray technology was at his disposal in a precarious emergency military infirmary in a remote Moroccan post in 1916. As the doctor explains, pointing to the X-ray, "Franco has forced inspiration" (a word that in Spanish means both the act of inhaling air and of being inspired) at the precise moment he was shot, so the bullet went straight through him without affecting any vital organs (Fig. 5.4). As he explains, "Had Franco had a normal respiration instead of an 'inspiration', the bullet would have hit the liver and consequently he would have died." The mise-en-scène of this interview is constructed to endow Dr Blasco-Salas's testimony with professional scientific credibility: interviewing him in his doctor's office wearing his doctor's attire while expertly handling an X-ray while providing an entirely irrational explanation of the natural event.[14] Franco's life was saved, we are supposed to infer from his story, not because of mere luck or the advances of modern medicine, but because Franco was divinely "inspired" at the particular moment he was shot. His miraculous survival was ultimately due to his "inspired" respiration. To further reinforce this hint at a supernatural intervention to ensure Franco's survival, the voice-over soon informs us that Franco had what the moors called *baraka*, that is, "the protection of prodigious forces."

The second expert interview takes place inside the Spanish pavilion at the 1964 New York World Fair and follows a similar narrative pattern. After a few establishing shots of the Manhattan skyline and of the numerous visitors attending the World Fair precinct, the camera cuts to a shot of

Figure 5.4 *Franco, ese hombre*, 1964

the building of the Spanish pavilion, which, as the voice-over reminds us, is known as the "Jewel of the Fair." Among its many attractions, including paintings by Velázquez, Goya, and Picasso, the pavilion boasted a gigantic statue of queen Isabela, the queen most admired by Spanish fascists, and a replica of *Tizona*, El Cid's famous sword, whose title *caudillo*, as mentioned earlier, Franco had opportunistically appropriated.

Cutting now to a medium long shot inside the lounge, we first hear the voice of Sáenz de Heredia—momentarily acting as Michel Chion's invisible acousmatic presence—and soon after we see him seated with Manuel Aznar at a table. Next to them stands a television set and in the back of the lounge we see a mechanical escalator leisurely transporting visitors—television sets and mechanical escalators being two clear markers of modernity in 1964 (Fig. 5.5). Like the scene in the film lab already discussed, this scene—located in the heart of the bustling New York City of the 1960s—also functions visually and narratively to isolate the traumatic events of the Spanish Civil War, the interview's main subject, from Spain's historical reality of 1964.

The mere presence of Manuel Aznar—a renowned author of an authoritative military history of the Spanish Civil War—is an obvious attempt to detach the peaceful historical present from the traumatic past. It serves to de-politicize the Civil War by discussing it as simply a matter of military strategy. Aznar, like Dr Blasco-Salas before him, also attributes to Franco supernatural powers and depicts him as the chosen leader of all Spaniards regardless of their political affiliation. He remarks without

Figure 5.5 *Franco, ese hombre*, 1964

hesitation: "Many years ago all Spaniards—green, white, red, or blue—knew that when we needed to entrust one of our generals to take control over the rudder of our national destiny our preferences would point towards Franco." After entrusting Franco with such a clear messianic mission, Aznar proceeds to map out the different military phases of the Civil War.

Similarly to Dr Blasco-Salas, Aznar, the erudite historian, suggests that Franco's victory in the Civil War was due to divine intervention, which was in line with the standard Francoist interpretation of the military uprising as a crusade against godless communism.[15] For example, to explain Franco's celebrated victory in the famous battle of Teruel, Aznar says that in response to heavy enemy fire, within Franco's camp "an incalculable capacity of defense, sometimes simply inexplicable emerged as a miracle that sprang from the earth." In this interview with a renowned expert in military strategy, as in the previous interview with Dr Blasco-Salas, the emphasis is again placed on the telluric, on the "miraculous," on the "simply inexplicable." Ironically, Franco's military success, like his miraculous survival early on, is ultimately attributed to his *baraka*, not to his military skills as commander. Franco is presented thus as demigod, as the chosen one, as the messiah, who *inexplicably* guides his troops to victory, instead of as skillful military strategist.

The interview comes to an end with Aznar's brief summary of Franco's main personal virtues: "a deep religious faith, which has only increased throughout his life; a very high estimation of the virtues of his people; and complete confidence in himself, in his own capacity, his will and his lucky star." This summary highlights Franco's blind faith (paralleling also the blind faith attributed/demanded to/of his viewers/citizens): in God, in himself, and in the Spaniards. As an example of Franco's main personality trait, Aznar tells an anecdote relating to Franco's famous meeting with Hitler in Hendaye. According to this story, the morning that Franco was scheduled to meet Hitler to discuss the possibility of Spain entering the war, the Spanish convoy left the railroad station an hour late because Franco insisted on personally dispatching some "major but also minor affairs." After a nervous official told Franco that it would be impossible to arrive in time for the interview because of the delay, Franco reassuringly replied, "Don't worry too much. This is a very important interview and it's important for me to arrive calm and for my interlocutor to be a bit nervous." The spectator is supposed to rejoice that Franco, our own beloved dictator, dictated his own terms even to Hitler, the uber-dictator.

Like the scene with the doctor in his office, this one with the Spanish ambassador at the UN serves a dual purpose: to give the impression that Spain is a modern country represented in the major world fairs—finally accepted into the international community—and to highlight the spiritual superiority of Franco's Spain over a secular modern world that has lost its faith. That is, *Franco, ese hombre* portrays Franco's Spain as "the spiritual reservoir of the Western world." It situated Spain at the heart of the modern civilized world but at the same time it gave her a special moral mission within that brave new world.

Franco, ese hombre portrays the rebellious general as a wise, able, and prudent statesman who is divinely "inspired" and embraced by all Spaniards. Every workers' strike and brutal retaliatory massacre is interpreted as a consequence of the subversive actions of a few anti-patriotic Spaniards, like the Asturian miners, radical conspirators belonging to the infamous "Jewish-Bolshevik-Masonic conspiracy" that Franco was obsessed with. Its root causes, deeply enmeshed in the grievous social and historical injustices resulting from the entrenchment of an oppressive oligarchic system that often resorted to brutal violence to preserve the status quo, are never even hinted at, let alone explored, despite the fact that they had already been addressed by the Spanish fascist parties themselves.

Despite its reflexive traits, *Franco, ese hombre*, as seen in both parts of the historical summary, follows mainly the model of the formal voice which strives "to explain a portion of the world to the viewer," and thus "reserves for itself a high degree of *epistemic authority*" (Plantinga 107). It adheres to what Bill Nichols calls the expository format, characterized by its straightforward narrative and extensive use of voice-over. Traditional expository documentary voice-over, commonly referred to as voice of god due to the omnipotence derived from its material disembodiment, inhabits a non-place unfettered by spatio-temporal constraints. The freedom from limitations of time and space grants this type of documentary voice-over ascendance over the images it helps endow with meaning. As Jonathan Kahana writes, "... the separation and recombination of voice and image puts the latter in the position of being structured and animated by the former" (93). It is through this "recombination of voice and image" that the film's ideology expressed through the voice-over contains the indexical, ambiguous nature of the archival footage. *Franco, ese hombre* exploits to the fullest this ability to separate voices from images, which, as Kahana reminds us, "is a mark of power, and the primary objection of both critics and subsequent generations of filmmakers" to the voice of god commentary style (93). Through this style of authoritative voice-over, predominant through the 1950s, to which images are subservient, *Franco, ese hombre* "imposed a single and obvious meaning on the documentary image" (93–4).

However, as Plantinga points out—and as *Franco, ese hombre* illustrates— the voice-over not only "disseminate[s] information or assert[s] authority" but "may express a wish, advocate, denounce, express solidarity, plead, hesitate, argue, postulate, and ruminate" (161–2). In *Franco, ese hombre*, the voice-over also wishes, argues, postulates, and ruminates. And, admittedly sharing the same space with the rest of the onlookers attending the military parade (unlike the canonical voice of god narration style that exists in an abstract space distinct from that of the projected images), it is closer to us, more intimately situated. The voice-over acknowledges sharing that space on two occasions. At the very beginning of the military parade, when it reveals its specific location: "The ovations of the audience [the onlookers contemplating the military parade] are getting closer to us," presumably referring to the place from where the documentary crew is filming, as a television anchor does when broadcasting a live event. And again, at the end of it to inform us that the whole film crew will now move their equipment to Franco's official residence to shoot the farewell scene. During the historical flashback of Franco, however, the voice-over inevitably inhabits a more neutral space characteristic of voice of god narration. The voice-over thus lives in a space located somewhere between us and the lofty historical space inhabited by Franco, the mythical character the voice helps to construct.

The voice-over in *Franco, ese hombre* can be more accurately described then as an intermediary between the ordinary Spaniard and its leader. As mentioned earlier, the voice-over is that of Spanish actor Angel Picazo, a successful theater and film actor who specialized in ladies' man roles and who was known for his good looks and velvety voice. Appropriately, the aim of Picazo's voice-over—aside from interpreting the truth of Spanish history—is to seduce the "feminine" masses into falling in love with their charismatic, fascist leader.[16] The voice-over becomes a matchmaker performing the seducer's role that, unlike Franco, Hitler and Mussolini entirely reserved for themselves.

Creating a seductive myth out of Franco the man was notoriously difficult due to the wanting human material. Franco was a short, portly man with a shrill voice, and whose hands were "feminine" and "always damp with perspiration" (Ashford 2). Even as a grown man, according to Ashford, "his military commands would sometimes burst forth in an ignominious squeak" (2).[17]

In *Franco, ese hombre* the difficult task of creating a myth out of the man cinematically hinges upon the symbiotic interaction between Chion's *acousmêtre*—the invisible presence of the voice-over—and the silent images of Franco culled from archival footage. In *The Voice in Cinema* (1982), Chion has persuasively argued that the character whose voice we hear but whose image is hidden from plain view becomes an "acousmatic" presence that acquires special powers and haunts the surface of the film (21). Due to his invisibility, the *acousmêtre* is endowed with special powers, particularly those of ubiquity, panopticism, omniscience, and omnipotence.[18] As he reminds us, the word 'acousmatic' derives from a Pythagorean sect "whose followers would listen to their Master speak *behind a curtain*," their focus of attention on his message supposedly enhanced by not being distracted by his image (19).[19] In *Franco, ese hombre* an ironic reversal takes place. It is not the image of the master—of Franco—that is hidden from his followers behind a curtain but his "shrill," "squeaky" voice, so it does not distract the audience from the imparted message. The voice-over makes the actions of the master—his master's voice—worth *listening* to. It bestows Franco the *caudillo*—the victorious leader and national savior—with the "radical otherness" it typically reserves for itself.

However, the *acousmêtre*, as Chion explains, cannot simply be a commentator completely removed from the image, as in the "voice of the magic lantern show" (24). It has to bear, "with the image a relationship of *possible inclusion*" (23). In *Franco, ese hombre* the voice-over is an off-screen voice whose body we never see, but it is not simply an appendix, exterior to the film diegesis. As the narrator admits, it also inhabits it, as when Picazo, as we saw, lets us know at the beginning that he hears the applause of the multitudes approaching, and then again, at the end, that the film crew will move from the site of the military parade to Franco's official residence to shoot the interview with Franco. Also, being the voice of a famous actor, whose face was well-known to Spanish audiences, the voice-over has already materialized in the mind's eye of the spectator.

The voice-over in *Franco, ese hombre* then could be aptly characterized as an already visualized *acousmêtre*, a figure "more familiar and reassuring" but who still retains a measure of power of the "complete *acousmêtre*" (Chion 21). This power of the voice-over derived from its "acousmatic" presence thus helps endow the image of Franco with a power of its own. In short, both voice and image work symbiotically to construct the myth of Franco.

In *Franco, ese hombre* the figure of Franco, rendered mute and spoken by the voice-over, also usurps the powers Chion ascribes to the peripheral mute character, which he describes as being "potentially omniscient, panoptic and omnipotent" (97). Thus, the mute, *the body without a voice*, displays many attributes of his counterpart, *the voice without a body*, the acousmatic voice, whose source we do not see (97). The mute character in film is often regarded as the keeper of a secret, which sometimes could be "a mythic or cosmogonic secret" (96). Franco, whom Serrano Suñer describes as a perennial chatterbox, is here rendered mute for political gain. Resorting to muteness was a political strategy deployed by Franco himself;[20] a strategy mocked by his own minister Pedro Sáinz Rodríguez, who famously described him as a sphinx who had no secret. Moreover, in *Franco, ese hombre*, Franco is assigned the role of moral compass of the nation, a role typically performed in film by the mute character (96). In *Franco, ese hombre*, therefore, the successful construction of Franco's myth depends on harnessing the powers of the *acousmêtre* to the powers of the mute.

In this symbiotic and ultimately self-defeating loop, Franco's image receives its power from the idolization of the "acousmatic" voice we never actually see, while the idolizing power of the voice resides in the prestige of the body of the mute we never hear, but which the narrator's voice nonetheless helps to create. The mute, the image of Franco himself, appears on screen but it does not speak; it is spoken for by the voice-over. The voice-over, whose image we never get to see (other than in the spectators' imagination of the famous actor Angel Picazo), derives what Steven Connor calls its "vocalic body"—"a surrogate or secondary body ... formed and sustained out of the autonomous operations of the voice" (35)—from the body of the mute. In *Franco, ese hombre* the voice-over fuses intimately with the body of the mute, Franco's silent image, to color and model its container (35). The voice-over, with its constant histrionic praise of

Franco as military hero, as saving messiah, hallucinates a full body—that of a mythical Franco—which seems to incarnate the political ideal, as expressed in the historical summary it wants its audience to embrace.

Therefore, Picazo's voice-over and the image of Franco—the bodiless voice and the voiceless body—can be understood as "the two disjointed halves of a single elusive entity" (Chion 101). This alliance between the *acousmêtre* and the mute haunts Sáenz de Heredia's documentary, giving power to both the image and the voice but, as we will see next, it also threatens its unraveling. Therefore, in *Franco, ese hombre* the successful creation of the myth of Franco depends on the strict separation of the voice from the body, of the sound from the image.

This separation of the voice from the mute body—of sound from image—suggests the kind of ventriloquial relationship that, ironically, as we will see through an analysis of the last scene of the film, unravels the myth of Franco that hinged on their separation. The appearance of Franco himself at the end of the film, reunited in image and sound, awkwardly reading lines written for him by the movie co-screenwriter, shatters the carefully constructed myth.

The tension created by the acousmatic presence is released when the source of the voice, in this case Franco himself, for whom the voice-over had served as surrogate throughout, becomes visible, a moment which for Chion is "always like a deflowering" (23). Its visibility anchors the *acousmêtre* to a specific location, making it lose some of its former powers (28). This last effort to bring Franco closer to the audience, in line with Adorno's understanding of fascist propaganda, backfires, setting in motion a triple process of disintegration: of the myth, of the human being behind, and, finally, of the overall fascist sublimating impulse to transcend corrupting bodily matter. Instead, this closing scene exposes Francoism for what it really is—a cacophony of clichéd narratives and kitsch utterances, which, by definition, come from elsewhere, ventriloquized, like the content of the cue cards read by Franco.

In the last scene of the movie, in yet another example of the film's self-reflexivity, the images of the military parade wane and the camera zooms out to reveal a movie screen. We are transported to *El Palacio de El Pardo* where Franco himself is watching the documentary of his own exploits. The camera cuts to a head shot of Franco, sitting alone in the semi-darkness of the projection room of his official residence. Sáenz de Heredia, microphone in hand, approaches submissively, as Franco, remaining seated, turns his head to the left to greet the director. Ceremoniously hovering over him, Sáenz de Heredia poses painfully banal questions about

Franco's main political influences, the task of governing, and the *caudillo*'s advice for the new generations of Spaniards who did not participate in "our glorious crusade."[21]

In the opening of the last scene, Franco is finally brought into the light and thus, like Chion's *acousmêtre*, is in the end "doom[ed] ... to the fate of ordinary mortals" (23). This final "embodiment" of the *acousmêtre* causes it to "lose its colossal proportions," to "deflate and become a wisp of a voice, finally speaking as a human" (29). His image, enveloped in shadows at first, crystallizes as the camera cuts from a head shot of Franco in semi-darkness to a well-lit shot of him. The omnipotent father of the nation is revealed to be an ordinary little fellow "who's speaking into a microphone and operating reverb and smoke machines," much like the Great Oz (29). Franco, the messiah and mythical figure, appears not to be much different from him, "a man who enjoys [hiding himself] and ... amplifying his voice" (29).[22]

But this ending should not be understood as an example of effective populist propaganda, which, according to Adorno, aims to humanize the leader. Instead, the interview with Franco, meant to bring him closer to the audience, reveals that Franco entirely lacks the spontaneity of the common man. Instead of being the moment when the dictator enters the "realm of human beings," Sáenz de Heredia's interview of Franco at the end of the movie suggests a conventionally staged act of a ventriloquist with his dummy. As Franco awkwardly reads the cue cards written by someone else, he resembles more a ventriloquist's dummy than an ordinary human. In fact, the entire scene's choreography mimics a typical ventriloquist act: Sáenz de Heredia stands slightly bent over a seated Franco, whose head turns to the left to be able to read the cue cards and deliver his answers (Fig. 5.6). Like most ventriloquist acts, it is also set inside a theater. The voice of Franco—the master's voice—is hijacked by that of another, the master ventriloquist: Spanish ideological ultra-conservatism. Incapable of transcending the totalitarian system he created, Franco the dictator, the sole source of authority and meaning, becomes Franco the dictated, a dummy spoken for by its ventriloquist master expressed, as mentioned earlier, in the banal content provided by the cue cards written by someone else stating the clichéd, ultra-right-wing ideological core of Spanish conservatism. Thus, unlike in Adorno's everyman of fascist propaganda, where the leader's commonality with ordinary citizens is the focal point, the appearance of Franco the man in *Franco, ese hombre* unravels not only the myth but also the *everyman*, leaving us only with a dummy who delivers somebody else's thoughts, in a semantic *mise-en-abîme* also suggested by the visual *mise-en-abîme* of the spectator watching Franco the spectator watching himself on the screen.

Figure 5.6 (upper and lower) *Franco, ese hombre,* 1964

The film's ventriloquism in this scene and the proliferation of the film's myriad voices—the different dubbed historical actors we hear throughout the historical summary—ultimately undermine Francoism's fascist sublimating impulse, its obsessive attempt to disassociate the purity of the voice from its residual, excremental body.[23] Borrowing heavily from fascism, Francoist metaphysics of presence was, as we saw in Chapter 3, based on an ill-informed Bergsonian attempt to liberate the self from deadening layers of abstraction. Like that of the Great Oz, the fascist voice, amplified by new kinds of technological advances, as seen in Hitler's and Mussolini's vocal acrobatics, pretends to have an unmediated access to the innermost recesses of the soul, which it distils in hysterical bursts. Nothing is more detrimental to this exultation of presence characteristic of fascist ideology than the displacement of the voice from the body implicit in the ventriloquial spectacle at the end of *Franco, ese hombre*.[24] Speaking from a place outside itself—represented here by the cue cards whose content was written by someone else—the voice ceases to have a direct, unmediated access to the inner self.

Fascism attempts to appropriate the pure speech of the divinity, present-to-itself, in order to announce its apocalyptic refashioning of the world. Fascist obsession with the purity of the voice may have to do with the fact that the voice is in itself an ideal sublimating mechanism: the voice as the purest emanation of the physical existence. Out of bodily secretion, the exhalation of used, contaminated air, comes pure ideal speech. Therefore, voice production is the ultimate example of successful sublimation, the complete recycling and elimination of corrupt residual matter—which fascism saw as the ultimate threat—into ethereal, uncontaminated speech.

In its obsession to forge a sublime, new language that would help remake the world according to its own will, fascism compulsively attempted to purify language from "historical excrescence" to find, as Steve Connor remarks, an Edenic, unmediated "correspondence between word and thing" (230).[25] This scene of Franco being interviewed, in which he is *not* the source of the content of the voice—as he delivers someone else's lines inside a theater—theatricalizes Franco's persona and de-sublimates the fascist self. Franco, who in the rest of the documentary is metaphorically rendered as messiah fully present to himself—as we saw cause and effect of his own being—not speaking with his own "voice," becomes alien to himself, a dummy, which undermines the sublime creation of the myth. Franco responds to the five questions the director asks with ready-made answers containing the main tenets of Francoist ideology: love of country, spirit of sacrifice, religious faith, Spain as spiritual reservoir of the Western world, and Spaniards as depositories of "a treasure of virtue."

Echoing the wooden, stale content of the answers, Franco's delivery is wooden and stale. He answers the banal questions with the lack of spontaneity and originality of an obsequious, obedient student seeking to impress his schoolmaster. Franco the dictator, the ultimate source of meaning, whose speech should be a natural emanation of his omnipotence, is reduced to the role of a dummy who speaks through his master's voice. In that sense, this scene is also a reversal of the traditional role of the dummy. The dummy is precisely the ventriloquist's unrepressed, unconscious other that irreverently speaks truth to power. Quite the opposite in *Franco, ese hombre*, Franco the dummy represents the repressed ventriloquist master. Instead of speaking truth to power, Franco, the powerful dummy, lies to the powerless audience, delivering only safe, paternalistic, politically banal remarks.[26]

The figure of the dummy is, as Connor reminds us, a "suturing agent" that actually keeps together the illusion of the spectacle—the separation of body and voice—"knitting together the evidence of eye and ear" (283). Similarly, Franco the dictator-dummy is the suturing device that ties the Francoist subject to its ideological position; it is the Lacanian "quilting point" that precariously holds together the symbolic ideological field. Interestingly enough, Franco described his regime as a monarchy without a monarch, but a monarchy nonetheless; because as he explained in a political speech after he passed the law of succession in 1947, monarchy is "a form that suits our content." Franco the dictator was the figure that allowed for that illusion of a monarchy without a monarch to be maintained.

Still, reducing the figure of the dictator to a dummy does not exonerate him from responsibility for his forty years of political repression. It simply expands the scope of responsibility of his criminal regime to encompass Spain's dominant classes. On the contrary, treating Franco as an ultimate source of evil exculpates the system he created, because it implies that had he not existed, Spain would have developed in sync with the rest of the Western nations. In actuality, although Franco occupied the highest position of power solely as guarantor of the "monarchy without a monarch," the military uprising was a conspiracy much larger than Franco himself. The revolution of "priests and bankers," as Manuel Vazquez Montalbán successfully labeled it, had actually been orchestrated long before Franco became its supreme commander. His regime, rather than the expression of *his* will to power, was the expression of the will to power of Spain's conservative elites. Franco himself was in that sense a cog in the machinery of Spanish fascism/ultra-conservatism. He was the ideological suturing device—the dummy—that held the system together. Ultimately, the system was in place not to satisfy his interests but those of the hegemonic class. In that sense, Franco was a screen, much like Peter Sellers in *Being There* (1979), upon which everybody—particularly the various factions of his conservative coalition—could project their own fantasies of power. As the closing scene reveals, even Franco himself, as spectator, used his screen image to project his own fantasies of power.

The ending of *Franco, ese hombre*, then, is the pinnacle of its kitsch aesthetic. Francoist ideological edifice was a mirage which promised the radical transformation of the country according to its fascist political agenda. In reality, Francoism was a revolution of "priests and bankers" that conspired to bring to a halt the Second Republic's social, cultural, and political reforms with the support of the military. Francoist rhetoric was nothing else other than a repertoire of traditional conservative clichés, formally wrapped in "Falangist kitsch." It was an ersatz ideology that heavily borrowed from other ersatz ideologies, particularly Spanish conservatism and Italian fascism. In short, it was a fake twice removed, a cliché made of clichés. Franco's wooden delivery of clichéd paternalistic answers to equally clichéd questions posing as edgy ones, such as, "Are we Spaniards as difficult to govern as we ourselves or others have observed?" exposes the smoke and mirrors of Francoist ideology, its mystifying, stupefying effects. Francoist kitsch reveals the other side of fascism's sublimating impulse; its supposedly beautiful, poetic form covers up its stale, putrid content.

In essence, as revealed by *Franco, ese hombre*, kitsch is an aesthetic without an originating identifiable source. Kitsch utterances, as we saw in previous chapters, are mere labels conveniently packaging their ready-made content. In that sense, they come from the outside—from nowhere—in the form of reductive, simplified prescriptions to reduce the complexity of reality to a network of useless but easily consumed and politically effective generalizations, as the content of the cue cards. The truth of kitsch speaks ventriloquially from a place where the subject is not, as the banal answers of Franco-the-dummy come to him from outside the visual field.

Insofar as it is a genre whose purpose is the honest examination of reality, it can be argued that documentary itself is intrinsically at odds with the escapism characteristic of kitsch aesthetics, whose main purpose is to mystify reality under the fantasy veil of cliché. Kitsch embodies fantasy to hide the traumatic core of social subjectivity. Yet, as *Surcos* had done a decade earlier through the appropriation of neorealist and noir aesthetics, *Franco, ese hombre* also attempted to smuggle its kitsch false historical content through the formal traits of a legitimate documentary cinematographic genre. As exemplified by the documentary's complete circumvention of the Civil War, Spain's traumatic core par excellence, kitsch is the ideal aesthetic for the Francoist revisionist veiling of the undesirable content.

The interview concludes with Sáenz de Heredia profusely thanking his excellency for his service to the fatherland and wishing that God will continue to guide his footsteps. Franco gets up and leaves the projection room with decisive step. The voice-over's final remarks focus on those footsteps, as the camera zooms in on them, as it also did in *Raza* in the beautiful and quintessentially kitsch beach execution scene. These steps, the narrator remarks, "walk with the same strength across the Moroccan hills and the Spanish mountain ranges as across the train stations of Hendaye and Bordighera. These steps always walk in a straight line," with the sole mission to "aggrandize Spain." The camera follows Franco's feet walking across luxurious carpets adorning the hallways of *El Palacio de El Pardo*. In the famous scene from *Raza*, the camera similarly focused on tenuous footprints left on the seashore by a group of monks about to be executed by Republican militiamen to suggest their purity and innocence. In *Franco, ese hombre* Franco's footsteps suggest that throughout his heroic exploits he always walked decisively without straying even in the most difficult historical moments. But the shot of Franco walking on the lush carpets of his palace also reveals that he, unlike the two unnamed others at Hendaye and Bordighera—Hitler and Mussolini—has made it safely home to Spain to stop the political chaos, like Ulysses in *The Odyssey*—a perennial subtext in Francoist cultural production. The camera cuts from his footsteps to a long medium shot of Franco with his back turned to us, as he slowly disappears like western heroes over the horizon (of his palace). But unlike the wild Nathan in *The Searchers* (1956), who after having fought to expand Western civilization into the wilderness is left behind— himself incapable of living in the civilized world—Franco, the benevolent grandfather, reaps the benefits of his victorious exploits by settling in his monarch-like palace.

Notes

1. This tendency, Neocleous writes, "to point to a glorious yet lost past which is nevertheless about to be reborn in an ever more glorious future is also the constitutive feature of nationalism" (73).
2. Ironically, due to his physical resemblance to King Alfonso XIII, Picazo was rumored to be the illegitimate son of the Spanish monarch, whom Franco came to replace.
3. During the marriage between Philippe II and Mary of Portugal, Castile and Portugal were supposedly part of the Spanish Empire, although in reality they were completely separate political entities.
4. The pinnacle of the disregard for the truth in *Franco, ese hombre* is the coverage of Franco's role in the brutal crushing of a miners' general strike in Asturias in 1917, for which he received the moniker "the butcher of Asturias." Displaying unimaginable political cynicism, the voice-over tells us that this action gave Franco the precious opportunity to get closer to the real problems of the Spanish working class. From then on, we are told, the concerns of the working class loomed large in his political thought, with the concept of "social justice" becoming "his most obstinate preoccupation."

5. In 1922, Franco is offered the rank of lieutenant by Millán Astray, a legendary figure in the history of the Spanish army, whom the voice-over describes as "passionate romantic of light bolted eloquence and paroxystic valor." Against the background of a photograph of the two men fused in an embrace, Astray's well-known bravado and erratic personality are contrasted with the traits of the steadier, more reserved Franco. Franco is characterized as "a methodical organizer. A studious person who himself ranks his well-proven valor second among the virtues that should characterize a military commander."
6. As Sánchez-Biosca points out, "telluric impregnation, foreboding, traces of memory, apocalyptic flashes: a detailed reading of this film would reveal a subtle use of mythical language" (436).
7. To strengthen the leitmotif of Franco as a nation-builder, we are informed of his vital role in the creation of Zaragoza's military academy. In March 1927, Miguel Primo de Rivera, the Spanish general who, under King Alfonso XIII, became Spain's dictator from 1923 until 1929, selects Franco for the challenging task of creating a military academy in the city of Zaragoza. The narrator brags about how Franco rose to the occasion to build in the short allotted time a "colossal building, finished even in its most minute detail." The military academy was such a marvel in technical sophistication and operational precision, we are told, that French war minister General Maginot reported soon after his visit, "Spain can already boast that its officers' school is the most modern center of its kind in the world."
8. In a speech Franco gave in 1969 explaining to the nation why he decided to elect Prince Juan Carlos to the throne, he said that this was a logical choice since his regime was "a monarchy without royalty, but a monarchy nonetheless."
9. Against the background of a photo of José Antonio sitting at his desk and wearing his Falangist outfit, the narrator mentions his famous letter, where these "prophetic words" could be read: "A socialist victory would have the same meaning as a foreign occupation."
10. Franco was completely convinced by "the Entente's paranoid bulletins" he subscribed to, which said that the Asturias uprising, for example, "had been 'deliberately prepared by the agents of Moscow'" (Ashford 76).
11. Interestingly enough, the motto of the 1964 World Fair was "Peace through understanding," although, in an ironic turn of events, Spain's showcasing in the international arena was hindered by the boycott of most European countries, Canada, and Australia due to an unsurmountable disagreement between the World Fair commissioner Robert Moses and the American organizers.
12. Although the documentary professes admiration for German military might and does not shy away from admitting "the friendly links that connected [Spain] with the Rome/Berlin axis," it maintains that Spain had remained

neutral during the war. In fact, its role in this new version of history had been strictly humanitarian, "offering the safe haven of its ports for the exchange of prisoners and the wounded," obviating the fact that it also made available those same ports to German submarines for refueling.

13. As Nancy Berthier writes: "Implicitly, behind this figure of legendary hero in contact with the Moors, the figure of another hero is profiled, Rodrigo Diaz de Vivar, called the Cid (precisely from the Arab word 'szidi' or 'señor'), in recognition of his exceptional virtues as a warrior. The Cid's privileged relationships with the Muslims, for example the poet king of Seville, Al-Mutamid, had been sung throughout history" (Berthier 291).

14. As Berthier writes: "Throughout the interview, there is an accumulation of elements which underline the association of this testimony and truth. First, all of the staging: the interview takes place in the professional office of the doctor, a place of objective science, with modern equipment in the background, with books and papers sitting on the table of the office in the foreground, signs of seriousness. Blasco-Salas is dressed with a white lab coat and he appears behind the desk of his office, as if it were a medical exam room. Also, the way in which they give the interview is similar to a police report: short questions in a cutting voice as if to be saying 'the truth, all the truth'" (290).

15. Francoist tanks were blessed by Catholic priests and numerous battle miracles were constantly recounted. The most famous was the episode of a bomb dropped by a Republican bomber in the *Basilica del Pilar de Zaragoza* which did not explode due to the miraculous intervention of the *Virgen del Pilar*.

16. In this sense, *Franco, ese hombre* notably differs from the propaganda of Portuguese dictator Oliveira Salazar, often cited as the dictatorship closest in nature to Spanish Francoism. While Salazar was usually represented, as Patricia Vieira has observed, following Adorno's notion of the little-big man, as the humble man who rose "almost fortuitously" to occupy "his governing position," Franco's propaganda presents Franco as the messiah, as the blessed, rightful heir to Spanish kings.

17. Given Franco's lack of charisma, as Vicente Benet, observes, "Franco's representation in the *Noticiario Español* was closely regulated since the founding of the *Departamento Nacional de Cinematografía* in April 1938. As Rafael Rodríguez Tranche explains, Franco was not photogenic, and this gave way to editing strategies designed to simultaneously show and hide the leader through multiple images of short duration or rapid flashes of his face and figure" (154).

18. As he explains, there are very different degrees in this characterization. From the complete *acousmêtre*, "the one who is not-yet-seen, but who remains liable to appear in the visual field at any moment," to the already visualized *acousmêtre*, "the one temporarily absent from the picture, is more familiar and reassuring—even though in the dark regions of the acousmatic field, which

surrounds the visible field, this kind can acquire by contagion some of the powers of the complete *acousmêtre*" (*The Voice in Cinema* 21).
19. "This inderdiction against looking, which transforms the Master, God, or Spirit into an acousmatic voice, permeates a great number of religious traditions" (Chion 19).
20. As we saw in a previous chapter, in fact, Franco's politically induced muteness was ridiculed by Pedro Sáinz Rodriguez, one of his early ministers during the 1940s, who described Franco as a sphinx—the mythological "guardian of a secret"—with no secret, referring to his capacity to remain impassively neutral: alluding both to his manipulative way of dealing with the various political factions he commanded but also to his lack of political vision.
21. Sáenz de Heredia reportedly said that he was impressed by the eloquence and naturalness of Franco's performance under the pressure of the cinematographic lens. Contrary to that, looking awkwardly off-camera, Franco's answers to the director's questions seem forced and staged, as he is quite obviously reading from cue cards.
22. In his ingenious reading of *The Wizard of Oz*, Chion observes how The Great Oz is revealed to be "an ordinary little fellow who's speaking into a microphone and operating reverb and smoke machines. The Great Oz is nothing but a man who enjoys playing God by hiding his body and amplifying his voice" (29).
23. Throughout the documentary we perceive Franco's image as a mute presence. The documentary resorts to a kind of ventriloquism whose various characters—from Dolores Ibárruri, King Alfonso XIII, and Maréchal Pétain, to a number of Franco's generals, Winston Churchill, José Antonio and Franco himself—are dubbed by professional Spanish actors, including Picazo, whose voice-over acts as that of master ventriloquist. The film generates, then, a multiplicity of voices which are not anchored to their sources, which hints at the uncoupling of subject from voice characteristic of ventriloquism.
24. The ventriloquial metaphor has also been used in a derogatory manner by Jeremy Treglown in *Franco's Crypt* (2013) in reference to Franco. In this case, Treglown describes Franco as an "incompetent ventriloquist" in a propaganda clip in which the dictator appears with his wife and daughter, eleven years old at the time. As Treglown writes, "The speech has clearly been rehearsed; if we were in any doubt about this, we're given a glimpse of the dictator behind his daughter, lips moving slightly ahead of hers like those of an incompetent ventriloquist" (218).
25. As Connor notes, in its obsession with the creation of a new language in which to forge the new political and social arrangements, the American Revolution performed also a sort of "elocutionary revolution" (231), which provided "the possibility of purifying language, stripping it of corruption and historical excrescence and returning to an Edenic correspondence between word and thing" (230).

26. About this scene, Sánchez-Biosca writes, "the little man, rigid, hieratic, turns to the camera to give advice to his subjects, both to those who lived through the *crusade* as well as those that did not. Once more, Franco's verbal discourse is incapable of 'engaging', still more incapable than its image, which is somewhat convincing particularly when mute and quasi-photographic, as it becomes manifest when hunting, fishing and in his family life as a grandpa" (NODO 436).

CHAPTER 6

Viridiana: The World, the Flesh, and the Devil

In mourning it is the world which has become poor and empty; in melancholia it is the ego itself

—Sigmund Freud, *Mourning and Melancholia*

The return of Luis Buñuel to Spain in 1960 for the filming of *Viridiana* coincides with the period of Spanish *apertura*, when, in an attempt to gain international legitimacy, Franco opened up the country to the outside world. Promised total creative control, Buñuel came to Spain after twenty-two years in exile to shoot the film, a welcome decision by the Francoist government, which saw in the return of the world-renowned filmmaker—a former close friend of Salvador Dalí and Federico García Lorca—a rare opportunity to score major political points. For Buñuel, however, it was an equally rare opportunity to burst from the inside the Francoist kitsch melancholy bubble to expose its perverse, repressive political contents.

The circumstances surrounding *Viridiana*'s scandal are widely known: *Viridiana* represented Spain at the Cannes Film Festival, where it won the prestigious *Palme d'Or*. Deeply humiliated by the condemnatory remarks made against the film by the Vatican's newspaper *L'Osservatore Romano* after the award was announced, accusing the film of blasphemy, the Francoist government withdrew its support and emphatically banned it. A Francoist censor issued a scathing new report: "blasphemous, profane. Cruel and contemptuous of the poor. Also morbid and savage. A poisonous, corrosive film with great cinematographic skill for coordinating images, overtones, and soundtrack" (quoted in Sánchez Vidal 256). More than just an anecdote revealing the inner contradictions of Francoist Spain during its *aperturista* attempt to modernize the country, *Viridiana*'s scandal is emblematic of a film, which—as we will see in the following pages—can be read as an allegory of the historical evolution of Franco's post-war Spain. Ironically, then, the external circumstances surrounding the film could be seen as thematically related to its script. *Viridiana* is a cinematic time bomb

Buñuel came to Franco's Spain to deliver; a film that not only accurately portrayed the first two decades of Franco's regime but also anticipated its dramatic transformation during the next fifteen years and beyond.

Pressured both by the failures of its isolationist policies and the changes in the politico-economic climate of the West during the second half of the 1950s, Franco's Spain was forced to open up to a process of modernization to secure the regime's political and economic survival. Leading a group of ambitious young technocrats culled from the highly influential religious group *Opus Dei*, finance minister Laureano López Rodó was the main architect of a new Spanish economic policy whose goal was to fully incorporate Spain into the Western capitalist system without altering the power structure of the Franco regime. The 1958 Principles of the National Movement (*Los principios del Movimiento Nacional*), drafted by Rodó himself, and the famous 1959 Stabilization Plan (*Plan de estabilización*) were the main pillars of the Francoist attempt to transform *latifundista* Spain, controlled by an ultra-conservative Church and a lethargic aristocracy—represented in the film by Don Jaime, Viridiana's uncle—into a modern industrialized country. In Francoist rhetoric, the goal was not to become just another nation on the European political map but to embrace the West without losing Spain's perceived role as the "spiritual reserve of the Western world."

In this chapter I argue that *Viridiana*, a film usually interpreted through the lens of Buñuel's surrealist aesthetics, is best understood as an allegorical attempt to upend Francoist ideology from within by exposing its use of melancholy as a means of political subjection. The film traces the historical evolution of Franco's Spain, a country which it describes as a religiously sublimated space characterized by the internalization of a fundamentalist version of Christian ethics, resulting in a vicious cycle of desire, guilt, repression, and perversion. As a narrative, *Viridiana* is organized to emphasize this evolution. Each half of the movie functions as a metaphor for a given moment and a given political discourse of Francoism: the autarky of the 1940s characterized, as we saw in the first part of this study, by its melancholic rhetoric of a lost idealized past to be re-created in the present, and the rapidly developing nation of the late 1950s and early '60s when the industrial bourgeoisie—represented in the film by Jorge, Don Jaime's illegitimate offspring—eventually gained the upper hand.[1] Yet it is precisely the character of Viridiana herself—a novice who, before swearing her vows, leaves the convent to meet Don Jaime, her uncle and benefactor—that can be read as an allegory of Spain, a national space traversed by the competing ideological factions that characterized the Spanish political landscape at the time.

The film follows Viridiana—a character loosely based on the life of St Verdiana, a medieval Italian saint who lived in seclusion for thirty-four years—to focus on the traumatic events she experiences at her uncle's mansion where she goes to thank him for his financial support.[2] Upon her arrival, she is welcomed by a startled Don Jaime, who cannot believe the uncanny resemblance between Viridiana and his deceased wife. As he informs his niece, his wife died in his arms of a heart attack on their wedding night. A few days after her arrival—after Viridiana reluctantly accepts her uncle's bizarre proposition to join him for tea wearing his wife's wedding dress—he drugs her with the intent of "consummating" his matrimony. Filled with shame at the last minute, however, Don Jaime is unable to perpetrate his crime, although the following day he tells Viridiana he took her virginity hoping she would give up her plan to become a nun and move in with him instead. After hearing the story, Viridiana decides to leave the mansion immediately, which prompts Don Jaime to commit suicide, in a final attempt to retain her forever at his house. As he shrewdly anticipated, feeling responsible for her uncle's death, Viridiana returns to the mansion, this time as Don Jaime's legal heiress. Don Jaime's passing is followed by a transitional period when the legal control of the house is shared between Viridiana, who is now entirely devoted to charitable work, and Jorge, Don Jaime's illegitimate son, whom he had included in his will thanks to Viridiana's intercession. This second part of the narrative ends with Viridiana being sexually assaulted by one of the beggars she has been housing. This second rape attempt results in Viridiana giving up all charity work and submitting her will to Jorge, who finally takes full control of Don Jaime's estate.

Structurally, the film is divided into three parts. The first takes place at Don Jaime's stately country manor before his suicide.[3] The manor is filled with objects that connote a closed, decadent world dominated by the economic, moral, and aesthetic values of the old Spanish nobility. Don Jaime's world is that of a gloomy aristocracy, cultured yet decadent, that sponsored aesthetic and moral codes that differ from those of the booming bourgeoisie that gradually is gaining power all around. The fact that Don Jaime's estate represents more a lifestyle—a *refuge* from the outside world—than a unit of economic production is stressed by the comment Viridiana makes to him upon her arrival: "You've been neglecting the farm, Uncle." For his part, Don Jaime replies, not without a hint of pride, "In twenty years the grass has invaded everything. There are spiders all over the house except on the first floor" (Buñuel 4); a state of affairs which not only hints at Spain's isolation from the world and at the spider's web into which Viridiana will unwittingly fall, but also at the mansion's decadent, gothic atmosphere.

The mise-en-scène of Don Jaime's manor, in fact, re-creates the oppressive atmosphere that interested Buñuel and the surrealists of gothic novels characterized by their passionate attachments and repressed traumas, which, in the form of ghostly figures, always return to haunt the living. Don Jaime's world—representing the old, decadent Spanish nobility—had already become a common theme in great works of Spanish literature, such as Emilia Pardo Bazán's *Los Pazos de Ulloa* [*The House of Ulloa*] (1886) and Ramón del Valle Inclán's *Romance de lobos* (1908). Furthermore, the decorative elements of the house—the fine linens, silver candelabras, delicate china, the family portraits on the walls, or the old harmonium that Don Jaime plays in a quasi-mystic trance—visually convey a world oscillating between exquisite refinement and inescapable decadence.[4]

The second part also takes place at the mansion, after Don Jaime's death. The film portrays his illegitimate son, Jorge, as a pragmatist, completely alien to the refined but decadent world of the dead patriarch. Jorge, an action-oriented bourgeois whom we are subtly informed has spent time abroad, barges in from the outside world with a clear modernizing project in mind. The film conveys the large scope of this project through Jorge's frenetic activity. He spends most of his time cataloguing, measuring, cleaning, repairing, and tilling the lands abandoned by his father with the goal of transforming the property from an aristocratic, ultimately parasitic lifestyle into a legitimate agricultural operation that will reap an economic benefit, thus legitimizing himself in the process. In short, Jorge represents the Spanish industrial bourgeoisie which, summoned by the will of the patriarch, took charge of the economic life of the country during the 1960s. His modernizing project is perfectly illustrated by the fact that he also brings electricity to the mansion, the classical symbol of modernity.[5]

Jorge's arrival at the mansion, however, like Franco's *aperturista* experiment, should not be interpreted as a radical break with Don Jaime's world, but as a deep restructuring of its economic priorities in order to save it from its self-inflicted deterioration. This intent becomes apparent in a sequence in which Jorge is making an inventory of the attic with the help of Don Jaime's devoted servant, Ramona. In this sequence, Jorge assesses the condition of the stored furniture and, while picking up a chair, optimistically remarks, "These chairs are in good condition. With a little varnish and some new covers this one will be quite presentable" (Buñuel 63). As this comment reveals, Jorge's renovations are merely cosmetic and aim more at "reupholstering" old structures with new fabric than at replacing them with new ones, a fact also underlined by the large portrait of a younger Don Jaime—sporting a Francoist-style moustache instead of the white beard we saw him wearing as an old man—hanging in the center of the living room wall as if he were still in full command of his estate.

The film, however, also makes clear that father and son represent two different classes, sensibilities, and lifestyles: Don Jaime that of a vanishing class of landowners, and Jorge that of a new upcoming bourgeoisie. The significant differences between father and son become immediately apparent when, upon Jorge's arrival, Ramona interrupts Jorge's attempt to play a few chords on his father's harmonium. Her gesture suggests that Jorge lacks the devotion needed to play the celestial instrument that used to stir Ramona's soul and transport her master into a state of spiritual frenzy. Somewhat removed from his father's lineage, as his illegitimate origin suggests, Jorge is a practical man who lacks his father's decadent refinement. Unlike his melancholically repressed father, he lives a life free from taboos or complexes. In Buñuel's own words, Jorge is "a positivist who believes in progress from a rational and bourgeois viewpoint" (Colina and Pérez Turrent 152).[6]

The third part of the film describes a transitional moment characterized by the convergence of Viridiana's charitable work—she decides to open the premises to a group of itinerant beggars, embodying the seven deadly sins—and Jorge's rational, modernizing enterprise aiming at transforming his father's decadent farm into a profit-oriented business. It is during this transitional moment—characterized by the uncertainty and ideological and social contradictions characteristic of transitional periods—that the film reaches its climactic resolution in the famous banquet scene, in which Don Jaime's pre-modern world and its repressive melancholy sublimation seem to vanish forever. In this seminal sequence, Viridiana's beggars intrude into the manor house to treat themselves to a succulent banquet while their masters are out on the town.

Gradually, the beggars' dinner degenerates into a sacrilegious parody of Christ's Last Supper, including a direct intertextual reference to Leonardo's painting of the same subject, which symbolizes like few others the sublimated *aura* that Walter Benjamin ascribed to Western art (Fig. 6.1). The arrangement in Leonardo's painting is spontaneously replicated by the drunken beggars as they pose for a group photograph taken by one of the female beggars, who, raising her skirt in the front, pretends to take a picture with the camera she received as "a present from [her] parents," obviously referring to her genitals (Buñuel 72).[7] In this group portrait, obscenely "taken" from the point of view of the beggar's sex, Leonardo's sublime representation of Christ and his disciples comes face-to-face with its repressed other, the female sexuality which both traditional Christianity and Francoism took pains to repress. More generally,

Figure 6.1 *Viridiana*, 1961

this "sacrilegious" scene also frees the unconscious desire, which provides the material for Francoist melancholy sublimation underlined by Handel's "Hallelujah," another masterpiece of Western civilization, diegetically playing in the background. Thus, in this sequence the repressed—represented by the beggars' intrusion into the mansion to enjoy themselves and scatter their filth on their masters' white tablecloths—return to contaminate both the biblical theme of The Last Supper and Don Jaime's refined space representing the melancholy sublimation of Francoism's repressive brand of *Nacional-catolicismo*.[8]

In this sequence—and this is a crucial point in my allegorical reading of the film—the ghost of Don Jaime's dead wife finally comes to the surface, embodied in the figure of the leprous beggar, who, wearing her bridal corset and veil, conducts his macabre dance to the music of Handel's "Hallelujah" (Fig. 6.2). Once again, as with the reference to The Last Supper, the sublimated/perverse space of Don Jaime's world is contaminated by its repressed other, which this time is incarnated in the rotting flesh of the leper. Like in the gothic novels on which the film draws, the dead bride, whose untimely death represents the mansion's repressed traumatic event, needs to make her spectacular appearance in order to finally exorcise the past.

The long banquet sequence ends up with the blind man—the leader of the group of beggars, a group of characters clearly indebted to Goya's dark paintings—trashing the fine china and the pieces of porcelain on top of the table with his cane, enraged because, supposedly, his girlfriend—whose genital camera took the group portrait—is engaging in sexual activity

Figure 6.2 *Viridiana*, 1961

with another beggar behind a sofa. The blind man's rage and his destructive frenzy—which opposes Don Jaime's spiritual frenzy playing his harmonium—signify the final bursting of Don Jaime's melancholic bubble, which causes the cathartic liberation of repressed instincts, symbolized by the beggars. When, finally, Jorge and Viridiana return to the house, the former is knocked unconscious by a blow to the head by one of the beggars, while Viridiana is sexually assaulted by another who, previously, had painted her portrait as the Madonna—as *La Virgen de los remedios*—and who is wearing as a belt the skipping rope with its phallic handles that Don Jaime used to commit suicide and the little girl used to skip. Once again, thus, sublimation confronts its repressed other. In this case, the sublimated image of a woman as the Madonna is violently debased, treated as a mere sexual object. After the process of de-sublimation and cathartic excess this sequence entails—which is ideally exemplified by the macabre dance of the ghost of Don Jaime's dead wife—has ended, and those responsible for attempting to rape Viridiana are arrested by the Civil Guard, the house is left definitively under Jorge's command; that is to say, under the sole authority of the rationalist and modernizing discourse of the industrial bourgeoisie. Therefore, at the end of the film, Jorge's project seems to prevail over the repressive, obscurantist, and decadent world represented by Don Jaime, the symbol of an anachronistic Spanish aristocracy, which, combining political repression with religious repression, represented the perverse moral universe of Francoism. This project is perfectly illustrated by Don Jaime's celebrated penknife, whose blade is hidden inside a cross, which drew the immediate attention of Francoist censors (Fig. 6.3).

Figure 6.3 *Viridiana*, 1961

A hasty reading of the film might conclude that, despite a series of scandalous scenes mixing eroticism with religiosity, Buñuel—as his brief presence in the country could also indicate—seeks to legitimize the reformist project of national transformation through which Franco sought to bring Spain into the future, as Dalí, Buñuel's former friend and artistic collaborator, had previously done. And, in fact, members of the Spanish exile community accused Buñuel of selling out to the regime.[9] However, a more detailed analysis of the film immediately negates any attempt to align it with Franco's overall propaganda campaign to seek legitimacy in the Western world.

Viridiana, I argue, bursts the Francoist ideological melancholy bubble—which, as we saw in the previous chapters, found perfect expression in totalitarian kitsch aesthetics—from within, to expose its toxic, nauseating, repressive effects. Don Jaime's isolated mansion illustrates the rarefied ideological atmosphere of Francoism, which also emitted that "faint but dreadful smell" of putrid lobster characteristic of kitsch aesthetics (Broch 72).

To understand *Viridiana* in all its complexity, one must pay attention to the various mechanisms of subjectification that shape Viridiana's character, which is cinematically constructed as a blank canvas,[10] a phantom subject, upon which the various political and moral discourses prevalent in Spain at the time try to impose their will. Essentially, Viridiana is constituted as a subject through the interpellation of four different discourses which combine to make up the contradictory ideological tapestry of Francoist

Spain: firstly, the religious discourse of the convent, which annuls her subjectivity; secondly, the sublimating/perverse discourse of Don Jaime, representing Francoist repressive melancholy; thirdly, the Christian principle of charity; and, lastly, the complacent materialistic-narcissistic discourse of the bourgeoisie, represented by Jorge.

The film begins in the convent where Viridiana spent her childhood, having been, as we saw, financially supported by her uncle, Don Jaime. By definition, the religious convent is the space where bodily desires are negated and individual subjectivity dissolves into the anonymity of the collective. In the first scene in the cloister of the convent, Viridiana is dressed in the typical white habit of the novice, which covers her entire body, leaving only her face, the "mirror of the soul," visible. A long medium shot of Viridiana visually emphasizes her lack of individuality, her belonging to the group. In this shot, Viridiana's upper torso and novice headscarf are shown against the rounded arches of the convent's cloister (Fig. 6.4). The curvature of her headscarf replicates the curvature of the round arches behind her, perfectly fitting into the convent's architectural religious space. As this opening scene visually suggests, at the beginning of the film Viridiana belongs to the repressive space of the convent. She is a subjectless void upon whom first Don Jaime and later Jorge will project their own desires, which, although distinct in their form and nature, attempt to make a subject out of this bodiless nun, allegorizing the Spanish nation.[11]

In the first part of the film, Viridiana is the subject of Don Jaime's religiously sublimating, yet perverse, gaze. In his pre-modern, Catholic

Figure 6.4 *Viridiana*, 1961

world dominated by the notion of sin and its vicious cycle of desire, guilt, repression, and perversion—characteristic of the excessive internalization of Christian behavioral codes typical of Francoism—the expression of instincts is fiercely repressed and sublimated. In the film, the traumatic loss Don Jaime suffered on his wedding night, during which his wife died in his arms, is a metaphor for his moral dysfunction. And it can also be read as the classic Freudian motif, recurrent in Buñuel's films, of culture as the sublimation of desire, as seen, for instance, in *The Exterminating Angel* (1962), *Simon of the Desert* (1965), or *The Discreet Charm of the Bourgeoisie* (1972).

Don Jaime's loss and his inability to mourn his dead wife render him as a character melancholically stuck in the past, like Captain Vidal in *Pan's Labyrinth*—a film which, as we will see in the last chapter of this study, pays homage to Buñuel and particularly to *Viridiana*. Following Freud's famous categorization in "Mourning and Melancholia," Don Jaime is a melancholic subject who, unable to properly mourn, is cursed to re-enact his loss through a series of fetishistic rituals.[12] Exemplary of a Freudian melancholic personality, the film implicitly suggests that Don Jaime's love for his wife was a narcissistic attachment to a loved object never fully accepted on its own. Don Jaime's love object, thus—and this is a critical point for my argument—was a projection of his thoughts right from the start. In this sense, Don Jaime's melancholic attachments replicated Francoism's melancholic projection of its own nostalgic desires over the fate of Spain.[13]

Building on Judith Butler's characterization of melancholy as the psychic portal through which social norms condition human subjectivity, Spanish scholar Alberto Medina examines how Francoism establishes "a constant exhortation to melancholy as instrument of political subjection," (20) based on a "sophisticated narrative of debt towards the dead" (20). As he explains, Franco's own death, offered as a spectacle carefully monitored by the state-owned media, constituted a veritable "theater of possession" used as a political strategy for the continuation of the dictator's regime after his death (20).[14] For Francoism, then, melancholy was an important tool for political manipulation, not only during the regime but also after Franco's demise.

In the film, the Francoist use of melancholy as political tool is seen both through Don Jaime's fetishistic rituals to keep his wife "alive," which reach their climax in his attempt to rape Viridiana, and by his manipulative suicide cynically executed to keep a guilty Viridiana imprisoned at his home. *Viridiana* shrewdly depicts Francoist political use of melancholy through Don Jaime's narcissistic attachment to his dead wife—a dead ringer for Viridiana, as seen in the portrait hanging next to that of her husband, and thus also sharing her allegorical traits. The uncanny resemblance between Viridiana and her dead aunt provide for Don Jaime a welcome opportunity to renew his efforts to keep his wife "alive" so that he can go on subjecting her to his narcissistic thoughts. This time the fetishistic ritual expands to include the attempted rape of an unconscious Viridiana, through which he hopes to consummate his marriage. Don Jaime's melancholic possession of his dead wife is also suggested in the staging of his own death as a literal "theater of possession" in Medina's terms. This is evident in the theatrical way Don Jaime writes his suicide note while caressing his chin and in his devilish smile as he continues to write it.

Accurately portraying the transformative phase Spain embarked upon during the 1960s, but also eerily anticipating the Spanish transition to come, the film depicts Don Jaime's suicide—a classic Freudian melancholic subject—as a manipulative attempt at keeping both Viridiana as well as his illegitimate son—representing the politically impure Spanish bourgeoisie—subjected to his political will after his passing. From then on, both will be indebted to the dead patriarch, who, as we saw, looks down upon them from his painting, as Franco did from his portraits: Viridiana because of guilt, Jorge because of power and economic opportunity. Don Jaime's comparison to Franco as a founding father of the nation is subtly implied by the choice of his first name, Jaime, which, as we saw in Chapter 1, was also the name Franco used as a pseudonym when penning *Raza*'s screenplay, and, also, of James, one of Jesus's apostles, who, in his Spanish variant of Santiago, became Spain's patron saint.[15]

The film portrays Don Jaime as a voyeur, and as a fetishistic old man melancholically stuck in the past, while also insinuating he is a child molester. One of the first scenes inside Don Jaime's property shows Ramona's daughter, Rita, playing with a skipping rope, through a medium shot of Rita's legs and feet. This is the first of several close-up shots of feet in the film, a conventional sign of fetishism. In the shot, the rope and the legs establish an imaginary circle on the ground—suggesting a state of innocence—which Don Jaime carefully circumvents while making an odd gesture with his fingers. A close-up shot of Viridiana's face immediately follows, in which she seems to recall something, her lowered gaze suggesting a mental flashback. We soon realize that the shot of Rita's legs and her skipping rope is a point of view shot corresponding to Don Jaime, a subtle hint of the fact that, as we later come to realize, he is a fetishist. Right from the start, then, the film seems to establish a link between the novice and the girl—both virginal, untarnished beings—and sexual perversion. This is a reading confirmed by a later scene in which a point of view shot shows Don Jaime looking down from a high window upon Viridiana and Rita skipping together with the same rope. He smiles to himself, happy to see that Viridiana is entering Rita's circle of innocence. The dialogue also seems to suggest that Don Jaime has an illicit relationship with the little girl, although its precise nature is never made explicit. Rita says that Don Jaime always makes her *jump* when he comes outside, and he calls her his little dog.[16] Furthermore, the camera emphasizes the phallic nature of the skipping rope handle, which, we are told, Don Jaime made himself so that Rita could jump better.

The parallel between the skipping rope handle and the phallus traverses the entire film, as Sánchez Vidal has pointed out (256).[17] The skipping rope handle/phallus is also visually displaced, as Gwynne Edwards suggests, to the cow's udder that in an earlier scene Viridiana is afraid to touch, only doing so with the help of one of Don Jaime's farmhands (31).[18] The camera gives us a close-up of the farmhand filling with milk the glass that Viridiana holds. The close-up of the peasant's hand touching the cow's udder unambiguously refers to the masturbatory act, an association further implied by the fact that once Viridiana's glass is filled, Rita empties out its content on the cow's head. Furthermore, in this scene Rita mentions how *well* Don Jaime does it, referring to the act of milking, reinforcing the initial suggestion that he is a pedophile. Moreover, when Don Jaime speaks with Viridiana for the first time, he marks his territory with a foot gesture that reminds us of a fighting bull before it charges, visually linking Don Jaime to the evil Minotaur—the devourer of young virgins such as Rita and Viridiana—which, as we will see in the last chapter, Captain Vidal also embodies in *Pan's Labyrinth*. This is an image also suggested by Rita's comment that a very big black bull entered her room during the night.[19] All this imagery and innuendo, then, clearly portrays mild-mannered Don Jaime—"timid," as Buñuel describes him—as the proverbial dirty old man.

As we have seen, Don Jaime's space is perverse, revolving around Catholic notions of sin, guilt, and religious sublimation. Viridiana, portrayed as a pure being from the opening shot, thus leaves the convent to enter Don Jaime's corrupt moral universe, where she will be subjected to Don Jaime's fetishistic gaze. The very night of her arrival, for instance, when Viridiana retires to her bedroom, Ramona spies on her through the keyhole.[20] As Viridiana starts to get ready for bed, the camera shows her taking off her novice habit, letting down her hair, and looking at herself in the mirror with a complete lack of vanity. Also, following convent customs, she places the mattress on the floor. Despite Viridiana's de-sexualized attitude toward her own body, the camera shows a close-up of her thighs, a shot that is linked by a straight cut to the face of Don Jaime, who in a state of mystical delirium plays religious music on his old harmonium, visually underlining his sublimating tendencies.

This scene is exemplary of Don Jaime's sublimation due to the displacement of the gaze that structures it. After the shot of Viridiana's thighs, the camera shows her getting up from the bed and heading to the table, where she opens her suitcase in which she keeps a hammer, some nails, and a crown of thorns, standard symbols of Christ's crucifixion, which reminds us of the redeeming power of suffering and the mortification of the flesh which were also central tenets of the Francoist moral universe. Immediately afterwards, Ramona runs to tell Don Jaime what she just saw in Viridiana's room. Here, it is not the act of spying that in itself holds interest, since it is a commonplace in stories about masters and servants, but rather the relayed gaze between Don Jaime and Ramona. Through two close shots of Don Jaime playing the harmonium and Ramona getting ready to spy on Viridiana, the camera conveys the continuity and parallelism of their gazes: both of them look to the lower right corner of the screen. Don Jaime delegates his gaze to Ramona, who has been transformed into a mere extension of her master's gaze. In her description, putting what she saw into words—a process that in itself already suggests the sublimation of matter into spirit—of flesh into language, Ramona focuses on the mortification to which Viridiana subjects her smooth, young skin; this is a vivid description which subtly registers in Don Jaime's face, establishing for the first time in the film the connection between bodily pain and sensual pleasure. The scene ends with a shot of Don Jaime playing his harmonium with renewed devotion after listening to Ramona's account of Viridiana's acts of penance (Fig. 6.5). The film thus clearly establishes a connection between the displacement of desire, via Ramona's verbal account of her scopophilic act, suggesting the repression of the flesh, and its perverted cultural sublimation.

Likewise, Viridiana's body is eroticized again (through the point of view of the camera, which now converges with Don Jaime's gaze) during the sequence of her somnambulant stroll, laden with symbolism. In pure gothic fashion, this sequence opens with a slow pan to the right from the fireplace to a close-up of a carillon wall clock whose chimes we get to hear amid the soundtrack of Handel's "Hallelujah" at precisely two o'clock in the morning. In this sequence—which has no dialogue with the exception of a short "Who is there?"—Don Jaime is caught by his sleepwalking niece during one of his transvestite fetishistic rituals while trying on his wife's wedding shoes and her corset. As her smooth walk—she "glides," according to the script—and white nightgown suggest, Viridiana has become the

Figure 6.5 *Viridiana*, 1961

mansion's ghost in the gothic tradition to which the film pays homage. Given Viridiana's uncanny resemblance to Don Jaime's wife, she becomes her surrogate, another ghost, which, appearing from nowhere, interrupts Don Jaime's nocturnal fetishistic ritual to deliver a message from the depths of the unconscious.

With a basket filled with wool in her hands, Viridiana walks differently in her sleep from the novice Viridiana; she glides like a ghost instead of walking. Don Jaime absorbedly contemplates the scene, which occurs just moments after he tries to conjure the appearance of his dead wife by opening a chest containing her wedding apparel, evoking a similar scene in *Un Chien Andalou* (1929) when a woman tries to resuscitate a man by intensely staring at his suit, which she has laid on the bed. In this sequence, engrossed in the stupor of sleep, Viridiana seems momentarily free from the rigidity of her persona—a sexually repressed novice—as her released hair and gliding walking style suggest. The sleepwalking Viridiana goes to the fireplace and throws the wool into the fire, collecting the ashes from the fireplace and spreading them on the bed where Don Jaime has thrown his wife's wedding bouquet. Her mere presence, as the ghost of the house, as well as her cryptic actions of throwing wool into the fire and spreading the ashes on top of the bed, expose Don Jaime's vain fetishistic attempt to resuscitate his dead spouse in order to satisfy his desire. When discussing with her uncle the following morning the meaning of her actions, Viridiana says to him that typically ashes mean penance or death, which leads him to immediately conclude, "Then it's penance for you who are going to be a nun; and for me, who am old, it's death" (Buñuel 15). As his words reveal, he has clearly misinterpreted the message encoded in his niece's actions, which—as the ashes on top of the bed seem to indicate—expose Don Jaime's futile fetishistic ritual as a melancholic "theater of possession" of his dead wife, by which he believes he controls her.

Wool also has a long symbolic tradition in both the Bible, in which sometimes its whiteness connoting purity was compared with snow (Psalms 147:16) or sins forgiven (Isaiah 1:18), as well as in Greek mythology. In the Bible, wool more generally refers to celestial truth, the truth of good love, which thus contrasts with Don Jaime's narcissistic attachment to his wife. In Buñuel's film, the hank of wool that Viridiana throws into the flames indirectly relates to the story of Penelope from the Odyssey. As we saw in Chapter 1 in the film *Raza*, the stoic mother of the protagonist is portrayed as Spain's Penelope, knitting silently in the family garden, while her husband recounts to his children the epic achievements of his heroic ancestor. In *Raza*, the image of Penelope was used metaphorically to convey Spain's desperate need for a savior, a powerful leader who would put an end to the pillage of the suitors who—as seen in the scene of the Republican parliament full of bickering politicians—were destroying the country. In this sense, Viridiana's throwing of the hank of wool into the fire points to the fact that she, who, as the mother in *Raza*, also allegorizes the Spanish nation, is emphatically putting an end to that fictional narrative by declaring, in cryptic fashion, that the country is not in need of a savior. Furthermore, Penelope's cloth was supposed to be a shroud for her father-in-law, Laertes, thus also hinting at proper burial and letting go, in contrast to Don Jaime's fetishistic ritual designed to keep his dead wife alive.

In this sequence, Viridiana's allegory is made visually explicit by showing the classical attributes of classical female statues, the conventional form of allegory. The scene's visual composition juxtaposes Viridiana's body and the cut-off silhouette of a statue on the hearth reminiscent of a Greek caryatid (Fig. 6.6). The cinematography plays with light and shadow to emphasize the statue's chest, which is silhouetted against the hearth's marble. The shadow cast by the statue is projected toward Viridiana, who is now seated in an armchair, revealing her white, sculptural legs, as if they were a continuation of the statue's torso. Besides being visually allegorized—made to look like a Greek caryatid herself—the novice Viridiana is also clearly eroticized in this shot. However, unlike in the second part of the film, the erotic rendition of Viridiana still falls within the parameters of Don Jaime's cultural sublimation, since Viridiana's female body is associated with Greek classical statuary, whose artistic prestige renders female sexuality culturally permissible.

Figure 6.6 *Viridiana*, 1961

Don Jaime's repeated attempts to "spectrify" his wife, to resuscitate her, have more tangible results in the parodic events of the "wedding night," when, as mentioned earlier, Don Jaime brings a drugged Viridiana to his room. His object of desire seems to physically materialize this time in the voluptuous feminine body of his niece.[21] Don Jaime's failed attempt to "consummate" his marriage, however, perpetuates his melancholy attachments; and, therefore, the vicious cycle of desire-guilt-repression-perversion continues to suffuse his entire estate, which, as Gwynne Edwards notes, is "a cathedral to her memory, the equivalent of Viridiana's convent" (29).[22] In this sense, Don Jaime's melancholic attachment to his wife neatly parallels Francoism's own "cathedral of memory" to an ideal of the nation which, as we already saw in the first part of this study, was also a narcissistically internalized lost object.

Don Jaime's perverse relationship with Viridiana remains strictly sublimated and codified through Christian iconography, while Don Jaime himself also displays—as does Gogol's Chichikov—clear diabolical connotations. He is seductive, friendly, and seemingly inoffensive; however, he uses all means at his disposal—deception, drugs, even suicide—to get what he wants: the total, willful submission of others to him. It is in this diabolical context that the apparently banal scene of Don Jaime offering a piece of fruit to Viridiana reveals its full meaning. Don Jaime's supposedly innocent, nurturing gesture alludes to Satan's temptation of Eve, which, as we saw in previous chapters, was a common subtext of Francoist cinema. In this scene, Don Jaime praises her skills as Viridiana peels an apple and feeds it to him. The long thread of twisted apple skin reminds us of Rita's phallic skipping rope handle and also of the snake into which Satan metamorphosed during his temptation of Eve, a snake which also subtly alludes to St Verdiana's iconographic representation usually with a snake on each side.[23] Don Jaime's gesture of offering Viridiana a bite of the apple that he is eating recalls the act of Eve's temptation, becoming another link in the process of subjectification of Viridiana from novice to fallen woman. However, more than an almighty Satan, Don Jaime—as we saw, a "timid" man in Buñuel's own description—is also a victim of his rigid internalization of Catholic orthodoxy and its notions of guilt and sin. Ultimately, Don Jaime lives and operates in the same sublimated religious space as Viridiana. He is nothing more than her necessary counterpoint: the saintly needs the devilish to sustain itself, just as the "Viridianas" need the "Don Jaimes" to be able to exist.

And, as we saw, Don Jaime's suicide (the supreme act of satanic rebellion against his creator) is a theater of melancholic possession, the only strategy that effectively succeeds in making Viridiana—feeling indebted to the dead patriarch—a prisoner in the house she wants to flee. It is in this context that the seminal role of Rita's skipping rope as a leitmotiv threading the entire narrative could be more productively understood. It signifies the powerful mechanisms of subjection that keep Viridiana and the other characters constrained, unable to free themselves from a repressive, right-wing version of Christian ideology.

In this transitional moment, after Don Jaime has disappeared from the scene[24] but before Jorge has definitively settled in the house, Viridiana has her first opportunity to constitute herself as a free, autonomous subject. Since she has inherited a portion of Don Jaime's estate, she no longer depends on anyone. Undoubtedly, her position has changed; she is not the object of Don Jaime's gaze anymore and, by her own choice, she no longer belongs to the religious community, the de-individualizing collectivity of the convent. Viridiana becomes, at least on a superficial level, the subject of enunciation, now freed from the repressive collectivity of the convent and Don Jaime's perverse moral universe that oppressed her.

However, this moment of Viridiana's apparent liberation, of her constitution as a free subject, is deconstructed by the film's critique of charity, which was one of the main vehicles of moral redemption sought by the Francoist upper classes mocked early on in critically acclaimed films such as *Plácido* (1961) or *La muerte de un ciclista* [*Death of a Cyclist*] (1955). Until now, Viridiana's identity was that of a virgin-novice or that of victim of Don Jaime's perversion, and surrogate of his dead spouse. Viridiana's new identity follows from a social institution developed by the Church and sanctioned by the Spanish King from the sixteenth century: the institution of charity. Believing that she is responsible for Don Jaime's suicide, Viridiana acquiesces to this new social identity, and the suppression of needs and desires it entails, because charity, in the radical Christian way practiced by her, requires sacrificing oneself to the needs of the other.[25] Therefore, despite having abandoned institutionalized religion, as represented by the convent, Viridiana still conducts herself according to Christian religious principles. Only now, paradoxically, she seems to be doing so freely. Thus, Viridiana's new identity also evolves from a process of ideological interpellation, though in this case through the Christian practice of charity.

Despite Buñuel's comments to the contrary, the film criticizes the validity of charity as a futile endeavor that makes its narcissistic practitioners feel temporarily better. It suffices to cite as an example the celebrated scene in which Jorge sees a peasant inhumanely walking his dog by tying it to his wagon. In an impulsive liberating gesture, Jorge buys the dog; meanwhile, he is unaware that another dog tied to another wagon in exactly the same way is passing by behind him. Moreover, Viridiana's charitable project enters into direct conflict with Jorge's plans for modernization. Viridiana and her beggars are a stain, a pathetic anachronism, on Jorge's civilizing project. That is, the film stages the conflict between a world centered on human relations and their transgressions, which is attached to the medieval idea of personal subjection to the master and to the concept of charity, and the world of modern capitalism, represented by Jorge, which revolves around notions of freedom, productivity, rationality, and profit. In contrast to the first part of the film, then, the subjectification of Viridiana no longer derives from the masculine perverted gaze—embodied by Don Jaime—but rather from an ideological-religious discourse that offers Viridiana an imaginary identity: an identity as spectral and as suppressive of feminine desire as Don Jaime wanted for her.

Until this moment, Viridiana's subjectivity has evolved from the asexual subject depicted at the beginning of the film to the eroticized yet sublimated subject of Don Jaime's fetishistic fantasies to the ideal charitable subject. In the last part of the film, Viridiana will finally become a sexualized female subject in accord with Jorge's more practical desires, as the scene of her attempted rape seems to indicate. In this scene, she becomes the victim of the beggar-painter who, as mentioned earlier, used her as the model for his portrait of the Virgin, thus pointing to the undoing of cultural sublimation, in a similar fashion to the beggars' banquet. When the beggar tries to rape her, Viridiana clutches one of the phallic handles of

Figure 6.7 *Viridiana*, 1961

Rita's skipping rope that the beggar is wearing as a belt, and then softly lets go of it (Fig. 6.7). This gesture—unlike her previous resistance to touching the phallic cow's udder—reveals Viridiana's reluctant acceptance/internalization of sexuality, thus ending the process of ideological sublimation that has characterized her as a virginal being.

Over the course of the film, as mentioned earlier, the rope Rita uses for skipping, Don Jaime for hanging himself, and the beggar as a belt suggests the different processes of interpellation mediating Viridiana's subjectivity. In the end, this process leads to her transformation into a sexualized female subject: a transformation that is implicit in the last scene, when Jorge, Ramona, and Viridiana play cards in Jorge's room while rock music plays on the record player in the background instead of the religious Baroque music previously prevalent. Before going to Jorge's room, Viridiana looks at herself with a handheld mirror, partially broken, as she puts on make-up in a clear contrast with the novice Viridiana at the beginning of the film, who meets her own gaze in the mirror with no vanity. Immediately after, a medium shot from behind shows her leaving her room to go to Jorge's bedroom (Fig. 6.8). In this shot, two ropes, their ends tied into a noose, hang from the ceiling, also reminiscent of the two snakes at St Verdiana's sides. As this shot powerfully suggests, and the broken mirror already implied, Viridiana "frees herself" from her old identity by "hanging" herself into a new one; that is, by assuming yet another oppressive role, as symbolized by the noose. That is to say, her new identity as a conventional, sexualized woman derives from her

Figure 6.8 *Viridiana*, 1961

internalization of Jorge's new rules and sexual demands in a space now purged of the anachronisms of melancholy sublimation, charity, and sin. This is a new reality subtly hinted at by Jorge's offer to help Viridiana move her hand to cut the card deck, which echoes the offer of the peasant to move her hand toward the cow's udder, which was loaded with sexual innuendo. Taking her as his lover, Jorge has finally succeeded in "modernizing" and commodifying both Viridiana and Don Jaime's mansion. The end of the transition from Don Jaime's pre-modern world to Jorge's new capitalist order is visually underlined by Rita's symbolic action of tossing Viridiana's crown of thorns into the fire, which, according to the script, "very soon becomes a crown of fire" (Buñuel 83)—an action which also reminds us of Viridiana's throwing of the wool into the fire. As Mercè Ibarz observes, "[i]n the montage, the fiery crown is substituted by a vinyl disk playing a popular rock and roll song on the record player in Jorge's room ..." (10). This match-cut clearly accentuates the transition from a sacred to a profane order. *Viridiana*, the film, can be understood as a political allegory of the contradictions emerging from the process of the historical evolution of Spain during the late 1950s and early 1960s. Viridiana, the character—that "green place" suggested by the word's Latin etymological origins—becomes the *locus amoenus* on which different conflicting discourses try to impose their dominance. Therefore, far from legitimizing the Francoist modernizing project, like some in the exile community had denounced, Buñuel's film reveals the different mechanisms of subjection that characterized different Francoist historical phases. In the end it is Jorge, representing the Spanish bourgeoisie, who is able to transform things just enough to make sure that nothing really changes, thus fulfilling Don Jaime's dream of possessing Viridiana, his true object of desire. In an ironic twist of fate, wanting to understand for himself the true causes of *Viridiana*'s scandal, Franco arranged for a private screening of the film at his presidential palace. Predictably enough, he missed the film's point entirely, just like Don Jaime had missed sleepwalking Viridiana's cryptic message. Unfazed by the film's content, he dismissively declared that he did not understand what all the fuss was about since the film did not amount to anything other than "a series of vulgar jokes strung together."

Notes

1. As Robin Fiddian and Peter Evans have pointed out: "... *Viridiana* looks very much like a microcosm of Spanish society in the 60s: five levels of society are represented through the beggars, or the dispossessed; the peasantry (the labourers on the estate); the proletariat (the workers brought in by the estate's new owner, Jaime's illegitimate son); the church (the convent where Viridiana is a novice); and the landed gentry (Jaime, and eventually his son and Viridiana)" (62).
2. Born Virginia Margaret del Mazziere in Tuscany, Italy (1182–1242).
3. The choice of Fernando Rey for the role of Don Jaime is significant in itself. As Peter Evans lucidly observes: "Rey's meanings, whether formulated through knowledge of the Cifesa or 'New' Cinema roles or exclusively on the basis of his international appearances, evolve from identifications with a contradictory mixture of convention and transgression. In all four Buñuel roles he represents authority. His status as landowner (*Viridiana*), guardian (*Tristana*), ambassador (*Le Charme discret*), or idle wealthy bourgeois (*Cet obscur objet*) emphasizes his identifications with tradition and privilege" (17).
4. Evans mentions this influence in other films by Buñuel: "Bécquer in Spain, but also the other gothic novelists—Lewis, Maturin, and so on—inspired Buñuel to introduce Gothic elements into his own work. *Los olvidados* [*The Young and the Damned*], *Le Charme discret* [*El discreto encanto de la burguesía*], and *Abismos de pasión*—the latter based on *Wuthering Heights*, a text so special to the Surrealists because of its eulogy of *amour fou*—are only three films that recreate the Poe-like atmosphere of deranged reverie and the uncanny in the most unexpected places ..." (7).
5. Jorge's lover is meaningfully named Lucía, reminiscent of the Spanish word *luz*, meaning "light".
6. Much like the choice of Fernando Rey for the role of Don Jaime (see note 3), choosing Francisco Rabal for the role of Jorge evokes a particular message. Peter Evans comments on this matter: "Rabal is a darker, Spanish Richard

Burton: powerful, sensitive, thoughtful, proletarian, hard-living and hard-drinking, and eroticized. All of these qualities are in evidence in his three Buñuel roles ... In *Viridiana* both the dark, sexually self-conscious maid and the fair, frigid novice of desire ultimately capitulate to him. Rabal is perhaps Buñuel's dream of masculinity, a wish-fulfilment of self-confident maleness of the sort to which he himself ... seems drawn as ego-ideal" (93–4).

7. Robin Fiddian and Peter Evans see in this "camera as *coño* ... more than just a typically Buñuelian way of seeking to *épater les bourgeois*. Much more significantly, while recalling Freud's suggestive analysis of scopophilia, the association simultaneously draws attention to Enedina's perspective on life, which is sketchily envisaged as sex-obsessed ... Viridiana, by contrast, at a superficial level sees everything through religion, Jorge through commerce, and Jaime through neurotic obsessions with death" (67).

8. In Lacanian terms, they are the outgrowths of the *real* climbing through the interstices of the *symbolic* and portrayed by Enedina's female sex, the *black hole*, whose brutal exclusion is the origin of subjectivity and culture, but at the same time it constantly threatens with its collapse.

9. For example, the journalist Mirabal wrote, "Little Buñuel, the false genius, is already going to Spain to serve Franco a film ..." (quoted in Colina and Pérez Turrent 157).

10. As Edwards points out, Viridiana's initial whiteness is developed over the course of the film: "[o]ur first glimpse of her in the film's opening sequence emphasizes the whiteness of her habit and the pale perfection of her face, the external manifestation of an innocence and purity as yet untouched by the sinfulness of the world outside the convent. This initial image, with all its associations, is then developed in a number of key sequences in Don Jaime's house" (28).

11. The alteration of the original script confirms our reading. The scene in which Viridiana is seen taking off her tights to reveal her thighs in a close-up shot was originally planned to take place in her convent cell, as she prepares to go to see her uncle. Yet Buñuel preferred to cut it from the convent scenes and insert it later, when Viridiana is already at Don Jaime's house. Without this scene, nothing suggests Viridiana's eroticism at the beginning of the film until confronted with Don Jaime's perverse world.

12. In fact, the film's three main characters—Don Jaime, Viridiana, and Jorge—seem to exemplify all the symptoms Freud ascribes to melancholy: Don Jaime, the acting out of his narcissistic attachment to his dead wife; Viridiana, the self-withdrawal from the world and the constant remorse and self-punishment; while Jorge becomes a model for mania, whose content is for Freud "no different from that of melancholia" (254), as manifested in his need for incessant action.

13. Cristina Moreiras remarks about melancholic subjectivity, "[t]he temporality of the melancholic is emptied out in the experience of the moment lived as eternal. A subject that is linked to his experience from a deep lack of

distinction between past and present because he remains stuck to a memory without an object ... " (*Cultura* 128).
14. As Medina writes, "[t]he 'spectacle' of his death through which the mass media, controlled by the power, aims to maintain a relationship of tutelage beyond death, to impede the process of emancipation that should happen upon the loss of Franco's paternal figure" (Medina 20).
15. Ironically, the real St Verdiana decided to seclude herself in a small cell for thirty-four years after returning from her pilgrimage to Santiago de Compostela, where the body of James, the apostle, is supposed to be buried.
16. Of Rita, Vicente Sánchez-Biosca observes, "[d]espite her wild and innocent appearance, the girl has two dark traits or, rather, Buñuel projects over her two enigmas that will never be revealed. The first has to do with the relationship that connects her to Don Jaime: he gives her a jumping rope as a gift ... and enjoys himself looking at her dirty legs while she jumps. The second has to do with the sudden and incomprehensible role she acquires through her gazing" (41–2).
17. On the other hand, in her article "Entró en mi cuarto un toro negro: la historia en el cine de Buñuel" ("A black bull entered my room: History in Buñuel's cinema"), Ibarz observes that in the film there are "three social and historical stages tied together with this subtle string of relationship, bond, and submission, which correspond to the women in the story: Ramona, Viridiana, and the girlfriend from the city who will be sent away once she no longer has value for Jorge" (10).
18. "The phallus motif occurs again in the form of a cow's teat which Rita urges her to grasp firmly. Viridiana cannot bring herself to do so, her deep-seated fears disguised in nervous laughter" (Edwards 31).
19. The fighting bull is charged with symbolism in Western culture, from the Minotaur of classical mythology that, shut in its labyrinth, devours the virgins who are sacrificed to him, to the symbol of the dark forces of the unconscious in more modern versions. Of course, in Spanish culture the bull has a prominent role both in art and literature. Moreover, the bull hide, because of its resemblance to the map of Spain, has been traditionally seen as a metaphor for the country. In this sense, Mercè Ibarz sees "the black bull of *Viridiana* as the image of history. One of the mythical representations of history contained in Buñuel's films" (2).
20. As Robin Fiddian and Peter Evans have observed, "The film is full of instances of voyeurism, or eavesdropping: Ramona spies on Viridiana as she undresses, her daughter Rita spies on Jaime as he attempts to seduce Viridiana once he has drugged her, the leading beggar is, crucially, blind, and so on" (68).
21. The influence of the gothic novel is obvious in Don Jaime's attempt to be with his dead love at any cost, both through the fetishist ritual and the vicarious resurrection of his lover through his niece's body. Thus, as Raymond Durgnat has pointed out, Don Jaime is reminiscent of Heathcliff in *Wuthering*

Heights: "Don Jaime as a lover is here as steadfast, as tragic as Heathcliff plundering Cathy's tomb in *Cumbres borrascosas* [*Wuthering Heights*]" (quoted in Edwards 39–40, note 4).

22. The house is described in this way: "At night it is filled with the sound of sacred music, played either by himself on the harmonium or in the form of gramophone records. Furthermore, the dead woman's clothing, preserved by Don Jaime, has become over the years the equivalent of religious relics, gazed upon, touched, even worn by him in a kind of sacred ritual; the counterpart of Viridiana's religious objects. When she assumes the bridal gown, she becomes in effect a reincarnation of the dead woman and, as he gazes at her on the bed, the candles around it suggest a shrine at which he worships" (Edwards 29).
23. Two snakes were supposed to enter through her small window and live with her, eat her food and bite her flesh, adding to her sacrificial torment.
24. In any case, despite Don Jaime's physical departure and Jorge's profound changes to the property, Buñuel often winks at the audience about the subjacent continuity from one stage to the next. As we have already seen, one of these winks is the sequence in the attic when Jorge recycles Don Jaime's objects. The other, as Robin Fiddian and Peter Evans have pointed out, is the portrait of Don Jaime that now hangs on the wall of the dining room: "[t]here is a superb irony in Jaime's suicide, for just as in life he had been possessed by a dead woman, so now with Jaime departed, but with his portrait symbolically very firmly placed in its cultural/ideological context, Viridiana and her cousin are very much controlled or haunted by a dead man" (70).
25. St Verdiana was characterized by her radical understanding of charity and by her love for the poor, whom she often fed through the small window of her cell.

CHAPTER 7

Balada triste de trompeta:
Of Ghosts and Clowns

In the work of mourning, it is not grief that works: grief keeps watch
—Maurice Blanchot, *The Writing of the Disaster*

Balada triste de trompeta [*The Last Circus*] (2010), Álex de la Iglesia's ninth feature film, recasts Francoist melancholy in a neo-Baroque, mournful light. As we saw in the previous chapter through Buñuel's *Viridiana*, Francoist melancholy served as a repressive political tool aiming to recreate the imagined glory of Spain's imperial past. Instead, *Balada* resorts to neo-Baroque aesthetics to mourn the victims of Spain's traumatic past.

In Sophocles's tragedy *Antigone*, Antigone dies in her attempt to give a proper burial to her brother Polyneices in defiance of Creon's edict. Polyneices had died during Thebes's Civil War against his brother Eteocles, who also died in battle. Unlike his brother who, celebrated as a hero, was buried with honors, Polyneices was declared a traitor of the state by Creon and left unburied on the battlefield.[1] Franco's treatment of Republicans during the Spanish Civil War and in its aftermath tragically resembles Creon's treatment of Polyneices. Deemed traitors to the state, Republican victims of Franco were denied proper burial and ceremonial mourning. In fact, many of them—including internationally renowned poet Federico García Lorca—still lie in unmarked mass graves scattered throughout the country. Antigone's choice of pursuing a moral law higher than Creon's political decree to provide a dignified burial for her brother—resulting in her death—powerfully resonates in Spain's stubborn unwillingness to properly mourn her dead.

In Spain, the political transition to democracy during the late 1970s and early '80s was based on what was referred to as *el Pacto del Olvido* (the Pact of Forgetting). While instrumental in securing a peaceful transition from dictatorship to democracy, the Pact of Forgetting came at a cost. The price Spain paid for "closing the books" on its violent past was to leave large sectors of the Francoist administration, the judiciary as well as the police and the military virtually intact. An unwelcome by-product of the Pact was that the official Francoist narrative of the past—a narrative developed during the forty years of Franco's dictatorship, which gravely distorted Spain's historical record in order to legitimize its fascist past—remained unchanged and unchallenged.[2] Francoist official memory is still in place—its monuments stand in many parts of the country—secured by forty years of official sanctioning. Republican memory, however, has been relegated to the private domain of the family and to the scholarly work of historians, which, due to a lack of state backing, has been unable to constitute a powerful counter-narrative.[3] So while Francoists have been able to openly mourn their dead, Republicans have been denied the right to do so.

It is the Pact's very regulation of Spain's relation to the past that helps explain why many cultural representations of the last four decades—ranging from literature to film and photography—have dealt obsessively with the ghosts of that past.[4] *Balada* is one of these works. Like Antigone, it wants to give proper burial to the dead and mourn Spain's tragic past.[5] *Balada*, nominated for fifteen Goya awards, the most prestigious Spanish film honor, is the director's most personal film to date, which he wrote on his own without the services of Jorge Gerricaechevarría, his habitual collaborator and childhood friend. Often dismissed as a film that proposes a bland form of national reconciliation to overcome Spain's traumatic past, *Balada*, I argue, makes an important contribution to the ongoing debate about how to deal with the ghosts of Spain's recent past through a re-elaboration of the theme of the sad clown, a traditional motif of kitsch aesthetics.[6]

The goal of this chapter is to examine *Balada*'s ethical gesture of opening the door to ghosts, based on its recognition of the act of mourning as a moral category.[7] Mourning here should be understood as a social and historical process of critically engaging with the past, and not a quiet remembrance of private grief without social and historical repercussions—not, that is, as a form of complacent silence that closes the door to the past.

This politics of mourning owes much to Derrida's concept of "hauntology," which envisions both a spectral notion of the self radically opened to the alterity of others and a non-teleological concept of time; that is, a multi-layered, non-linear conception of time which, like the self, is also traversed by the ghosts of the past and the potentialities of the future (*Specters of Marx* 20). Derrida's concept of hauntology helps clarify *Balada*'s critique of the idea that, conventionally, justice comes about only with revenge, an idea embedded in Francoist teleological historical narratives. Francoism legitimized itself, as we saw in the previous chapters, by arrogating to itself the role of avenging angel charged with setting the time right, with putting Spain back on the "right" track after the historical derailment caused by the revolutionary chaos of the Second Republic. Through this teleological concept of history, Francoism claimed to bring stability and prosperity back to Spain.[8] In contrast to how Spain attempted to move on after Franco, justice as mourning empathically invites the ghosts of the past to freely and openly appear alongside us.

Balada follows the dramatic transformation of the main character, Javier, from a sad clown to an avenging angel. Javier is the son of a happy clown who, having fought in the Civil War on the Republican side, was imprisoned and forced to work—like tens of thousands of Republican soldiers—in the construction of the Valley of the Fallen, Franco's monumental mausoleum on the outskirts of Madrid. After trying to liberate his father in an unsuccessful sabotage operation at the Valley's construction site, Javier finds a job in a circus controlled by Sergio, a successful, happy clown adored by children, who is also a sadist involved in a physically abusive relationship with Natalia, a femme fatale Javier falls for. To free Natalia from Sergio's grip and win her over, he assaults the abusive clown with a trumpet, horribly disfiguring his face. To Javier's surprise (he considered his act to be gallant and heroic), Natalia rejects him, horrified at the savagery of Javier's attack against Sergio. After being rejected, and following his late father's plea for revenge, which he hears in a dream, as well as being prompted by a vision of Natalia as the Virgin Mary, he transforms himself from a sad clown into an angel of death, determined to avenge his father and himself, and thereby fulfilling his destiny.

The movie is in this way an allegory arguing against revenge and in favor of properly burying the dead and thereby mourning Spain's traumatic past, even while it understands mourning not simply as a ritual necessary to leave the past behind but as a "creative process mediating a hopeless relationship between loss and history," to use David L. Eng's and David Kanzanjian's definition of the politics of mourning (2). By attending to the remains of the past in the present, they argue, one can generate "a politics of mourning that might be active rather than reactive, prescient rather than nostalgic, abundant rather than lacking, social rather than solipsistic, militant rather than reactionary" (2). *Balada* suggests mourning to be an ongoing historical and social process of dealing with loss—loss not only understood as a psychological category, but, as Judith Butler explains in her afterword to *Loss*, also encompassing the social and the political (467).[9] Instead of being pathologically fixated on the past, like in Francoist cinema, *Balada* opens the door to the ghosts of the past in order not only "to remember them sorrowfully," as the etymological definition of mourning would have it, but also to engage "in an ongoing and open relationship with the past," so as to never forget it (Eng and Kanzanjian 4).

Balada's visual style goes into overdrive to make its allegorical point. It draws on the aesthetics of the *Trauerspiel* ("mourning play"), the allegorical German Baroque drama that, according to Walter Benjamin, was influenced by Spanish playwright Calderón de la Barca (81). These were dramas characterized, like *Balada*, by a melodramatic tone, a depiction of courtly politics, the downfall of a sovereign, and a "crude emphasis on violence, suffering and death."[10]

De la Iglesia's Baroque, visually saturated sensibility, which displays the main features of what Cuban writer Severo Sarduy characterizes as neo-Baroque aesthetics—parody, condensation, substitution, proliferation, intertextuality, and what he calls "textual erotics"—strives to keep the spectator dazed and confused, experiencing a sort of aesthetic vertigo. His films also produce a kind of semantic vertigo by alluding to a wide range of cultural references—from high to pop culture—and wildly mixing film genres and literary sources. This dazzling display of styles and narrative sources does not simply constitute a postmodern pastiche but is filtered through de la Iglesia's personal, critical vision of reality.

As Pedro Almodóvar did during the early 1980s, de la Iglesia in these ways also engaged in a camp reappropriation of clichéd Spanish motifs from the 1990s onwards. As I argued in a previous study on the cinema of Almodóvar, camp aesthetics was the main strategy deployed by the most influential Spanish artists during the Spanish political transition to liberate the Francoist iconographic repertoire both from the ideological grip of the right and the disdain of the left. Resorting to irony as a main weapon, camp artists recycled Francoist kitsch parodically and mixed it with a vast array of styles prevalent in popular Western culture—from melodrama to pop art to punk aesthetics—imbuing it with new meaning. It was through this aesthetic cocktail—which mixed the artists' own personal styles with recognizable Spanish motifs—that the most influential artists of the Spanish transition were able to contribute to the international artistic arena without becoming mere imitators of foreign trends—and, more importantly, to critique Francoism.

Álex de la Iglesia was a protégé of Pedro Almodóvar, whose own production company, *El Deseo*, financed his first feature film, *Acción mutante*, a low-budget science fiction/horror/comedy film. Sixteen years younger that Almodóvar, de la Iglesia became one of Spain's most successful young film directors at the box office. His film aesthetic is inspired by comic books and various mainstream film genres, ranging from screwball comedy to horror and science fiction. It is also inspired by Almodóvar's own earlier films and by the Spanish black humor comedies of the 1950s. But, unlike Almodóvar's cinema, whose earlier ironic punch was replaced by what could be described as a visually refined high camp cinematic style veering towards the melodramatic, de la Iglesia has continuously opted for a more provocative and daring ironic film aesthetic, which strikes a balance between the serious and the frivolous, comedy and horror, highbrow and lowbrow. As various critics have observed, his films are a high adrenaline turbo mix of genres and aesthetic traditions: from the comic books of Hergé, Tardi, or Guido Crepax to the films of George Lucas, Alfred Hitchcock, Luis Buñuel, or Ingmar Bergman.[11]

Balada, I will show, not only draws from this wild mix of genres, and from a wide range of prestigious literary and film subtexts—particularly Shakespeare's *Hamlet* (1603) and Hitchcock's *Vertigo* (1958)—but also from the more traditional circus characters originating in commedia dell'arte, particularly Pierrot, Clown, and Columbine.[12] Through all this, the film proposes an allegorical reading of Spain under Francoism. De la Iglesia's Baroque sensibility explains his preference for the allegorical mode through which he is able to simultaneously explore the particularities of his dark, ex-centric characters, while at the same time commenting on Spain's larger historical themes. His use of allegory is filtered through late Goya's distorted images and Valle-Inclán's literary *esperpentos*, distorted mirrors both artists held to the world in order to represent it more accurately.

The text the movie most depends on for creating its allegory is *Hamlet*. As in *Hamlet*, the father is murdered in *Balada*—here by Francoists, of which Sergio, the sadist clown, is a clear allegorical representation—and the new tyrannical despot, like Claudius in *Hamlet*, sleeps with the protagonist's "mother," who is also complicit in the parricide. And, as in *Hamlet*, Javier's father reappears as a ghost to ask his son for revenge, as a victim demanding reparations. As he tells Javier, "revenge is the only way to be happy [...] the only way to escape your destiny." And as in *Hamlet*, in *Balada* the degrading moral consequences of revenge are also explored.

Balada, I argue, proposes a form of mourning and justice that serves as a radical critique of the Francoist notion of justice as revenge disguised as Christian moral redemption. *Balada* not only implicitly unmasks Francoist notions of justice as redemptive violence; it also criticizes the rigid social polarities solidified by forty years of dictatorship. In its critique of Christian redemption and political revenge, the film proposes a structural moral realignment of Spanish society in order to leave behind the old idea of the two Spains, a fratricidal society on the verge of self-destruction, as visually captured in paintings such as Goya's *Duelo a garrotazos* (1823), which constitutes one of the main visual references for the film. *Balada* wants to do away with the confusion of not knowing who is buried where so that mourning can do its work, because, as Javier tells Natalia inside the Valley of the Fallen as he kicks one of the skulls surrounding them, "one of these *could* be my father."

To provoke what he thought at the time to be a complacent Spanish film establishment, de la Iglesia famously declared that his films would never talk about the Civil War, adapt a prestigious literary source, or re-create childhood traumas: the three main traits of the critically acclaimed films in Spain of the 1980s and 1990s. By his own admission, *Balada* transgresses all three of his self-imposed cinematic rules; it addresses the Civil War, it deals with childhood traumas, and although it does not directly adapt a prestigious literary source, consciously or not, it draws from prestigious literary and cinematic sources including, as we saw, Baroque drama and Shakespeare's *Hamlet*, but also Mark's Gospel, Hitchcock's *Vertigo* and *North by Northwest* (1959), and Marcel Carné's *Les Enfants Du Paradis* [*Children of Paradise*] (1945).[13]

Balada traces the protagonist's transformation from sad clown to avenging angel against the background of Spanish history, from the Civil War to the end of Francoism. It pays special homage to popular culture—particularly popular music and television programs—a pseudo-official kitsch culture closely monitored by Franco's censors, which features prominently from the opening credits to the closing of the film. Echoing Hitchcock's *Vertigo*, the film reaches its climax at the top of the gigantic cross of the Valley of the Fallen, from which Natalia leaps to her death to save Javier from Sergio's blows. It is through the catharsis brought on by Natalia's death that the film symbolically reclaims Franco's monumental burial site as an entry point for the proper burial of the dead and mourning in Spain. The film comes to an end with the two clowns—the happy one and the sad one—facing each other inside a police van, sobbing uncontrollably for the death of Natalia, the object of their love. The last shot is a medium close-up of the faces of the two clowns, whose expressions change subtly, tears gradually mixing in with laughter, in a crescendo in which we are no longer sure if they are crying or laughing. This shot emphasizes the structural resemblances of opposites, of the two clowns as eternal nemeses, and suggests that despite their fierce antagonism both end up mourning for Natalia's death, Spain's allegorical representation.

Balada begins with a brief sequence set in Madrid in 1936, at the onset of the Spanish Civil War, thus firmly anchoring the film in Spain's traumatic past. Here we first encounter Javier as a child mesmerized by his father's clown routine. In order to distract their young audience, after the performance is suddenly interrupted by the sound of the fascist bombardment of the capital, the two clowns resort to their signature act: the "opening of the door" routine, which metaphorically refers to the major conflict which will engulf the country for almost three years. Through the fake circus door first enter the fascists, as suggested by one of the clowns getting his face painted blue—the traditional Falangist color—and immediately after the "reds," led by a militia commander, burst through the real door to interrupt the clown act.[14] The opening sequence clearly suggests that the traumatic conflict has invaded the innocent space of the circus primarily filled with children. The "opening of the door" act the clowns employ as an imaginary safety space to keep the children calm—a fantasy screen, as it were, first proposed by Javier's father, the happy clown—proves however to be a failed attempt at keeping conflict at bay since the traumatic conflict still comes in through both doors. It is the "opening of the door" as a moral act, not as an escapist kitsch blindfold against historical trauma, which the film proposes as a way to deal with traumatic loss. The film, I will argue, reflects on "what it would mean to open the door again", and to prolong "the moment of the opening of the door" to the ghosts of the past.

The appearance of a Republican militia officer who, in the name of the legendary communist general Enrique Líster, bursts in through the door to recruit the performing clowns "and anyone else who wants to follow [him]" for the Republican cause, mocks the infamous lack of military discipline within Republican quarters, as well as the lack of adequate training and equipment on the Republican side. In the following sequence, the most threatening militiaman in the assault on the Francoists is Javier's father who, still dressed as a clown in female garb and swinging a machete with lethal fury, inflicts serious harm on an entire Francoist battalion.[15]

The sequence ends with a shot of a helpless Javier alone against a dimly lit background. Seconds later, a circus lion joins him to keep him company. This is an image reminiscent of Mark the Evangelist's traditional iconography, usually represented with a lion beside him. Mark's Gospel—considered by many scholars to be a drama which, like *Balada*, draws from multiple literary sources—ends abruptly with the sight of Jesus's empty tomb, from which the women "fled from [...] for terror and amazement had seized them; and they said nothing to anyone, for they were afraid" (*Holy Bible* 56). Mark's Gospel's subtext is underlined by the recurring appearance of Mark's bust (and the lion) throughout the movie. Mark's head appears not only in Javier's dreams, as when Javier needs to climb the Evangelist's giant headstone in order to get to Natalia, but also at the beginning of the film, at the Valley's construction site, and at the end of the film, when Javier and Natalia climb the headstone in order to access the cross as they run away from Sergio. The subtle reference to Mark's Gospel, which for modern Bible scholars is considered to be firmly inscribed in the eschatological tradition of the messianic secret of Jesus in the ends of time, lends a sense of apocalyptic urgency to the narrative's exploration of Spanish history, while also underlining the film's main theme: the proper burial of the dead.[16] The reference to Mark's Gospel thus calls subliminal attention to the "fear of the empty tomb" and to the subsequent ghostly apparition of Jesus to his followers. The spectral apparition of Jesus to seek acknowledgment from his followers, so that he can finally vanish, contrasts, as we will see, with the ghost of Hamlet's father, who comes back to demand revenge. The former preaches a form of justice based not on forgetting but on forgiveness, while the latter offers a form of justice that avenges the past, that sets "time back right." This polarity is overcome by *Balada*'s understanding of mourning as an active process that engages critically with the ghosts of the past.

The ghosts of the past first appear in the movie in the guises of well-known monsters and villains—Dracula, Frankenstein's monster, the Werewolf, the Phantom of the Opera and Fu Manchu—in the credit sequence following the battle scene that sets the historical coordinates of the film and visually underlines its theme of revenge disguised as Christian redemption. In *Balada*, as Jo Labanyi has observed for other Spanish contemporary narratives, the ghosts of the past appear in their menacing, vengeful forms—as "victims demanding reparation"—because the past has not been properly mourned (66).

The credit sequence neatly condenses the entire history of Francoism, from the brutally repressive, murderous Francoism of the aftermath of the Civil War and the onset of the Second World War, to the relatively softer version of Francoism that evolved in the late 1950s onwards until another spike in violent political repression occurred from 1969 until Franco's death in 1975.[17] It contains a large series of still images, which appear on the screen as background to the rolling film credits, as we also saw in the case of the opening of *Franco, ese hombre*, examined in Chapter 5, visually summarizing the film's intention to recuperate Spain's historical collective memory which was put on hold by the Pact of Forgetting. This series of images is set to the musical chords of a saeta, a mournful flamenco-inflected song traditionally played in the public processions of Spain's Holy Week (Easter). Unlike *Franco, ese hombre*, however, in which the still photographs replicate the format of a family photo album to project a mood of political and social normalcy by mixing Franco's official appearances as head of state with his private family moments, *Balada*'s credit sequence is designed to evoke the darker side of Francoism.

The editing of the sequence advances rhythmically to the musical chords of the saeta and is meant to elicit a powerful, mournful, emotional response from the spectator. The series opens with a few shots of details of the Falange's red-and-black banner, each respectively intercut by a headshot of the three main characters: Javier, Sergio, and Natalia, followed by two headshots of the Virgin Mary as *Mater Dolorosa*, a shot of the giant headstone of Mark the Evangelist sculpted in the Valley of the Fallen, and by two shots of details of Grünewald's Crucifixion—Christ's nailed feet at the cross and Christ's agonizing face. The Grünewald's Crucifixion shots are followed by the infamous Francoist eagle printed on the Spanish currency, by a dramatic shot of the giant cross at the Valley of the Fallen, filmed bottom-up to emphasize its sheer size, and by a close-up shot of Grünewald's painting representing a detail of the crowds witnessing the Crucifixion of Christ. Finally, the title of the film, *Balada triste de trompeta*—referring to a sentimental song about a "dying past" performed by Raphael, Spain's renowned musical kitsch icon, which features prominently in the film's narrative—is superimposed on an old map of the Iberian Peninsula, indicating the former imperial glory Franco frequently evoked.

This opening serves the purpose of introducing us to the film's main characters and to Spain's dark Francoist past, both of which are woven into the main Christian narrative theme of the Crucifixion. The overarching Christian theme of redemption through sacrifice is visually connected—via the gigantic cross of the Valley of the Fallen—to its Francoist ideological reinterpretation, the Francoist special brand of *nacional-catolicismo* characterized by its sadomasochistic violent overtones and its "politics of revenge", as Paul Preston calls it, that ultimately defined the regime.[18] Franco's ideological petrification of reality, as we saw in Chapter 1, is perfectly crystalized in the monumental architecture of the Valley of the Fallen, Franco's burial site, directly excavated from the rock and Spain's most controversial *Lieux de Mémoire*, which appropriately provides the location for the climactic final scene of the movie.

This brief set-up is followed by a series of shots of strictly Francoist motifs: Franco haranguing his troops; Nationalist soldiers arresting Republican militiamen; Franco being given the fascist salute by the members of the Spanish *Cortes*; and a dramatic shot of a photograph of Francoist fighter planes writing Franco's name in the sky on the upper part of the photograph, while on its lower part fascist soldiers carry coffins of the dead. This series comes to an end with a shot of a defiant Millán

Astray, the eye-patched, sinisterly charismatic founder of the Foreign Legion and mentor of the young Franco in Morocco. Reminiscent of the close-up of the eye in the opening of *Vertigo*, in which the camera, as also in *Pan's Labyrinth*, seems to spiral down to the other side of consciousness, here it rapidly zooms in on Millán Astray's portrait to pass through his eye socket to take us to the other side: the even darker side of Spanish history, filled with images of clowns, monsters, fascist leaders, Francoist politicians, and religious figures. These images range from photographs of the famous meeting of Franco and Hitler at Hendaye to discuss the possible entry of Spain into the Second World War, to images of female corpses hanging from butcher's hooks from Spanish gore film *Holocausto Caníbal*—reminiscent of Charles Perrault's "Bluebeard" (1697), which, as we will see, is one of the multiple intertexts of the film—to images of famous Spanish clowns like Tonetti and classic monsters and film villains such as Frankenstein's monster, Dracula, the Werewolf, and Fu Manchu, which are all interspersed with images of Francoist politicians such as Fraga Iribarne and Arias Navarro, and religious figures such as Father José María Llanos, Franco's personal confessor later turned communist militant. The series ends with a rapid montage of iconic Spanish TV personalities of the 1960s and '70s comprised of several shots including those of the Eurovision Song Contest winner Massiel, international sex icon Raquel Welch in her famous role in *One Million Years B.C.*, critically acclaimed Spanish humorists Tip y Coll, and the television comedy troupe *Los Chiripitifláuticos*. The final series alludes to Spain's rapid modernization during the 1960s, as suggested by various shots of tourists sunbathing on Spain's crowded beaches. Tourism, of course, was part and parcel of the "Spanish miracle," the economic boom made possible by the protective umbrella of the United States, as a shot of a young Ronald Reagan dancing with a flamenco dancer clearly suggests. The credit sequence closes with an homage to the work of iconic figures Chicho Ibañez Serrador and Antonio Mercero, two of Spain's television producers who in the early 1970s pushed the envelope of the possible in the sluggish Spanish television of the period with their daring programming style.[19]

The entire credit sequence combines historical figures with fictional ones culled from both the Western popular cultural imaginary and the more idiosyncratic Spanish pop culture of the Francoist era, which from the 1960s onwards became prevalent due to the rapid development of Spanish television.[20] The striking appearance of monsters and film villains alongside real historical characters points toward a rich fictional space at the interstices of memory, a symptomatic dark side, as it were, in which the symbolic imagination attempts an imaginary resolution of Spain's traumatic social contradictions. More simply put, the scary monsters represent the return of the repressed of history who haunt the living in their ghostly, monstrous form. They are "the victims of history" who, in disguised form, "return to demand reparation; that is that their name instead of being erased, be honored" (Labanyi 66). "The victims of history" are also the tormentors who threaten the imagination of the living with their grotesque forms.

The scene of Javier's bombing of the Valley's construction site in order to liberate his father—which opens the narrative, echoing the credit sequence just described—also helps sets the film's allegorical entryway to the darker side of Francoism. In the bombing sequence, a colonel mounted on a horse kills Javier's father by making the horse repeatedly strike his face. As a result of the commotion caused by the explosion of the dynamite set by Javier inside a tunnel, however, the fascist colonel loses his right eye when he is violently taken down from his horse by a Republican prisoner. The one-eyed colonel reminds us of the shot of Millán Astray, the legendary one-eyed fascist general founder of the Spanish Foreign Legion and author of its "Long live Death" slogan, whose photograph we saw in the credit sequence. In that opening shot, as we saw, the camera zooms in to pass through his empty eye socket to give us access to the darker side of history, which is populated by monsters. Similarly, the colonel's loss of the eye inside the tunnel in the bombing sequence suggests an entrance into an allegorical narrative mode; the more stylized narrative space of the circus, which is also populated by allegorical figures, including monsters and villains, alongside the main characters—Natalia, Sergio, and Javier.

In *Balada*, the circus itself and its power structure is an allegorical representation of Spain under Francoism. Sergio, the sadistic clown, who became a clown because, by his own admission, he otherwise would have become a murderer, represents a brutal dictator. Through violence and financial intimidation, he maintains complete control over the circus, overpowering its legal owner, who, admittedly, is scared to do anything about it because he desperately depends on Sergio's popularity for financial gain. Sergio's fascist character is mocked when he kicks two "dwarfs"—a traditional staple of any circus—out of his trailer after firing them because, as he complains, "Damn it, I'm sick of fucking midgets! Their bowed legs and oversized heads. Jesus!" Sergio claims to be in love with Natalia but he keeps abusing her. The extent of the abuse is made patently clear in the diner scene examined below in which Sergio brutally beats her. When Javier explicitly asks Natalia after the beating if Sergio behaves like this toward her often, she replies, "Only when he drinks," which, as she immediately confesses, is every night.

The circus's three different physical locations throughout the film represent the different stages of the evolution of Francoism. At the beginning, the circus is located on the outskirts of Madrid, as it would be typical of circuses touring Spain's major cities. However, coinciding with the years of Sergio's dominance, the urban landscape surrounding the circus tents is in utter ruin, a reminder of Spain's Civil War landscape. After Sergio is violently assaulted by Javier in 1973—Franco died in 1975—in order to avoid financial ruin, the owner takes Natalia and most of his crew members to perform inside a music hall called Kojak, in honor of the famous American series of the 1970s with Telly Savalas in the role of a tough American detective, which was a huge hit on Spanish television. Finally, toward the end of the film, the entire circus without Sergio—animals included—finds temporary housing at the Valley of the Fallen, inside the belly of the beast, as it were, where Javier has constructed a personal memorial, reminiscent of Maria's shrine to her beloved Diego in Almodóvar's *Matador* (1986).

Balada's allegorical tale of political revenge is structured as a classical Oedipal story.[21] As the events of the movie attain a deeper level of meaning if read allegorically to refer to Spain's recent history, the Oedipal dynamics underlying the psychological motivation of the main characters also gain sharper focus when understood as embodying the historical conflict between the "two Spains" that have characterized Spain's modern history: the triangle between Javier, Natalia, and Sergio obviously alludes to the power struggle between the despotic patriarch and his repressed "adopted" son for the love of Natalia, Spain's allegorical representation. Javier, who is motherless from the beginning of the movie, becomes an orphan after his father is brutally murdered by the fascist colonel during his son's failed attempt to rescue him from forced labor at the site of the Valley of the Fallen. Following in his grandfather's and father's footsteps, he joins a circus as a sad clown because, as his father tells him, "You were robbed of your childhood by the war, so you will never be able to make people laugh." Javier, his own name deriving from the Basque *Etxeberri*, meaning "new house," is now a homeless child looking for a new home. The circus becomes a surrogate family ready to adopt him. In the circus, as mentioned above, Javier becomes entangled in a classic Oedipal triangular relationship with Natalia and Sergio. In his psychic imagination, Javier associates Natalia, a Latin word referring to Christmas Day (to the birth of Christ), with the Virgin Mary in her role as *Mater dolorosa*. This link is also established by the film itself, which, as we saw, juxtaposes still shots of Natalia and the Virgin Mary in the credit sequence. Natalia will be, however, not only a *Mater Dolorosa* for Javier but also a surrogate incestuous mother, who treats him as if he were a baby—affectionately pulling his chubby cheeks while mockingly calling him *mi chiquitín* ("my little thing")—but whom she also attempts to seduce on numerous occasions. In turn, Natalia will be Javier's object of desire with whom he falls in love at first sight, like Scottie does with Madeleine in Hitchcock's *Vertigo*. Finally, Sergio, whose name, ironically, is etymologically linked to the words "protector" and "guardian", becomes the terrifying, castrating father. He physically harms Javier, and symbolically castrates him both onstage (in the act they perform together) but also offstage, as when, after catching him with Natalia in an amusement park, he beats Javier so brutally that he needs to be hospitalized.

The Oedipal tensions of the film reach a dramatic climax early on in the sequence of the first dinner that Javier shares with several members of the circus crew. Immediately after Javier's arrival, Sergio proceeds to tell a joke about a father who is anxiously waiting in a maternity ward for his wife to give birth. After a while, a nurse comes with a baby in her arms and passes him along to the father. While the father is affectionately looking at his baby, the nurse takes the child away and, without further explanation, smashes the baby repeatedly against the father's face—while Sergio imitates the nurse by smashing a grilled chicken against the diner's large glass window. The father, desperately crying, tells the nurse, "You've killed my baby, you've killed my baby," to which the nurse calmly replies, "No, no, it was already dead at birth." Sergio's punch line is greeted with enthusiastic laughter by the members of the crew seated at the table, with the exception of Javier, who remains impassive. A visibly irritated Sergio asks him why he is not laughing. Javier admits to not understanding the joke. "Where is the mother?" he replies, deadpan. Humiliated at Javier's perceived personal offense in front of the crew, Sergio throws a violent fit, shouting uncontrollably. As he reminds everyone, "I decide what's funny around here. I'm the clown! The kids come to see me. I'm your meal ticket, assholes! Me!" After eventually calming down, Sergio blames Javier for making him lose his temper. As he tells everyone, a perfectly harmonious dinner "goes to shit because some idiot doesn't get the joke." And menacingly staring at Javier, he concludes: "There is NO MOTHER, you got that?"

The joke's violent punch line is a typical example of what is often referred to as Spanish black humor, characterized by its crude tone and bleak, dark vision of reality. As Juan F. Egea writes in *Dark Laughter* (2013), his book on Spanish comedy and the nation, "who gets the joke and who doesn't is the benchmark for measuring the possible communal and hence exclusionary properties of film genres" (10). Javier's not getting the joke, characteristic of typical Spanish "black humor," immediately positions him outside the group, an outsider whose resistance to accepting the code is perceived as a subversive act by Sergio.[22]

This scene—which clearly follows the model of the scary-psychotic-clownish-thug made famous by Joe Pesci in Martin Scorsese's *Goodfellas* (1990)—also gives greater emphasis to the fact that Javier is a motherless child. In fact, Javier's lack of mother serves as the narrative structuring absence suffusing his relationship with Natalia with forbidden Oedipal desire. When Natalia, encouraged by Javier's resistance to laugh, also objects to the joke as not being funny, Sergio hits her and savagely kicks her. Javier is now subjected to the whim of a hostile substitute father, a brutal clown adored by children who has become a clown because, in his own words, otherwise "I would be a murderer." Javier is completely alone in the world. His own father is dead and "there is NO MOTHER." Sergio—like *Hamlet*'s Claudius married to his brother's wife—is now the usurper to the throne, the brutal despot (and surrogate father) who controls the circus affairs through a mixture of sheer physical force and psychological and financial intimidation, because, as he reminds the real circus owner on one occasion, "the public comes to see me."

For Javier, the Oedipal tension reaches a painful climax in the next scene, in which a drunken Sergio returns to the diner—the scene of the crime—to pick up Natalia. Javier has also gone back to the diner in order to take care of her. Upon seeing Sergio arriving, Natalia rushes out of the restaurant so as not to be seen with Javier. Through the large window against which Sergio had smashed the chicken while telling the joke, Javier sees the two of them making up. Sergio apologizes to Natalia for having hit her and begins to seduce her. Natalia is seemingly aroused, and the two of them proceed to have rough sex, pressing Natalia's breasts against the diner's window. Javier, hidden from view on the other side of the glass, listens to the scene unfold, intrigued and terrified as the proverbial Freudian child witnessing the primal scene. Panic-stricken and squatting down on the floor, Javier whispers to himself, "Please don't hurt her. Don't hurt her." Sergio's previous assertion that there is no mother, thus, is suddenly put into question. There is a mother, but she is being violated by the abusive stepfather. And, as the grease stain left by the smashed chicken against the window reminds us, the baby is not literally dead but severely traumatized, impotently crying on the other side, "robbed of his childhood" as Javier's father told him, much like most of the Republican children living in postwar Francoist Spain. Unbeknown to Javier, however, the camera eroticizes the entire scene as a sadomasochistic sex act in which Natalia also plays the role of femme fatale, a seductive role she will also play toward Javier in the first half of the movie. The shot fades out while for an instant we hear children's laughter in the background, an ironic aural counterpoint to Javier's loss of innocence after witnessing the primal scene.

It is through the Oedipal family drama, thus, that the movie explores the aftermath of Spain's Civil War, a fratricidal war whose psychic scars branded a generation of children effectively robbed of their childhood; the same children that at the beginning of the film were innocently watching the clowns perform. The scene also suggests that Natalia—the allegorical representation of the country—is somewhat complicit in her own abuse. That is, it implies that large sectors of Spanish society encouraged and supported Franco's rule, thereby becoming responsible for contributing to the political repression.

From this moment on, the film walks a thin line between the private sphere of Oedipal family dynamics and the public sphere of politics. As mentioned earlier, *Balada* draws substantially from Shakespeare's *Hamlet*, for Freud a quintessential Oedipal narrative, and, as Simon Critchley and Jamieson Webster remind us, a play that accurately describes what it feels like to live under a totalitarian regime (48). From the private domain of the family, *Hamlet*'s subtext carries us into the public sphere of politics. From the "rotten kingdom of Denmark," we are directly plunged into Franco's rotten dictatorship in Spain. And, as in *Hamlet*, as we will see soon, in *Balada* the degrading moral consequences of revenge are also explored. As in *Hamlet*, in *Balada* the father has also been murdered—here by Francoism, allegorically represented by Sergio—and the new tyrannical despot, like Claudius in *Hamlet*, sleeps with the protagonist's mother, who is also complicit in the parricide. And, as in *Hamlet*, Javier's father reappears as a ghost to ask his son for revenge, as a victim demanding reparation. As he tells Javier, "revenge is the only way to be happy ... the only way to escape your destiny."

The scene in which Javier falls in love with Natalia underlies the need to recuperate Spain's historical memory kidnapped by Franco. Upon first arriving at the circus, Javier is taken under the wing of Ramiro, the trainer and caretaker of Princesa, the circus elephant. He shows Javier around the premises and introduces him to the rest of the crew. When he finally introduces him to Princesa, the elephant hits Javier hard with her trunk and he falls to the floor. It is at this particular moment, still shaky from the blow, that Javier sees Natalia descending from her trapeze for the first time. The shot is constructed to suggest an enchanted, magical moment of love at first sight—as when Scottie first lays eyes on Madeleine at Ernie's in *Vertigo*—punctuated by lyrical musical chords and the word

Figure 7.1 *Balada triste de trompeta*, 2010

entrada, Spanish for "entrance," written against the upper side of the shot. Natalia, who Javier first sees wrapped in the veil of her long red flowing scarf—similar to the one she wears around her waist when plunging to her death at the end of the film—seems to descend from heaven, hypnotically swaying her body above him (Fig. 7.1). Ramiro helps Javier to get up, as if ushering him into this new world Javier is "entering," but also warns him to be careful because Natalia "has an owner." The shot is crafted in such a way that while Javier looks at Natalia completely transfixed, we also notice a juggler right behind him practicing his routine. The shot is visually deceiving, and for a second it seems that it is Javier himself who is doing the juggling due to Natalia's sudden appearance—his true object of desire. Javier is not a baby anymore, having acquired a new sense of wholeness and portentous motor coordination.[23] But as we will see through the analysis of their two dating scenes, Javier's masculinity is tied to his mournful acknowledgment of the past. Until then, his sense of maturity will be as illusory as the shot itself.

Natalia—and this is a crucial point—is wearing red, yellow, and purple, the colors of the Republican flag. It is only after the elephant—an animal associated with its capacity for extraordinary memory—knocks Javier to the floor that he finally "remembers" and is able to reconnect with his lost Republican past by "entering"—as the Spanish word *entrada* above his head indicates—the forbidden space of memory. Natalia, like Sergio and the circus itself, then, is thus constructed as an allegorical figure. Wrapped in the colors of the Republican flag, she is the lost mother, an allegorical representation of the Republican mother Javier never knew. Natalia's allegorical meaning, and that of the other characters in the film, however, is not so simple. Although her outfit's color scheme reminds us of the colors of the Republican flag, she can also be associated with the Virgin

Mary, mother of Christ, in her role of *Mater Dolorosa*, both in the credit sequence and in the final transformation of Javier to killer clown, which symbolizes the motherland and the sacrifices she has to endure for her children.[24] But Natalia is also described as an enchantress, a femme fatale, who, having lost her way, betrays her children. Only at the end of the film does she sacrifice her own life to redeem her children. In an interesting twist on Christian mythology, then, in *Balada* it is the Virgin Mary, mother of Christ—and of the nation—and not her son who dies on the cross to expiate her own historical betrayal; in other words, the nation's betrayal of its own legitimate Republican government.

The kidnapping of historical memory is underlined in a later scene in which Sergio and Javier perform "the elephant and the baby" act, which reinforces the traditional metaphorical association between the elephant and memory. For this act, Sergio appears mounted on top of Princesa while Javier stands on top of a podium, from where he is supposed to pass a baby from one of the spectators, mostly mothers, to Sergio. Javier realizes that the elephant has moved away and tells Sergio that it is too dangerous to proceed. Annoyed at Javier's warnings, Sergio orders him to throw the baby to him anyway. Noticing that the elephant has moved again, Javier refuses to obey, but he eventually gives in and throws the baby up in the air to Sergio. Sergio fails to catch the baby, which is about to hit the ground, but at the last moment Ramiro saves it and returns it to its frightened mother.

If interpreted from the lens of the recuperation of historical memory, the scene calls critical attention to the fact that Spanish babies have been denied access to Spain's historical past—a fact accentuated by the moving away of the elephant controlled by Sergio—because Spain's history was completely rewritten by Francoist historiography. This lack of historical memory, the scene seems to imply, endangers the future of the newborns, as suggested by the baby's dangerous flight through the air. In short, the lack of historical grounding (ignoring the facts) compromises the ability of new Spanish generations to move safely forward. It is no coincidence that it is precisely Ramiro, the elephant's caretaker, the custodian of memory, who saves the baby from falling.[25]

Javier's first date with Natalia is the first time the ghosts of the past appear to disrupt the present. It also emphasizes Natalia's complicity in her own abuse, suggesting once again the motherland's betrayal of her Republican children. Impressed by how Javier has endured Sergio's abuse in their first circus act together, Natalia invites him for a night out. Hesitant at first, Javier is finally convinced by Ramiro, who mediates between the two and confirms that "he'll be ready at 8:00 pm."[26] They go to the Museum of Horrors, where for the first time since the credit sequence the mise-en-scène brings in the dead, in the form of human skulls and Halloween-like ghostly figures. This scene also alludes to the story of Bluebeard, which is another important subtext for the film. After having killed his previous wives, Natalia reminds Javier, Bluebeard provides his new wife with a bunch of keys to his mansion, but warns her, "You can go wherever you like, but this little key opens a door that I don't want you to open." Natalia continues her story while advancing seductively toward Javier, who, visibly frightened, begins to retreat.[27] With a faltering voice, he tells her, "Right. And you opened the door." Natalia answers affirmatively, mischievously adding, "And I loved what's inside," referring to the gory contents of the forbidden room which in Charles Perrault's story hides the corpses of Bluebeard's previous wives hanging from hooks, reminding the spectator of similar images of female corpses hanging from hooks during the credit sequences, which are immediately followed by Hitler's photograph standing next to Franco in Hendaye.

Natalia, an allegorical representation of the nation, thus admits being aware of Sergio's fascist criminal past and of her own complicity in Sergio's control of her. Regardless of this knowledge, or perhaps because of it, she seems drawn to Sergio. As she will later confide to the circus owner who advises her to stay away from Sergio, " ... have you never felt trapped by a love you know might kill you but still you can't help yourself? Have you never been attracted to something that you know is bad for you but there's nothing you can do to avoid it?" The film thus seems to suggest that Sergio's dominance over Natalia, symbolizing Franco's rule over Spain, was not simply imposed by brute force from the outside but was also propped up and nurtured from the inside.

Natalia's ambiguous Oedipal relationship with Javier deepens when she asks him to take her out to the amusement park in a sequence where the "ghosts of the past" lurk around them, threatening Javier's regained sense of self. Dismayed at Natalia's invitation, Javier first questions Natalia's sanity, warning her that if Sergio catches them together he will kill them both. A defiant Natalia mocks Javier's prudence by telling him, "Ooh, my baby is scared," once again treating him as if he were a child. Visibly upset, Javier asks her why she is toying with him, to which Natalia, now wearing her black wig, confesses, "With you I feel safe," a statement that she makes while erasing Javier's large clown tear from his white face, as if suggesting that Javier's sad lonely days are over.

It is precisely at this point of the diegesis that Javier naïvely thinks that he is finally able to steal Natalia away from Sergio, who later savagely attacks him. But, as the mise-en-scène reveals, his infatuation with Natalia is just infantile wishful thinking. He will not have a real chance at love until the second part of the movie, when he gradually begins to come to terms with the ghosts of the past, which until then linger in the background. This is a crucial moment in Javier's Oedipal development. The film's narrative builds up his precarious masculinity to its highest peak moments before subjecting him to a devastating blow, which physically harms him and symbolically castrates him. Enchanting, mysterious music—similar to that in the scene in which he saw Natalia for the first time—connects the previous shot of Natalia wiping Javier's tear with a shot of the two of them taking a ride inside a boat in the amusement park, like lovers do. On the other side of the river, a mechanical figure of King Kong defiantly pounds his chest in front of what seems like a large cross made of tree trunks. Next to King Kong is a crocodile on the riverbank, and several mechanical figures of native warriors wielding their spears behind a protective wooden fence; their black bodies are painted partially white, reminding us of skeletons or ghosts from a past long gone. Javier's regained sense of masculinity and fullness of being, projected onto King Kong's image, however, is, as the mise-en-scène subtly implies, only disposable kitsch theme park material, as the final scene at the park will reveal. Like the rest of the figures around them—made of papier mâché—it is a precarious construct. King Kong's display of strength alludes to the new powerful male instinct inside Javier: he is the strong lover and protector of Natalia. It also prefigures the end of the film at the top of the giant cross which, as we will see, also draws from *King Kong*, whose theme of the beauty and the beast—the latter alluding to the lingering presence of the traumatic past haunting the present in its distorted, monstrous form—is also a subtext of the film.

Javier's sense of prelapsarian bliss experienced while sitting next to Natalia in the small boat—cinematically captured by the magical lighting and enchanting musical soundtrack—is not stable; rather, it is haunted by the ghosts of the past and exposed to Natalia's mocking. In this scene, as in the one inside the Museum of Horrors, Javier's subjectivity and his real connection to Natalia is "threatened" by the native warriors painted in white who, like ghosts of the past, agitate wildly their threatening spears (Fig. 7.2). As in the museum scene, these ghosts linger without receiving proper notice. In this scene, however, although still contained within their protective wooden fences, they are becoming increasingly visible, "wildly agitating" their weapons as if waiting to be reckoned with, to be directly acknowledged, as they will finally be at the end of the film inside Franco's crypt at the Valley of the Fallen.

Figure 7.2 *Balada triste de trompeta*, 2010

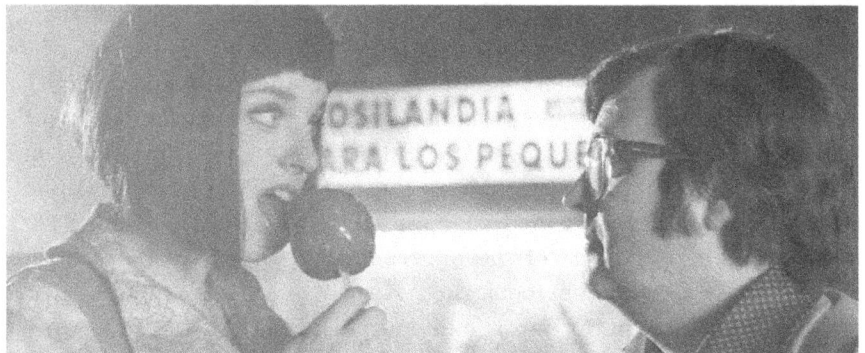

Figure 7.3 *Balada triste de trompeta*, 2010

Javier's Oedipal fantasy is made explicit in the next scene, when he confesses his love to Natalia, who, as a modern-day Eve, temptingly licks her apple.[28] As he nervously puts it, "Being with you like this really affects me." Pressed by Natalia to clarify his statement, he finally confesses, "I could end up loving you." "Loving me. How much?" she replies sarcastically while continuing to lick her apple. "A lot. More than a lot," he exclaims. Warmed by Javier's loving words, Natalia makes a facial expression suggesting pity, which offends him to the core. The shot's visual composition shows both of them in profile while the letters of the name of the stall where they just bought candy—*Golosilandia, todo para los peques* (Candyland, everything for the little ones)—feature prominently on the upper frame, reducing Javier's love declaration to nothing more than an infantile wish (Fig. 7.3).

As she did in the past, Natalia lures Javier in but keeps him off balance: "You're the only one who stood up to him [in reference to Sergio]. You didn't laugh at his jokes. That's what I call a man," Natalia reassuringly tells him while she leans over to kiss him. Ecstatic, Javier kisses her back. After a few seconds, she moves slowly away from him while still seductively licking her apple, curving the tip of her tongue as she had done previously in the sex scenes with Sergio. The mise-en-scène, however, pokes fun at Javier's newly found male confidence with a shot of fireworks over a fake Eiffel Tower. Instead of being expelled from the Garden of Eden through sexual temptation, as in the Francoist films, where the Garden of Eden is a recurring theme, Javier has found his inner paradise by succumbing to it. Of course, this is a kitschy, illusory state of mind, made obvious by the romantic cardboard cut-out, clichéd setting of the city of Paris around them.

At this point of the narrative, Sergio seems to appear from nowhere to beat Javier to a pulp after brutally assaulting Natalia. Sergio's beating puts an emphatic end to Javier's illusory state of mind, deflating his precarious masculinity. For the beating, Sergio makes use of one of the fair's staple attractions—the device in which the contestants measure their strength by hitting the base of a vertical pole with a mallet, which, of course, has clear phallic connotations, referring both to Javier's castration and Sergio's need to use violence against the vulnerable, as Francoism did in its later days with renewed impetus, when feeling itself vulnerable.[29] Sergio places a semiconscious Javier at the base of the attraction's device and repeatedly pounds his stomach and chest with the mallet—a movement that insinuates castration while ironically replicating King Kong's self-congratulatory chest pounding—with such force that he ends up hitting the bell at the top, after which Sergio demands his teddy bear from the attendant.

Echoing the previous scene at the Museum of Horrors, the theme park sequence thus subtly underlies the idea that Javier's Oedipal development—and therefore his ability to win over the woman of his dreams—is closely tied to his recognition of Spain's traumatic past. Until then he will only be able to experience an illusion of wholeness, which, as the mise-en-scène ironically suggests, is a theme park, kitsch fantasy of a traumatized child. In other words, it is only by reopening the door to the past as Pierrot—a sad, melancholy clown open to loss—and not as his father did as mere distraction from social conflict in his role of happy clown, that Javier will be able to mature. Only by replacing the kitschy clown tear Natalia wipes off with her finger with real tears, as we will see in a later scene, will Javier, and the country along with him, finally grow up; only a nation that respectfully mourns its past can offer a historically grounded future to its children. That is, only by coming to terms with the ghosts of the past, the film seems to suggest, will the nation mature. So, while an adolescent-like Javier can only engage in violence and revenge, Javier the grown-up can finally properly mourn the loss of his father.

The brutal beating that sends Javier to the hospital, however, also sends him down the wrong path, toward vengeance instead of mournful recognition of the traumatic past, setting in motion the narrative of revenge Javier's father—as Hamlet's father before him—demands from his son. While in the hospital, Javier has a vivid dream in which Natalia appears before him as his true object of desire, dressed in her trapeze outfit with an alluring peacock design, the conventional visual code for vanity. In his dream, Javier enters Natalia's bedroom and, removing her bed covers, contemplates her naked body. Suddenly, Sergio appears from nowhere, as in the amusement park, dressed in his silly clown gear to spoil Javier's erotic wish. In the next dream scene, Javier, still clad in his hospital gown, must climb the giant headstone of St Mark at the base of the cross of the Valley of the Fallen. On the other side of the headstone, Natalia appears as if she were an angel suspended by the red flowing cloth she will die in, wrapped around her at the end of the film. Javier smiles at the sight of Natalia, but Sergio pops up again to spoil Javier's erotic vision, this time holding a knife to Javier's father's throat. Before slashing his throat, though, the father still manages to yell to his son, "Remember me," replicating the exact words of Hamlet's ghost to his son. These two dreams make Javier realize that his only chance of happiness with Natalia is by following his father's advice and seeking revenge against Sergio, who as the representative of Francoism is the true murderer of his father.

The legitimacy of revenge, though, is put into question from the outset in the dream sequence by the subtle reference to Mark the Evangelist and to the giant headstone Javier is forced to climb to access Natalia. As we saw, Mark's Gospel points to the theme of the "empty tomb," and implicitly to the idea of acknowledgment and proper burial instead of vengeance. Thus, as the dream suggests, in *Balada* Javier has to properly address the past in order to get the girl.[30]

Prompted by the dream, and possessed by rage, Javier decides to take justice into his own hands and honor his father's plea. However, as we will come to realize, when he avenges his father by assaulting Sergio with a trumpet, Javier is mishandling the instrument as a weapon to inflict punishment instead of using it as an instrument for remembering and honoring the dead, as the song "Balada triste de trompeta" and the film itself want us to do. Leaving the hospital bed with blind determination, he goes straight to the circus looking for Sergio. He finds him inside a circus tent, surrounded by anxious caged animals, having rough sex with Natalia from behind a screen made of canvas. Javier first sees Sergio's and

Natalia's silhouettes projected against the screen as in a magic lantern show. A close-up shows Natalia's head in profile with her tongue sticking out of her mouth with that characteristic seductive curve we have already seen, indicating she is complicit in her own abuse. A crazed Javier grabs a metal hook from the top of a crate and runs toward them. As at the beginning of the film, he is once again witnessing the primal scene. However, unlike the first time, when he hid in a corner as a hopeless sobbing child, Javier now takes action to protect his "mother" from the sadistic stepfather. The camera shows a close-up of the hook tearing the canvas. Javier is finally able to shatter the fantasy–reality screen that separates them (the previous time he was separated from them by a large sheet of glass stained by the grease mark of the smashed chicken which bespoke of his infant impotence) and move to the other side where Sergio and Natalia, confused and frightened, look at him. With a trumpet in hand as his only weapon, Javier assaults Sergio, horribly disfiguring his face. Petrified, Natalia, her face spattered with blood, witnesses the brutal beating. The camera cuts to a close-up of the broken trumpet Javier has used as a weapon, which he now casts aside. Smiling, his face also drenched in blood, Javier delivers the good news to Natalia: "You don't have to worry about him anymore," as Natalia looks at him horrified. Noticing Natalia's shocked reaction to her liberation, he asks, "What's wrong? You're free. I freed you from the monster." As several members of the crew approach the scene, Javier, covered in blood and transformed into a monster himself, runs away.

This revenge scene, when Javier finally tears the veil of his projected primordial fantasy—also suggested by the projected silhouettes against the screen—is the first time he allows himself to impulsively act on his Oedipal desire. The violent sinful act, the "tearing of the veil," grants Javier access to the other side of allegorical reality. Empowered through Oedipal struggle, he is now stepping into historical temporality, leaving allegorical time behind. The tearing of the veil allows him to regain his lost agency, to grow up, and "enter" the real space of history, as the word *entrada* written on top of the frame when he first saw Natalia subtly seems to foreshadow. He is still an infant, though, a fact stressed by Javier's outfit, the scanty hospital gown which exposes his baby fat and chubby buttocks. But this time the child, instead of crying inconsolably from the other side, as he did earlier, attempts to kill his stepfather, as Hamlet is supposed to do, in order to occupy his place and thus claim his rights over his mother.

Javier hits Sergio in the face, replicating the brutal disfiguring of his own father by the kicks of the colonel's horse, thus following the logic of "an eye for an eye, a tooth for a tooth." The chosen weapon, a trumpet (a word whose original Spanish is related to the word *trompa*, the elephant's trunk that hits Javier at the beginning, setting in motion his quest for Natalia and therefore for historical memory) obviously alludes to the film's title, *Balada triste de trompeta*, "A Sad Trumpet Ballad," which refers to a song by Raphael, one of Spain's foremost entertainers. This is a mournful, sentimental song that Raphael sings in an important scene we will discuss later; a song which mourns for "a past that died, which moans and cries like I do." In the song, the trumpet is the perfect vehicle to properly honor and mourn the dead, in stark contrast to Javier's handling of it as a weapon for revenge against Sergio, as he does in his angry adolescent phase.

Javier's vicious attack on Sergio divides the film into two parts. In the second part, after having liberated Natalia from Sergio's grip, Javier becomes a monster himself, who, after acting out his rage in a terrifyingly vengeful manner, gradually acknowledges his moral debt to the past. He, as the trumpet, will finally become a conduit for mourning instead of revenge. But for now he is a runaway, an outlaw chased by the Francoist police, whom the film compares to *El Lute*—the legendary Spanish fugitive who had Spanish police in a state of high alert for two months in 1972—who appears on the news.[31] After his symbolic parricide, Javier has lost his innocence and, stigmatized like Cain, another biblical subtext of the film, turns back the clock of time. From symbolic being he is now transformed, like Cain, into historical being for having committed a heinous crime, treated in the movie as a sort of original sin. Javier is expelled from his newly found circus home and condemned to experience nakedness, cold, hunger, and loneliness inside what looks like an underground man-made shelter. Feeding on roots and animals, Javier becomes like a prehistoric cave man, an anachronistic historical being—out of joint—in the midst of rapidly developing Spain, as a shot of him eating the raw entrails of a deer in the bottom of his dwelling during the winter suggests.

The dwelling itself also reminds us of a grotto, a sort of natural or artificial cave, which in modern times was mainly used for ornamental and devotional purposes, often associated with saintly apparitions. The term grotto is related both to the word "grotesque" and the word "crypt," both of which are at the core of the fictional universe of the film: grotesque, to *Balada*'s distorted representation of reality, and crypt, to Franco's crypt at the Valley of the Fallen—the epicenter of Francoist kitsch ideology—and to burial sites more generally. Because of their common function as sites of cheap transcendental religiosity—particularly as preferred sites of religious apparitions—grottoes, and the grotesque associated with them, are part and parcel of kitsch aesthetics; in fact, inside the grotto Natalia does "appear" to Javier in an advertisement for the circus in the newspaper he uses as wrapping paper. This scene, then, not only foreshadows the apparition of Natalia as *Mater Dolorosa* that prompts Javier's transformation into an avenging angel in a sequence we will examine later, but also prefigures the last sequence of the film, which takes place inside Franco's crypt, as Franco's monumental burial at the Valley of the Fallen is sometimes referred to. It is from this inner core of Francoist kitsch, symbolized by the crypt itself, that the film resignifies the most exclusionary and sacred of Francoist places to include all Spaniards.

The turn to historicity is also suggested by his means of escape from the police: an abandoned sewerage system where an official warning sign at the entrance reads, "No Trespassing. Danger." As this implies, Javier has retreated into a clandestine mode of existence navigating a host of forbidden time tunnels, which also reminds us of the maze of galleries inside the Valley of the Fallen. Leaving behind a circus life characterized by role-playing and fanciful clothes, Javier has finally reached the other side of historical reality, alone and naked. Only after this trial period away from civilization, living among nature, eating raw meat and without clothing, is he ready to assume his avenging mission and confront the real historical monsters of this fable: Franco himself, and the fascist colonel who actually killed his father. To do this, Javier will transform himself into an *esperpento*, a murderous avenging ghost who will punish the real perpetrators.

Chased out of his prehistoric underground dwelling by a wild boar that falls inside, Javier is finally discovered and caught by the fascist colonel who murdered his father and his aide, who are hunting nearby. The colonel immediately realizes who Javier is by recognizing the medallion of the Virgin Mary Javier wears around his neck. The colonel throws Javier into the back of his Jeep, along with the wild boar, as if he were a beast himself. The colonel, we learn, is in charge of organizing a hunting party to honor Franco—hunting being one of Franco's favorite hobbies and most cherished rituals—at his country mansion. The sequence of the hunting party, the only time in the film when Franco appears, while illuminating the level of de-humanization Republicans were subjected to during Francoism, also provides the narrative alibi for Javier's metamorphosis into the avenging angel of history, which, as mentioned earlier, was prompted by the vision of Natalia as *Mater Dolorosa*, a traditional representation of Spain.

During the hunt, Javier is forced by the colonel to imitate a dog and instructed to bring the dead prey back to the hunters clutched between his teeth. As such, he appears twice in front of Franco. Not fully amused by the situation, a mere distraction in the enjoyment of his precious hobby, Franco tells the colonel off: "I always liked you, Salcedo, but this is not a very Christian thing to do." Finally, Franco tells Javier, who on all fours and surrounded by men with guns cannot do much about his current state of humiliation, not to let himself be mistreated like this. Javier, unable to do anything else, behaves like a dog, severely biting the dictator's hand, in retaliation for his useless comment. Immediately arrested, he is thrown into a small chapel of the palace the colonel uses as a temporary jail, where Javier will undergo his terrifying transformation from sad clown (and viciously hunted animal) into an exterminating angel.

Javier's transformation takes place inside the small chapel which serves as a jail that perfectly encapsulates the nature of Francoism, and the important role the Catholic Church in legitimizing Franco's "glorious crusade," as Pope Pio XII referred to Franco's military uprising against the Republic. It is the manner of his transformation, though, which really concerns us for our argument about Javier's maturation and the film's progressive recuperation of historical memory. The chapel/prison is used as a kind of storage room of Francoism, which reminds us of *Viridiana*'s attic, where, as we saw in the previous chapter, Don Jaime stored the old furniture his nephew Jorge wanted to recycle. Unlike Jorge, who makes few cosmetic changes in his uncle's house so everything can stay the same, Javier creates his new horrific identity by recycling the old clothes of an ultra-conservative Spain so that everything can change.

The chapel contains a large medieval cross, a large statue of the Virgin Mary, and trunks filled with expensive fabric, as well as many scattered objects mostly covered in cobwebs. Upon noticing the statue of the Virgin, Javier devotedly falls to his knees and, as if he were a modern-day Baroque Spanish mystic, has a rapturous vision. In Javier's vision, the Virgin's face becomes that of Natalia who, in a reversal of the traditional motif of the annunciation, where the angel appears to the Virgin Mary to deliver the news, announces to him that "[t]he day of wrath is here. You'll become my angel of Death. Save me from evil and fulfill your destiny, my beloved." (Fig. 7.4). After this vision, Javier falls unconscious to the floor.

When he finally regains consciousness, Javier rapidly begins to design a new costume for himself. The soundtrack now plays the mournful chords of the saeta we heard in the credit sequence. In the old trunk, he finds a cardinal's miter and some priestly robes, a few big colored Christmas baubles and a pair of what resemble bullfighter leggings. And he proceeds to sew all these together with a large wooden needle, while a medium shot shows the crucified Jesus looking at him as his only witness. The new outfit is part clown, part cardinal, part bullfighter: three figures, as de la Iglesia points out, characterized by their role of performing ritual sacrifices, and also characterized by their feminized appearance. When he

Figure 7.4 *Balada triste de trompeta*, 2010

Figure 7.5 *Balada triste de trompeta*, 2010

finally supplies himself with weapons and ammunition from the colonel's arsenal, he also reminds us of Antonio Das Mortes, the Brazilian *cangaceiro*, protagonist of Glauber Rocha's famous film, who roamed the *sertão*, his country's backlands. Javier has finally become the avenging son who will redeem his father's death. He has become a monster who with the discarded fragments of the past has turned himself into a horrific spectral presence haunting those who hunted him (Fig. 7.5).

Javier's new look thus becomes a distorted mirror image, an *esperpento*, which like Valle-Inclán's famous concave mirror at the *callejón del gato*, reflects back at Francoism a grotesque monstrous representation of itself. And, as in the case of Valle-Inclán's *esperpento* or Goya's grotesque faces, which do not mask a purer inner self behind them but instead bring it to the surface, Javier's grotesque eclectic representation exposes the inner, grotesque, murderous truth of Francoism. In addition to designing his new outfit, he also disfigures his face with caustic soda and then burns his chubby cheeks and lips with a hot iron. His face now resembles Sergio's monstrous face, which after Javier's savage attack was coarsely stitched back together by a veterinarian. It also resembles his father's face, which, as we saw earlier, was brutally disfigured by the colonel's horse. And the red color of his burned cheeks together with the yellow and purple of the miter replicate the colors of the Republican flag, which Natalia was also wearing the first time he saw her. The aesthetic/visual transformation is now complete, including a pair of ridiculous white shoes with bows on top, also reminiscent of cardinals' and clowns' footwear. Javier is no longer Pierrot, the sad, white-faced, passive clown desperately in love with Natalia, but a terrifying evil clown determined to conquer her. When the colonel's aide finally comes to take him to his master, he is utterly shocked by Javier's new appearance: "What are you dressed up as? A priest or a lady? If the colonel sees you dressed like that, he'll have a fit."[32] Without uttering a word, Javier strikes his face and then, grabbing two irons, one in each hand, proceeds to finish him off with a series of movements replicating those made by the horse of the colonel toward his father's face; movements that also are reminiscent of the iron branding he has performed on himself.

Javier's transformation opens up the realm of vengeance, where "an eye for an eye and a tooth for a tooth" is the measure of justice that the film, however, rejects all along as a legitimate moral option. His transformation now complete, Javier begins his search for the colonel, the murderer of his father. Like the little chapel, the colonel's large, aristocratic living room is also a cluttered space filled with objects of a past long gone—full body armor, imperial banners, tapestries illustrating historical feats, and a large portrait of Franco presiding over the room. But unlike the chapel's interior, a storage room of the past, the colonel's living room is fully functional, clean, and orderly, an ideal representation of Franco's Spain. It also exhibits a multitude of stuffed animals, including a tiger, several skulls of hunted animals, and a large polar bear extended on two legs, possessing a ghostly quality which reminds us of the white ghosts haunting the empty hallways of old castles in gothic novels.

Javier bursts into the colonel's living room and shoots dead the assistant, a Francoist high-ranking official with whom the colonel has been discussing Javier's punishment, who is explaining that given the pressure the international community is putting on Spain lately they should resolve the matter discreetly. Finally, after a struggle, Javier manages to tackle the colonel to the floor and, now sitting on top of him, aims his gun at him. The colonel dares him to kill him: "You don't have the balls!" Javier hesitates for a second but then he fires shots with the last two bullets.

Exhausted by the physical exertion and extreme violence of the scene, he falls to the floor with his arms crossed, framed upside down by the camera. He starts laughing, but a shadow around his mouth, and the fact that he is shot upside down, makes the laughter sound and look like a cry, in an indistinguishable undecidable mixture, which foreshadows the last shot of the film with the two clowns facing each other in the back of a police car crying/laughing inconsolably. As we will see, this is a shot in which for the first time both clowns, like "Balada" the song, mourn for a past that died. Javier's happiness at accomplishing his vengeful mission is tainted by the ambiguity of the shot in which laughter and crying fuse into one. The moral validity of revenge is thus put into question by the film as this shot implicitly robs Javier of the hard-earned satisfaction of his vengeful act.

The scene at the diner when we first hear the song of the film's title further questions the moral soundness of Javier's vengeful rampage to create a mournful melancholic mood embracing the ghosts of Spain's traumatic past. The scene reveals its deeper meaning when interpreted as being at the intersection of kitsch aesthetics and historical memory, which emerged in the scene at the Francoist chapel. In this scene, *Balada* turns the flatness of Francoist kitsch, its lack of historical depth, on its head, finally breaking Francoism's rhetoric to disorienting ideological effect. The scene is visually crafted à la Sergio Leone/Quentin Tarantino, and shot with a similar stylistic sensibility of sharp angles and extreme close-ups, also characteristic of the aesthetic of comic books, which is the artistic background from which de la Iglesia originally comes. At the diner, an average Spanish family of two exhausted parents and their three kids are ordering sandwiches at the counter, in a humorous scene mocking the banality of everyday life. The camera then cuts to a diagonal close-up of a jukebox, where someone whose face initially we do not see is selecting a song. The song is "Balada triste de trompeta," the mournful song originally performed by Raphael dressed as a clown in Vicente Escrivá's film *Sin un adiós* (1970). As the lyrics tell us, the singer mourns "for a past that died, and that cries and moans like I do."[33] And as the singer exclaims, "with such trumpet crying/my desperate heart/goes on crying/remembering my past/a sad trumpet ballad of a broken heart."

When the song begins to play, the camera cuts to a close-up of a postcard that Javier is holding in his hand. It is a quintessential kitsch postcard of a boy clown sitting morosely in the gutter against a wall, reminiscent of Chaplin's character "The Little Tramp." The postcard reads, "How beautiful it is to have a friend to lean on." Like Javier, the little clown boy is also lonely, without anyone in the world. In this sad situation, as the postcard obviously announces, a friend would be the most precious gift to have. Upon hearing the first chords of Raphael's song, Javier suddenly gets up from his table and approaches the old man who picked the song, and anxiously asks him, "Who is Raphael?" The old man responds, "A great singer and a great person."

The song is about mourning the past, and thus is appropriately selected on the jukebox by the oldest person in the place, who can still remember that past. The song's theme and its melancholy mood immediately grab Javier's attention. The postcard of the lonely boy clown Javier holds contrasts starkly with his renewed sense of empowerment provided by his monstrous appearance and the weapons he brandishes, as if he were an invincible superhero from a comic book. But Javier's vengeful acts have not made him happier or stronger, or brought him any friends or any sense of justice. On the contrary, he is still as lonely and vulnerable as the little clown on the postcard, as the shot suggests. This is why the song, sung by a broken-hearted singer like himself, also dressed in a clown outfit, resonates so powerfully with Javier. He has now found an imaginary friend in Raphael, someone he can trust and lean on.

The song, however, opens up the echo chambers of the crimes of the past, like Bluebeard's little room. Unlike Bluebeard, though, Raphael is a "great singer and a great guy," whose sad trumpet ballad cries for "a past that died" which "cries and moans like myself." This is a self who, like Javier, goes on remembering and crying, haunted by the past everybody seems to ignore around them.

While a lonely Javier contemplates the kitsch postcard, the first chords of the song bring back echoes of Spain's suppressed memory of the recent past. The old man who selects the music serves as a guarantor for the good quality and integrity of the voice's source, who cries and moans for the past, which the singer tells us is also moaning and crying itself and which, we should infer, cannot be dead, but rather represents a specter haunting the living. This depth of memory seems to be ignored by the new Spain, represented by the family and everybody else in the place who, unlike Javier, do not even notice the song playing. *Balada*, the film, like "Balada," the song, mourns for the past. Javier is thus turning himself into a monstrous anachronism—'out of joint' with the times—a Derridean ghostly presence, lonely as the boy clown in the postcard, but, like Raphael, increasingly attuned to the ghostly presence of the past in the present, to its whispers and cries, in the midst of a society that has made a social contract to forget.

The kitsch motif of the lonely clown boy on the postcard is replicated in a sort of *mise-en-abyme* by Raphael's performance dressed as a clown moaning for a past as well as by Javier, dressed as a monstrous lonely clown while holding the postcard in his hand. It creates a house of mirrors, which, as in a famous scene from Chaplin's *Circus* (1928)–which also has a similar plot of a controlling circus owner who oppresses his own daughter and in which The Little Tramp also ends up being chased by the authorities—creates a disorienting effect that keeps the characters caught in a spatial labyrinth, unable to move forward and find their exit. As kitsch was the preferred aesthetic of Francoism, it was instrumental in projecting a nostalgic clichéd vision of Spanish history. As we saw in our reading of *Raza*, *Romancero*, and *Los últimos*, it was kitsch's historical flatness which allowed Francoism to "hallucinate ideological empty spaces" through which to hypostasize historical reality: historical time was thus emptied, spatialized, distorted in the beauty of the smoke and mirrors of Francoist rhetoric. In Francoist Spain, as we saw, reality was petrified, replaced by a nostalgic ahistorical account of the glorious Spanish past, in the same way that the postcard Javier holds reduces the tragic dimension of the human condition to self-pity, to the mere sentimentality of a little child abandoned by his friend. Against this kitsch ideological flattening of reality, this scene, and the whole film, attempts to bring Spain's tragic historical dimension back to the fore, thus rejecting both the Francoist mythologized, kitsch version of the past and the Pact of Forgetting consensual ignoring of the recent traumatic past evoked by the song.

Sad and lonely, isolated from those around him who keep ignoring the ghostly past conjured by the song but still filled with vengeful rage and thus unable to properly acknowledge the moral debt to the dead, Javier wanders the city crying inconsolably. The faintly ghosts of the Museum of Horrors and of the amusement park materialize in this scene as a large piece of dead meat a butcher is carrying on his shoulder, and into which Javier sinks his face still sobbing, which reminds us more literally of the corpses of the dead. As if seeking consolation, Javier now enters a movie theater, where *Sin un adiós* [*Without a Goodbye*] (1970) is being shown—a film whose title ironically also suggests a lack of proper mourning.

The scene inside the movie theater, during which Javier stands in front of the screen absorbed by the projected images of Raphael performing "Balada triste de trompeta," the song that gives the film its title, is important for understanding *Balada*'s attitude toward revenge. It exposes the dilemma that Franco's dictatorship, in its failure to administer justice, precipitated the subject's quest for vengeance, even if vengeance is deemed immoral.[34] Javier watches Raphael, dressed as a clown, singing dramatically. In the song's chorus Raphael begins to moan, imitating the mournful sound of a trumpet. Javier is again visibly moved to tears. Singer and song are the visual and emotional mirror image of Javier, who is also dressed as a clown and feeling sad. He is so immersed in the performance that he begins lip-synching to it, oblivious to the fact that he is standing in front of the screen and blocking the view of the spectators.

It is at this moment, in front of the film screen, that Javier has his second vision. This time, instead of a vision of Natalia as *Mater Dolorosa*, Javier sees the images of both Raphael and his father, who appear on the screen to directly address him. An actor impersonating Raphael, also dressed as a clown, advises him to leave Natalia who, as he says, is not good for him, and to turn himself in to the police because, as he warns him, "You cannot keep on killing people." Suddenly, Javier's father pops up in the scene and, as Hamlet's father's ghost, admonishes his son to take revenge, to "go after her and kill that bastard [Sergio]. He doesn't deserve her." Morally outraged, Raphael replies to Javier's father, "How dare you talk like that to your own son?" Irritated, Javier's father asks Javier, "Who is this creep, son? What is he doing inside your head?" Lost for words, Javier just shrugs his shoulders, timidly replying, "I like the way he sings." Echoing the words of Hamlet's father's ghost, Javier's father tells his son, "Remember your father. Remember your destiny. There's only one way to be happy," implying that revenge is the only way for Javier to set time back on track.

The scene at the cinema is the first time that Javier, as Hamlet, shows clear signs of ambiguity toward his destiny as an avenger. As was established earlier in the diner scene, Raphael is a source of value, a man of moral integrity, as the old man described him, who instead of preaching revenge like his father is telling Javier to stop killing people. Raphael himself, as the song he sings suggests, has opted for a very different path to Javier's: a path between revenge and forgiveness where he can mourn the dead by attentively listening to their voices. As we see in his performance, he and the trumpet are in perfect harmony. Raphael even imitates the sound of the trumpet, replicating the moans of the dead suggested by the trumpet's lamentations. In other words, the song mourns for a past that is absent yet present, which, like Javier's father and Hamlet's father's ghost, is dead but also "undead," spectral, a past haunting the present.

As Avery Gordon observes, "[b]eing haunted draws us affectively, sometimes against our will and always a bit magically, into the structure of feeling of a reality we come to experience, not as cold knowledge, but as transformative recognition" (8). Thus, Raphael's mournful song turns similar personal melancholy longings into "transformative recognition" of the suffering of the victims.[35] The scene at the film theater thus instills doubt in Javier's heart, who nonetheless keeps on denying his responsibility for the actions committed. At the end of the film, he lies to Natalia by telling her that both Raphael and his father commanded him to do all that he did. We know this is not true. Beginning a process of a "transformative recognition," from vengeance to mournful acknowledgment, Raphael acts in this scene as Javier's moral conscience, suggesting that revenge is not the moral thing to do. However, unlike the seventeenth-century revenge plays it draws from, which are somewhat ambiguous toward the moral status of revenge, *Balada* is crystal clear about it.[36] It condemns it unequivocally. As the film makes obvious, the quest for revenge Javier embarks upon does not enable him to resolve his grief but turns him into a monster like Sergio, thus further alienating Natalia, who is horrified with Javier's new identity.

In the movie theater scene, as in *Hamlet*, Javier's father angrily demands that his son avenge him and thus set things right. In *Hamlet*, the conflicted Prince of Denmark pronounces these famous lines in response to his father's plea: "The time is out of joint, O cursed spite,/That ever I was born to set it right" (23). In *Balada*, Javier, increasingly conflicted about his avenging mission, admits to liking Raphael, thus implying that he might be susceptible to listening to him, "a man of moral integrity." From the diner scene onwards, Javier is thus progressively "out of joint" with his own mission, as he tries to follow his father's advice instead of his own feelings, which are clearly sympathetic to Raphael and to properly mourn.

As Hamlet, thus, Javier is also cursed from birth for having been born to fulfill his destiny to rectify the "originary wrong." His curse being, as Derrida writes of Hamlet's curse, "the birth wound from which he suffers, a bottomless wound, an irreparable tragedy ... [a] murderous, *bruising origin*" (24–5, emphasis added). It is precisely the "bruising origin" that *Balada* wants to leave behind, by confronting the past in the present. Since, as we saw at the beginning of the chapter, the law that forces Hamlet, or Javier, to set things right inexorably "stems from vengeance," it also invites the following question: "Can one ... yearn for a justice that one day, a day belonging no longer to history, a quasi-messianic day, would be finally removed from the fatality of vengeance?" (24). *Balada*, I argue, welcomes such a day. It exposes the moral degradation implied in the fatality of vengeance as Goya's painting *Duelo a garrotazos* surely did, which, as mentioned earlier, was one of the main visual references for de la Iglesia in making the film.

Javier, as avenger, as "righter of wrongs," like Hamlet, can only come after the crime, a second generation "destined to *inherit*," as the Republican children inherit the fate of their forebears. And as Derrida writes, "one never inherits without coming to terms with ... some specter" (24). The specter Javier has to come to terms with is that of his own father and his father's demand for revenge, but he also has to come to terms more generally with the specters of the war's victims and of the subsequent Francoist repression; a pile of corpses, whose ghosts remain present, demanding reparation. Vengeance, *Balada* suggests, is a poor way to come to terms with the ghosts of the past, since it only perpetuates the cycle of violence, making the traumatic past continuously alive in the present. Although, as Martha Minow explains, vengeance "is the wellspring of a notion of equivalence that animates justice ... the same vengeful motive often leads people to exact more than necessary, to be maliciously spiteful or dangerously aggressive or to become hateful themselves by committing the reciprocal acts of violence" (10). Javier has become such a person. Vengeance is corroding his sense of self as the caustic soda he used corroded his face. He has turned into a monster like his nemesis Sergio. Only by properly coming to terms with the ghosts of the past, this time as Derrida writes, "to grant them the right ... to ... a hospitable memory ... out of a concern for justice," could he do Spain's past proper justice (220).

In the movie theater scene, when Javier reacts emotionally to the song, he continues to follow the moral path of mournful acknowledgment he began to follow at the diner. Rejecting vengeance as justice in favor of properly mourning the dead is his only chance at not becoming like Sergio and thus avoiding his monstrous fate. Inside the movie theater, his tears express most eloquently Javier's inherited "bottomless wound, and irreparable tragedy." They are neither the petrified kitsch tears of Franco described in Chapter 1, which flowed from a melancholic narcissistic identification with his own avenging historical mission, nor the sad clown's painted tears Natalia wiped off with her finger, which are the kitsch sentimental tears that turn real emotion into self-pity. Javier's tears, elicited by the emotion conveyed by Raphael's song, are empathic tears.

Javier's empathic crying in front of the screen for the memory of the dead prompted by the mournful song suggests a rejection of kitsch's promotion of timeless sentimentality and narcissistic self-indulgence suggested by the clichéd sad clown—which is still inscribed in the postcard Javier was holding at the diner—in favor of a more vulnerable, empathic sort of identification with the fate of the dead expressed in the trumpet's lamentation. Javier's tears are the emotional response to Raphael's "tears."[37] His tears, elicited by Raphael's performance, suggest a desire for "transformative recognition" of the past in the present. "Balada," the song, as *Balada*, the film, projecting a mournful melancholic mood, aspires to make the society aware of its loss—a communal sense of loss. Loss, as Butler writes, is a "condition and necessity for a certain sense of community, where community *cannot* overcome loss without losing the very sense of itself as community" (468). *Balada*'s imagined community, unlike that of Spain resulting from the Pact of Forgetting, can only move forward by not ignoring its traumatic past.

However, in *Balada*, not only the past comes back in its ghostly form to haunt the present, but the present itself dissolves into a "ghostly matter," to use Avery Gordon's phrase, particularly as the end of Francoism rapidly approaches. This happens for instance after Sergio is expelled from the party where he has been performing his routine, aided by Natalia, for the child of a rich family; the only kind of event he is hired to after having lost the circus he once controlled with an iron grip. In this sequence, Sergio appears with a fake bear to cover his monstrous face and with a cut-out of a ghost stuck to his back, but one of the children pulls Sergio's beard and screams in horror upon seeing his disfigured, monstrous face. The house owner and his friends order Sergio to get away from the children, since for a moment they mistake him for Javier, the killer clown who has been appearing in the news.

Sergio's expulsion from the party by the rich parents signifies the moment of Natalia's final liberation from the abusive clown. It marks the transitional moment in which even Spain's upper bourgeoisie is looking for further political integration within Europe, after Francoism's repressive apparatus has become more of a hindrance than a help to successful capitalist expansion. We see them wandering the streets at night. A long shot shows Sergio sitting on the gutter crying and complaining that kids don't love him anymore. An increasingly confident Natalia tells him, "Forget it Sergio. Enough! Your clown years are over." Visibly upset, Natalia moves away from him and begins to walk away. Sergio lies on the pavement with his back turned to us. The shot emphasizes the cut-out of the ghost stuck to his back (Fig. 7.6). As this shot suggests by giving us the outline of his figure against the pavement with the ghost attached to his back, he is now gradually becoming a ghost himself, living somewhere between the living and the dead. The love affair with Natalia is over.

The following sequence of the assassination of Admiral Carrero Blanco—Spain's president of the government at the time (1973) and Franco's right-hand man—by Basque separatist group ETA is the moment in the movie in which reality finally disintegrates and becomes spectral; a moment equally marked by the weight of the past and the potentiality of the future. It reveals the competing forces at play in Spain during the transitional time. This is an important sequence in a film that, like *Balada*, wants to portray the entire history of Francoism. Carrero Blanco's death was a lethal blow to Francoism, bringing in its wake—while the dictator was still in power—the anticipated possibility of a future without Franco.

Figure 7.6 *Balada triste de trompeta*, 2010

Natalia, a specter of her former self after ending her affair with Sergio, walks zombie-like through the early-morning streets of Madrid when an ice cream truck driven by Javier with an ad for Alaska Ice-cream—which could be read as a humorous reference to the preservation of memory—appears from nowhere and begins to follow her. At the precise moment that Javier gets out to kidnap Natalia, a car carrying Admiral Carrero Blanco slowly passes by. And after a brief close-up of Carrero's face we hear the tremendous explosion of the bomb planted by ETA, which kills the person who was supposed to be Franco's successor.

In the midst of the confusion which ensues after the explosion, Javier gets back up a little shaken while, almost subliminally, we see a shadowy figure which reminds us of Sergio crossing the shot, although the camera never reveals his identity. This subliminal apparition is repeated once again a few shots later, as if indicating that Sergio was also in pursuit of Natalia, refusing to let her go, and suggesting that this is the time that the nation is traversed by competing political agendas: Javier's, signifying the oppositional stand against Francoism; Sergio's, which, in his desperate attempt to cling to Natalia, represents the refusal of the old political order to go away; and ETA's, which symbolizes the push to end Franco's oppression of Spain's peripheral nationalities (Basque, Catalonian, and Galician). It also constitutes a humorous critique of the narrow concept of nationality itself, as when Javier finally turns a corner and sees some young people inside a car, who are obviously members of the ETA commando that are about to flee the scene of the crime. Javier approaches the car to ask them, "[w]hat circus are you from?" This question not only brings to the fore our reading of the circus as an allegorical representation of Spain, but also expresses de la Iglesia's suspicion of nationalist political agendas, regardless of their source, since as he declared in an interview, "I hate the circus."

The transformative energy of the transitional moment precipitated by Carrero Blanco's death crystallizes in the last sequence of the film, which takes place in Franco's monumental burial site built at Cuelgamuros valley near Madrid. Choosing a moral path between vengeance and forgiveness, *Balada*'s last sequence at the Valley of the Fallen aspires—as Minow recommends nations transitioning from regime crime do—to symbolically memorialize Spain's traumatic past so that it may never be forgotten (23).[38] The movie does this by cinematically resignifying the "most imposing piece of Fascist architecture still active anywhere," as Jeremy Treglown describes "Franco's crypt" (63), transforming this beacon of *nacional-catolicismo* at the core of Francoist ideology into a memorial for *all* victims of the Civil War, thus communicating, as Minow writes, "the aspiration of 'never again'" (23).[39]

In connivance with Ramiro and the rest of the circus crew, Javier moves the animals and the remnants of the circus equipment to the Valley of the Fallen, described by one of the characters as a cave with a giant cross on top. The Valley is not just a spectacular architectural frame to the last climactic sequence, but also becomes central to *Balada*'s theme of mourning the dead.[40] Given its visibility—its ominous cross can be seen miles away presiding over the Castilian mesa—the monument remains for Treglown Spain's "elephant in the room" (84) (Fig. 7.7).[41] Despite the fact that according to Francoist rhetoric the site was built to remember the casualties of war from both sides, as Patricia Keller writes, "the monument was designed not to show the horrors of war ... nor to perpetuate memory ... but to consecrate war, to glorify and sanctify it within the visual and discursive logic of Imperial Christian-militarism" ("The Valley, the Monument, and the Tomb ..." 75). Thus, despite Franco's effort to bury almost 40,000 bodies of fallen soldiers from both camps, the Valley of

Figure 7.7 *Balada triste de trompeta*, 2010

the Fallen is a monument that instead of honoring the victims from both sides, as Katherine Hite observes, materializes the Francoist "'doctrine of redemption'" (quoted in Keller, "The Valley, the Monument, and the Tomb ..." 75).[42] The Valley of the Fallen, as Keller instructively concludes, "in monumentalizing its defiance of 'el olvido' (forgetting), in fact, re-inscribes the logic (and burden) of forgetting into its very foundation" ("The Valley, the Monument, and the Tomb ..." 77).[43]

Although the monument contains tens of thousands of bodies, Gilles Tremlett shrewdly remarks, "I could ... find only two names on the tombstones inside. One was that of Falange founder José Antonio Primo de Rivera ... [t]he owner of the other one, General Franco, reserved his spot well before his death. 'When my turn comes, put me here,' he told the architect, pointing to the floor behind the altar" (Tremlett 44).[44] Thus, despite the Francoist rhetoric of redemption, as Nicolas Sánchez Albornoz categorically affirms, Franco's remains "are buried in a monument to cruelty and corruption" (quoted in Tremlett 50).[45]

The last sequence of *Balada* not only resignifies Franco's monumental burial, reversing its logic of forgetting, but also upends the Francoist rhetoric of redemption. After successfully kidnapping Natalia, Javier takes her to see his new-found home at the Valley—Javier's own name, as mentioned earlier, meaning "new house." Javier has moved what remained from the circus—animals included—to Franco's monumental burial site with the help of the rest of the crew, who have decided to help him win Natalia's love. Surrounded this time by thousands of real human skulls instead of the fakes that we saw at the Museum of Horrors and the amusement park, Javier has created a shrine to Natalia's love, similar to the one María made to honor her beloved Diego in Almodóvar's *Matador*.

The place resembles a cave, a grotto, a space associated with the fake transcendence of kitsch aesthetics, and reminds us of Franco's crypt which Javier has decorated with the circus memorabilia and thus allegorically alludes to the nation's recent past.[46] He has adorned the place with the old circus lighting and the extant letters of the word *entrada* which appeared in the scene at the beginning of the film in which Javier saw Natalia for the first time, suggesting a point of entry into Spain's dark past, this time from the very epicenter of the monument symbolizing Francoist dictatorship (Fig. 7.8). He has even installed a film projector which replays the performance of Raphael's mournful song on one of the walls of the crypt. Excited as a child would be in anticipation of showing his own room to a loved one, Javier tells a terrified Natalia, "You're in for a surprise. Look what I've got for you," while he pulls her through the maze of corridors of the Valley—the labyrinth, as we will see in the next chapter on *Pan's*

Figure 7.8 *Balada triste de trompeta*, 2010

Figure 7.9 *Balada triste de trompeta*, 2010

Labyrinth (2006), being a common visual metaphor for the intricate paths of memory. When the two finally reach Javier's inner shrine at the core of the Valley, to the left of the frame we first see a pile of skulls shown against the musical background of Raphael's song. Natalia, truly frightened, looks around while Javier eagerly jumps up and down on an elastic circus bed, as the camera cuts to another shot of more skulls piled up against the wall (Fig. 7.9). Javier's childish behavior starkly contrasts with the macabre spectacle around him, elevating the dramatic tension of the scene.[47] Finally, the camera cuts to a shot of Ramiro—the guardian of memory— now in charge of the film projector showing Raphael's images, who gives Natalia an ominous look (Fig. 7.10). Javier has thus reoccupied Franco's crypt, the most sacred site of Francoism, endowing it with his personal sensibility, as suggested by the new decorating arrangements made by recycling the circus memorabilia, and also historical depth, as implied by the projected images of Raphael's performance, connoting a mournful

Figure 7.10 *Balada triste de trompeta*, 2010

Figure 7.11 *Balada triste de trompeta*, 2010

remembrance of the past and appropriately controlled by Ramiro, the guardian of memory. When Javier finally invites Natalia to dance, she, horrified, attempts to flee. Javier soon captures her and the two of them begin to slow dance below the screen on which Raphael is singing the song.

The dance echoes their previous parodic romantic scene—the shot is even filled with snowflakes—in the amusement park, shot, as we saw, against the background of a cut-out of the Eiffel Tower (Fig. 7.11). But unlike the earlier scene, where Javier's romantic ambitions were mocked by the mise-en-scène as mere childlike wishful thinking, now the dance scene opens up the space for the two characters' moral transformation.[48] And it is Javier's last attempt at reconciling with Natalia after his violent and murderous episodes have completely alienated the two of them. After a few seconds, however, Natalia stops dancing and tells him, "It's difficult to dance with those huge shoes," alluding to the clown shoes he is wearing and, implicitly, to his monstrous transformation. As she resumes the dance, Javier apologizes to Natalia for everything he has done, while simultaneously, and childishly, renouncing all responsibility for his actions by blaming them on the advice his father and Raphael gave him, although the spectator knows that Raphael urged him against vengeance, as we saw in the scene inside the movie theater. While dancing, Javier opens his heart to Natalia: "I know you don't love me." To which she sarcastically replies, "Who told you that? Raphael?" Ignoring the snide comment, Javier continues, "Maybe in time, I will learn to pretend to be like Sergio." To which Natalia replies, "You're well on your way. I'm scared of you now too," making clear that everything Javier has done was based on the mistaken assumption that the only way to gain Natalia's respect (and win her heart) was by becoming like Sergio. And releasing herself from his embrace, she claws Javier's face with her fingernails as if she were a tigress, and manages to flee.

While Javier himself has been labouring under the wrong assumptions, even possibly lying to himself to justify his own behavior, however, the mise-en-scène of the shrine he built for Natalia speaks the truth: the only way to gain Natalia's heart is by acknowledging the presence of the dead, by offering them cohabitation, as both the many real human skulls piling up against the wall and the projection of Raphael's song of mourning for them seem to suggest. This is why Natalia perceives Ramiro's look as ominous in the point of view shot referred to above. She is about to confront the past she had previously denied.

Machine gun in hand, Javier soon catches up with Natalia against a wall of the tunnel filled with human bones. She gets scared by the rattling of the circus lion in its cage, a subtle reference to Mark's Gospel and the fear of the empty tomb. Reflecting on their surroundings, filled with the remains of the dead—in an irreverent way similar to the gravedigger's handling of human bones which leads to Hamlet's famous reflections on Yorick's skull, a jester just like Javier's father he played with as a child—Javier asks Natalia, "The Valley of the Fallen. Did you know about it? There are fifteen caves here full of bodies. One of these has to be my father," and he goes on while kicking a skull as if it were a soccer ball, Spain's national sport: "Some fascists, others reds. But they all ended up here together. Death unites people," thus replicating the careless manner of *Hamlet*'s gravedigger, who tosses away the bones of the grave he is preparing for Ophelia.

This is a crucial comment in the film's larger theme of dealing with the ghosts of the past, but it should not be understood as evidence that the film is suggesting both sides are equally complicit and thus clearing Franco's side of moral, political, or criminal responsibility for the crimes committed, since, as the standard narrative goes, after all war is a dirty affair in which both fascists and Republicans committed gross human rights violations. This, of course, is the preferred line of argument of the Spanish political right, which I argue the film strongly opposes. In *Balada*, both sides are not equal. There is a huge difference between Sergio—the brutal sadist despot, and Javier, a sensitive person who mistakenly tries to impress his love by becoming like his rival because he is led to believe that Natalia only loves men like Sergio. It also makes a clear distinction between Javier's father, a good-hearted silly clown adored by children, who demands revenge after being arrested, reduced to slave status and forced to work in the Valley by the fascists, and the fascist colonel who savagely murders him while cowardly mounted on his horse.

Nor surprisingly, according to our reading of the film, is it inside "Franco's Crypt," surrounded by the skulls of the dead, that Javier and Natalia finally begin to understand each other. For the first time, Natalia implicitly admits her own moral responsibility for the tragic turn of events when she tells Javier that she doesn't love Sergio anymore, confessing she would consider being with Javier "but not like this ... ," referring to his monstrous transformation. And for the first time Javier opens his heart to Natalia, revealing his true feelings for her. As in the standard romantic comedy, when after a truth-revealing monologue the boy is able to get the girl back, here Javier also seems to have touched Natalia's heart with his declaration of love, and they fuse in a passionate kiss. This romantic moment, which for the first time is not treated ironically by the mise-en-scène, is interrupted, as in the amusement park, by Sergio who, pointing a gun at Ramiro's head, suddenly shows up: "How sweet! Can I be the best man?" (Fig. 7.12). Ramiro—the guardian of memory—instructs the couple to escape through the exit door that leads to the cross, and Sergio shoots him in the head, as if attempting to efface forever the historical record Ramiro is in charge of keeping.

Figure 7.12 *Balada triste de trompeta*, 2010

The long sequence of the physical struggle ending in death involving Sergio, Javier, and Natalia, which takes place on top of the cross of the Valley, becomes the narrative climax of the movie. Through Natalia's death—by jumping from the top of the cross in order to save Javier from Sergio's persecution—the film upends Francoist notions of redemption derived from an ultra-conservative hijacking of Christian ethics as symbolized by the giant cross of the monumental site. Natalia's death could be understood as a ritual sacrifice which, like the ending of Almodóvar's *Matador*, is also contemplated by a community of onlookers gathered below, in this case constituted by security forces, paramedics, and the media, as well as several members of the circus crew.[49]

This last scene with Natalia and Javier chased by Sergio on the cross is crafted as a homage to both Hitchcock's *North by Northwest* and *Vertigo*, whose daring mise-en-scène and ingenious narrative twists are here revisited to enrich the film's larger theme of redemption through mourning instead of through violence. Like Thornhill and Eve, in *North by Northwest*, they start climbing a giant headstone, in this case not that of former US presidents but that of Mark the Evangelist, whose appearance has already been foreshadowed by the shot at the beginning of the film of young Javier next to the lion—the traditional iconographic representation of St Mark—and also by Javier's dream sequence. Their climbing through Mark's headstone to escape from Sergio suggests that the only way for Spain to heal and become whole again is to address its fascist past by filling "the empty tomb" and giving the dead a proper burial. They finally reach the inner staircase of the cross and proceed to ascend in a scene reminiscent of that of Scottie and Madeleine inside the tower of the Mission Dolores—a Spanish word meaning "pain" and etymologically related to the word *luto*, Spanish for "mourning"—at the end of *Vertigo*, a film which, like *Balada*, is also haunted by the ghosts of the past. As de la Iglesia explained, he likes ending his films on the tops of buildings—three of his films have endings like this—because people tend to tell the truth in extreme situations (46).[50]

Natalia and Javier climb the stairs to reach the top of the cross, which like *Vertigo*'s mission tower also has obvious phallic connotations—both Scottie and Javier can only get the women of their dreams by mastering themselves in these vertical, phallic structures. In *Vertigo*, the middle-aged Scottie—his nickname referring to his arrested psychic development symbolically represented by his fear of heights—is given a second chance at conquering his fear in the tower at the end of the film. In *Balada*, Javier becomes an adult by breaking the cycle of revenge, by ceasing to be his father's vengeful errand boy. Only then, the film suggests, will he grow up and begin living in the present, a temporal multilayered present that instead of denying the past, finally acknowledges it. The film symbolically reclaims the cross's vertical structure for all Spaniards so that the society as a whole can also mature and begin to mourn its loss. This is still a necessary step since, as the next few shots reveal, the cross's inner walls are branded with the yoke and arrows of Falange—a visual reminder of Franco's reappropriation of Christianity—which, as we saw in Chapter 3, branded Spain's urban landscape long after the transition to democracy began.

The scene of Javier and Natalia running up the stairs inside the cross reinforces the idea of healing, of coming to terms with the past by playing with the color scheme of the Spanish flag. Natalia runs upstairs first, followed by Javier being chased by Sergio. In the last flight of stairs before reaching the cross's horizontal arms, the frame reveals four big rolls of cloth—two red and two yellow—which together form the colors of the Spanish flag. During her fast ascent, Natalia inadvertently hits them with her body and the two yellow rolls get separated from the red, an action that symbolically suggests the tearing of the Spanish flag, the rift within Spain (Fig. 7.13). Javier, running immediately behind her, is careful enough to put them back together, an action which acquires great symbolic significance. Like Hamlet, he might be unable to "set the time right" through vengeance, but he can at least try to restore a torn community, to let it heal, as his gesture of putting the colors of the Spanish flag back together seems to infer. This is a fleeting moment of synchronicity, though, since immediately after having reached one of the arms of the monumental cross, Javier goes back to pick up the red roll of fabric, which Natalia ties around her waist as a means of escape—the red color suggesting her own sacrifice, thus foreshadowing the tragedy about to happen—before jumping to her

Figure 7.13 Balada triste de trompeta, 2010

death. Still unsure of Natalia's change of heart, Javier probes further, "Are we escaping together?" To which Natalia convincingly responds, "Yes sweetie, we are escaping together and fast," using the Spanish term of endearment *cielo* (Spanish for "Heaven"), as if anticipating her own death.

As in *North by Northwest*—a film whose title, supposedly, derived from a line from *Hamlet*—the villain finally catches up with the couple, stepping on Javier's hand, which desperately clings to the edge of the precipice. Unlike in Hitchcock's movie, though, Sergio's appearance at the top of the cross will precipitate the tragic end of Natalia and implicitly the symbolic reclaiming of the Valley of the Fallen for all Spaniards by deconstructing Francoist/Christian notions of redemption. Sergio attacks Javier and Natalia, and ends up holding a knife to Natalia's throat like he did to Javier's father in the dream sequence.

It is at this critical moment in the film that the appearance of the circus's ghost rider—a daredevil who in his regular act always misses his mark and crashes against a wall—brings us back to Derrida's argument in favor of a notion of justice based on a disjointed temporality. The ghost rider tries to convince the rest of the circus crew that since he has boosted his motorcycle's turbo motor, he can now break the sound barrier and reach the top of the cross in time to help Natalia and Javier. His plan is received with skepticism by the circus owner, who says, "It's not us. It's this country that's gone to the dogs," an obvious comment on Spain's collective malady.

As it always happened in his circus act, the ghost rider fails once again, this time crashing against the hard surface of the cross and falling down to hit St Mark's giant headstone (Figs. 7.14 and 7.15). The ghost rider's failed attempt to rescue Natalia and Javier reveals its deeper meaning if interpreted through Derrida's concept of "hauntology," which, as mentioned earlier, argues for a spectral notion of subjectivity which, inhabiting a non-teleological notion of time, opens up the possibility for a non-abstract, singular concept of justice. As Derrida writes, justice not simply as "*rendering* that would be limited to sanctioning, to restituting, and to *doing right*" (26). In other words, justice not as generalizable abstraction but as hospitality, an empathic opening to others as others, which is the kind of justice championed by the film. This concrete, non-abstract notion of justice is also at the heart of any true notion of forgiveness.[51] It is precisely the abstract kind of forgiveness—imposed at the institutional level by Spain's Pact of Forgetting—*Balada* refuses to endorse. The movie thus shares in Derrida's notion of justice and rejects the notion of revenge against the fascists as it rejects the attempts to forgive their crimes. Memory serves as guardian of the just reckoning against the two.

Figure 7.14 (upper and lower) *Balada triste de trompeta*, 2010

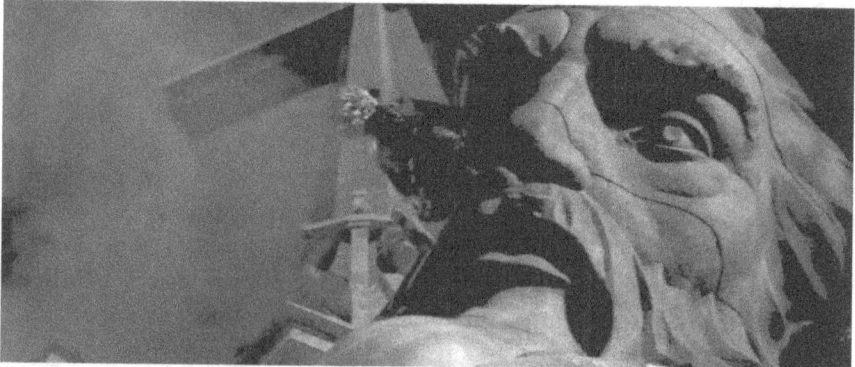

Figure 7.15 *Balada triste de trompeta*, 2010

The ghost rider's flight through space in order to get to the top of the cross simulates the crossing of the sound barrier by creating a visual ripple effect that could be understood—to use Keller's phrase—as a "rupture of time," a tear in the smooth veneer of linear temporality

(*Reading the Ghost* ... 10). In his failed attempt to rescue Javier and Natalia, the ghost rider has metaphorically chipped the synchronous armor of fully present temporality and reintroduced a sliver of the spectral past that helps contemplate history as "ghostly time situated somewhere between the past, the present, and future" (11).[52] As his name strongly suggests, the ghost rider himself—always missing his mark—embodies Derrida's notion of spectral subjectivity, "out of joint" with itself. This is a kind of subjectivity haunted by the ghosts of the past which is able to "transformatively recognize" the past in the present, as the singer Raphael was able to do through his lamentation song.[53] In the film, the time out of joint and the self out of joint thus open the possibility for non-closure and "disadjustment," which for Derrida paradoxically is the condition of justice (22). In this way *Balada*, like Almodóvar's earlier films, proposes a different way to conceive the subject and its relation to the social from Francoist polarizing categories. This emerging new subject should be like post-Francoist Spain, not "unified" or "divided" but "multiple" and "contradictory." The film invites us to imagine the possibility of redeeming the past by acknowledging it, by burying the dead, by properly mourning "out of concern for justice."

The attempt by the ghost rider to rescue the couple is also important for understanding the film's conscious effort to avoid a facile narrative closure and thus closing too soon the books on the past. At this point it would have been very easy to succumb to the temptations of closure and turn the frustrated ghost rider, allegorically embodying the spectral national past, into the proverbial hero who at the last minute saves the couple in peril. The film, however, refuses a conventional happy ending, as the ghost rider not only crashes against the hard surface of the cross but also, as we saw, St Mark's headstone, reminding us of the film's theme of the "empty tomb" above our heads. *Balada* thus refuses closure as it opens itself up to "what remains inevitably indeterminate, elusive, and inexplicable about collective horrors" (Minow 24).[54] Unlike Almodóvar's *Matador*'s final scene, then, in which everything converges in a moment of social and cosmic closure offering a final imaginary resolution to social contradictions by showing cosmic continuity in the death of discontinuous beings, in *Balada* such cathartic closure does not occur. Instead it opens a space for reflection and for remembering the past sorrowfully, as its own title demands.

After a series of lucky moves, Javier manages to liberate Natalia from Sergio's grip. Feeling triumphant despite his extremely precarious situation, Javier tells Sergio: "See? In the end, I'm the smart one and you're the dummy. Who cares if you're funny when it's time to die?" Prompted to tell the truth from these heights, as de la Iglesia had promised of his characters,

Natalia insists again that she does not want him to be like Sergio: "You have to believe me. Nobody wants you to be funny. You have to believe me. I love you, sad clown." In her love declaration, Natalia thus makes perfectly clear that she loves Javier as the sensitive melancholic character the sad clown has come to signify.[55] It is the sad clown, like Pierrot, with his white face and a large black tear rolling down his cheek, not the happy clown, who the film proposes as the ideal vessel for mourning the dead. It is in this exact moment of truth, similar to *Vertigo*'s moment of truth, that the ghost rider crashes against the hard surface of the cross to become literally a "ghost" rider, as if underlining the melancholy nature of their relationship, traversed by the ghosts of the past.

This climactic scene at the top of the cross also undermines the Francoist redemptive function of the Valley. A giant cross on top of a cave, as described earlier by one of the characters, the Valley materializes Francoism's obsession with martyrdom and redemptive violence. The monumental site could be read thus as a giant sacrificial altar on which Republicans were sacrificed in order to expiate their sins against the state. Noticing that Sergio's foot is encircled by the red cloth that she tied around her waist, and in order to save Javier's life, Natalia hits Sergio and plunges into the abyss. Her plan works and Sergio—entangled in the cloth—falls with her but gets stuck, dangling safely in mid-air. Natalia, her body circling down at incremental speed to the soundtrack of operatic music and wrapped in red cloth and a yellowish bodice—the colors of the Spanish flag—keeps falling. After running out of cloth, she comes abruptly to a full stop. Her spine is broken. As does Antigone, Natalia also dies tragically. The camera cuts to a close-up of her bloody face and then to the red cloth, to the cross and to the faces of the circus crew contemplating the spectacle, as in Grünewald's Crucifixion painting in the opening sequence. The police finally arrest Sergio and Javier, locking them up in the back of a police van.

Through Natalia's tragic end, which saves Javier's life, the film's ending upends Franco's logic of redemption, which was based on the idea of a good Spaniard always being ready to die for his motherland, thus reclaiming the Valley of the Fallen for every Spanish citizen. In so doing, it also rewrites the traditional meaning of the Christian Crucifixion. As we saw in earlier chapters, for Francoism Spaniards should fulfill their destiny by sacrificing themselves literally or figuratively for the well-being of the nation, for the *Madre Patria*, the fatherland. In *Balada* it is Natalia, the *Mater Dolorosa*, the allegorical figure of the *Madre Patria*, who traditionally mourns her son, the one who sacrifices herself to redeem its citizens from their tragic fate, and not the other way around, becoming thus as mentioned above a subject of mourning herself. In this new narrative, Natalia, the Virgin Mary of the nation, becomes a Christ-like figure who sacrifices herself so her son can live. In *Balada*'s inversion of Franco's logic of redemption, then, Spaniards are no longer ideologically interpellated to sacrifice themselves for the fatherland, but it is the motherland which sacrifices itself for its citizens.

Natalia's death by jumping into the abyss from the top of the giant cross at the end of this sequence has turned her into a ghost herself, so at the end the film transforms Spain's allegorical representation into a subject of mourning. The final scene, as mentioned earlier, is a medium shot of the two clowns facing each other in the back of the police van. The camera intercuts shots of each face sobbing inconsolably (Fig. 7.16). Following their preordained roles and their subsequent facial transformations, though, Sergio, the funny clown, seems also to be simultaneously laughing. After a while, Javier's uncontrollable crying also seems to have a tinge of laughter in it. As mentioned earlier, these final shots emphasize the structural resemblance of opposites as tears and laughter fuse, ultimately

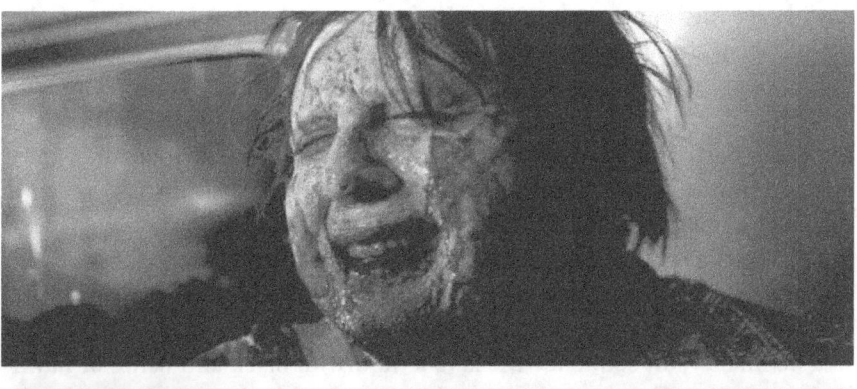

Figure 7.16 (upper and lower) *Balada triste de trompeta*, 2010

deconstructing the binary oppositions that have for too long characterized Spanish society.⁵⁶ This final scene not only undermines binary categories but also has both antagonists equally share in the role of mourners of Natalia, the personification of the motherland. At the end, thus, the film itself accomplishes the "transformative recognition" from forgetting to mournful acknowledgment that had begun at the diner scene in which Javier first heard "Balada triste de trompeta," the song which cries for a past to which Natalia now belongs.

The closing credit sequence embodies in its very form the idea of mourning the film proposes throughout. Until that point, according to de la Iglesia, "the film is a circus of striking colors" which for him represents what is going on in Spain, where it is very difficult "to contemplate reality from an ex-centric point of view. Either you are with me or against me. It's our way of thinking. Violence is not in the film, it is in everyday life" (Angulo and Santamarina 286). In that sense, Javier is not the only one who is "out of joint," at odds with his avenging mission; the film itself is off its hinges inasmuch as it plays off the idea of revenge to end all revenge. As de la Iglesia has declared, *Balada* was born precisely out of his own rage, his "desire for vengeance to confront a situation that I was not responsible for either at a political or at a social or personal level."⁵⁷ Paradoxically, the motivation behind making *Balada*, admittedly his most personal film, was his vengeful feeling against vengeance; he was frustrated and tired of the rigid polarities that have traditionally characterized Spanish society. His reaction to this frustrating situation was to make a film that redraws the rules of the game. Like Maria's shrine in *Matador*, which is a space of integration that offered itself to difference and heterogeneity, *Balada* also offers itself as such a space for overcoming the ideological dichotomy that has traditionally characterized Spanish society.

The final credit sequence turns to a mournful black and white of familiar images from Spanish television; black-and-white images that invite the spectator to reflect on the black-and-white political ideology imposed by Franco. They are the familiar images of entertainers recognizable to any Spaniard growing up under Franco: the clowns Tonetti, Gabi, Fofó, and Miliki; cartoons such as *La Familia Telerín*; the famous Spanish lion tamer Angel Cristo, whose name and profession remind us of important figures in the film (the exterminating angel, Jesus Christ, and the emblematic lion of Mark the Evangelist); and comedians such as *Los hermanos malasombra*, Torrebruno and *El Capitán Tan*.

The saeta's musical chords at the beginning of the film, whose powerful emotional resonance is normally associated with the mass spectacle of Easter, are now replaced by mournful piano music, quiet and introspective.

Not coincidentally, the last flickering image is that of Charlie Rivel, the internationally renowned Spanish clown whose signature was to howl as if he were a wolf standing on top of a chair. The clown as a howling wolf, a staple figure of the gothic imagination, which immediately conjures up images of moonlit cemeteries at midnight, brings the film to an end. Here, as in Shakespeare's plays—where gravediggers are also clowns representing the common man who, armed solely with wit, stands against the mystifications of ideology—the clown is the perfect character to conjure up the dead. The film is personally dedicated by de la Iglesia to the common person, that is, to "all who suffered and died during those years but nobody remembers them and to the TV clowns for making me laugh."

Notes

1. In the 1921preface to his novel *La Tía Tula*, Miguel de Unamuno describes Oedipus's daughter Antigone as "that saint of Helenic paganism ... she suffered martyrdom for her love for her brother Polyneices, and because she confessed her faith in the eternal laws of conscience, the laws that rule the eternal world of the dead, the immortal world, and not the laws forged by despots and tyrants of the earth such as Creonte" (39).
2. As Oxana Shevel has observed, "[b]y drawing a curtain over the past in the name of national reconciliation, the pact [of forgetting] left the historical narrative created under Franco undisturbed and thus suppressed the memory of the Republican side" (139).
3. Thus, although the Spanish transition was deemed "the paradigm of a peaceful transition from an authoritarian to a democratic regime" other countries aspire to imitate (Aguilar 93), as Spanish political scientist Josep Colomer writes, "the virtues of the transition have become the vices of democracy" (quoted in Aguilar 117). As Aguilar writes, "[i]t is indubitable that Spanish democracy is consolidated and has high levels of social legitimacy. Many of the defects mentioned above as institutional remnants of the dictatorship are also found in other countries for very different reasons. However, I have tried to point out which of the worst aspects of Spanish democracy are at least partly attributable to its authoritarian past and to the fact that it took politicians at least ten years to engage in certain institutional reforms" (Aguilar 118).
4. As José Colmeiro writes, the "avalanche of memoirs, autobiographical novels, films, documentaries, and revisionist historical accounts [...] coincides with the official politics of collective forgetting" ("A Nation of Ghosts" 24).
5. Bringing Derrida's theoretical framework to better understand the Spanish case, in her influential essay "History and Hauntology," Jo Labanyi sets out to answer the following question: "What does a society—in particular, Spanish society of the transition and since—do with history; that is, what

does it do with the ghosts of the past?" (65). Following Derrida, she proposes that "ghosts must be exorcised not in order to chase them away but in order 'this time to grant them the right to a hospitable memory'" (66). The ghost in *Balada* is understood in Avery Gordon's definition as "not simply a dead or missing person, but a social figure," which, if investigated, "can lead to that dense site where history and subjectivity make social life" (8).

6. In *Machiavelo frente a la gran pantalla*, for instance, Pablo Iglesias criticizes the film's reconciliatory impulse.
7. In *La estela del tiempo: imagen e historicidad en el cine español contemporáneo*, Cristina Moreiras-Menor sees in de la Iglesia's film *La comunidad* (2002) a clear need to deal with the ghosts of the past. As she writes, in this film "the past ... is rendered in its spectral presence, as a reality radically present in its absence" (155).
8. This is a narrative still promulgated by many members of the governing *Partido Popular*.
9. Like the active and prescient politics of mourning described above, *Balada* tries to complicate the traditional separation of mourning and melancholia as delineated by Freud's famous essay "Mourning and Melancholia," in which the former is described as a healthy working through of the loss of the love object, and the latter as a pathological attachment to it which impedes the subject from moving forward.
10. As Benjamin writes, "Nowhere but in Calderón could the perfect form of the baroque *Trauerspiel* be studied" (81). Firmly rooted in history rather than in tragic myth, as George Steiner writes in the introduction to Benjamin's *The Origins of German Tragic Drama* (1963), "the baroque dramatist, allegorist, historiographer, and the personages he animates, cling fervently to the world" (16). Given its grounding in historical reality, the *Trauerspiel*, he concludes, "is counter-transcendental" and "empathically 'mundane,' earthbound, corporeal" (16). Instead of positing what he calls tragedy's "aesthetic of reticence," the "sorrow-play" (*Trauerspiel*), like *Balada*, is "emphatically ostentatious, gestural and hyperbolic" (18).
11. This wide range of influences obviously reflects his cultural background. He has a degree in philosophy from the University of Deusto in the Basque Country, and began working in the entertainment industry first as a comic-book writer and then as an artistic director.
12. As Butler writes, in Benjamin's conception of *Trauerspiel* "pantomime becomes the index of mourning," since the gesture "has lost its referent" so it operates "through a non-mimetic semiotic of its own" (470). This is an idea emblematically personified by Pierrot's pale melancholy face, immediate precursor of the white face of the sad clown represented by Javier.
13. As de la Iglesia explains, once the counter-cinema he proposed during the 1990s became the new norm he decided to contradict his own guidelines by telling himself: "Let's do a film about clowns during the Civil War" (Angulo and Santamarina 148).

14. The "opening of the door" routine also reveals the historical referent of the allegorical form of the film by combining the realistic style of depicting historical events (the militia officer bursting through the real door) with the metaphorical quality of the fake circus door (through which fascism intrudes).
15. Marta Rivero Franco noticed how this scene is inspired by Goya's etchings and "reminds us of *Los desastres de la Guerra*. Here the cinematography has faded tones where a harsh and contrasted black predominates suggesting a grotesque *aguafuerte*" (22).
16. As biblical scholar Karen Armstrong writes, Mark's Gospel "ended on a note of terror. When the women went to anoint the body, they found that the tomb was empty. Even though an angel told them that Jesus had risen, 'the women came out and ran away from the tomb because they were frightened out of their wits; and they said nothing to a soul, for they were afraid'" (70).
17. This incipient capitalist Spain was made entirely possible with the blessing of the US and the close monitoring of the International Monetary Fund working alongside Franco's "technocrats," as the regime's *Opus Dei* cabinet members were commonly called, whose goal was to integrate Spain into the global capitalist system.
18. See Paul Preston, *The Politics of Revenge: Fascism and the Military in 20th-Century Spain*.
19. The credit sequence also suggests, as Juan Pablo Pacheco Bejarano writes about *Balada*'s overall aesthetic approach, "that, just as the regime was solidified through culture, the subversion of its legacy must also take part of such cultural dialogue, radically questioning and deconstructing official narratives through deforming an already absurd and fragmented past" (117–18).
20. As he stated in an interview, "[t]here are generations that remember some television programs better then certain political events or they remember those events that had to do with television better" (Buse, Triana-Toribio, and Willis 98). As Buse, Triana-Toribio, and Willis write in relation to *Muertos de Risa*, "[w]ithin the film ... the medium of television, rather than the press or other forms of historical record, becomes the authenticator of the fictional world and the medium that de la Iglesia clearly links most closely with popular memory" (101).
21. As Buse, Triana-Toribio, and Willis have written, the cinema of Álex de la Iglesia is "for the most part ... a ludic, pre-Oedipal cinema, or, to translate Freudian vocabulary into Lacanian, a cinema of pre-symbolic play. Although it embraces the kinetic values of Hollywood, it foregoes the standard Oedipal trajectory that tradition favours" (31–2).
22. The idea of the stillborn baby, and the fact that "there is no Mother," also links the joke with the larger theme of the movie of the crimes of Francoism and of the mourning of the dead, particularly to the newly exposed fact that during the 1940s and '50s thousands of babies were stolen from their mothers to be adopted by Francoist families.

23. Or one could say that Javier now feels that the "apparent contradictions locked together in a numinous intimation of wholeness," as Armstrong writes describing the experience of those who recognized Jesus's ghostly apparition (73).
24. *Mater Dolorosa* is precisely the term historian José Álvarez Junco chose for the title of an important book on Spanish history (2001).
25. Princesa, as her caretaker Ramiro reveals to Javier, is profoundly jealous of women. In fact, we learn she killed Ramiro's own wife by sitting on her until crushing her to death. The immense weight of historical memory crushes the only person who potentially could distract Ramiro from his priestly task as a guardian of memory.
26. Ramiro in this sense is also the equivalent of the *Intrigant* in the *Trauerspiel* "whose intimacy with the tyrant or royal victim," as Steiner writes, "makes of him a key witness and also the weaver of murderous plots" (18).
27. Natalia is now wearing a blonde wig instead of the black one she alternates with throughout the film, the blonde and the brunette being the two stock female characters of film noir.
28. The whole scene, with its "fullness of being" and jungle setting, could be seen as a postmodern variation on the theme of Eve's temptation in the Garden of Eden—as we saw in earlier chapters, a common subtext of Francoist kitsch cinema.
29. As the small skull moving up and down the vertical pole suggests, the deadly legacy of Francoism is still alive and kicking. This is similar to what happened historically. Francoism's final years were characterized by a renewed political and social repression; as Sergio, like a wounded animal, becomes most dangerous when he senses that Javier could win Natalia over. Finally, the police arrive to arrest him, which they do only after he puts up a struggle.
30. Unlike in the tongue-in-cheek Mount Rushmore sequence in *North by Northwest*, in which Cary Grant acquires sexual empowerment by climbing Roosevelt's face, as suggested by the last shot of the film showing a train—where the two protagonists share a compartment—rapidly entering a dark tunnel.
31. *El Lute* excited the Spanish popular imagination, in which he was deemed a new Dillinger, a type of working-class rebel against the tyrannical Francoist regime. He earned a law degree while in prison and was even the subject of a song by the then famous musical group *Boney M*.
32. The comment of the colonel's aide regarding Javier's sexual ambiguity reminds us of a similar comment, made by Ramiro, when he explains to Javier that the elephant hit him in the first place because his sad clown attire reminded her of a female. Javier's sexual ambiguity, also characteristic of Hamlet, is a leitmotif throughout the movie. It bespeaks of Javier's useless attempt to transform himself into a terrifying killing monster. No matter how hard he tries, he cannot entirely escape his softer, Hamlet-like, feminine nature. By reminding us of this side of him that he desperately tries

to repress, *Balada*, as *Hamlet*, is already questioning the moral validity of revenge.
33. As mentioned earlier, the interpreter is Spanish kitsch icon Raphael—who, incidentally, is the subject of de la Iglesia's film *Mi gran noche* [My Big Night] (2015). The original song itself appeared in Vicente Escrivá's film *Sin un adiós* (1970), whose main protagonist is also Raphael, who, in a famous sequence, sings the song in a clown's make-up.
34. And to use an example also characterized by its gore and sensationalism which brings things closer to home, Catherine Belsey mentions that in one of the main sources of *Hamlet*, Thomas Kyd's *The Spanish Tragedy* (1587), Hieronimo "rips the bowel of the earth with his dagger, calling for 'justice, O justice, justice, gentle king'" (154). For Belsey, revenge understood as an act that is supposed to remedy a lack of justice has an ambiguous moral status, since "[t]o uphold the law revengers are compelled to break it" (157).
35. Unlike Japanese songs of lamentation analyzed by Alan Tansman, which "could become songs endorsing violence because they posited a self that was willing to give itself up," thus "serving the war effort best" (261). As he writes, these songs contribute "to the atmosphere of self-sacrifice to the state, not so much because of their clichéd lyrics as because of the melancholy of their musical rhythms" (260).
36. As Vanessa Pupavac explains, "Shakespeare's drama takes us to the historic juncture between the old feudal order and the rise of the modern, and their conflicting values ... Hamlet's psychological crisis is precipitated by his inability to ... reconcile contradictory normative imperative: the ancient warrior's honour, Christian ethics, Machiavellian secular politics and faithfulness to himself" (15).
37. Unlike the tears of "Mournful Sake," for instance, the Japanese melancholy song whose tears taste "of parting" and, simultaneously, of a defiance to let go, and that, as Tansman writes, they were invariably shed onstage by her famous performer Misora Hibari—through which a "generation of Japanese have claimed to see their suffering, forbearance, and hope" (265). As Hibari's, Raphael's performance is also able to "express 'communal sentiment',", but, unlike hers, Raphael's does not present the listener with a "moment of fusion that harbors the potential for a fascist moment" but with a community of loss (266).
38. As she writes, these regimes should devise "art and memorials to mark what happened, to honor victims, and to communicate the aspiration of 'never again'" (23).
39. In January 2017, the Spanish government maintained its response to the Catalan political formation *Compromís*, which asked to *desfranquizar* the monument, citing the fact that currently the place "does not have the signification implied by them" ("*El gobierno niega que el Valle de los Caídos sea un lugar de exaltación franquista*"). Soon after, Spain's Supreme Court rejected a petition by former judge Baltasar Garzón to move Franco's remains out of

the Valley of the Fallen and to dedicate the monument to a "space of memory" ("*El Supremo rechaza la petición de Garzón sobre el Valle de los caídos*"). This rejection was followed by a proposal by the *Partido Socialista Obrero Español* (PSOE) and approved by the *Comisión Constitucional del Congreso* in early March, with the sole objection of *Partido Popular* (PP), asking the government to implement the Law of Historical Memory of December 2007 and to "follow the recommendations of a group of experts who in 2011 proposed to move Franco's remains out of the Valley of the Fallen in order to 'resignify' the space" ("*El Congreso respalda exhumar a Franco del Valle de los Caídos*").

40. As de la Iglesia stated, after being forced to build a replica of the site in the studio because the Francisco Franco Foundation (in charge of managing the site) did not allow him to shoot on location: "[t]o shoot that scene at the Valley of the Fallen was essential because I was making a film about two Spains, in a country that continues to mentally torture itself for not having resolved a problem ... For my part, I had to show that gigantic cross—the symbol that best expresses the nation's pain—both for narrative and cinematographic purposes. For me this is the moment of the recuperation of historical memory ... There are 34,000 corpses underneath that cross" (Angulo and Santamarina 288).

41. As Treglown observes, "In the 2007 Law of Historical Memory, the valley has a section to itself. Article 16 requires the place to be run 'strictly along lines applicable to places of worship and public cemeteries.' It prohibits, everywhere in the valley, 'acts of a political character and celebrations of the civil war, its leaders, and of Francoism'" (60).

42. And in an article on "coming to terms with the past," historian Helen Graham analyzes the "violence of exclusion of the defeated," asserting that "[h]istory itself became a weapon in this work of exclusion" not only under Francoism in general, but also specifically with the "vision" for the Valley (29).

43. As Tremlett writes, "Nowhere is the silence more eloquent than in the state-owned gift shop at the Valley of the Fallen. There are only two guidebooks on sale here. One is a cheap picture book. The other is written by the state body that owns it, *Patrimonio Nacional*. One does not even mention the fact that Republican prisoners of war were used to build the Valley. The other observes, briefly, that prisoners of war could redeem part of their sentence by working here" (Tremlett 48).

44. "Nominally, and according to the literature published by *Patrimonio Nacional*, it is a monument to all the dead of the Civil War. Damiana González, mayoress of Poyales del Hoyo, had insisted to me that it remained exactly that—a symbol of forgiveness and peace between the two, bitterly opposed, Spains of yesteryear. The bodies of some 40,000 dead were brought here" (Tremlett 44).

45. Professor Emeritus at New York University, Nicolas Sánchez Albornoz was himself a Republican political prisoner working, like Javier's father in the film, at the construction site.

46. The cave always had an important place within Francoist historiography, as symbolized by the famous cave of Covadonga in Asturias, believed to be the site of an apparition of the Virgin Mary, and considered as the birthplace of the Spanish nation.
47. For Nieves Corral Rey, this scene also points to Javier's return to his own past, "to an infancy he could not live, to the jumps he was denied, because as his father told him ... he did not have a happy childhood and was on the verge of death several times" (91–2).
48. As Steiner reminds us, "[t]he Dance of Death depicted in sixteenth- and seventeenth-century art and ritual is the crowning episode in the game or play of lamentation" (18).
49. As Steiner observes, unlike tragedy that "does not require an audience ... *Trauer* ... signifies sorrow, lament, the ceremonies and memorabilia of grief. Lament and ceremonial demand an audience" (17).
50. Despite the similar visual motif of climbing through the headstones of patriarchal figures, however, *Balada* is in fact much closer to *Vertigo*'s psychic bleakness than to *North by Northwest*'s tongue-in-cheek narrative charm. Like Scottie, Javier also loses the girl just brief moments after thinking he would finally be able to be with her. In *Vertigo*—a film also dealing with the ghosts of the past based on a French short novel titled *D'entre les morts* ("From among the Dead")—it is the sudden apparition of the nun's ghostly figure at the end who literally scares Madeleine to death. In *Balada*, it is Natalia who voluntarily jumps to her death to save Javier from Sergio. In *Vertigo*, which, as *Balada*, is structured as an Oedipal story, it is the castrating phantasmal presence of the mother which ultimately thwarts Scottie's chance at happiness. Scottie regains his masculinity just in time to lose the girl and therefore, as Robin Wood wrote, "triumph and tragedy are indistinguishably fused" (129). In *Balada*, triumph and tragedy are also inextricably bound but here, on the contrary, it is the mother figure—the allegorical representation of the nation—that sacrifices herself for the sake of her children.
51. As Martha Minow observes, forgiveness cannot be abstract but only particular, respecting the specificity of individual experience. Otherwise, as she writes, "[f]orgiveness can slip into forgetting or else elude those from whom it must come" (20).
52. *Balada*'s temporality is thus close to "the temporality of the allegorical," which is "dynamic, mobile and fluid," in contrast to what for Benjamin is the "measure of time for the experience of the symbol [which] is the mystical instant" (165).
53. This, as Keller observes following T. S. Eliot, Benjamin, and Derrida, "point[s] to a simple fact: that we obtain entrance into history as a lived experience of the present, not by severing it from our reality or attempting to remember it 'as it was,' but rather by embracing it as an integral and transformative force in the present—through which the fabric of our relation to

contemporaneity, and our understanding of time and space in or out of sync with itself is woven" (*Reading the Ghost* ... 13).

54. As Minow reminds us, following Saul Friedländer, it is "imperative for people to render as truthful an account as documents and testimonials will allow, *without giving in to the temptations of closure*, because that would avoid what remains inevitably indeterminate, elusive, and inexplicable about collective horrors" (24).

55. Robert F. Storey, in *Pierrot: A Critical History of a Mask* (1973), in fact compares Pierrot to Hamlet: "[l]ike the melancholy Dane, Pierrot is largely a static figure, one who is even given to occasional fits of morose brooding" (73).

56. As Steiner writes of the *Trauerspiel* then, in *Balada* "[i]t is not the tragic hero who occupies the centre of the stage, but the Janus-faced composite of tyrant and martyr, of the Sovereign who incarnates the mystery of absolute will and of its victim (so often himself). Royal purple and the carmine blood mingle in the same emblematic persona" (16–17).

57. As he says, "full of feelings of vengeance in the face of a situation that I had not generated or provoked at either a political, social or familiar level. And, then, as I told you all before, you end up feeling trapped and trying to escape the situation on all fronts."

CHAPTER 8

Under the Sign of Saturn: The Labyrinth of Moral Choices in Francoist Spain

The true fairy tale must be at once a prophetic representation—an ideal representation—an absolutely necessary representation. The maker of true fairy tales is a prophet of the future
—Novalis, *Philosophical Writings*

According to internationally renowned Mexican filmmaker Guillermo del Toro, *Pan's Labyrinth* (2006) is a film about "disobedience, choice and memory" (Diestro-Dópido 84). His critically acclaimed film is set in Spain in 1944 in the midst of brutal Francoist post-Civil War repression. The film upends Francoist kitsch ideology and symbolically ends the Francoist melancholic repressive cycle, delineated in the first part of this study, by rescuing Captain Vidal's newborn baby son from his fascist grip. Through the eyes of Ofelia, the film's young protagonist, we experience the intricate labyrinth of moral choices that citizens faced in Francoist Spain. Although many critics have argued that the supernatural events that take place in the film are a figment of the imagination of a dying child, I will try to show—in agreement with the filmmaker himself—that they are real occurrences. The film, I argue, is in fact a fairy tale for adults through which we are invited to confront our own moral responsibility in the proper mourning of a traumatic past.

Enhancing its emotional appeal through its fairy-tale narrative mode, *Pan's Labyrinth* revisits one of the bleakest periods of Spanish history to establish an emotional connection with contemporary spectators by inviting them to identify with its vulnerable child protagonist.[1] Through this emotional identification with the travails of Ofelia in fascist Spain, the audience gets to relive their traumatic experiences while, through the fairy-tale "structures of wonder and magic" (Warner 74), ironically envisioning a future grounded in historical fact and not turned into a kitsch myth. Through a reading of the film's melancholic temporality, I hope to show how the film moves its spectators to work through the trauma of the nation's troubled past. It is my argument that it can only do this through the fairy-tale form, whose magic is, ironically, all that remains to oppressed peoples struggling to see through the spell of fascism to a vision of moral clarity.[2]

As del Toro explains, it was the opening image of the fatally wounded Ofelia—the film's child protagonist—whose blood flows backwards as she lays on the ground, which enabled him to fully understand that the film "was not about a girl dying, but about a girl giving birth to herself the way she wanted to be."[3] The theme of the moral construction of the self—of "giving birth" to oneself—implicit in del Toro's words, is encapsulated in the scene of Ofelia's mother's funeral, who dies after giving birth to a son she had with Captain Vidal, the film's villain and Ofelia's murderer. This small scene encapsulates the film's ethical positioning. At Carmen's funeral, the priest recites the following words from the New Testament:

> Because the paths of the Lord are inscrutable; because the essence of His forgiveness lies in His word and in His mystery; because although God sends us *the message, it is our task to interpret it*; because when we open our arms the earth takes in only a *hollow and senseless shell, far away is now the soul in its eternal glory*; because it is in pain that we find the meaning of life and the *state of grace* that we lose when we are born; because in His infinite wisdom, [God] puts *the solution in our hands*; and because it is only in His physical absence, that the place He occupies in our souls is reaffirmed. (Emphasis added)

These words, perfunctorily delivered by a Francoist priest, are met with indifference by the funeral participants, as a medium shot of an absent-minded Captain Vidal holding his newborn baby flanked by two visibly bored Civil Guards suggests. However, for the spectator they embody the film's ethical core, calling attention to the "message" of moral freedom in politically oppressive times. The scene does this by visually counterpointing a shot of Ofelia picking up the bottle of the potent sedative she will use to drug Captain Vidal—her evil stepfather—at the end of the film to rescue her baby brother with the following words of the priest's recitation: "because [God] in His infinite wisdom puts the solution in our hands," thus highlighting not only Ofelia's determination to decide her own fate and fight the fascist Captain, but also the film's larger theme of choice and disobedience, and of moral responsibility in dangerously oppressive times. This is a message also highlighted by the Latin inscription at the entrance of the old labyrinth standing next to the Captain's headquarters, which reads "In your hands is your destiny." Ofelia's body will soon become the "hollow and senseless shell" described in the Gospel, while her soul, as in the biblical passage, will bask in "eternal glory," as suggested by the final shots of the movie in which Ofelia is reunited with her long-lost parents in the magical kingdom she once inhabited.

It is a main argument of this chapter that Ofelia's newly recovered "state of grace" is not the fake, kitsch state of being—the aura—that, as we saw in the first part of this study, Francoism wanted to restore to the country by unleashing a brutal wave of redeeming political violence. Ofelia's "state of grace" is a "moral" state of grace she achieves by making the right moral choice in the relentless pursuit of truth and justice, which the film counter-poses to the dehumanizing vindictive morality of Francoist *nacional-catolicismo* embodied by Captain Vidal and propagated, as we saw in earlier chapters, by Francoist kitsch aesthetics. The priest himself, who mechanically delivers Ofelia's eulogy, has sabotaged his own moral authority by collaborating with the military, as the institutional Church did in Spain when it sanctified Franco's crusade against the Republic. Yet his words evocatively describe Ofelia's moral path, her fervent desire to stay true to herself by following her inner moral compass, unlike most (but not all) of the film's characters, who choose to compromise their integrity for their own personal gain or—like her own mother—to simply survive Franco's new Spain.

Pan's Labyrinth's plot builds up two distinct storylines that gradually intersect. The first is the story of Ofelia, a curious, imaginative child and voracious reader of fairy tales, who is taken against her own will by her pregnant mother to a remote Civil Guard post in the mountains of northern Spain to be with her mother's new husband, the post's ruthless Captain Vidal. The second storyline comprises a classical fairy-tale narrative in which Ofelia is not a terrified child forced to move to a remote, dark corner of the country, but Princess Moanna—a princess of a magical kingdom—who leaves her kingdom to explore the human world above. In this second, fairy-tale story, a faun—part animal, part vegetable, resembling a goat with horns and hoofs but also made of stems and leaves—is sent by her parents to find the princess (Fig. 8.1). However, once the faun finds her, it is instructed not to bring her back to the magical kingdom until she can pass three tests designed to prove that her "princessly" essence is intact. The final and most important of these tests is the demand that Ofelia allow him to spill a few drops of the blood of her baby brother using a magical dagger during a full moon at the center of the old labyrinth. It is through this sacrificial act, the faun informs her, that the portal to return to the magical kingdom at the center of the labyrinth will open. But Ofelia categorically refuses to obey the faun's demand to let him harm her little brother, despite the enormous reward. During the final scene, which ties the two storylines together, Ofelia is fatally shot by Captain Vidal, who

Figure 8.1 *Pan's Labyrinth*, 2006

chases her in order to recapture his baby son, who has been kidnapped by Ofelia. Ofelia thereby becomes the victim hero of her own fairy tale.[4]

In this way, *Pan's Labyrinth* upends Francoist kitsch ideology—juxtaposing Ofelia's authenticity and moral conviction against Captain Vidal's blind obedience to fascist rules and sadistic violence—by reconnecting the fairy tale, a genre prone to kitsch and, as in the case of the Brothers Grimm, cooptable by fascism, to its darker roots in historical reality.[5] As Marina Warner points out, despite the wishful thinking and happy endings that have come to define the genre, fairy tales "are rooted in sheer misery" (74).

As a genre, fairy tales have undergone a wearisome process of "Disneyfication" that has enhanced their kitsch, escapist traits, while abandoning their darkest, most disturbing features.[6] Against this escapist, ideologically conformist use of the genre, del Toro's film opposes the fairy tale as "connective tissue between a mythological past and the present realities," in Warner's words (xvi).[7] The film revisits one of the bleakest periods of Spanish history to establish an emotional connection with contemporary spectators, by inviting them to identify with its vulnerable child protagonist. Through this emotional identification with the struggle of a child in fascist Spain, the audience relives Ofelia's traumatic experience while, through the tale's "structures of wonder and magic," as we saw, envisioning a morally just future "when suffering will be over."[8] The fairy tale, I argue, is a particularly effective mode of representation to portray Spain's traumatic and silenced past.

At the heart of fairy tales there has always been a duality between an emancipatory potential and a repressive pedagogical social function.[9] As purely behavioral corrective narrative devices, fairy tales function ideologically to instill obedience in the heart of children by describing, sometimes in gruesome detail, the great harm experienced by those who dare to disobey their parental commands, particularly in their absence, as in the case of Little Red Riding Hood, a fairly evident subtext of del Toro's film.[10] In that sense, its primary pedagogical purpose is thus to help children internalize parental laws that protect them from peril and allow them to grow up conforming to dominant social norms after their parents' final absence.

Unlike in fairy tales, however, or in biblical scriptures, in *Pan's Labyrinth* parental absence does not allude to a higher authority—"the almighty God Father"—to be internalized but to the image of a frail and vulnerable mother allegorically representing a prostrated Spain.[11] Ofelia's mother's absence will not be filled by the internalization of adult patriarchal law prompting the child's transition to adulthood, but by Ofelia's Cinderella-like desire to honor the memory of her mother and to liberate herself and her baby brother from the Captain's fascist grip. In this sense, like traditional fairy tales, *Pan's Labyrinth* is also a tale of moral growth to adulthood. But in order to grow up, instead of following orders, Ofelia becomes the tale's hero by developing a sense of self, unlike the Captain, whose self is obliterated by the large shadow cast by his father's heroic death.

Pan's Labyrinth, then, does not work ideologically as a delectable pill for the moral edification of children, but instead it deconstructs the narrative structure of fairy tales to promote its message of moral freedom in politically oppressive times. Against the reactionary ideological function of the fairy tale typical of the more "prettified and simplified versions," which, according to Bettelheim, "subdued their meaning and rob them of all deeper significance," *Pan's Labyrinth* chooses to reconnect with their original emancipatory potential (24). Del Toro's film thus partakes of a recent wave of revisionist accounts of the genre, particularly from feminist writers, "whose retellings," Warner explains, "often take the form of what have been called 'anti-tales,'" in the sense that "they seize hold of the old story and 'tell it slant'" (Warner 138). In short, *Pan's Labyrinth* summons the spirit of the fairy tale—what Bettelheim saw as the tale's ability to endure a traumatic reality and emerge victorious.

The film drops three typical fairy-tale characters—Ofelia, the faun, and the Captain—in the midst of Spain's early post-Civil War historical reality.[12] Princess Moanna, the fairy-tale hero, goes to another "kingdom"—Francoist Spain—in this case located above, in search of her true moral essence, which she will only discover through suffering and death. The faun functions as a fairy-tale classical "donor," who, in

Vladimir Propp's taxonomy, is a character typically "encountered accidentally, in the forest, along a roadway," from whom the hero "obtains some agent (usually magical) which permits the magical liquidation of misfortune" (39). Captain Vidal, Ofelia's stepfather, is the fairy tale's villain, whose role is "to disturb the peace of a happy family, to cause some misfortune, damage, or harm" (27). Echoing the horrific Pale Man's—a monster inspired by Goya's painting *Saturn Devouring His Son*—frenzy in the underworld in a seminal scene that we will examine later, the Captain becomes a true ogre, ready, like the big, bad wolf, to devour Ofelia, as suggested by the gaping knife wound at the side of his mouth inflicted by his landlady, Mercedes, who befriends Ofelia and secretly collaborates with the rebels.

The film gradually blends both of its storylines so that the fairy-tale world and the real world become intertwined to create a moral fable of civil and moral disobedience, which in its defiance of the fatalism of myth also ironically shares the moral universe of traditional fairy tales. The merging is represented visually by the mixing of the color palette: at the beginning the real world is dominated by cold, bluish tones while the magical world is depicted in warm, golden ones; by the blending of its fantasy and real narrative elements: the actual chalk Ofelia uses to open magical doors, for instance; by the visual rhyming of the mise-en-scène of the two worlds, as in the scene of the Captain's banquet which is re-created in the Pale Man's sequence in the underworld; and, finally, by the characters' gradual participation in both tales as, for example, when the Captain's movements chasing Ofelia echo those of the Pale Man's chase.

By blending two distinct narrative modes, fairy tale and realist drama—the former characterized by flights of fancy and the inclusion of the supernatural, the latter by its sober representation of reality—*Pan's Labyrinth* alters both. Unlike in prettified, kitschy versions of fairy tales that serve as moral fables that instill dominant ideological values, or propose an illusory escape from the suffocating material conditions of the working class in times of crisis, *Pan's Labyrinth*'s reworking of the genre uses the fairy tale to question blind obedience and the surrender to fate. It thereby reveals both fascist ideological and political oppression, and also the mystifying escapism of fantasy tales themselves. *Pan's Labyrinth* refuses fairy tales' "easy catharsis" that, as we saw in previous chapters, was characteristic of kitsch aesthetics, to propose instead a tale of moral self-fashioning. In doing so, the film also undermines the realist cinematic mode by bringing back to the representation of reality its own repressed shadow, which, as we saw in the chapter devoted to *Viridiana*, was also characteristic of Buñuel's aesthetic, a cinematic presence being palpable throughout the film.

Undoing the fairy tale through the fairy tale opens up the film to the world of history. The film opens with a black screen to the soundtrack of the humming of a haunting, mournful, and melancholy lullaby. As in *Balada*, the opening suggests times of darkness and despair alleviated only by motherly affection; Ofelia's mother's name, Carmen, meaning "song" or "tune," is also the name traditionally associated with the allegorical representation of Spain. Ofelia's mother, like the female protagonist of *Balada*, is also oppressed by a tyrannical lover, both representing the fate of the nation under Francoist dictatorship.

Ofelia is shown in close-up in a vertical position, but as the camera tilts to the right, we realize that she is in fact lying down, gravely wounded, blood dripping from her nose and hand (Fig. 8.2). But her blood, we soon notice, flows in reverse, as do the pages of a book of fairy tales next to her. A narrator's voice utters the conventional fairy-tale words, "Once upon a time ... ," creating in the spectators the expectation that they are about to step into the magical world of fairy tales. At the same time, the camera begins its investigation into the reality of Ofelia's mind as it zooms in through Ofelia's left eye.

This exploration of the inner recesses of Ofelia's consciousness is immediately followed by images of the magical world the princess wants to escape, filled with fantastic-looking circular buildings reminiscent of Romanesque architecture.[13] As the princess leaves her kingdom to venture into the human world above, the narrator tells us that "the sunlight blinded her and erased her memory" as the screen turns to a blinding white. From the black screen of the opening fairy-tale image to the white screen of the

Figure 8.2 *Pan's Labyrinth*, 2006

beginning of the tale in the human world, the film's opening sequence takes us from Ofelia's other side of consciousness to the dark reality of Spanish history outside. The blinding white screen which mimics the erasure of her memory also suggests, as in Buñuel's *Viridiana*, that Ofelia's self is being emptied out, ready to register Spain's traumatic history, and thus opening her to the possible development of her own moral character.

After the whiteness fades out, we are introduced to a series of images of Spain's post-war ruined landscape, while the narrator informs us that "after many years the princess died." His words are punctuated by a shot of a human skull and bones, an ambiguous image referring both to the princess's fate and to that of all the victims of the Spanish Civil War.

Given these intersecting storylines, one might assume that the fairy-tale narrative is the compensatory fantasy Ofelia tells herself while writhing in agony from her fatal wound.[14] However, over the course of the movie fantasy and reality gradually blend into one single representation of reality—a representation made more complex by simultaneously mixing objective and subjective points of view. For del Toro himself, the fairy-tale story in the movie is not a self-comforting imagined flashback before Ofelia dies, but a narrative reality. It is not a figment of Ofelia's vivid imagination derived from her resistance to growing up, as her mother suggests on many occasions, or an escapist route to bear the bleakness of reality. *Pan's Labyrinth* is thus not a realistic story about a girl who believes in fairy tales so that she can endure Francoist Spain; instead, it is an actual fairy tale for adults—set in post-Civil War Spain—that helps us mourn our lost innocent moral selves and also a more just Republican Spain, which Ofelia's death has come to symbolize.

That Ofelia has a vivid, fairy-tale-like imagination is beyond dispute. But it is my argument that her imagination is not fantastical; quite the contrary, it is born of the strength of her moral gaze that allows her—and those "who know how to look," as the narrator's last words tell us—to see beyond the surface and understand reality more fully.[15] Her ability to see more than those around her is suggested by a brief scene early on in which the motorcade bringing her and her mother to the Captain's military post makes a final stop in the middle of the road so her pregnant mother can rest. Ofelia wanders away and picks up from the side of the road a stone with the image of an eye carved in it that piques her curiosity. Nearby there is a statue, also made of stone, of a standing figure, seemingly a faun, with a deep hole for a mouth and a missing eye. Ofelia approaches the statue and inserts the stone eye in its socket, echoing the threading camera movement through her eye at the beginning of the film. The stone clicks into place and a strange insect resembling a praying mantis, which later transforms itself into a fairy guide, comes out through the statue's mouth.[16] Ofelia's action of giving full stereoscopic vision to the statue has brought it alive—she has begun the process of creating an imaginary world out of the terrible conditions of her time, and of becoming, by the power of that imagination, a moral force and exemplum.[17]

Anchoring this transformation is the figure of the labyrinth. From its beginnings in Greek culture, where it suggested an image of human entrapment threatened by evil, the labyrinth morphed in medieval times into an image of spiritual pilgrimage.[18] Like the Greek Minotaur living at the heart of the maze, Captain Vidal is a monster, a true ogre who kills innocent Ofelia at the center of the labyrinth. However, the true center of the film's labyrinth is not the place where Ofelia dies but the one inscribed vertically below the pit. At the center of this smaller labyrinth stands a monolith, with a carved image of Ofelia holding a baby with her back to the faun—representing the three main characters of the film's sacrificial triangle—symbolizing Ofelia's correct moral choice. As in the medieval labyrinth, in *Pan's Labyrinth* it is the innocent victim, the sacrificial lamb, not the evil Minotaur, who triumphantly stands at the center.

To return to the scene of Ofelia's demise: after she is fatally shot by Captain Vidal (which is often given as evidence that Ofelia's fairy tale takes place entirely in her mind), Ofelia runs away from the Captain and meets the faun under a full moon at the center of the pit for her third and final test. Chasing her into the labyrinth, Captain Vidal arrives at the scene just seconds later; he shoots her and takes the baby away. From the Captain's point of view, we realize that Ofelia, whom we just saw talking to the faun, is actually talking to no one. The faun is nowhere to be seen. The scene thus seems to suggest that Ofelia's entire fairy tale has been a figment of her imagination. Del Toro himself has argued that the scene proves only that the Captain is unable to see him: being morally corrupt, he, unlike Ofelia, cannot see the creatures from the magical kingdom.

It is still possible to object to del Toro's reading. In the film we see two shots of Ofelia in agony: at the beginning, when she is mortally wounded, and at the conclusion, when she takes her last breath. In the first instance, we also see her blood flowing backwards into her nose and the book pages flipping in reverse. We could logically adduce, then, that all the magical elements in the story come from Ofelia's last-moment flashback, a comforting fantasy she runs through her mind before dying. Yet there is another, more intriguing way of understanding this temporal reversal at the film's opening which stands in perfect accord not only with del Toro's interpretation but also with the true spirit of the medieval labyrinth as a figure of moral development. In this medieval rendering, Ofelia's story follows Christ's own story of descent and ascent, his recursive journey.[19] She is a sacrificial lamb; she contains within her, as did Christ, both the beginning and the end, the Alpha and the Omega (letters which Ofelia's own name, meaning "help" or "aid," also contains in reverse as if reflected in a mirror). Her death, like Jesus's own, points to salvation and rebirth, a journey to hell and back to save the trapped souls visually represented. The story of Ofelia, like that of Jesus, is also that of a recursive journey from the magical kingdom to Franco's Spain and back to the magical kingdom.[20]

But it is not my intention to suggest a Christian reading of the film. In fact, as Craig Wright explains, "[t]he story of a conquering god who descends into the land of the dead and does battle with the forces of evil is not unique to Christianity" (82). It was also a common theme in Babylonian, Egyptian, and Greek mythology (82). For del Toro, the biggest influence in creating Ofelia's moral universe was in fact Carl Jung's archetypal view of reality. And the film makes every effort to dress the labyrinth in Celtic pagan clothes, not in medieval Christian ones. As del Toro explains, the art design of pit, labyrinth, faun, and monolith are all made of circles and curves, which make this world feel very Celtic.[21]

The labyrinth Ofelia encounters immediately after arriving at the remote military post is only partially recognizable as such, and reminds us of the many stone ruins scattered throughout the north of Spain. Mercedes, the Captain's housemaid who secretly collaborates with the guerrilla fighters, appears out of nowhere to tell Ofelia, "It's a labyrinth. Just a pile of old rocks that have always been there, even before the mill." Mercedes, the first character in the film to be associated with the labyrinth's secret underworld, who is also connected to the clandestine real underworld of anti-Franco guerrilla warfare, is also the one who pronounces the classical fairy-tale injuncture to Ofelia: "Do not go there." These words call attention to the fact that the labyrinth—"a pile of old rocks that have always been there, even before the mill"—belongs to an ethico-magical world predating the current state of the nation, represented by the mill, where the fascist Captain has arranged his headquarters.[22] It is a dangerous space in which a child might easily get lost. But it is only the innocent child Ofelia who will learn to navigate its twists and turns, its moral secrets; only Ofelia whom the labyrinth will fully embrace at the end by magically opening a corridor for her to escape. Within minutes of her arrival at the mill, Ofelia enters the moral labyrinth where her battle not to get ethically lost—her own recursive moral journey—begins. Atop its entrance reads the Latin inscription: "In your hands is your destiny." It is only the labyrinth that will deliver her moral character.[23]

In the development of her moral character, Ofelia must battle the Captain. From the outset, the film equates the Captain's obsessive, calculating, and mechanical behavior with the watch he carries. The watch is the second in the triad of figures (along with the labyrinth and Goya's art, to be discussed below) that anchor the film's development toward a critique of Francoism and fascism. The watch is the object through which the Captain's fascist mind is revealed.

Upon Ofelia's arrival at the mill, the camera transitions from the flight of the fairy/insect, who welcomes her to her new home, to a close-up of the Captain's watch, while in the soundtrack we hear the tick-tock of time passing. Through this close-up we realize that the glass face of the watch the Captain is holding in his black leather glove is broken. From the face of the watch the camera cuts to a close-up of the face of the Captain, whose first words in the film are to complain that the motorcade is fifteen minutes late. In their precise, mechanical movements, the Captain and the watch are synchronized devices, extensions of each other—and of the fascist state. The Captain is thus associated from his first appearance with a broken watch that we will later learn belonged to his father. As del Toro observes, the watch is "the only memory he has of his father pressing him to be a famous, really large man." To enhance his characterization of the Captain as a man oppressed by his father's shadow, del Toro sets the mill's mechanical gears in the Captain's living quarters, to echo "the fact that he is trapped in his father's watch."[24]

The Captain's obsession with time, as indicated by his constant cleaning and repairing of the watch, suggests a fascist state of mind, obsessed with control. Even more than José Churruca, Franco's alter ego in *Raza*, Captain Vidal becomes the perfect embodiment of a mind that has filled the moral vacuum left by his failed ethical stand with material icons. The broken watch is such a material icon or fetish, like the crosses and flags which crowd the cinematic space in *Raza* and *Los últimos*. It suggests that he is not an authentic being living in his own time, as his own last name of Vidal would suggest, but is entirely fixated to a point in time marked by his father's "heroic" death: a glorious moment his father dutifully recorded by breaking the watch against a rock at the precise moment he died in battle for his son to remember.[25] The Captain's obsession with mechanical gears and his father's watch embalms the past in a fixed, irretrievably lost point in time. This suggests a melancholy notion of time—an epic, heroic time—that, as we saw in *Los últimos* and *Viridiana*, was a defining trait of Francoism.

The moral vacuum and death drive implicit in Captain Vidal's obsession with the time of his father's heroic death inevitably fills him with self-hatred, as becomes apparent in an important scene depicting the Captain's shaving ritual. In this scene, wearing a T-shirt, suspenders, military pants, and boots, the Captain stands in front of the mirror with a shaving blade in hand, while on the gramophone he listens to the music of a Spanish paso doble ironically titled "I'm a prisoner" and performed by Angelillo, a Spanish musical icon of the 1930s who went into exile after the Francoist victory. Pasodobles were traditionally used in bullfights and favored by Francoists because they were thought to embody the truest essence of the Spanish character. In this scene, besides underlining the fact that the Captain is indeed a prisoner of his rigid, authoritarian personality, the song helps to establish an association between the Captain and the evil Minotaur, half man and half bull, trapped inside the labyrinth. On the soundtrack we hear the tick-tock of the Captain's watch. In front of the mirror, Captain Vidal looks first at the watch and then to his face reflected in the mirror. The camera cuts now to a close-up of his mirror reflection while a crescendo of the ticking of the watch saturates the soundtrack. The elevated dramatic tension created by the ticking and by the scrutiny the Captain subjects himself to is resolved with a sudden and precise hand movement with which he simulates slashing his own throat with the blade (Fig. 8.3). As this intimate moment reveals, the Captain is full of self-loathing because he deems himself unworthy of his father's heroic legacy. This is an insight subtly implied earlier in the banquet scene, in which an officer who had met the Captain's father in Morocco reveals to him,

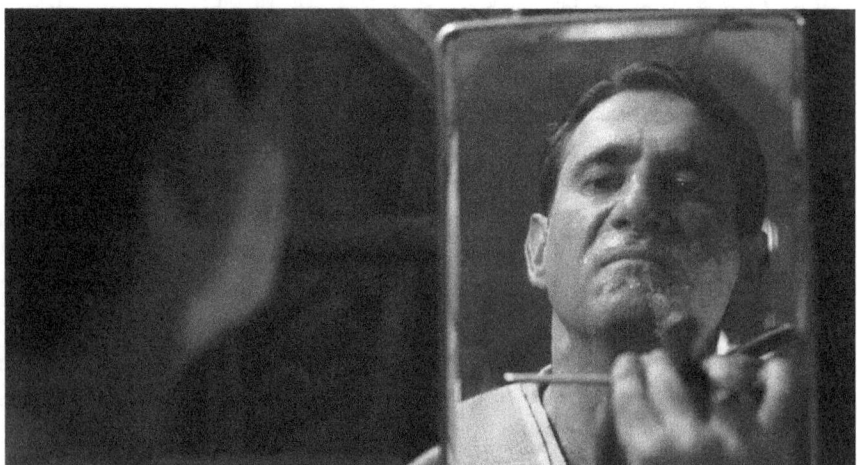

Figure 8.3 *Pan's Labyrinth*, 2006

"I knew [your father] only briefly but [he] left a big impression," to which a visibly upset Captain dryly replies: "An excellent soldier." When the officer relates to everyone the story that "the men in his battalion said that when General Vidal died on the battlefield, he smashed his watch against a rock so that his son would know the exact hour and minute of his death, so he would know how a brave man dies," the Captain abruptly puts an end to the conversation, replying, "Nonsense. He didn't own a watch." Feeling unmanly and castrated, the Captain publicly humiliates his wife.

The Captain's death drive, and his pathological obsession with detail, make him thus a chained character—as the title of the song, "I'm a prisoner," clearly suggests—trapped inside his rigid, immoral, world view. He cannot budge from fascist conduct. This intolerant, self-destructive behavior starkly contrasts with Ofelia's moral struggle for freedom and authentic self-expression. This contrast is markedly apparent in the difference between the warm, rounded, uterine, protective nature of the magical world ruled by motherly affection and the deadly, bluish, straight-line, toxic real world dominated by the father's injunction to die. To this pathological notion of melancholy, as we will see next, the film opposes a different kind of melancholy, an artistic, neo-Baroque melancholy, as we also saw in *Balada*, that in engaging with the past generates sites of memory and history for the rewriting of the past and the reimagining of the future.

The scene in the Pale Man's lair, one of the most celebrated in the film, brings us to the third visual metaphor—Goya's painting *Saturn Devouring his Son*—which the film uses to address its larger themes of memory and history, and arrive at its strong ethical form of melancholy. The Pale Man's physical appearance, as well as his grotesque action of eating two of Ofelia's guiding fairies, is inspired by the famous Goya painting, which was del Toro's main visual reference for the scene[26]. This close resemblance of the Pale Man to Goya's Saturn imbues the scene, and the entire film, with Saturn's veil of melancholy and the allegorical political meanings often associated with the painting, which has been read as a critique of the totalitarian regime of Ferdinand VII, one of the more repressive kings of modern Spanish history. From the traditional negative characteristics of melancholy associated with Saturn, the film, I argue, proposes a notion of melancholy as a moral and artistic category as seen, for instance, in Goya's famous etching *The Sleep of Reason Produces Monsters*, whose owls, associated with Minerva, the goddess of wisdom, discreetly decorate Ofelia's own bed.[27]

It is both through the mythological readings of Saturn as the melancholic, cruel god of time and the political allegorical meanings conveyed by

Goya's painting—all of which are displaced onto Captain Vidal—that the Pale Man becomes a seminal figure in del Toro's film.[28] And it is as if by descending into the visual world of a Goya painting that Ofelia makes her journey toward gaining a moral character. Measuring time with an hourglass and using a piece of chalk to carve out a magical door in her bedroom wall, Ofelia goes to the underworld to retrieve the magical element she needs to complete the second of her three tests. As del Toro has explained, in this scene "the violence of the real world is about to enter the magical world in the shape of the Pale Man and his banquet room." Before entering the Pale Man's underworld, Ofelia reads the book of crossroads for further guidance, as instructed by the faun. In typical fairy-tale fashion, the book tells her to "let the fairies guide you," to "not eat or drink anything during your stay" and to "come back before the last grain of sand falls," in a shot with the characteristic bluish tint corresponding to the real world. Simultaneously, a drawing of the Pale Man she is about to encounter gradually emerges in the pages of the book. In the drawing, the arms of the Pale Man form a similar arch as the fallopian-like branches of the dying tree, and his open mouth and body posture are also strongly reminiscent of the image of the tree, indicating that the protective, motherly uterine world of nature has been devoured and kidnapped by the saturnine monster. As revealed in the pages of the book, the overall shape of the Pale Man seems to combine both the image of the tree and the image of the faun. The film's art design suggests, then, that the Pale Man is not only a creature of the underworld, alien to the real space above, but that his saturnine evil influence has permeated the entire cinematic space, including the scene in which Captain Vidal chases Ofelia inside the labyrinth, mimicking the sluggish movements of the Pale Man.

After Ofelia has carved a magical door with her piece of chalk, the camera cuts to a counter-shot of her looking down the corridor that appears in front of her. The corridor has dominant red tones and reminds us of the insides of an animal, like Jonah's whale, ready to swallow her, an impression also enhanced by the camera's slow movement backwards in a sucking motion that reveals to us the corridor's entire length.[29] Being swallowed up and devoured also points to the dissolution of the self, as Ofelia's magical name of Moana, meaning "ocean," also seems to indicate. Ofelia's task, like that of Little Red Riding Hood, is to avoid being swallowed, to establish herself in this hostile adult world. In short, her mission is to give birth to a moral self by carving an individual moral core out of the primal oceanic state of indifference.[30]

The space below, inhabited by the Pale Man—who, according to del Toro, echoes "the facelessness of a fascist organized politics or organized religion"—also looks like the interior of a church. Ofelia walks carefully down the corridor and soon reaches the large dining room, where the Pale Man sits motionless at the head of the table, occupying the exact same place as the Captain in the banquet scene above (Fig. 8.4). The movie set, with the fireplace behind him and the large table displaying a culinary extravaganza of elaborate dishes, where a red tonality predominates, clearly replicates the Captain's banquet scene. In this scene, thus, the two worlds—the Francoist one above and the magical one below—finally conflate. Through this merging, the film colors reality with the foreboding intensity of fairy tales.[31] It tinges the cruel, arbitrary oppressiveness of the totalitarian Francoist regime with the ominous unreality of

Figure 8.4 (upper and lower) *Pan's Labyrinth*, 2006

nightmares. But unlike in fairy tales and nightmares, in *Pan's Labyrinth* there is no waking up from Franco's Spain's historical reality to a more human state of affairs. In turn, the fairy-tale world acquires an explicit political meaning usually absent from traditional fantasy literature. After all, as del Toro remarked, in this scene "the violence of the real world enters the magical world."

The Pale Man's lair's mise-en-scène mixes references to the real horror of fascist concentration camps with the horror induced by the gothic narrative imagination, thus capturing the nightmarish quality of 1940s Spain. On the walls of the Pale Man's banqueting hall hangs a series of paintings depicting the Pale Man's murdering of children. To the left of the dining table stands a large pile of old, dark children's shoes, sadly familiar from documentary footage of the Holocaust. As del Toro explains, "I wanted to echo a church-like feel and a concentration camp with the shoes piled up in the corner so I'm telling you that this is an ogre, which is a classic element in a fairy tale. This ogre who eats children is a perverse figure that has a lot of food in front of him but only eats innocents."[32]

In typical fairy-tale fashion, Ofelia's mission in the underworld is to strictly follow the instructions from the book of crossroads in order to retrieve her next magical object. One of the fairies, whose guidance she is supposed to follow, points to the small door in the center—out of the three she is supposed to choose from, a typical element of fairy tales—to let her know it is the right one. But instead of obeying blindly, after inserting the key in that door, Ofelia changes her mind and exclaims "This is not the one," and chooses the left one instead. It clicks open to let Ofelia extract her precious content: the sacrificial golden dagger to be used in the final test. Dagger in hand, she is momentarily tempted by some luscious grapes placed at the edge of the table, and disobeying the command— "Do not eat or drink anything during your stay"—proceeds to eat a couple of them. Ofelia's transgression causes the Pale Man, who has been motionless until this moment, to wake from his slumber. He suddenly moves his claw-like hands, picks up his eyeballs, which are on a tray in front of him, and inserts them into the stigmata at the center of each of his palms.[33] He then brings his hands up to his face in dramatic fashion so as to be able to see, an action that echoes Ofelia's insertion of the right eye—giving vision—into the stone statue at the beginning of the film, which sets the tale in motion (Fig. 8.5). He quietly approaches Ofelia from behind, who, ignoring the warning of the fairies, keeps eating the grapes. Finally, Ofelia realizes that the Pale Man is behind her and she attempts to flee from his grip, while the fairies try to distract him by hectically flying around his head. The Pale Man catches two fairies and bites their heads off (Fig. 8.6). Blood

Figure 8.5 *Pan's Labyrinth*, 2006

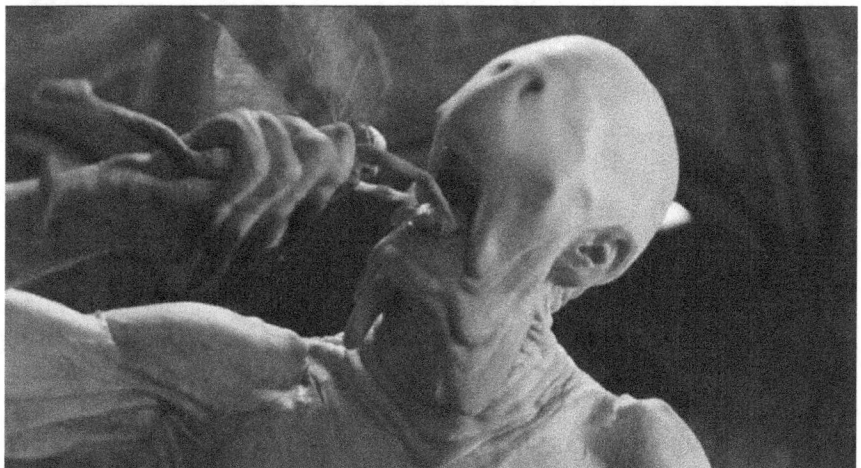

Figure 8.6 *Pan's Labyrinth*, 2006

now running down his chin, he begins to chase Ofelia through the corridor with the slow menacing movements the Captain will replicate when chasing her at the end of the film. Ofelia barely escapes alive by opening another door only seconds after the time in the hourglass has run out and the original door has magically vanished.

This scene underlines the importance of Ofelia's right moral choice, as if she were a character in a fairy tale. However, unlike in traditional fairy tales, or the Bible, the scene does not lay out a moral scenario where transgression is severely punished by physical harm. After all, despite being frightened, Ofelia escapes unscathed. On the contrary, the lesson Ofelia learns through such a dramatic and dangerous experience is precisely the opposite: never to follow orders, and to trust her own judgment instead. This is made patently clear by the fact that she retrieves the magic dagger by ignoring the advice of her "guardian" fairies, which, according to the book of crossroads, Ofelia was supposed to follow. Ofelia becomes a moral being precisely by transgressing adult commands and thus preserving her innocence.[34] Her minor transgression of eating two small grapes from a table displaying such an enticing banquet reveals not her flawed character—resulting in her loss of innocence and expulsion from paradise—but the cruelty and arbitrariness of the adult commands, which stand for Francoist law represented and controlled by the Captain.

The Pale Man's physical appearance and his grotesque behavior closely resemble Goya's painting *Saturn Devouring His Son*, which belongs to a series commonly referred to as "The Black Paintings."[35] Goya's series comprises fourteen paintings depicting menacing, bleak scenes featuring biblical and mythological characters, as well as stock characters from Goya's traditional witchcraft repertoire. In the context of early nineteenth-century Spanish politics, the painting of Saturn has often been understood as a cryptic visual metaphor for the cruel, repressive reign of Ferdinand VII, and, by extension, for Franco's totalitarian regime, where "'tradition,' imagined as the absolute reign of total authority" not only justified but also necessitated murder for its political survival (Hughes 383). It is my contention that the film also alludes to the painting of Judith killing Holofernes, hanging next to Saturn's, whose liberating act of killing the occupying despot is now displaced to both Ofelia's and Mercedes's courageous act of resistance.[36]

Pan's Labyrinth harnesses the power of Goya's image to signify the repressive regime of Franco, and thus by transferring to the Pale Man the allegorical meanings and terrifying qualities found in Goya's Saturn, by displacing these qualities onto Captain Vidal, and by displacing onto Ofelia the liberating narrative found in Judith's painting. The film does this by visually rhyming the two banquet scenes and by having the Captain, who, like the Pale Man, now has a menacing, gaping hole for a mouth, imitate the physical movements of the Pale Man during the chase sequence at the end of the film. The allegory seems clear: Franco, like Ferdinand VII, wanted to turn back the clock in order to erase all traces of the Enlightenment's progressive agenda. As in the painting, which references Cronus, the Greek god of time, who murders his own children, in the movie, Francoist political repression also murders its own children to avoid being dethroned.

In the film, Saturn's traditional association with melancholy is linked to Captain Vidal—who, like Saturn, is a devouring monster—and his obsession with memory and time. The reference to Cronus, the god of time, devouring his progeny also alludes in the film to the notion of a "lost" historical time devouring itself by impeding social progress. And it is linked as well to the notion of Spain as a labyrinth, as being in an historical loop, a space where totalitarian forces, represented here by Captain Vidal as the Minotaur—the bull-like creature clearly referencing Spain, as seen, for instance, in Picasso's *Minotauromachia* (1934)—lurk at its center. Like Cronus, the mythological creator of time, who, unable to move forward, paradoxically arrested time, the Captain's melancholic obsession with the time of his father's heroic death also freezes him in time. The Captain not only impedes his own growth but, being obsessed with the past, as is Cronus, mercilessly terrorizes those around him. The film symbolically ends this Francoist melancholic repressive cycle by rescuing Captain Vidal's newborn baby son—as if he were a modern-day Zeus—from his fascist grip. The film, as mentioned earlier, replaces Francoist repressive melancholy temporality with an ethical mournful one also characteristic of fairy tales.[37] Like Cinderella, Ofelia mourns the traumatic death of her mother, representing the motherland. Similarly, the whole film, suffused with a veil of mournful melancholy, mourns the country's troubled past. This is what the opening scene, which, as we saw, juxtaposes an empty black screen with the sound of a hummed lullaby—the mother's primordial song, appropriately titled "Long, Long Ago/The Funeral"—that returns at the end, is supposed to signify. It is both an ironic mournful lullaby for the tragic future and an elegy to its traumatic past.

All the various meanings of the film, anchored, as we have seen, in the fairy-tale structure and in three visual metaphors—the labyrinth, the Captain's watch, and Goya's paintings—converge in the long sequence of the Captain's chase of Ofelia into the center of the labyrinth, which brings the film to its climactic resolution. In this sequence we witness the final transformation of the classical labyrinth as the embodiment of the battle between good and evil—with the Minotaur at its center—into the medieval labyrinth as metaphor of spiritual pilgrimage. A Christ-like Ofelia will triumphantly stand now at its center, both as sacrificial lamb and savior. The faun's horned head, a figure traditionally associated with Saturn, adorns the top of the arch at the entrance of the labyrinth, thus bringing with it the allegorical meanings of melancholic temporality and political repression discussed in the Pale Man's scene.[38] The Captain's watch, reminding us of his father's heroic death, also alludes to the totalitarian regime devouring its children, as Goya's painting does. Saturn's devouring frenzy materializes in the Captain's fascist political repression, reminding us of the figure of the Minotaur trapped inside the Cretan labyrinth, whose bull's head also happens to be one of the many classical representations of Cronus, the original Greek god of time. The film's allegorically kaleidoscopic message starkly contrasts with Francoist kitsch cinema, which, as we have seen throughout this study, is characterized by the semantic impoverishment of its ideological propaganda.[39]

The chase scene at the end of the film is modeled on the Pale Man's scene, thus coloring the real world above with the allegorical meanings ascribed to the underworld. In fact, the chase sequence could be understood as a re-enactment of the Pale Man's scene, providing a symbolic resolution to the film's oppressive world. It depicts Ofelia's attempt to rescue her baby brother from the Captain and save him from becoming yet another victim of the fascists. It begins in exactly the same manner, with Ofelia escaping the confines of her room by opening a magical door using the same piece of chalk, provided by the faun, as she had done before.[40]

Once downstairs, Ofelia is able to put a few drops of a potent sedative in the Captain's drink, thus fulfilling the words of the priest in the funeral scene: "because in its infinite wisdom [the Lord] puts the solution in your own hands." After a medium shot of the Captain looking at his watch, as if sensing his end is near or fantasizing that time has still stopped, he finally discovers Ofelia. She is holding her baby brother in her arms, an image reminiscent of the stone monolith carving at the center of the labyrinth. This shot, in which Ofelia is bathed in flashes of light caused by the bombing of the partisan attack of the military post, also reminds us of Goya's painting of Judith.[41]

Captain Vidal chases Ofelia down to the center of the labyrinth, where she is supposed to meet the faun for her final test. Feeling the effects of the potent sedative that Ofelia slipped into his drink, the Captain begins to make sluggish movements reminiscent of the Pale Man. The gaping wound in the side of his mouth further reminds us of the Pale Man, of Saturn, and of the proverbial devouring ogre of fairy tales, all of whom the Captain represents. The entrance of the labyrinth, formed by a round arch, suggests a large oral cavity ready to swallow anybody who dares to venture inside, and echoes both Cronus's and the Pale Man's menacing jaws (Fig. 8.7). This is an impression clearly reinforced by the carving of the faun's head with a menacing dropping jaw at the arch's center. But, as we soon come to realize, unlike the lethal jaws of the monster, the labyrinth entrails are a uterine, protective space for those like Ofelia who have learned to navigate their moral twists and turns. The Latin inscription

Figure 8.7 *Pan's Labyrinth*, 2006

marking the labyrinth's entrance is now fully disclosed: "In your hands is your destiny," accentuating the fact that Ofelia is creating her own future, unlike the Captain, who is destined to repeat the past. At the end of the film, then, Ofelia is ready to cross the threshold of the morally intricate space of the labyrinth that Mercedes warned her not to cross because she "may get lost." Ofelia, like the medieval pilgrim, has learned to navigate its intricate moral waters. She has also learned to break the spell of the fairy tale. Now the labyrinth makes itself accessible to Ofelia, helping her in her cause, as when after reaching a dead end[42] it magically opens one of its thick bush walls, enabling her to reach the center where the faun is waiting for the final test, momentarily escaping the Captain—a move which also obviously introduces the biblical idea of the parting of the waters to allow the innocents to pass through.

It is Ofelia's moral innocence that enables her to pass the third and final test. At the center of the pit awaits the faun who, dagger in hand, asks Ofelia to let him get a few drops of her baby brother's "innocent" blood so he can perform the sacrificial act needed for the portal to open. Ofelia refuses to obey the faun's demand. When asked again by the incredulous faun, "You would give up your sacred rights for this brat you barely know?" Ofelia categorically replies, "Yes, I would." At that precise moment the Captain arrives at the labyrinth's center, sees Ofelia alone holding the baby, takes the baby away from her and shoots her in the chest.

Gravely wounded, Ofelia falls to the ground at the edge of the center of the pit. The camera cuts to a close-up of her hand dripping blood of an intense red color, reminiscent of the opening of "Snow White," which contrasts with the monochrome bluish palette of the rest of the frame. The intense redness of Ofelia's blood in this shot speaks of Ofelia's moral maturation, just as in "Snow White."[43] As at the beginning of the film, the two worlds, the real and the magical, seem at the time of Ofelia's death to come apart.

As del Toro explains, "this brings us full circle to the opening of the film and the first time we saw her," thus forming a narrative circularity which is also suggested by the circularity of the labyrinth and the full moon above, and by the full circle formed by the letter O of Ofelia's name and by her princely name of Moanna, meaning "ocean"—Oceanus—the first-born Titan who was the brother of the "treacherous-minded Cronus," representing "that liquid belt that rings the universe and flows in a circle, so that he ends where he begins" (Vernant 86). In short, what we have here at the end is the full circle contained in the Alpha and Omega of Ofelia's Christ-like, triumphant "act of submission," which is also the second meaning of her princely name of Moanna. This recursive nature of Ofelia's moral journey is further reinforced by the close-up at the center of the labyrinth down below, which shows her blood dripping from her hand into a pool of water where another perfect circle, this time that of a full moon, is poetically reflected.

The film's opening shots showed us Ofelia on the ground with her blood flowing backwards. At the end, we see Ofelia in the exact same place, but this time her blood is running down, indicating that time has resumed its normal forward flow. As del Toro explains, "the first time we saw her she is dying and the second time we see her, in my mind, she is being reborn..." The dramatic experiences the film makes us go through are thus no other than the pangs of Ofelia's moral birth. She has achieved a moral victory in the corrupt Francoist world by disobeying official state law to follow instead the "moral law within."

As we are about to learn, it is her own innocent blood, not that of her baby brother, that is the real key granting her access to the magical kingdom. Passing this final test, Ofelia has proven that her moral essence is still touched by magic and has not been corrupted by her experience on earth. Or, more precisely, we could say that she has retained her magical essence because through her earthly traumatic experience she has remained authentic to herself. She has chosen the right moral path at every twist and turn of the story. Like the pilgrim often represented in medieval labyrinths, Ofelia too has conquered evil.

When the Captain exits the labyrinth carrying his baby son, he, like the Minotaur, is finally killed by a modern-day Theseus, collectively represented by the partisans. Before his execution, the Captain, *caught*

Figure 8.8 *Pan's Labyrinth*, 2006

melancholically in time, attempts to replay his father's heroic death when he reaches for his watch. Like a character from *Raza* or *Los últimos*, he bombastically tells Mercedes, who has brought the partisans into the labyrinth: "Tell my son. Tell him what time his father died. Tell him that I ..." But his attempt at a heroic speech is immediately interrupted by Mercedes, who denies the Captain his final wish: "No, he won't even know your name." Now the leader of the partisans, Pedro—Mercedes' brother—shoots him right under the eye. The Captain's eye becomes gradually bloody, bringing back to mind the grotesque world of Goya's Saturn (Fig. 8.8).

All of this allegory is leading us back to history, as Ofelia has been led from fairy tale to reality. The long chase, Captain Vidal's killing of Ofelia and his stealing of her baby brother underline the idea of the labyrinth as a representation of historical memory. The fact that Ofelia is thirteen years old in 1944 means that she was born in 1931, the year of the creation of the Spanish Second Republic. Her death represents the death of the Republic, and can now be seen to represent "all those whose deaths have been locked in silence" (Diestro-Dópido 75).

The chase and the Captain's final snatching of Ofelia's baby brother away from her thus signify not only the traumatic turbulence of Spanish history but also the intricacies of the historical record. They refer to the Francoist military uprising against the Spanish Republic and also to the Francoist attempts to bring up a new generation of Spaniards, symbolized by the baby, in a "New Spain." Through this fairy-tale narrative, though, the film envisions an alternative ending to the Francoist victory by having the partisans kill the Captain and take the baby away from him. Ofelia's baby brother will now grow up within the exiled Republican community. It is in this way that *Pan's Labyrinth* redresses the Francoist distortion of Spain's historical record.

A vertically ascending camera reveals now the spatial layout of the two labyrinths: the one above where the Captain, as the evil Minotaur, has killed Ofelia, and the smaller miniature circular labyrinth right below the pit, representing Ofelia's final moral victory. Through her death, she, as the true daughter of time, not as the stepdaughter of the Captain, time's usurper, has given a "solid testimony of truth," forever memorialized by the stone monolith of Ofelia holding the baby next to the faun standing triumphantly at the center of the labyrinth.[44] Still breathing, Ofelia is gradually bathed in a magical golden light coming from her right side, which throughout has signified the magical kingdom. The portal has opened and Ofelia is finally able to return to her kingdom where she appears dressed with a red cape and red shoes—reminiscent of Dorothy in *The Wizard of Oz*—and a red rose embroidered on her shirt, referencing the copper rose of her own fairy tale that nobody dared to pluck (Fig. 8.9). The rose, which was the object of desire in the fairy tale that Ofelia told her brother still in the womb, symbolizes the dangers but also the rewards of following the true moral path. Ofelia is now welcomed by her parents, who are sitting on tall thrones in an imposing space which looks like a gothic cathedral with a radiant round window echoing the rosette of medieval labyrinths. Magical light fills the screen; the camera cuts to a close-up of Ofelia's face back at the pit. She sketches a brief smile, as if responding to the standing ovation

Figure 8.9 *Pan's Labyrinth*, 2006

she receives from the crowd in her kingdom, and finally exhales, magical pollen swirling around the frame.

The narrator's voice returns to inform us that Princess Moanna went back to her kingdom, where "she reigned with justice and a kind heart for many centuries." A dissolve takes us now from the labyrinth to the tree, and the narrator brings the tale to an end by letting us know that the princess "left behind the small traces of her time on earth visible only for those who know how to look," while the camera cuts to a close-up of a budding white flower on one of the branches of the tree. It suddenly begins to open, while an insect, like the one at the beginning of the film, flies next to it.[45] Ofelia's legacy in this world is a tiny fragile flower, like herself, symbolizing organic, moral growth only visible to "those who know how to look;" that is, only visible to those willing to look attentively and compassionately at the world around them. In contrast, the Captain's unfulfilled legacy is a broken mechanical watch marking the hour of his father's heroic demise.

Pan's Labyrinth is a dark fairy tale for grown-ups. Fairy tales are narrative conduits of moral awakening, stories that help children mature by enabling them to deal with their unconscious fears and desires. Del Toro's film also wants to help its spectators—particularly the generations of Spaniards who have endured times of abomination—to grow up morally without forgetting to mourn their troubled past. *Pan's Labyrinth* enlists the power of the moral imagination of the fairy tale against Francoist kitsch political escapism. Because far from being a Neverland lacking a sense of reality, as G. K. Chesterton wrote, "Fairyland is nothing but the sunny country of common sense" (49).

Notes

1. In *The Child in Spanish Cinema*, Sarah Wright points out that, "[d]el Toro was seen as spiking a renewed interest in the (child-centred) 'genre film' ..." (4). As she writes, "[c]ritics also drew attention to the intertextual reliance of Guillermo del Toro's film on another globally famous Spanish film: Víctor Erice's *El espíritu de la colmena* (*The Spirit of the Beehive*, 1973)" (4). Wright lucidly observes that, "Torrent's mute gaze," referring to Erice's child actress, "might be seen as a reaction to the excesses of the *película con niño* (child-centred films) which had dominated in Spain during the 1950s and 1960s ... " (4). Del Toro's restrained, honest portrayal of childhood in *Pan's Labyrinth* follows Erice's model against the kitsch representation of childhood of this earlier Spanish cinema.
2. Film itself is no stranger to the world of fairy tale and several of its most celebrated pioneers, such as Georges Méliès, early on adapted its dreamy, fantastic scenarios to the magic of celluloid. According to Kristian Moen,

"Georges Méliès was the genre's most well-known and influential filmmaker, having produced ... the first film feerie, *Cinderella* (1899) ... Other major filmmakers, such as Edwin S. Porter, Cecil Hepworth and Ferdinand Zecca, worked within this genre as well" (40). As he explains, "These films presented cinema's first fairy tales, including "Bluebeard", "Little Red Riding Hood," Sleeping Beauty" and "Aladdin ..." (40).

3. In "Under the Sign of Saturn," Susan Sontag observes that the idea of the self as a project to be built is the true mark of a saturnine, melancholy character, which also defines artists and martyrs (117).
4. In Vladimir Propp's classical definition, the hero is a "character who either directly suffers from the action of the villain in the complication ... or who agrees to liquidate the misfortune or lack of another person." As Propp explains, in the course of the action the fairy-tale hero, like Ofelia, is "supplied with a magical agent (a magical helper)," in this case represented by the faun, and the insect fairy who becomes Ofelia's guide throughout the film (50).
5. In fact, the Brothers Grimm's famous collection of tales became an important pedagogical tool of the Third Reich, which found in the Brothers Grimm's tales a pure expression of the German spirit. As Warner writes, "The Grimms became part of the swelling movement to retrieve a record of the German spirit, through an encyclopedical account of the German language, myths, history, custom, beliefs and knowledge. They called it 'folk poesy', and they thought of it as part of nature—untutored, uncontaminated by book learning, wild as the forest and the mountains" (56).
6. According to Marina Warner, society's censoring of the darkest, most disturbing aspects of fairy tales is not entirely new and has been denounced by writers such as Dickens, Tolkien, and Windling, and psychoanalysts such as Bettelheim, who "for different reasons, have declared that sweetening the tales is tantamount to vandalism" (172).
7. As Warner writes, "for this reason, many readers have found in fairy tales a powerful 'consolatory fable' for the suffering that ordinary people went through, and the proof of the emancipatory spirit of the oppressed in action" (94). Additionally, for Italo Calvino—himself an indefatigable compiler of fairy tales—despite their flights of fancy, these tales "speak of poverty, scarcity, hunger, anxiety, lust, greed, envy, cruelty" (74).
8. Reflecting on what has been described as the national cathartic effect that the TV series *Holocaust* had in Germany when first shown on television in the late 1970s, Rainer C. Baum observes that only "modes of representation that adequately capture" historical trauma are able to bring back suppressed emotions and with them "morally compelling aspects of the truth." These cathartic representations—as *Roots* was for American viewers around the same time—are emotionally resonant because they are able to convey what "concrete historical subjects felt" and thus successfully capture the "emotional reality of past experience," bringing back from the past to contemporary audiences what has moral relevance to them (54).

9. As Benjamin writes in "The Storyteller," fairy tale "tells us of the earliest arrangements that mankind made to shake off the nightmare which the [fatalism of] myth had placed upon its chest" (102). Through its "liberating magic," for Benjamin, the fairy tale shows nature's "complicity with liberated man" (102).
10. As Bettelheim argues, Charles Perrault's version of "Little Red Riding Hood," for instance, becomes "a cautionary tale which deliberately threatens the child with its anxiety-producing ending" (167). As he concludes, "it seems that many adults think it is better to scare children into good behavior than to relieve their anxieties as a true fairy tale does" (167).
11. The mother in the film has been sequestered by the fascist Captain she seeks protection from and whom she is too weak to resist: her name, after all, is Carmen, derived from the Latin word meaning "poem" or "tune"; and *La Virgen del Carmen* (Our Lady of Mount Carmel) has, since the eighteenth century, been the standard allegorical representation of Spain.
12. As Propp observes, most fairy-tale heroes search for an object, which is typically "located in 'another' or 'different' kingdom," which "may lie far away horizontally, or else very high up or deep down vertically" (50).
13. Del Toro explains that the "opening went through many changes," including Borges's inspired motifs "with labyrinths, circular ruins, etc.," to be finally dramatically streamlined. The opening as it originally appeared in the Spanish-language published version of the original screenplay gives us a hint not only of del Toro's original narrative intentions but also of his overall poetics of representation. In the original screenplay, after the camera goes through Ofelia's eye we first see an image of a dark mirror "floating in the absolute nothingness" (9). The mirror itself explodes and swallows the camera that now swerves around the penumbra for a few moments to the sound of subterranean wind. This opening metaphorically indicates we are entering the mysterious dark world of the subconscious, but it also seems to suggest that the narrative is holding a dark mirror to reality, like in *Balada*'s case, to capture more accurately its grotesque, twisted nature.
14. In a similar way to that of Naomi Watts' character in David Lynch's *Mulholland Drive* (2001), a film with a similar narrative structure. In this regard, Diestro-Dópido writes that "... both *Pan* and *Mullholland Dr* can be read as the death dreams of their protagonists; both begin and end with their respective deaths, and the codas follow them into their chosen versions of paradise" (73).
15. In short, Ofelia, as Jung writes of the "primitive mind," unlike the rest of us who have learned in our daily experience "to discard the trimmings of fantasy both in our language and in our thoughts ... is still aware of [the] psychic properties" of everything around her, and she "endows animals, plants, or stones with powers that we find strange and unacceptable" (30).
16. Jack Zipes points out that, "from that point on, this vision, which is really an imaginary projection, changes her life. In fact, she has *real* double vision,

unique visionary powers that enable her to see two worlds at the same time, and we watch as she tries to navigate through two worlds, trying to use the characters, symbols, and signs of her imaginary world to survive in a social world destitute of dreams and filled with merciless brutality and viciousness" (356).

17. Ofelia's action reminds us of little Ana in *The Spirit of the Beehive* (1976), a cult Spanish film and an important referent of *Pan's Labyrinth*. In that film, Ana provides the eyes to a school cut-out on which the children hang the different organs for pedagogical purposes, which in the film alludes to Frankenstein's monster. Víctor Erice's film, which like del Toro's blends fairy tales with gothic narratives, is about a small girl in a desolate Castilian village who, like Ofelia, is capable of seeing beyond the range of the adults surrounding her. In her case it is not a faun she sees but Dr Frankenstein's monster, who in the film is metaphorically represented by the wounded resistance fighter of whom Ana takes care.

18. The labyrinth, like the famous one inscribed in the floor of Chartres Cathedral, for example, came to represent the moral twists and turns of the Christian soul in its search for spiritual perfection. But instead of the evil Minotaur, Jesus stood triumphantly at its center.

19. The film, I argue, finds a visual equivalent to the musical symbol of the "retrograde motion" of the Agnus Dei in the visual motif of time flowing literally backwards in order to represent Ofelia's recursive moral journey. Therefore, this scene is not definite proof that Ofelia's fantasy is simply a figment of her imagination, but, on the contrary, the temporal reversal suggested by the dripping of her blood running backwards and the turning back of the pages of the fairy-tale book point to Ofelia's own harrowing of Hell. Like Christ, whose cross rose triumphant in the middle of the medieval labyrinth, signifying the liberation of the innocent souls trapped in purgatory, Ofelia's carved relief holding the baby she came to rescue also stands triumphant at the center of the labyrinth, suggesting her baby brother's liberation as well as her own.

20. Another important component of medieval labyrinth iconography, which is also prominent in *Pan's Labyrinth*, is that of the rose. In the famous labyrinth of Chartres, as Wright observes, "Christ is signified by the rosette at the center of the maze," which symbolized the "apotropaic powers of Christ no less than the cross stamped upon the tracks of the maze" (42). In *Pan's Labyrinth* the image of the rose figures prominently as one of the film's main visual leitmotifs. The first fairy tale that Ofelia narrates to her baby brother still inside his mother's womb is the story of a rose made of copper. It represents the flower of immortality standing on top of a peak nobody dared to pluck because it was surrounded by a "forest of thorns that were full of deadly poison." As del Toro observed, echoing Nietzsche, the rose signifies the rewards available to those able to live a full, moral life: "So only if you dare to die would you reach true immortality."

21. For del Toro, Celtic art exhibits "very simple traces but very elaborate patterns. That is the essence of Celtic art. And most people link Celtic with Ireland or the UK but the Celtic culture actually came through Spain and through the north of Spain and to the islands above."
22. The other main architectural structure of the film is that of the old mill, where the Captain has made his living quarters. The word "mill" immediately conjures up Cervantes's *Don Quixote*, whose protagonist fights windmills as if they were threatening giants because he is an idealist, like Ofelia, who sees the world filtered through his obsessive reading of chivalric novels, like Ofelia does through fairy tales. Unlike the curvilinear shapes that configure the labyrinth, also inscribed in the faun's forehead, Captain Vidal's living quarters in the old mill are characterized by the coldness and severity of straight lines. As del Toro observes, "The fantasy is very warm, very round, very uterine because I believe it should echo the belly of the mother . . . and the reality is all cold, rust, grey, blue colors . . . So other than the gears and the wheel of the mill the rest of the world outside is straight lines."
23. As Wright points out, "The maze suggested a code of ethical conduct for this present world by making more apparent—indeed, by making visible on the floor of the church—a zone of penance and punishment. It helped humans understand circumstances in this world by clarifying the next" (86).
24. As he explains, " . . . I tried to rhyme it visually with gears, with the gigantic gears behind him so he looks that he is repairing a watch inside a watch."
25. It also reminds us of Franco's near-fatal wound in Morocco, recorded for posterity by a standing monument, as we saw in Chapter 5.
26. Goya is, in fact, admittedly one of del Toro's favorite painters, "whose etchings and black paintings became very important in my life from an early age." As he explains, "after he puts his eyes in the stigmata we are going to see almost a verbatim quote of one of Goya's most famous paintings which is *Saturn Devouring His Son*."
27. Goya's most famous etching, as Folke Nordström points out, represents, as in Dürer's *Melencolia I*, "a type of *Melancholia artificialis* or artist's melancholia" (Kindle 2248).
28. In fact, the film brings back through the back door some of the traditional iconographic attributes of Saturn which, according to Bozal, as mentioned earlier, were left out of Goya's representation, such as: the swaddled stone, the key, the wings, and the water, and also the horns of the male goat representing the zodiac sign of Capricorn under his sphere. All these iconographic motifs traditionally associated with Saturn/Cronus sprinkle the entire movie in subtle ways.
29. Referring to Jonah's biblical episode, Bettelheim points out that "everybody who hears this story knows intuitively that Jonah's stay in the fish's belly was for a purpose—namely, so that he would return to life a better man" (179), just as Ofelia will emerge more morally developed after the encounter with the Pale Man.

30. This is an extremely traumatic experience. In Ofelia's case, it requires being thrown out into the real world, leaving behind her princely cozy magical kingdom to experience loneliness and pain. To achieve moral authenticity in the "real" world, she needs to avoid being devoured by the big bad wolf of the Francoist patriarchal order, symbolized both by the Captain and by the Pale Man down below.
31. As Diestro-Dópido remarks, "one of *Pan*'s most striking and unusual traits is the juxtaposition of a fairy tale with the raw cruelty and horror of fascism in post-war Spain, which is braided with other similarly structuring contrasts: between reality and fiction, feminine and masculine, innocence and adulthood, material and spiritual, our world and the underworld, and good and evil; all of which are primarily conveyed through the figures of Ofelia and Vidal" (40).
32. As del Toro explains, as typical in fairy tales, "you're going to see the three doors which is an element in fairy tales."
33. The idea behind the detachable eyes came from a statue of Santa Lucía that del Toro once saw as a kid in a church. According to him, the other major visual influences for the film came from "Arthur Rackham, Edmund Lacker Nielsen, who were golden age fairy tales' illustrators."
34. In del Toro's own words, by "disobeying and eating a single, measly grape in a huge banquet table ... she almost gets killed but she learns the most important lesson, which is to trust herself." As he concludes, "I think it is very important that she chooses for herself in the film regardless of danger, regardless of influence, she remains true to herself."
35. Originally conceived for purely decorative purposes in *La Quinta del Sordo*, the painter's own farmhouse on the outskirts of Madrid, and now hanging at the Prado Museum, The Black Paintings have been the subject of intense speculation and numerous critical studies and interpretations. In his study on Goya, for example, Robert Hughes argues that in this series Goya "did not care about creating a unified allegory or a coherent story" (379). Folke Nordström, however, claims to have found the interpretive key to the series in the notion of melancholy—traditionally associated with Saturn—which, emanating from the painting of Saturn, according to him, resonates in the other six paintings hanging next to it. As Nordström writes, the series offers "... a completely pessimistic vision of life, created by a deaf old man, isolated for a long period of time ..." (Kindle 3827).
36. According to Bozal, "Judith is a character of complex symbolism. She represents Temperantia [Temperance] or Justitia [Lady Justice], but also humility defeating Pride, embodied this time by Holofernes. Temperantia defeating lust is, according to Moffit ... the meaning of a pechina [the space between two arches, or spandrel] painted by Mariano Bayeu [Goya's father-in-law] in the Carthusian church of Valdemosa. On the other hand, Nordström warns of the relationship between Judith and Saturn in a ceiling painted by Girolamo Mocetto in display in Paris at the Jacquemart André museum. Naturally, I am

not suggesting that Goya had seen these paintings but only that their symbolism could have been known by the artist and acknowledge when decorating his house" (Kindle 1147).

37. In this sense, the film, playing with the profound duality which, as Axl, Klibanski, and Panofsky observe, characterized Cronus, distinguishes two distinct types of political melancholia: a cruel, Francoist, destructive, deadly, ahistorical melancholia, and a positive, mournful, ethical, artistic melancholy which the film embraces. As they write, in none of the other Greek gods "is this dual aspect so real and fundamental as in Kronos" (134). On the one hand, "he was the benevolent god of agriculture, whose harvest festival was celebrated by free men and slaves together, the ruler of the Golden Age when men had abundance of all things and enjoyed the innocent happiness of Rousseau's natural man." But on the other, Cronus "was the gloomy, dethroned and solitary god." On the one hand "the father of gods and men." On the other, "the devourer of children, eater of raw flesh, the consumer of all 'who swallowed up all the gods' and exacted human sacrifice from the barbarians" (135).
38. As del Toro explains, the faun is actually the Pale Man, both characters appropriately being performed by Doug Jones.
39. Allegory, as Max Pensky observes, is "a creative cognitive mode inseparably connected to the melancholy disposition." As he writes, "melancholics need not be allegorists, but allegory arises from melancholia" (117). And for Walter Benjamin allegory is "the only pleasure the melancholic permits himself" (quoted in Sontag 124). As del Toro observes, "*Pan* is a game of interpretation where the reward for repeated viewings is not the addition but the multiplication of meanings" (quoted in Diestro-Dópido 24).
40. The film does not show her doing this but subtly alludes to it in a later scene which reveals the outline of a door drawn with chalk on the wall of her room; and also by the fact that when we see Ofelia downstairs in the Captain's living quarters she is holding a piece of chalk. Besides, as del Toro explains, there is no other possible rational explanation since she would never be able to escape from her room given that the Captain has assigned two officers to watch her door.
41. As Bozal explains, "this nocturnal character, this expressive light, which behaves like lightning, substantially alters Judith traditional iconographic interpretation now transformed into an aggressive daughter of the night, related to the three fates, and not with the chaste Temperantia or Justitia" (Kindle 1176).
42. As del Toro admits in his DVD commentary, "this is a cheat, a [unicursal] labyrinth would never have a dead end. And I apologize and I'm admitting fully and openly."
43. According to Bettelheim, the "redness of the apple evokes sexual associations like the three drops of blood which led to Snow White's birth, and also menstruation, the event which marks the beginning of sexual maturity" (213).

In this regard, Jack Zipes, a foremost scholar of fairy tales, comments on the association of Ofelia with Snow White: "Ironically, del Toro's Snow White will *not* refuge in a large lodge in which the atmosphere is gothic and sinister. Instead of living happily with the seven dwarfs as protectors, she will be menaced by the cruel Captain Vidal and be killed by him" (357).

44. In this sense, she actually embodies truth as traditionally represented as the daughter of time—who, according to Democritus, lay, like Ofelia, at the bottom of a deep well.

45. The insect at the end could be read in the same vein as Bettelheim reads the little white bird which comes to answer Cinderella's prayers. As he writes, "the white bird is easily recognized as the mother's spirit conveyed to her child through the good mothering she gives him; it is the spirit which originally became implanted in the child as basic trust. As such it becomes the child's own spirit, which sustains him in all hardships, giving him hope for the future, and the strength to create a good life for himself" (259–60).

Works Cited

Books

Adorno, Theodor W. (1982), "Freudian Theory and the Pattern of Fascist Propaganda," in *The Essential Frankfurt School Reader*, pp. 118–37.

Afinoguénova, Eugenia (2006), "'Esto se llama Raza, hijo mio.' El mito fascista y las visualizaciones del nuevo estado en el cine de la propaganda del primer franquismo: *Prisioneros de Guerra* (1938) y *Raza* (1941)" *Filmhistoria* online, Vol. XVI No. 3.

Agamben, Giorgio (1994), *The Man Without Content*, Stanford: Stanford University Press. Print.

Aguilar, Paloma (2001), "Justice, Politics, and Memory in the Spanish Transition," in Alexandra Barahona de Brito, Carmen González-Enríquez, and Paloma Aguilar (eds), *The Politics of Memory: Transitional Justice in Democratizing Societies*, New York: Oxford University Press, pp. 92–118. Print.

Alberich, Ferrán (1997), "Raza. Cine y propaganda en la inmediata posguerra," *Archivos de la filmoteca* 27: 50–61. Print.

Allinson, Mark (2005), "Calle Mayor/Main Street," in Alberto Mira (ed.), *The Cinema of Spain and Portugal*, London: Wallflower Press, pp. 79–87. Print.

Althusser, Louis (1971), "Ideology and Ideological State Apparatuses," *Lenin and Philosophy, and Other Essays*, London: New Left Books.

Álvarez Junco, José (2001), *Mater Dolorosa: La idea de España en el siglo XIX*, Madrid: Taurus. Print.

—(2016), *Dioses útiles: naciones y nacionalismos*, Barcelona: Galaxia Gutenberg. Print.

Anderson, Benedict (2006), *Imagined Communities*, Rev. edn, London and New York: Verso. Print.

Andrade, Jaime de (1942), *Raza: anecdotario para el guión de una película*, Madrid: Ediciones Numancia. Print.

Angulo, Jesús and Antonio Santamarina (2012), *Álex de la Iglesia. La pasión de rodar*, San Sebastián: Filmoteca Vasca. Print.

Armstrong, Karen (2007), *The Bible: A Biography*, New York: Atlantic Monthly. Print.

Ashford Hodges, Gabrielle (2000), *Franco: A Concise Biography*, New York: St Martin's Press. Print.

Augé, Marc (2008), *Non-Places: Introduction to an Anthropology of Supermodernity*, Trans. John Howe, New York and London: Verso. Print.

Aumont, Jacques (2003), "The Face in Close-Up," in Angela Dalle Vacche (ed.), *The Visual Turn*, New Brunswick, NJ and London: Rutgers University Press, pp. 127–48. Print.

Balázs, Béla (2003), "The Close-Up and The Face of Man," in Angela Dalle Vacche (ed.), *The Visual Turn*, New Brunswick, NJ and London: Rutgers University Press, pp. 117–26. Print.

Ballesteros, Isolina (2016), "Exodo rural, migración e inmigración en el cine español," *Hispanófila*, Vol. 177, June, pp. 249–61.

Baskett, Michael (2009), "All Beautiful Fascist? Axis Film Culture in Imperial Japan," in Alan Tansman (ed.), *The Culture of Japanese Fascism*, Durham: Duke University Press, pp. 212–34. Print.

Bataille, Georges (1986), *Eroticism: Death and Sensuality*, Trans. Mary Dalwood, San Francisco: City Lights. Print.

Bazin, André (2005a), "The Ontology of the Photographic Image," *What Is Cinema?* Vol. 1, Trans. Hugh Gray, Berkeley: University of California Press, pp. 9–16. Print.

—(2005b), "An Aesthetic of Reality: Cinematic Realism and the Italian School of the Liberation," *What Is Cinema?* Vol. 2, Trans. Hugh Gray, Berkeley: University of California Press, pp. 16–40. Print.

—(2005c), "The Evolution of the Language of Cinema," *What Is Cinema?* Vol. 1, Trans. Hugh Gray, Berkeley: University of California Press, pp. 23–40. Print.

—(2005d), "De Sica: Metteur en Scène," *What Is Cinema?* Vol. 2, Trans. Hugh Gray, Berkeley: University of California Press, pp. 61–78. Print.

—(2005e), "In Defense of Rossellini," *What Is Cinema?* Vol. 2, Trans. Hugh Gray, Berkeley: University of California Press, pp. 93–101. Print.

Belsey, Catherine (1992), "Revenge in 'Hamlet'," in Martin Coyle (ed.), *Hamlet: William Shakespeare*, Basingstoke: Palgrave, pp. 154–9. Print.

Ben-Ghiat, Ruth (2004), *Fascist Modernities: Italy, 1922–1945*, Berkeley: University of California Press. Print.

Benet, Vicente J. (2012), *El cine español: una historia cultural*, Barcelona: Paidós Comunicación. Print.

Benjamin, Walter (1968), *Illuminations: Essays and Reflections*, Trans. Harry Zohn, Ed. Hannah Arendt, New York: Shocken Books.

—(1998), *The Origin of German Tragic Drama*, Trans. John Osborne, London and New York: Verso. Print.

Bentley, Bernard P. E. (2008), *A Companion to Spanish Cinema*, New York: Tamesis. Print.

Bergson, Henri (2001), *Time and Free Will: An Essay on the Immediate Data of Consciousness*, Trans. F. L. Pogson, 3rd edn, Mineola, NY: Dover Publications. Print.

Berlin, Isaiah (1999), *The Roots of Romanticism*, Princeton: Princeton University Press. Print.

Berthier, Nancy (1994), "El combate del Biutz en *Franco ese hombre*: Historia de un milagro," *Mélanges de la Casa de Velázquez* 30.3: 285–97. Print.

Bettelheim, Bruno (2010), *The Uses of Enchantment: the Meaning and Importance of Fairy Tales*, New York: Vintage Books. Print.
The Holy Bible (1989), New York: Oxford University Press.
Blanchot, Maurice (1995), *The Writing of the Disaster*, Lincoln: University of Nebraska Press. Print.
Bogdanovich, Peter (2004), "Interview with Orson Welles," in James Naremore (ed.), *Orson Welles's Citizen Kane: A Casebook*, Oxford: Oxford University Press, pp. 19–71. Print.
Bollas, Christopher (1993), "The Fascist State of Mind," *Being a Character: Psychoanalysis and Self Experience*, London: Routledge, pp. 193–217. Print.
Borau, José Luis, Carlos F. Heredero, and María Pastor (eds) (1998), *Diccionario del cine español*, Madrid: Alianza Editorial. Print.
Borraz, Marta (2017), "El Gobierno niega que el Valle de los Caídos sea un lugar de exaltación franquista," eldiario.es, 18 January.
Bozal, Valeriano (2015), *Pinturas negras de Goya*, Kindle edn, La balsa de la medusa No. 170.
Broch, Hermann (1969), "Notes in the Problem of Kitsch," in Gillo Dorfles (ed.), *Kitsch: An Anthology of Bad Taste*, New York: Universe Books, pp. 49–76. Print.
Brooks, Peter (2005), *Realist Vision*, New Haven: Yale University Press. Print.
Buñuel, Luis (1996), *Viridiana*, Trans. Piergiuseppe Bozzetti, Portsmouth, NH: Heinemann, 1996. Print.
Burke, Kenneth (1957), "The Rhetoric of Hitler's 'Battle'," *The Philosophy of Literary Form: Studies in Symbolic Action*, New York: Vintage Books, pp. 164–89. Print.
Buse, Peter, Núria Triana Toribio, and Andy Willis (2007), *The Cinema of Álex de la Iglesia*, Manchester: Manchester University Press. Print.
Butler, Judith (1997), *The Psychic Life of Power*, Stanford: Stanford University Press. Print.
—(2003), "After Loss, What Then?" Afterword, in David L. Eng and David Kazanjian (eds), *Loss: The Politics of Mourning*, Berkeley and Los Angeles, CA: University of California Press, pp. 467–73. Print.
Calinescu, Matei (1987), *Five Faces of Modernity: Modernism Avant-Garde, Decadence, Kitsch, Postmodernism*, Durham: Duke University Press. Print.
Camporesi, Valeria (1994), *Para grandes y chicos: un cine para los españoles 1940–1990*, Madrid: Turfan. Print.
Carr, Raymond (2000), "Liberalism and Reaction, 1833–1931," in Carr (ed.), *Spain: A History*, New York: Oxford University Press, pp. 205–42. Print.
Casals Meseguer, Xavier (2006), "Franco 'El Africano'," *Journal of Spanish Cultural Studies* 7.3: 207–24. Print.
Chesterton, G. K. (1959), *Orthodoxy*, New York: Image Books. Print.
Chion, Michel (1999), *The Voice in Cinema*, Trans. Claudia Gorbman, Ed. Claudia Gorbman, New York: Columbia University Press. Print.
Coira, Pepe (2004), *Antonio Román: un cineasta de la posguerra*, Madrid: Editorial Complutense. Print.

Colina, José de la and Tomás Pérez Turrent (1992), *Objects of Desire: Conversations with Luis Buñuel*, New York: Marsilio. Print.
Colmeiro, José F. (2000), "Nostalgia colonial y la construcción del nuevo orden en *Los últimos de Filipinas*," Ed. Florencio Sevilla y Carlos Alvar, Actas del XII Congreso de la Asociación Internacional de Hispanistas, Madrid: Castalia.
—(2011), "A Nation of Ghosts?: Haunting, Historical Memory and Forgetting in Post-Franco Spain," *452°F. Electronic journal of theory of literature and comparative literature* 4: 17–34.
Connor, Steven (2000), *Dumbstruck: A Cultural History of Ventriloquism*, Oxford: Oxford University Press. Print.
Corral Rey, M. Nieves (2016), "La Manipulación de las mentes en la infancia: *Balada triste de trompeta* y *El niño con el pijama de rayas*," Revista de Comunicación Vivat Academia, December, Vol. XIX, No. 137, pp. 78–107.
Cortés Salinas, Carmen (2002), "Ciudades y vecindades: de la autarquía al desarrollo a través del cine español," *La dimensión artística y social de la ciudad*, Ed. Juan Antonio Sánchez García-Saúco, Madrid: Secretaría General Técnica, Subdirección General de Información y Publicaciones, pp. 83–98. Print.
Costa, Joaquín (1998), *Oligarquía y caciquismo como la forma actual de gobierno en España; urgencia y modo de cambiarla*. Madrid: Editorial Biblioteca Nueva. Print.
Critchley, Simon and Jamieson Webster (2013), *Stay, Illusion! The Hamlet Doctrine*, New York: Pantheon Books. Print.
Crussells, Magí (2000), *La Guerra Civil española: cine y propaganda*, Barcelona: Ariel. Print.
—(2001), *Las brigadas internacionales en la pantalla*, Ciudad Real: Universidad de Castilla-La Mancha. Print.
De Man, Paul (1978), "The Epistemology of Metaphor," *Critical Inquiry* 5.1: 13–30. Print.
Del Molino, Sergio (2016), *La España vacía: viaje por un país que nunca fue*, Madrid: Turner. Print.
Del Toro, Guillermo (2006), *El laberinto del fauno: guión cinematográfico de Guillermo del Toro*, Madrid: Ocho y Medio. Print.
Deleuze, Gilles (1986), *Cinema 1: The Movement Image*, Trans. Hugh Tomlinson and Barbara Habberjam, Minneapolis: University of Minnesota Press. Print.
Denning, Michael (2004), "The Politics of Magic: Orson Welles's Allegories of Anti-Fascism," in James Naremore (ed.), *Orson Welles's Citizen Kane: A Casebook*, Oxford: Oxford University Press, pp. 185–216. Print.
Derrida, Jacques (2006), *Specters of Marx*, Trans. Peggy Kamuf, New York and London: Routledge. Print.
Diestro-Dópido, Mar (2013), *Pan's Labyrinth*, New York: Palgrave Macmillan. Print.
Diez Puertas, Emeterio (2002), *El montaje del franquismo: la política cinematográfica de las fuerzas sublevadas*, Barcelona: Laertes. Print.

D'Lugo, Marvin (1997), *Guide to the Cinema of Spain*, Westport, CT: Greenwood Press. Print.
Dodds, Frank Loring (1909), Introductory to *Under the Red and the Gold: Being Notes and Recollections of the Siege of Baler* by Saturnino Martín Cerezo, Trans. Dodds, Kansas City: Franklin Hudson Publishing Company, pp. 5–10.
Domínguez Búrdalo, José Manuel (2009), "*La canción de Aixa* o la racial *marroquinada*: una apuesta perdida del africanismo cinematográfico español," *Revista de Estudios Hispánicos* 3.43: 609–36. Print.
Dorfles, Gillo (1975), *Kitsch: The World of Bad Taste*, New York: Universe Books. Print.
Eco, Umberto (1989), *The Open Work*, Trans. Anna Cancogni, Cambridge, MA: Harvard University Press. Print.
Edwards, Gwynne (1995), *Indecent Exposures: Buñuel, Saura, Erice and Almodóvar*, London: Marion Boyars. Print.
Egea, Juan F. (2013), *Dark Laughter: Spanish Film, Comedy, and the Nation*, Madison: University of Wisconsin Press. Print.
Egurbide, Peru (1995), "Franco fue 'una esfinge sin secretos' según Javier Tusell," *El País*, Rome, 7 November.
Eisner, Lotte (1969), "Kitsch in the Cinema," in Gillo Dorfles (ed.), *Kitsch: An Anthology of Bad Taste*, New York: Universe Books, pp. 197–217. Print.
"El Congreso respalda exhumar a Franco del Valle de los caídos," Público.es., 8 March 2017.
Elena, Alberto (1997a), "*Romancero marroquí*, 1939," in Julio Pérez Perucha (ed.), *Antología crítica del cine español 1906–1995: Flor en la sombra*, Madrid: Cátedra, pp. 122–4. Print.
—(1997b), "Los últimos de filipinas, 1945," in Julio Pérez Perucha (ed.), *Antología crítica del cine español 1906–1995: Flor en la sombra*, Madrid: Cátedra, pp. 196–8. Print.
—(2004), *Romancero marroquí: el cine africanista durante la guerra civil*, Madrid: Filmoteca Española/ICAA/Ministerio de Cultura. Print.
—(2010), *La llamada de África: estudios sobre el cine colonial español*, Barcelona: Edicions Bellaterra. Print.
Eng, David L. and David Kazanjian (eds) (2003), *Loss: The Politics of Mourning*, Berkeley and Los Angeles, CA: University of California Press. Print.
—(2003), "Mourning Remains," Introduction to Eng and Kazanjian (eds), *Loss: The Politics of Mourning*, Berkeley and Los Angeles, CA: University of California Press, pp. 1–25. Print.
Evans, Peter William (1995), *The Films of Luis Buñuel: subjectivity and desire*, New York: Oxford University Press. Print.
Fanés, Félix (1982), *Cifesa, la antorcha de los éxitos*, Valencia: Institución Alfonso el Magnánimo. Print.
Faulkner, Sally (2013), *A History of Spanish Film: Cinema and Society 1910–2010*, London: Bloomsbury. Print.
Fernández, Miguel Anxo (2011), *Las imágenes de Carlos Velo*, Mexico, d.f.: Universidad Nacional Autónoma de Mexico. Print.

Fiddian, Robin and Peter William Evans (1988), *Challenges to Authority: Fiction and Film in Contemporary Spain*, London: Tamesis Books. Print.
Flaxman, Gregory (2000), "Cinema Year Zero," in Flaxman (ed.), *The Brain is the Screen: Deleuze and the Philosophy of Cinema*, Minneapolis: University of Minnesota Press, pp. 87–108. Print.
Foucault, Michel (1970), *The Order of Things: An Archaeology of the Human Sciences*, New York: Random House. Print.
Franco, Francisco (1949), *Franco ha dicho*, Madrid: Ediciones Voz. Print.
Fraser, Benjamin (2010), *Encounters with Bergson(ism) in Spain: Reconciling Philosophy, Literature, Film and Urban Space*, Chapel Hill: University of North Carolina Department of Romance Languages. Print.
Freud, Sigmund (1957), "Mourning and Melancholia," *The Standard Edition of the Complete Psychological Works of Sigmund Freud*, Vol. XIV (1914–16): On the History of the Psycho-Analytic Movement, Papers on Metapsychology and Other Works, Trans. J. Strachey, London: The Hogarth Press and the Institute of Psycho-Analysis, pp. 243–58. Print.
Freud, Sigmund, "Fetishism," *The Standard Edition of the Complete Psychological Works of Sigmund Freud*, Vol. XXI (1927–31).
Friedländer, Saul (1986), *Reflections of Nazism*, New York: First Discus Printing. Print.
—(1990), "Preface to a Symposium: Kitsch and the Apocalyptic Imagination," *Salmagundi* 85/86: 201–6. Print.
Ganivet, Ángel (1999), *Idearium español*, 2nd. edn, Madrid: Editorial Biblioteca Nueva. Print.
Gerow, Aaron (2009), "Narrating the Nation-ality of a Cinema: The Case of Japanese Prewar Film," in Alan Tansman (ed.), *The Culture of Japanese Fascism*, Durham: Duke University Press, pp. 184–221. Print.
Giménez Caballero, Ernesto (1938), *España y Franco*, Madrid: Ediciones "Los combatientes". Print.
—(1944), *El cine y la cultura humana. Conferencia pronunciada en la facultad de Filosofía y Letras de la ciudad universitaria de Madrid*, Bilbao: Ediciones de Conferencias y Ensayos. Print.
Golomstock, Igor (2011), *Totalitarian Art: in The Soviet Union, The Third Reich, Fascist Italy, and The People's Republic of China*, New York: Overlook Duckworth. Print.
Gómez de La Serna, Ramón (1943), "Lo cursi y otros ensayos," Buenos Aires: Editorial Sudamericana.
González Aja, Teresa (2005), "Monje y soldado. La imagen masculina durante el Franquismo," *Revista Internacional de Ciencias del Deporte* 1: 64–83. Print.
González, Luis Mariano (2009), *Fascismo, kitsch y cine histórico español (1939–1953)*, Cuenca: Ediciones de la Universidad de Castilla-La Mancha. Print.
—(2012), "Francoist Spaces: *Un hombre va por el camino* (Manuel Mur Oti, 1948) and *Surcos* (José Antonio Nieves Conde, 1951)," in David R. Castillo and Bradley J. Nelson (eds), *Spectacle and Topophilia: Reading Early Modern*

and Postmodern Hispanic Cultures, Nashville: Vanderbilt University Press, pp. 213–30. Print.
Gordon, Avery F. (2008), *Ghostly Matters: Haunting and the Sociological Imagination*, Minneapolis and London: University of Minnesota Press. Print.
Gubern, Román (1977), *Raza: un ensueño del general Franco*, Madrid: Ediciones 99.
—(1986), *1936–1939: La Guerra de España en la pantalla*, Madrid: Filmoteca Española. Print.
Hardcastle, Anne E. (2009), "Melodramatic Victimization and The Spanish Civil War: The Cases of *Raza* and *El Lápiz del Carpintero*," *Vanderbilt e-Journal of Luso-Hispanic Studies* Vol. 5.
Herralde, Gonzalo (1977), *Raza: el espíritu de Franco*, Barcelona: Editrama.
Herzberger, David K. (1995), *Fiction and Historiography in Postwar Spain*, Durham and London: Duke University Press. Print.
Hughes, Robert (2003), *Goya*, New York: Alfred A. Knopf. Print.
Ibarz, Mercè (2000), "Entró en mi cuarto un toro negro: la historia en el cine de Buñuel," Conference paper read at the International Luis Buñuel Conference, 1900–2000, Zaragoza, España.
Iglesias Turrión, Pablo (2013), *Maquiavelo frente a la gran pantalla*, Kindle edn, Madrid: Ediciones Akal.
Jordan, Barry and Rikki Morgan-Tamosunas (1998), *Contemporary Spanish Cinema*, Manchester: Manchester University Press. Print.
Jung, Carl (1964), *The Man and His Symbols*, Garden City, NY: Doubleday.
Kafka, Franz (1999), *The Trial*, Schocken. Print.
Kahana, Jonathan (2008), *Intelligence Work: The Politics of American Documentary*, New York: Columbia University Press. Print.
Keller, Patricia M. (2008), *Reading the Ghost: Toward a Theory of Haunting in Contemporary Spanish Culture*, Dissertation, University of Michigan.
—(2012), "The Valley, the Monument, and the Tomb: Notes on the Place of Historical Memory," *Hispanic Issues On Line* 11: 64–86.
Kellogg, Catherine (1999), "The Question of Marx and Justice Revisited: Derrida's Marx and Messianic Time," *Problématique* 5: 118–43. Print.
Kermode, Frank (2000), "Solitary Confinement," *The Sense of an Ending: Studies in the Theory of Fiction*, New York: Oxford University Press, pp. 155–80. Print.
Kinder, Marsha (1993), *Blood Cinema: The Reconstruction of National Identity in Spain*, Berkeley: University of California Press. Print.
Kirby, Lynne (1997), *Parallel Tracks: The Railroad and Silent Cinema*, Durham: Duke University Press. Print.
Kjellman-Chapin, Monica (2010), "The Politics of Kitsch," *Rethinking Marxism* 22:1, 27–41.
Kleist, Heinrich von (1972), "On the Marionette Theater," *The Drama Review*, Vol. 16, No. 3, pp.22–6.
Klemperer, Victor (2002), *The Language of the Third Reich: LTI-Lingua Tertii Imperii. A Philologist's Notebook*, Trans. Martin Brady, London: Continuum. Print.

Klibansky, Raymond, Erwin Panofsky, and Fritz Saxl (1964), *Saturn and Melancholy: Studies in the History of Natural Philosophy, Religion, and Art*, New York: Basic Books.
Koepnick, Lutz (1999), "Fascist Aesthetics Revisited," *Modernism/modernity* 6.1: 51–73. Print.
Koestler, Arthur (1937), *Spanish Testament*, London: Victor Gollancz Ltd. Print.
Kracauer, Siegfried (2004), *From Caligari to Hitler: A Psychological History of the German Film*, Rev. edn, Trans. Leonardo Quaresma, Princeton: Princeton University Press. Print.
Kulka, Tomas (2002), *Kitsch and Art*, 2nd edn, University Park, PA: The Pennsylvania State University Press. Print.
Kundera, Milan (1984), *The Unbearable Lightness of Being*, New York: Perennial Library. Print.
Labanyi, Jo (2000), "History and Hauntology; or, What Does One Do with the Ghosts of the Past? Reflections on Spanish Film and Fiction of the Post-Franco Period," in Joan Ramon (ed.), *Dismembering the Dictatorship: The Politics of Memory in the Spanish Transition to Democracy*, Amsterdam and Atlanta, GA: Rodopi, pp. 65–82. Print.
Lacoue-Labarthe, Philippe and Jean-Luc Nancy (1990), "The Nazi Myth," *Critical Inquiry* 16.2: 291–312. Print.
Lim, Bliss Cua (2011), *Translating Time: Cinema, the Fantastic, and the Temporal Critique*, Durham: Duke University Press. Print.
Llorente, Ángel (1995), *Arte e ideología en el franquismo: 1936–1951*, Madrid: Visor. Print.
Llovet, Enrique (1954), *Los últimos de Filipinas*, Madrid: La novela del sábado. Print.
Loureiro, Ángel (2003), "Spanish Nationalism and the Ghost of Empire," *Journal of Spanish Cultural Studies* 4.1: 65–76. Print.
Macey, Samuel L. (2010), *Patriarchs of Time: Dualism in Saturn-Cronus, Father Time, the Watchmaker God, and Father Christmas*, Athens: The University of Georgia Press. Print.
Macherey, Pierre (1999), "Marx Dematerialized, or the Spirit of Derrida," in Michael Sprinker (ed.), *Ghostly Demarcations: A Symposium on Jacques Derrida's Specters of Marx*, London: Verso, pp. 17–25. Print.
Madariaga, María Rosa de (2002), *Los moros que trajo Franco: La intervención de tropas coloniales en la Guerra Civil*, Barcelona: Ediciones Martínez Roca. Print.
Maeztu, Ramiro de (1938), *Defensa de la hispanidad*, 3rd edn, Valladolid: Aldus. Print.
Manovich, Lev (2001), *The Language of New Media*, Cambridge, MA: MIT Press. Print.
Maravall, José Antonio (1986), *Culture of the Baroque: Analysis of a Historical Structure*, University of Minnesota. Print.
Marsh, Steven (2006), *Popular Spanish Film under Franco: Comedy and the Weakening of the State*, New York: Palgrave Macmillan. Print.

Martín Cerezo, Saturnino (1909), *Under the Red and the Gold: Being Notes and Recollections of the Siege of Baler*, Trans. F. L. Dodds, Kansas City: Franklin Hudson Publishing Company. Print.

Martín Corrales, Eloy (1995), "El cine español y las guerras de Marruecos (1896–1994)," *Hispania* 190.55/2: 693–708. Print.

Martín Gaite, Carmen (2006), *Esperando el porvenir: Homenaje a Ignacio Aldecoa*, Madrid: Ediciones Siruela. Print.

Mayne, Judith (1993), *Cinema and Spectatorship*, London: Routledge. Print.

Medina Domínguez, Alberto (2001), *Exorcismos de la memoria: políticas y poéticas de la melancolía en la España de la transición*, Madrid: Ediciones Libertarias. Print.

Menéndez y Pelayo, Marcelino (2014), *Historia de los heterodoxos españoles. Libro VIII*, Barcelona: Linkgua. Print.

Metz, Christian (1986), *Psychoanalysis and Cinema. The Imaginary Signifier*, Trans. Celia Britton and Annwyl Williams, Bloomington: Indiana University Press. Print.

Minow, Martha (1998), *Between Vengeance and Forgiveness: Facing History after Genocide and Mass Violence*, Boston: Beacon Press. Print.

Mitchell, W. J. T. (2005), *What Do Pictures Want? The Lives and the Loves of Images*, Chicago: University of Chicago Press. Print.

Moen, Kristian (2013), *Film and Fairy Tales: the Birth of Modern Fantasy*, London: I. B. Tauris. Print.

Monsiváis, Carlos (2009), "The Neobaroque and Popular Culture," *PMLA* Vol. 124, No. 1, January, pp. 180–8.

Moreiras-Menor, Cristina (2002), *Cultura herida: literatura y cine en la España democrática*, Madrid: Ediciones Libertarias/Prodhufi.

—(2007), "War, Post-War, and the Fascist Fabrication of Identity," in Noël Valis (ed.), *Teaching Representations of the Spanish Civil War*, New York: MLA. Print.

—(2011), *La estela del tiempo: imagen e historicidad en el cine español contemporáneo*, Madrid: Iberoamericana Vervuert.

Moretti, Franco (1983), *Signs Taken for Wonder*, London: Verso. Print.

Mulvey, Laura (1986), "Visual Pleasure and Narrative Cinema," in Philip Rosen (ed.), *Narrative, Apparatus, Ideology. A Film Theory Reader*, New York: Columbia University Press, pp. 198–209. Print.

—(1993), "Some Thoughts on Theories of Fetishism in the Context of Contemporary Culture," *October* 65: 3–20. Print.

—(2006), *Death 24x a Second: Stillness and the Moving Image*, London: Reaktion Books.

Murray, Timothy (2008), *Digital Baroque: New Media Art and Cinematic Folds*, Minneapolis: University of Minnesota Press. Print.

Nabokov, Vladimir (1971), *Nikolai Gogol*, 13th edn, New York: New Directions Books. Print.

Ndalianis, Angela (2004), *Neo-Baroque Aesthetics and Contemporary Entertainment*, Cambridge, MA: MIT Press. Print.

Naremore, James (2004), "Style and Meaning in *Citizen Kane*," in Naremore (ed.), *Orson Welles's Citizen Kane: A Casebook*, Oxford: Oxford University Press, pp. 123–60. Print.

Neocleous, Mark (1997), *Fascism*, Minneapolis: University of Minnesota Press. Print.

Ngai, Sianne (2012), *Our Aesthetic Categories: Zany, Cute, Interesting*, Cambridge, MA: Harvard University Press. Print.

Nichols, Bill (2001), *Introduction to Documentary*, Bloomington: Indiana University Press. Print.

Nordström, Folke (2015), *Goya, Saturno y melancolía: consideraciones sobre el arte de Goya*, Kindle edn, La balsa de la medusa No. 193.

Olalquiaga, Celeste (1998), *The Artificial Kingdom: A Treasury of Kitsch Experience*, New York: Pantheon Books. Print.

Ortega y Gasset, José (1998), "Sobre el fascismo. Sine ira et studio," *El espectador*, Madrid: Editorial EDAF, pp. 105–18. Print.

Pacheco Bejarano, Juan Pablo (2014), "Unveiling the Monster: Memory and Film in Post-Dictatorial Spain," self-designed Majors Honors Papers. Paper 10. New London: Connecticut College.

Palacio Atard, Vicente (1949), "Menéndez y Pelayo, historiador actual," *Arbor* 14.47: 254–9. Print.

Paxton, Robert O. (2004), *The Anatomy of Fascism*, New York: Alfred A. Knopf. Print.

Payne, Stanley G. (1984), *Spanish Catholicism; An Historical Review*, Madison: University of Wisconsin Press. Print.

Pelzer, Peter (2001), "The Melancholic Manager–For Goodness Sake!" The 2nd Critical Management Studies Conference, Manchester, 11–13 July, pp. 1–14. Print.

Pensky, Max (2001), *Melancholy Dialectics: Walter Benjamin and the Play of Mourning*, Amherst: Massachusetts Press.

Pippin, Robert B. (2012), *Fatalism in American Film Noir: Some Cinematic Philosophy*, Charlottesville: University of Virginia Press. Print.

Plantinga, Carl (1997), *Rhetoric and Representation in Nonfiction Film*, New York: Cambridge University Press. Print.

Prado, Ignacio (1995), "Del espíritu de Franco al espíritu de la colmena: Raza y rizoma en el cine español," *Anuario del cine español*, pp. 101–10. Print.

Preston, Paul (1994), *Franco: A Biography*, New York: Basic Books. Print.

—(2001), *The Politics of Revenge: Fascism and the Military in Twentieth-Century Spain*, London and New York: Routledge.

Primo de Rivera, José Antonio (1945), *Obras Completas*, Madrid: Ediciones de la Vicesecretaría de educación popular de F.E.T. y de Las J.O.N.S. Print.

Propp, Vladmir (2013), *Morphology of the Folktale*, Austin: University of Texas Press. Print.

Pupavac, Vanessa (2008), "Hamlet, the State of Emotion and the International Crisis of Meaning," *Mental Health Review Journal* 13.1: 14–26. Print.

Rancière, Jacques (2013), *Béla Tarr, the Time After*, Trans. Erik Beranek, Minneapolis: Univocal.
Renov, Michael (ed.), (1993), *Theorizing Documentary*, New York: Routledge, pp. 58–89. Print.
Richards, Michael (1998), *A Time of Silence: Civil War and the Culture of Repression in Franco's Spain, 1936–1945*, New York: Cambridge University Press. Print.
Richardson, Carl (1992), *Autopsy: An Element of Realism in Film Noir*, Metuchen, NJ and London: The Scarecrow Press. Print.
Richardson, Nathan E. (2002), *Postmodern Paletos: Immigration, Democracy, and Globalization in Spanish Narrative and Film, 1950–2000*, Lewisburg: Bucknell University Press. Print.
Rincón, Reyes (2017), "El Supremo rechaza la petición de Garzón sobre el Valle de los Caídos," elpaís.com, 1 March.
Rivero Franco, Marta (2015), "El esperpento en el cine de Álex de la Iglesia," *Fonseca, Journal of Communication*, No. 10 (January–June), pp. 360–92.
Rose, Jacqueline (1998), *States of Fantasy*, New York: Oxford University Press. Print.
Rosen, Philip (1993), "Document and Documentary: On the Persistence of Historical Concepts," in Michael Renov (ed.), *Theorizing Documentary*, New York: Routledge, pp. 58–89. Print.
Sánchez-Biosca, Vicente (1999), *Luis Buñuel. Viridiana: estudio crítico*, Barcelona: Paidós. Print.
Sánchez Casado, Antonio (1988), *El Kitsch Español*, Madrid: Ediciones Temas de Hoy, S.A. Print.
Sánchez-Mazas, Rafael (1939), *Discurso*. Edición de la editora nacional, Bilbao: En la casa Elexpuru Hermanos. Print.
Sánchez Vidal, Agustín (1984), *Luis Buñuel: obra cinematográfica*, Madrid: Ediciones J.C. Print.
Santaolalla, Isabel (2005), "Los últimos de Filipinas. Last Stand in the Philippines," in Alberto Mira (ed.), *The Cinema of Spain and Portugal*, London: Wallflower Press, pp. 51–9. Print.
Sarduy, Severo (1980), *"The Baroque and the Neobaroque." Latin America in its Literature*, New York: Holmes and Meier Publishers, Inc. Print.
Saz, Ismael (2004), *Fascismo y franquismo*, Universitat de Valencia. Print.
Schivelbusch, Wolfgang (2014), *The Railway Journey: The Industrialization of Time and Space in the Nineteenth Century*, Berkeley: University of California Press. Print.
Schrader, Paul (1998), "Notes on Film Noir," in Alain Silver and James Ursini (eds), *Film Noir Reader*, 4th edn, New York: Random House, pp. 53–63. Print.
Shakespeare, William (1992), *Hamlet*. New York: Palgrave. Print.
Shaw, Spencer (2008), *Film Consciousness: From Phenomenology to Deleuze*, London: McFarland & Company. Print.
Sherover, Charles M. (2003), *Are We in Time? And other Essays on Time and Temporality*. Ed. Gregory R. Johnson. Evanston, IL: Northwestern University Press. Print.

Shevel, Oxana (2011), "The Politics of Memory in a Divided Society: A Comparison of Post-Franco Spain and Post-Soviet Ukraine," *Slavic Review* 70.1 (Spring): 137–64. Print.
Sontag, Susan (1981), *Under the Sign of Saturn*, New York: Vintage Books. Print.
Stam, Robert (1991), "Hitchcock and Buñuel: Authority, Desire and the Absurd," in Walter Raubicheck and Walter Srebnick (eds), *Hitchcock's Rereleased Films: From* Rope *to* Vertigo, Detroit: Wayne State University Press. Print.
Steimatsky, Noa (2008), *Italian Locations: Reinhabiting the Past in Postwar Cinema*, Minneapolis: University of Minnesota Press. Print.
Steiner, George (1998), "Introduction," in Walter Benjamin, *The Origin of German Tragic Drama*, Trans. John Osborne, London and New York: Verso, pp. 7–24. Print.
Stone, Rob (2007), "Spanish Film Noir," in Andrew Spicer (ed.), *European Film Noir*, Manchester: Manchester University Press, pp. 185–209. Print.
Storey, Robert F. (2014), *Pierrot: A Critical History of a Mask*, Princeton: Princeton University Press. Print.
Tansman, Alan (2009), *The Aesthetics of Japanese Fascism*, Berkeley: University of California Press. Print.
Tolentino, Roland B. (1997), "Nations, Nationalism, and *Los últimos de Filipinas*: An Imperialist Desire for Colonialist Nostalgia," in Marsha Kinder (ed.), *Refiguring Spain: Cinema, Media, Representation*, Durham: Duke University Press, pp. 133–53. Print.
Tranche, Rafael (2002), "La imagen de Franco 'Caudillo' en la primera propaganda cinematográfica del Régimen," *Archivos de la filmoteca. Revista de estudios históricos sobre la imagen* 42-3.1: 76–95. Print.
Tranche, Rafael and Vicente Sánchez-Biosca (2001), *NO-DO: El tiempo y la memoria*, Madrid: Cátedra/Filmoteca Española. Print.
Treglown, Jeremy (2013), *Franco's Crypt: Spanish Culture and Memory Since 1936*, New York: Farrar, Straus & Giroux. Print.
Tremlett, Giles (2006), *Ghosts of Spain: Travels Through Spain and Its Silent Past*, New York: Walker & Company. Print.
Triana-Toribio, Núria (2003), *Spanish National Cinema*, London: Routledge.
Unamuno, Miguel de (2013), *Aunt Tula*, Trans. Julia Biggane, Oxford: Arts & Phillips. Print.
Valis, Noël (2002), *The Culture of Cursilería: Bad Taste, Kitsch, and Class in Modern Spain*, Durham: Duke University Press.
Varderi, Alejandro (1996), *Severo Sarduy y Pedro Almodóvar: del barroco al kitsch en la narrativa y cine posmodernos*, Madrid: Editorial Pliegos. Print.
Vernant, Jean Pierre (2001), *Universe, the Gods and Mortals: Ancient Greek Myths*, New York: HarperCollins. Print.
Vernon, Kathleen M. (1998), "Scripting a Social Imaginary: Hollywood in/and Spanish Cinema," in Jenaro Talens and Santos Zunzunegui (eds), *Modes of Representation in Spanish Cinema*, Minneapolis: University of Minnesota Press, pp. 319–30. Print.

Vieira, Patricia (2013), *Portuguese Film, 1930–1960: The Staging of the New State Regime*, London: Bloomsbury. Print.
Viscarri, Dionisio (1996), "Political Ideology and Orientalism: The Pre-Fascist Narrative of the Moroccan War (1921–1923)," Dissertation, Ohio State University. Print.
Warner, Marina (2014), *Once Upon a Time*, New York: Oxford University Press. Print.
Wollen, Peter (2002), "Architecture and Film: Places and Non-Places," *Paris Hollywood: Writings on Film*, New York: Verso, pp. 199–215.
Wood, Robin (2002), *Hitchcock's Films Revisited*, Rev. edn, New York: Columbia University Press. Print.
Wright, Craig (2001), *The Maze and the Warrior*, Cambridge, MA: Harvard University Press. Print.
Wright, Sarah (2013), *The Child in Spanish Cinema*, Manchester and New York: Manchester University Press. Print.
Yarza, Alejandro (1999), *Un caníbal en Madrid: la sensibilidad camp y el reciclaje de la historia en el cine de Pedro Almodóvar*, Madrid: Ediciones Libertarias-Prodhufi. Print.
Zipes, Jack (2011), *The Enchanted Screen: the Unknown History of Fairy-Tale Films*, New York: Routledge.
Žižek, Slavoj (1989), *The Sublime Object of Ideology*, London: Verso. Print.
Zumalde Arregui, Imanol (1997), "*Surcos* 1951." *Antología crítica del cine español 1906–1995: flor en la sombra*. Ed. Julio Pérez Perucha. Madrid: Cátedra, pp. 294–6. Print.
Zunzunegui, Santos (1994), *Paisajes de la forma: Ejercicios de análisis de la imagen*, Madrid: Cátedra. Print.

Films

1898. Los últimos de Filipinas. Dir. Salvador Calvo. Perf. Luis Tosar, Javier Gutiérrez, Álvaro Cervantes. CIPI Cinematográfica S.A., 2016. Film.
Aguirre, the Wrath of God [*Aguirre, der Zorn Gottes*]. Dir. Werner Herzog. Perf. Klaus Kinski, Ruy Guerra, Elena Rojo. Filmverlag der Autoren, 1972. Film.
Agustina de Aragón [*The Siege*]. Dir. Juan de Orduña. Perf. Aurora Bautista, Fernando Aguirre, Valeriano Andrés. Compañía Industrial Film Español S.A. (Cifesa), 1950. Film.
¡Ahí va otro recluta! Dir. Ramón Fernández. Perf. José Luis Ozores, José Luis Carbonell, Manuel Zarzo. Aspa, 1960. Film.
Alba de América [*Dawn of America*]. Dir. Juan de Orduña. Perf. Antonio Villar, María Martín, José Suárez. Cifesa, 1951. Film.
Alhucemas. Dir. José López Rubio. Perf. Julio Peña, Nani Fernández, José Bódalo. Peña Films, 1948. Film.
Amaya. Dir. Luis Marquina. Perf. Susana Canales, Julio Peña, José Bódalo. Cifesa, 1952. Film.

El ángel exterminador [*The Exterminating Angel*]. Dir. Luis Buñuel. Perf. Silvia Pinal, Jacqueline Andere, Enrique Rambal. Producciones Gustavo Alatriste, 1962. Film.

Aquellas palabras. Dir. Luis Arroyo. Perf. José María Seoane, Ana Mariscal, Isabel de Pomés. Galatea Films, 1949. Film.

Balada triste de trompeta [*The Last Circus*]. Dir. Álex de la Iglesia. Perf. Carlos Areces, Antonio de la Torre, Carolina Bang. Films Distribution, 2010. Film.

Bambú [*Bamboo*]. Dir. José Luis Sáenz de Heredia. Perf. Gabriel Algara, Manuel Arbó, Imperio Argentina, 1945. Film.

El barbero de Sevilla. Dir. Benito Perojo. Perf. Miguel Ligero, Estrellita Castro, and Roberto Rey. Hispano Filmproduktion, 1938. Film.

Bataan. Dir. Tay Garnett. Perf. Robert Taylor, George Murphy, Thomas Mitchell. Metro-Goldwyn-Mayer, 1943. Film.

Beau Geste. Dir. William Wellman. Perf. Gary Cooper, Ray Milland, Robert Preston. Paramount Pictures, 1939. Film.

Being There. Dir. Hal Ashby. Perf. Peter Sellers. New Gold Entertainment, 1979. Film.

Berlin, Symphony of a Great City [*Die Sinfonie der Großstadt*]. Dir. Walter Ruttmann. Deutsche Vereins-Film, 1927. Film.

The Birds. Dir. Alfred Hitchcock. Perf. Rod Taylor, Tippi Hedren, Suzanne Pleshette. Alfred J Hitchcock Productions, 1963. Film.

Boda en el infierno. Dir. Antonio Román. Perf. Conchita Montenegro, José Nieto, Tony D'Algi. Hércules Films, 1942. Film.

Cabiria. Dir. Giovanni Pastrone. Perf. Italia Almirante-Manzini, Lidia Quaranta, Bartolomeo Pagano. Itala Film, 1914. Film.

Carmen (la de Triana). Dir. Florián Rey. Perf. Imperio Argentina, Pedro Barreto, J. Noé de la Peña. Hispano Filmproduktion, 1938. Film.

Casablanca. Dir. Michael Curtiz. Perf. Humphrey Bogart, Ingrid Bergman, Paul Henreid. Warner Bros. Pictures, 1942. Film.

El Cid. Dir. Anthony Mann. Perf. Charlton Heston, Sophia Loren, Raf Vallone. Dear Film Produzione, 1961. Film.

Circus. Dir. Charles Chaplin. Perf. Charles Chaplin, Merna Kennedy, Al Ernest García. United Artists, 1928. Film.

Citizen Kane. Dir. Orson Welles. Perf. Orson Welles, Joseph Cotten, Everett Sloane. RKO/Mercury Theatre Productions, 1941. Film.

La corona negra [*Black Crown*]. Dir. Luis Saslavsky. Perf. María Félix, Rossano Brazzi, Vittorio Gassman. Suevia Films, Cesáreo González, 1951. Film.

Cristo Negro. Dir. Ramón Torrado. Perf. René Muñoz, Jesús Tordesillas, María Silva. Copercines, Cooperativa Cinematográfica, 1963. Film.

El crucero Baleares. Dir. Enrique del Campo. Perf. Roberto Rey, Marta Ruel, Elena D'Algy. RKO Radio Pictures/Radio Films Española, 1941. Print.

Deliverance. Dir. John Boorman. Perf. Jon Voight, Burt Reynolds, Ned Beatty. Warner Bros., 1972. Film.

De Salamanca a ninguna parte. Chema de la Peña. Artimaña Producciones S.L., 2002.

Dog Day Afternoon. Dir. Sidney Lumet. Perf. Al Pacino, John Cazale, Penelope Allen. Warner Bros., 1975. Film.
El laberinto del fauno [*Pan's Labyrinth*]. Dir. Guillermo del Toro. Perf. Ivana Baquero, Ariadna Gil, Sergi López. Estudios Picasso, Tequila Gang, Esperanto Filmoj, 2006. Film.
Escuadrilla. Dir. Antonio Román. Perf. Alfredo Mayo, José Nieto, Luchy Soto. Productores Asociados S.A., 1941. Film.
État de siège [*State of Siege*]. Dir. Costa-Gavras. Perf. Yves Montand, Renato Salvatori, O.E. Hasse. Reggane Films, Euro International Film (EIA), Unidis (co-production), Dieter Geissler Filmproduktion, 1972. Film.
Franco, ese hombre. Dir. José Luis Sáenz de Heredia. Perf. Francisco Franco. Castilla Films, 1964. Film.
Frente de Madrid [*Carmen fra i rossi*]. Dir. Edgar Neville. Perf. Fosco Giachetti, Rafael Rivelles, Conchita Montes. Film Bassoli, 1939. Film.
Gallipoli. Dir. Peter Weir. Perf. Mel Gibson, Mark Lee, Bill Kerr. Paramount, 1981. Film.
Germania Anno Zero [*Germany Year Zero*]. Dir. Roberto Rossellini. Perf. Edmund Moeschke, Ernst Pittschau, Ingetraud Hinze. Tevere Film, 1948. Film.
Goodfellas. Dir. Martin Scorsese. Perf. Robert De Niro, Ray Liotta, Joe Pesci. Warner Bros., 1990. Film.
¡Harka! Dir. Carlos Arévalo. Perf. Alfredo Mayo, Luis Peña, Luchy Soto. Cifesa, 1941. Film.
Héroes del 95 [*Heroes of '95*]. Dir. Raúl Alfonso. Perf. Alfredo Mayo, Maria Eugénia, Rafael Calvo. Faro Producciones Cinematográficas, 1946. Film.
High Noon. Dir. Fred Zinnemann. Perf. Gary Cooper, Grace Kelly, Thomas Mitchell. United Artists, 1952. Film.
La battaglia di Algeri [*The Battle of Algiers*]. Dir. Gillo Pontecorvo. Perf. Brahim Hadjadj, Jean Martin, Yacef Saadi. Igor Film, Casbah Film, 1966. Film.
La canción de Aixa. Dir. Florián Rey. Perf. Imperio Argentina, Manuel Luna, Ricardo Merino. Hispano Filmproduktion, 1939. Film.
La leona de Castilla [*The Lioness of Castille*]. Dir. Juan de Orduña. Perf. Amparo Rivelles, Virgilio Teixeira, Alfredo Mayo. Cifesa, 1951. Film.
La llamada de África. Dir. César Fernández Ardavín. Perf. Ali Beiba Uld Abidin, Yahadid Ben Ahmed Lehbib, Farachi Ben Emboiric. Hesperia Films S.A., 1952. Film.
La mies es mucha. Dir. José Luis Sáenz de Heredia. Perf. Fernando Fernán Gómez, Sara Montiel, Enrique Guitart. Chapalo Films S.A., 1948. Film.
La muerte de un ciclista [Death of a Cyclist]. Dir. Juan Antonio Bardem. Perf. Lucia Bosé, Alberto Closas, Bruna Corrá. Guión Producciones Cinematográficas, 1955. Film.
Land Without Bread. Dir. Luis Buñuel. Perf. Abel Jacquin, Alexandre O'Neill. Ramon Acín, 1932. Film.
La princesa de los Ursinos. Dir. Luis Lucía. Perf. Ana Mariscal, Roberto Rey, Fernando Rey. Cifesa, 1947. Film.

L'assedio dell'Alcazar [*The Siege of the Alcazar*]. Dir. Augusto Genina. Perf. Fosco Giachetti, Mireille Balin, María Denis. Film Bassoli, 1940. Film.
Las últimas banderas. Dir. Luis Marquina. Perf. María Arias, Mario Berriatúa, Félix Dafauce. Velázquez P.C., 1954. Film.
Les Enfants du Paradis [*Children of Paradise*]. Dir. Marcel Carné. Perf. Arletty, Jean-Louis Barrault, Pierre Brasseur. Pathé Consortium Cinéma, 1945. Film.
Lifeboat. Dir. Alfred Hitchcock. Perf. Tallulah Bankhead, John Hodiak, William Bendix. 20th Century Fox, 1944. Film.
Locura de amor. Dir. Juan de Orduña. Perf. Aurora Bautista, Fernando Rey, Sara Montiel. Cifesa, 1948. Film.
Lola la piconera [*Lola, the Coalgirl*]. Dir. Luis Lucía. Perf. Juanita Reina, Virgilio Teixeira, Manuel Luna. Cifesa, 1952. Film.
Los últimos de Filipinas [*Last Stand in the Philippines*]. Dir. Antonio Fernández Román. Perf. Tony Leblanc, Fernando Rey, Nani Fernández. Alhambra, 1945. Film.
Man of Aran. Dir. Robert J. Flaherty. Gaumont British Picture/Gainsborough Pictures, 1934. Film.
Man with a Movie Camera [Человек с киноаппаратом]. Dir. Dziga Vertov. VUFKU, 1929. Film.
Mariquilla Terremoto. Dir. Benito Perojo. Perf. Estrellita Castro, Antonio Vico, Ricardo Marino, Rafaela Santorrés. Hispano Film-Produktion, 1938. Film.
Matador. Dir. Pedro Almodóvar. Perf. Assumpta Serna, Antonio Banderas, Nacho Martínez. Compañía Iberoamericana de TV, Televisión Española (TVE), 1986. Film.
Misión Blanca. Dir. Juan de Orduña. Perf. Julio Peña, Manuel Luna, Elva de Bethancourt. Colonial AJE, 1946. Film.
Moana. Dir. Robert J. Flaherty. Famous Players-Lasky Corporation, 1926. Film.
Nanook of the North. Dir. Robert J. Flaherty. Revillon Frères, 1922. Film.
Night-mail. Dir. Basil Wright and Harry Watt. Associated British Film Distributors, 1936. Film.
North by Northwest. Dir. Alfred Hitchcock. Perf. Cary Grant, Eva Marie Saint, James Mason. Metro-Goldwyn-Mayer, 1959. Film.
Novios de la muerte. Dir. Rafael Gil. Perf. Julián Mateos, Juan Luis Galiardo, Ramiro Oliveros. Coral Producciones Cinematográficas, 1975. Film.
Out of the Past. Dir. Jacques Tourneur. Perf. Robert Mitchum, Jane Gerr, Kirk Douglas. RKO Radio Pictures, 1947. Film.
Paisà. Dir. Roberto Rossellini. Perf. Maria Michi, Gar Moore, Carmela Sazio. O.F.I., 1946. Film.
Paths of Glory. Dir. Stanley Kubrick. Perf. Kirk Douglas, Ralph Meeker, Adolphe Menjou. United Artists, 1957. Film.
Plácido. Dir. Luis García Berlanga. Perf. Cassen, José Luis López Vázquez, Elvira Quintillá. Jet Films, 1961. Film.
Porque te vi llorar. Dir. Juan de Orduña. Perf. Pastora Peña, Manuel Arbó, and Eloísa Muro. Cifesa, 1951. Film.

Power and the Land. Dir. Joris Ivens. Perf. William Adams, Stephen Vincent Benet, Hazel Parkinson. United States Film Service, 1940. Film.
Ran. Dir. Akira Kurosawa. Perf. Tatsuya Nakadai, Akira Terao, Jinpachi Nezu. Greenwich Film Productions, 1985. Film.
Raza, el espíritu de Franco. Dir. Gonzalo Herralde. Septiembre P.C., 1977. Film.
Raza. Dir. José Luis Sáenz de Heredia. Perf. Alfredo Mayo, Ana Mariscal, José Nieto. Cancillería del Consejo de la Hispanidad, 1941. Film.
Rojo y Negro. Dir. Carlos Arévalo. Perf. Conchita Montenegro, Ismael Merlo, Quique Camoiras, Luisita España. CEPICSA, 1942. Film.
Romancero marroquí. Dir. Carlos Velo and Enrique Domínguez Rodiño. Alta Comisaría de España en Marruecos/C.E.A., 1939. Film.
Simón del desierto [*Simon of the Desert*]. Dir. Luis Buñuel. Perf. Silvia Pinal, Claudio Brook, Enrique Álvarez Félix. Sindicato de Trabajadores de la Producción Cinematográfica, 1965. Film.
Sin un adiós. Dir. Vicente Escrivá. Perf. Raphael, Lesley-Anne Down, Antonio Pica. Aspa Producciones Cinematográficas, 1970. Film.
Surcos [*Furrows*]. Dir. José Antonio Nieves Conde. Perf. Luis Peña, María Asquerino, Francisco Arenzana. Atenea Films, 1951. Film.
Straw Dogs. Dir. Sam Peckinpah. Perf. Dustin Hoffman, Susan George, Peter Vaughan. ABC Pictures, 1971. Film.
Suspiros de España [*Sighs of Spain*]. Dir. Benito Perojo. Perf. Miguel Ligero, Estrellita Castro, Roberto Rey. Hispano Filmproduktion, 1939. Film.
The Alamo. Dir. John Wayne. Perf. John Wayne, Richard Widmark, Laurence Harvey. Batjac Productions, 1960. Film.
The City. Dir. Ralph Steiner, Willard Van Dyke. Perf. Morris Carnovsky. American Institute of Planners, 1939. Film.
The Discreet Charm of the Bourgeoisie [*Le charme discret de la bourgeoisie*]. Dir. Luis Buñuel. Perf. Fernando Rey, Delphine Seyrig, Paul Frankeur. Greenwich Film Productions, 1972. Film.
The Killers. Dir. Robert Siodmak. Perf. Burt Lancaster, Ava Gardner, Edmond O'Brien. Universal Pictures, 1946. Film.
The New Earth [*Die Tochter des Samurai*] [新しき土]. Dir. Arnold Fanck and Mansaku Itami. Perf. Setsuko Hara, Sessue Hayakawa, Ruth Eweler, Isamu Kosugi. T&K Telefilm, 1937. Film.
The Plow that Broke the Plains. Dir. Pare Lorentz. Perf. Thomas Chalmers, Bam White. Resettlement Administration, 1936. Film.
The River. Dir. Pare Lorentz. Perf. Thomas Chalmers. Farm Security Administration, 1937. Film.
The Searchers. Dir. John Ford. Perf. John Wayne, Jeffrey Hunter, Vera Miles. Warner Bros., 1956. Film.
They Died with Their Boots On. Dir. Raoul Walsh. Perf. Errol Flynn, Olivia de Havilland. Warner Bros., 1941. Film.
Triumph des Willens [*Triumph of the Will*]. Dir. Leni Riefenstahl. Leni Riefenstahl-Produktion, Reichspropagandaleitung der NSDAP, 1935. Film.

To Have and Have Not. Dir. Howard Hawks. Perf. Humphrey Bogart, Walter Brennan, Lauren Bacall. Warner Bros. Pictures, 1944. Film.
Una cruz en el infierno [Flame Over Vietnam]. Dir. José María Elorrieta. Perf. Elena Barrios, José Nieto, Manolo Morán. Universitas Films, Universum Film (UFA), Westside International Films, 1956. Film.
Un Chien Andalou. Dir. Luis Buñuel. Perf. Pierre Batcheff, Simone Mareuil. 1929. Film.
Vertigo. Dir. Alfred Hitchcock. Perf. James Stewart, Kim Novak, Barbara Bel Geddes. Paramount, 1958. Film.
Viaggio in Italia [*Journey to Italy*]. Dir. Roberto Rossellini. Perf. Ingrid Bergman, George Sanders, María Mauban. Italia Film, 1954. Film.
Viridiana. Dir. Luis Buñuel. Perf. Silvia Pinal, Fernando Rey, Francisco Rabal. Films 59/UNINCI/Producciones Alatriste, 1961. Film.
Ya viene el cortejo. Dir. Carlos Arévalo. Cifesa, 1939. Film.
Zulu. Dir. Cy Endfield. Perf. Stanley Baker, Jack Hawkins, Ulla Jacobsson. Diamond Films, 1964. Film.

Index

Note: *italic* page number indicates illustration; n refers to an endnote

Acción mutante, 14, 206
acousmatic voice, 141, 162, 166, 167, 168, 169
Adorno, Theodor W., 11, 52, 83, 143, 169
aesthetics, 3, 4, 7, 10
   Baroque, 15–16
   camp, 12, 13, 14, 16, 206, 207
   fascist, 43, 84
   Francoist, 233
   and indoctrination, 11
   kitsch, 23–4, 49, 65, 74, 82, 83–4, 107, 128, 136, 173, 186, 204
   Neo-baroque, 12, 14, 15, 16, 206
   noir, 103, 104–5
Afinoguénova, Eugenia, 40n11
Africa: Second World War, 151, 159; *see also* Morocco; Oran
"Africanist" cinema, 56
Agamben, Giorgio, 18n18
Aguilar, Paloma, 253n3
Aguirre, the Wrath of God, 65
Alas, Leopoldo, 18n16
Alba de América [*Dawn of America*], 24, 105
Alberich, Ferrán, 9
Alcázar, El (journal), 58n6
Alfonso XIII, King, 174n2, 175n7, 177n23
Algeria *see* Oran
allegory: definitions, 291n39
Allinson, Mark, 104, 136n2
Almodóvar, Pedro, 13–14, 83, 207; *see also* Matador
Almogávares, 27–8, 29
Álvarez Junco, José: *Mater Dolorosa*, 256n24
American Revolution, 177n25
Anderson, Benedict, 46, 77
Andrade, Jaime de (pseudonym of Franco), 3, 23; *see also* Raza
Angelillo (singer), 272

anti-Semitism, 18n13
Antonio, José, 153, 160
apertura, 179, 180
Armstrong, Karen, 255n16, 256n23
Arrarás, Joaquín, 151
Arriba España (newspaper), 18n17
Art Nouveau, 5
Ashford, Gabriel, 6, 166
Assedio dell'Alcazar, L' [*The Siege of the Alcazar*], 39n5, 57n4, 97n14
audiences: receptivity of, 10–11
Augé, Marc, 73, 77
Avalos, Juan de, 39n8
awards
   film, 9, 67, 97n20, 98n22, 204
   military: Laureate Cross of St Ferdinand, 91, *92*, 94
Aznar, José María, 155
Aznar, Manuel, 38n4, 150, 155, 160, 162–4, *163*

Balada triste de trompeta [*The Last Circus*], 203–53, *218*, *222*, *229*, *238*, *242*, *244*, *246*, *251*
   abuse of women, 213, 216, 225
   allegory, 205, 207, 208, 213, 214, 217, 218–19, 250–1, 255n14, 259n50
   Biblical references, 214, 218–19, 226, 227, 228, 243, 245, 249, 250, 251, 252
   black humor, 215
   and Civil War, 208
   clowns, 204, 205, 207, 208, 209, 213, 219, 223, 224, 230, 231, 232–3, 234, 237, 244, 250, 251, 253
   color, 218, 230
   community, 236–7
   credit sequence, 210–11, 212, 220, 252
   death, 208, 220, 238, 244, 246–7, 250, 251, 256n25
   dedication, 253

Balada triste de trompeta (cont.)
   dream sequence, 224
   as film noir, 256n27
   forgiveness, 247, 248
   Francoist motifs, 211–12
   Francoist truth, 229
   ghosts, 205, 210, 219, 220, 223, 227, 230, 232, 233, 235–6, 237, 247, 248–9, 250, 254n5
   Goya award nomination, 204
   grottoes, 226–7, 240, 241
   historical memory, 219
   hunting scene, 227–8
   iconography, 209
   influences, 206, 207, 208, 212, 215, 217, 231, 245, 247
   justice, 204, 207
   King Kong image, 221
   kitsch motif, 231–3
   labyrinth, 240–1
   locations, 214
   masculinity, 223, 245–6
   metaphor, 209, 228, 255n14
   morality, 243
   mourning, 203, 205–6, 208, 210, 218, 223–4, 232, 236, 239, 251, 252
   musical score, 252
   Oedipal dynamics, 214–15, 216–17, 220, 221, 222, 223, 224, 225
   phallus motif, 223
   and popular culture, 208
   redemption, 207, 211, 219, 229, 240, 245, 247, 249
   Republicans, 209
   revenge, 204, 205, 207, 210, 214, 217, 224, 225–6, 231, 233, 235, 236
   sexual ambiguity, 256n32
   song, 224, 226, 231–2
   soundtrack, 228
   space, 230
   symbolism, 220
   tears, 208, 220, 221, 223, 233, 236, 251
   temporality, 225, 247, 248–9
   theme, 205, 208, 210
   title, 211
   trumpet motif, 224, 225–6
   visual references, 207–8, 212, 214, 218, 235, 255n15
   visual style, 206
Ballesteros, Isolina, 139n22
Barcones, Enrique Alfonso and Sánchez Campoy, Rafael: *El fuerte de Baler*, 95n3, 98n22

Baroque, 15–16, 21n35; *see also* Neo-baroque
Baskett, Michael, 43
Bataan, 69
Bataille, Georges, 36–7
Baum, Rainer C., 286n8
Bazin, André: "An Aesthetic of Reality," 109, 113–14
Becker, George J., 119
Beigbeder, Colonel Juan, 44
Being There, 172
Belsey, Catherine, 255n34
Benet, Vicente, 176n17
Ben-Ghiat, Ruth, 58n5
Benjamin, Walter, 1, 52, 78, 183, 206, 259n52, 291n39
   "The Storyteller," 287n9
Bentley, Bernard P. E., 137n3
Bergson, Henri, 17n6, 65, 95
Berlin, Isaiah, 17n6, 26
Berthier, Nancy, 176nn13,14
Bettelheim, Bruno, 265, 286n6, 287n10, 289n29, 291n43, 292n45
Birds, The, 120
Blancanieves [Snow White], xi–xiii, *xii*, *xiii*, 281–2
Blanchot, Maurice: *The Writing of the Disaster*, 203
Blasco-Salas, Dr, 160–1, *162*
Bollas, Christopher, 26, 31–2, 73–4
bourgeoisie, 182, 183, 189, 237
Bozal, Valeriano, 290n36, 291n41
Brazil, 150
Broch, Hermann, 3–4, 6, 24, 53, 101n41, 103
Brooks, Peter, 81, 100n39
bull motif, 190
bullfighting, xi, 13, 75, 123, 124–5
Buñuel, Luis, 14, 38n3; *see also Viridiana*
Burke, Kenneth, 53
Buse, Peter, Triana-Toribio, Núria and Willis, Andy: *The Cinema of Álex de la Iglesia*, 255nn20, 21
Butler, Judith, 205, 236, 254n12

caciquismo, 95n4
Calderón de la Barca, Pedro, 15, 206
Călinescu, Matei, 8, 30, 75
Calvo Sotelo, José, 153–4
camp, 12, 13, 14, 16, 206, 207
Camus, Mario, 136n2
Carmen, 3
Carr, Raymond, 61

Carrero Blanco, Admiral Luis, 105, 237, 238, 239
Castile, 174n3
Catholic Church
  and "cultural manufacturing," 15
  and Francoism, 48, 79, 188, 228
  guilt and sin in, 195
  Nacional-catolicismo, 184, 211, 263
  protective role of, 81
  Republicans and, 152
caves, 226, 239, 240, 243, 250, 259n46; *see also* grottoes
CEDA (political party), 152
censorship, 9, 105, 185, 208
Cerezo, Lieutenant Martín
  La pérdida de Filipinas, 62–4, 71, 83
  and *Los últimos de Filipinas*, 77, 96n7
Cervantes, Miguel de: *Don Quixote*, 289n22
change: historical, 5, 7–8, 15, 29, 30
Chaplin, Charlie, 232, 233
Chesterton, G. K., 285
Chien Andalou, Un, 192
child-centered films, 285n1
Chion, Michel, 141, 162, 166, 167, 168, 177n22
Christianity, 159, 164, 211, 246; *see also* Catholic Church
Cid, El, 160, 162
Cifesa (production company), 9–10, 19n20, 80
cine de cruzada 9, 24–5
cities
  and country compared, 107–8, 112, 135
  migration to, 105–6, 107, 116
  see also Madrid; Seville; Zaragoza
Citizen Kane, 17, 104, 106, 114, 115–16, 129
Clarín, 18n12
Cleinow, Marcel, 45
Code of the Spanish, 98n24
Colmeiro, José, 95n1, 96n12, 253n4
Colomer, Josep, 253n3
comedies, 10
Comisión Constitucional del Congreso, 258n39
commedia dell'arte, 207
communism, 154, 158, 159
community: and loss, 236–7
Compromís (Catalan political formation), 257n39
comunidad, La, 254n7
Connor, Steven, 167, 171, 172

conservatism, 172
Corral Rey, M. Nieves, 259n47
Corrales, Martín, 48
Costa, Joaquín, 61
counter-cinema, 254n13
Cristo, Angel, 252
Critchley, Simon, 217
Cronkite, Walter, 160
Cronos, 14
crucero Baleares, El, 39n6
Cua Lim, Bliss, 48, 50–1
Cuba, 150
Cuelgamuros valley *see* Valley of the Fallen
currency, 211
cursi/cursilería, 5–6

Dalí, Salvador, 186
Darío, Rubén: "Marcha triunfal," 80
Dark Habits, 14
Das Mortes, Antonio, 229
Daston, Lorraine, 51
de Man, Paul, 134, 136
death
  Dance of Death, 259n48
  fear of, 52
  fetishization of, 33–4, 36, 37, 91, 94
  glamorization of, 8, 26, 29, 30, 40n12, 55
  kitsch and, 8
  and mourning, 203, 204
  and narratability, 135
decadence, 61, 95n6, 182
Delegación Nacional de Prensa y Propaganda, 8–9
Deleuze, Gilles: *Cinema I*, 93, 101n46
democracy, 57, 98n23, 147; *see also* general election (1936)
Departamento Nacional de Cinematografía, 8, 58n10, 67, 98n22, 176n17
Derrida, Jacques, 204, 235, 236, 247, 249
Deseo, El (production company), 206
Devil's Backbone, The, 14
día de la bestia, El, 15
Diestro-Dópido, Mar, 283, 287n14, 290n31
D'Lugo, Marvin, 136n2
documentaries, 154
Dodds, Major F. L.: *Under the Red and Gold: Being Notes and Recollections of the Siege of Baler*, 62–3, 71–2, 83
Domínguez Búrdalo, José Manuel, 48, 50
Domínguez-Rodiño, Enrique, 44, 45; *see also Romancero marroquí*
Dorfles, Gillo, 2

dubbing, 11, 42, 43, 56
Durgnat, Raymond, 201n21

Eco, Umberto, 25, 28–9
Edwards, Gwynne, 190, 194, 200n10
Egea, Juan F.: *Dark Laughter*, 215–16
Eisenhower, General Dwight, 150
Eisenstein, Sergei Mikhailovich, 93
Eisner, Lotte, 35
Elena, Alberto, 57n2, 58n8, 59n14, 67
Emmer, C. E., 17n8
Eng, David L., 16, 205
Enlightenment, 40n16
Epstein, Jean, 101n46
Erice, Victor *see espíritu de la colmena, El*
Escrivá, Vicente: *Sin un adiós*, 257n33
Escuadrilla, 39n6
"españoladas," 19n21
Espasa Calpe (publishing house), 18n17
espíritu de la colmena, El (*The Spirit of the Beehive*), 285n1, 288n17
ETA (Basque separatist group), 238
Evans, Peter, 199nn1, 3, 4, 6, 200n7, 201n20, 202n24

fairy tales, 264, 265, 285
Falange
  anthem, 147, 153
  and artistic liberation, 119
  banner, 211
  displacement of, 98n24
  Falange Española, 4, 152
  and historical cinema, 9
  symbol, 6, *49*, 77
Fanck, Arnold and Itami, Mansaku: *The New Earth* [*Die Tochter des Samurai*], 43, 55–6
Fanés, Félix, 10, 19n23
fantasy, 4, 10, 11, 51
fascism
  aesthetic of, 43, 84
  birth of, 2
  and change, 7–8
  defascistization, 68
  "fascist moments," 8, 36
  and identity, 43
  and nostalgia, 6
  rise of, 152–3
  and Romanticism, 17n6
  and self, 8, 26, 73–4
  and speech, 171
Faulkner, Sally, 20n27, 137n5
Ferdinand VII, King, 273, 278

Fernández, Miguel Anxo, 44
Fernández Cuenca, Carlos, 9, 45
fetishes/fetishism, 31, 81–2, 88, 100n39, 124–5
  Freud on, 82, 100n40
Fiddian, Robin, 199n1, 200n7, 201n20, 202n24
film feerie, 283n2
film legislation, 43, 56
film noir, 102, 103, 117–19
Filmófono (production company), 38n3
First World War films, 70
Flaherty, Robert, 48
Foucault, Michel: *The Order of Things*, 37
Fraga Iribarne, Manuel, 3, 212
Franco, ese hombre, 141–74
  credits, 143, 210–11
  as a documentary, 141, 154–5, 157, 173
  Franco's appearance in, 155, 168–9, *170*, 171–2, 173–4
  as a history lesson, 150–2
  kitsch aesthetic, 173
  metaphor, 145, 147, 177n24
  military parades, 147–8, 149–50, 165
  narrative purpose, 142–3, 157, 164
  soundtrack, 143
  structure, 146
  time, 148
  ventriloquism, 142, 168–9, 171–2, 177n24
  voice-over, 141, 145, 147, 148–9, 150–1, 152, 158, 159–60, 165–8, 173–4
Franco, Francisco
  and Africa, 151
  appearance, 166
  in *Balada triste de trompeta*, 227–8
  birth, 149
  burial site, 239, 240, 241
  and Christianity, 246
  coup d'état by, 61, 62, 153, 154
  courage, 1
  critiques of, 102
  cruelty, 1
  death, 40n12, 57
  and fetishism, 81
  as a film subject, 8, 24; *see also Franco, ese hombre*; *Ya viene el cortejo*
  and filmmaking, 48; *see also* Andrade, Jaime de
  and hunting, 227
  images of, 80–1, 93, 101n48, *144*, *146*, *170*
  as kitsch-man, 38, 142

meeting with Hitler, 158–9, 164, 212, 220
as a messiah, 148, 156, 157, 160, 161, 162–3
military honors, 91
myth of, 141–2, 143, 148–9, 160–1, 165–6, 167, 168
and "organic democracy," 98n23
political ideology, 252
and postcards, 6
and *Raza*, 38, 141
and *Romancero marroquí*, 45, 50
and self, 8, 26, 74
and social justice, 164, 174n4
and Spanish Foreign Legion, 151–2
and Spanish history, 64
speeches, 42, 98n26
totalitarianism, 278
treatment of Republicans, 203
Francoism
and Catholic Church, 48, 79, 188
contradictions of, 43, 44, 56
critiques of, 105
definitions of, 17n5, 172–3
as "ersatz" fascism, 56
film portrayals of, 142, 168, 210
isolation of, 98n25
justification of, 204–5
kitsch aesthetic of, 233
legacy of, 256n29
and melancholy, 73
and *nacional-catolicismo*, 73
and politics of survival, 57
post-Second World War, 98n24
redemption rhetoric of, 240, 244, 250, 263
and revenge, 207, 211
siege metaphor of, 64
and Spanish character, 272
and time, 71, 76
Freud, Sigmund
on fetishes, 82, 100n40
and *Hamlet*, 217
Mourning and Melancholia, 75, 179, 188, 254n9
Friedländer, Saul, 2, 8, 16n2, 33–4, 40n13, 52

Gaite, Carmen Martín, 136n2
Ganivet, Ángel, 62
Garau Planas, Father Antonio, 105
García Escudero, José María, 105, 136n2
García Lorca, Federico, 203

García Viñolas, Manuel Augusto, 9
Garden of Eden, 223, 256n28
Garnett, Tay: *Bataan*, 69
Generación del 98, 62
general election (1936), 153
Genina, Augusto, 39n5, 58n4, 97n14
Gerricaechevarría, Jorge, 204
Giménez Caballero, Ernesto, 5
El cine y la cultura humana, 60
España y Franco, 81
Golomstock, Igor, 18n15
Gómez de la Serna, Ramón: "Lo Cursi," 4–7, 18n17, 52
González, Damiana, 258n44
González, Luis Mariano
Fascismo, kitsch y cine histórico español, 19n20, 99n31
"Francoist Spaces," 136n1, 137n8, 138nn10, 14
González Aja, Teresa, 70
Gordon, Avery, 234, 237, 254n5
Goya, Francisco de, 229
Desastres de la guerra, 37, 255n15
Duelo a garrotazos, 207–8, 235
Judith killing Holofernes painting, 278, 280
Saturn Devouring his Son, 16, 266, 273, 278
The Sleep of Reason Produces Monsters, 16, 273
Goya awards, 204
Graham, Helen, 258n42
Grierson, John, 154
Griffith, D. W., 93
Grimm Brothers, 264
grottoes, 226–7
Grünewald, Matthias: Crucifixion, 211
Gubern, Román, 24, 38n5, 39nn6, 7, 8

Halcón, Manuel, 24
Halpern, Jorge, 89
Hardcastle, Anne E., 41n19
¡Harka!, 45
haunting, 234
hauntology, 204, 247
Labanyi, Jo: "History and Hauntology," 253n5
Hayworth, Rita, 131
heroes, 286n4
Herzog, Werner: *Aguirre, the Wrath of God*, 65
Hispania Tobis (production company), 44

Hispanidad, 19n21, 123
   concept of, 87
   Consejo de la Hispanidad, 24
   peasants and, 3, 120, 138n13
   in *Raza*, 94
   in *Surcos*, 128–9
   in *últimos de Filipinas, Los*, 60, 85
Hispano-Film-Produktion, 57n4
historical cinema, 9, 10
historical memory, xii, 217, 219
   Law of Historical Memory (2007), 258nn39, 41
Hitchcock, Alfred
   Birds, The, 120
   Lifeboat, 69, 245
   North by Northwest, 208, 245, 247, 256n30
   Vertigo, 207, 208, 215, 245
Hite, Katherine, 240
Hitler, Adolf
   and anti-Semitism, 18n13
   and Franco, 154, 158–9, 164, 212, 220
   and kitsch, 6
   suicide of, 57
   in *Triumph des Willens* [*Triumph of the Will*], 148
Hollywood, 11, 56, 80
Holocaust (TV series), 286n8
Hopewell, John, 104
Hughes, Robert, 278

Ibarz, Mercè: "Entró en mi cuarto un toro negro: la historia en el cine de Buñuel," 201nn17, 19
identity, 10, 43, 73
Iglesia, Álex de la
   aesthetics, 206–7
   on *Balada triste de trompeta*, 228
   and counter-cinema, 254n13
   political views, 238
   see also Acción mutante; *Balada triste de trompeta*; *comunidad, La*; *día de la bestia, El*
Iglesias, Pablo: *Machiavelo frente a la gran pantalla*, 254n6
imperialism, 88
indoctrination, 11
irony, 206, 207
Itami, Mansaku *see* Fanck, Arnold and Itami, Mansaku

James, St, 189
Japan, 8, 36, 40n18, 43, 57

Jones, Doug, 291n38
Jordan, Barry and Morgan-Tamosunas, Rikki: *Contemporary Spanish Cinema*, 19n21
Juan, Pedro de, 95n3
Juan Carlos, Prince (later King), 153

Kafka, Franz: *The Trial*, 60
Kahana, Jonathan, 165
Kazanjian, David, 16, 205, 206
Keller, Patricia, 239, 248–9, 260n53
Kermode, Frank, 100n32
Killers, The, 119
Kinder, Marsha, 34, 39n9, 68, 98n25, 102, 118, 137n5
Kirby, Lynne, 138n11
kitsch
   aesthetic of, 23–4, 35–6, 49, 65, 74, 82, 83–4, 107, 128, 134, 136, 173, 186, 204
   common, 34, 52
   definitions of, 1–2, 3–4, 17n9
   and emotions, 2, 11, 30
   essence of, 53
   function of, 11
   pseudo-official, 208
   as a refuge, 52
   totalitarian, 29
   unmaking of, 12
   uplifting, 34, 52
kitsch-man: definition, 18n18
Kjellman-Chapin, Monica, 17n8
Klein, Norman, 12
Klemperer, Victor: *The Language of the Third Reich*, 18n12
Koepnick, Lutz, 10, 43
Koestler, Arthur, 99n32
Kuleshov effect, 124
Kulka, Tomas, 97n16
Kundera, Milan: *The Unbearable Lightness of Being*, 1–2, 4, 17n9, 24, 29
Kyd, Thomas: *The Spanish Tragedy*, 255n34

Labanyi, Jo: "History and Hauntology," 210, 213, 253n5
Laclau, Ernesto, 56
Lacoue-Labarth, Phillip, 8
Law of Historical Memory (2007), 258nn39, 41
legislation
   Code of the Spanish, 98n24
   film, 43–4, 56

Law of Historical Memory (2007), 258nn39, 41
Succession Law, 98n24, 172
Leonardo da Vinci: *The Last Supper*, 183
Lifeboat, 69, 245
Llanos, Father José María, 212
Llorente, Ángel: *Arte e ideología del Franquismo*, 98n24
Llovet, Enrique, 95n3, 100n35
López Rodó, Laureano, 180
Loureiro, Angel, 95nn5, 6
Lumière brothers, 108, 109
Lute, El, 226
Lynch, David: *Mulholland Drive*, 287n14

Madrid
  in *Balada triste de trompeta*, 208–9
  Palacio de El Pardo, 168, 174
  Plaza de Oriente, 159
  in *Surcos*, 103, 112, 118, 138n14
  traumatic past of, 147
Maeztu, Ramiro de, 60, 87
Maginot, General André, 175n7
Maistre, Joseph de, 26
Manet, Edouard, 3
Manovich, Lev: *The Language of New Media*, 102
Maravall, José Antonio: *Culture of the Baroque: Analysis of a Historical Structure*, 15
Marcelino, pan y vino, 11, 14
Mark, St, 209–10, 211, 224, 243, 245
Marsh, Steven, 19n22, 20n27
Martialay, Félix, 58n6
Marxism, 153
mass-media, 3
Matador, 14, 240, 244, 249, 252
Mayne, Judith: *Cinema and Spectatorship*, 11
Medina, Alberto, 73, 96n9
melancholia, 7, 12, 14, 15, 16, 75, 188, 203
Méliès, Georges, 285n2
melodrama, 10, 132
Menéndez Pelayo, Marcelino, 77
Mérimée, Prosper: *Carmen*, 3
metaphor
  Foucault on, 37
  Franco, ese hombre, 145, 147, 177n24
  Francoist historiography, 64
  Giralda tower, Seville, 47
  and language, 136
  Pan's Labyrinth, 279
  Raza, 30, 32, 38, 193

Romancero marroquí, 53, 55
Surcos, 107, 134
and symbolism, 77
últimos de Filipinas, Los, 64, 68, 73
Viridiana, 12, 180, 188
Metz, Christian, 82
Millán Astray, General José, 48, 175n5, 211–12, 213
Ministerio de Información y Turismo, 142
Minow, Martha, 236, 239, 249, 259n51
Mitchell, W. J. T., 88
modernity, 52, 55, 212
Moen, Kristian, 285n2
Molino, Sergio del, 139n21
  La España vacía: viaje por un país que nunca fue, 137n9
monarchy, 153, 172; *see also* Alfonso XIII, King; Juan Carlos, Prince
Monsiváis, Carlos: "The Neobaroque and Popular Culture," 20n33
Montes, Eugenio, 106, 107, 108
Moreiras-Menor, Cristina, 21n34, 41n20, 200n13, 254n7
Morgan-Tamosunas, Rikki *see* Jordan, Barry and Morgan-Tamosunas, Rikki
Morocco
  Alta Comisaría de España en Marruecos, 44
  and fascism, 47, 55
  and Francoism, 45–6
  as an ideological fantasy, 51
  Partido de la Unidad Marroquí, 57n2
  propaganda, 57n2
  Second World War, 159
  Spanish filmmaking in, 47–8; *see also Romancero marroquí*
  Spanish Foreign Legion in, 151–2
  Al-Wahda al-Maghribya (newspaper), 57n2
mourning
  Freud, Sigmund: *Mourning and Melancholia*, 75, 179, 188, 254n9
  and ghosts, 205
  politics of, 204–5
Muertos de Risa, 255n20
Mulholland Drive, 287n14
Mulvey, Laura
  on *Citizen Kane*, 115–16, 138n17, 139nn18, 19
  Death 24x a Second, 132, 133, 135
  "Some Thoughts on Theories of Fetishism in the Context of Contemporary Culture," 82

Mulvey, Laura (*cont.*)
  "Visual Pleasure and Narrative Cinema," 31, 123, 137n7
Murray, Timothy, 21n35
musicals, 9
Muslims, 42, 48, 50
Mussolini, Benito, 18n15, 57, 127, 154
mute characters, 167
myths, 2, 19n21

Nabokov, Vladimir, 3
names, 87, 189, 214, 240, 267, 274, 282
Nancy, Jean-Luc, 8
National Film Library, 136n1
National Movement: Principles (*Los principios del Movimiento Nacional*), 180
nationalism, 238
Nazis, 35, 43
Ndalianis, Angela, 15
Neo-baroque, 12, 14, 15, 16, 206
Neocleous, Mark, 52, 101n42, 147–8, 174n1
New Earth, The [*Die Tochter des Samurai*], 43
New Spanish Cinema, 136n2
New York World Fair (1964), 155, 157, 161
Ngai, Sianne, 17n4
Nichols, Bill, 155, 164–5
Nietzsche, Friedrich, 17n6
Nieves Conde, José Antonio, 102, 120, 139nn23, 24; *see also* Surcos
Nordström, Folke, 289n27, 290n35
North by Northwest, 208, 245, 247, 256n30
Noticiario Español, 176n17
Novalis (German poet), 261

Odyssey, The, 174, 193
Olalquiaga, Celeste, 55, 128
Oliveira Salazar, António, 176n16
Opus Dei (religious group), 180, 255n17
Oran (Algeria), 159
Orduña, Juan de, 24
Orientalism, 3, 83, 84
Ortega y Gasset, José, 56, 138n14
Out of the Past, 119

Pacheco Bejarano, Juan Pablo, 255n19
Pacto del Olvido (Pact of Forgetting), 203–4, 210, 233, 247
Palacio Atard, Vicente, 77

Pan's Labyrinth, 261–85, *264, 267, 272, 275, 277, 281, 283, 284*
  allegory, 265, 278, 279, 280, 283
  bull motif, 190
  circularity, 282
  death, 262, 263–4, 269, 273, 279, 281–2
  ethics, 262
  as a fairy tale, 261, 263, 264, 265–6, 267, 268, 274, 276, 285
  influences, 188
  labyrinth, 240–1, 263, 269–71, 279, 280–1, 282, 283, 284
  metaphor, 279
  morality, 266, 269, 277–8, 281, 282, 284
  mournful melancholy, 14, 16, 273, 279
  opening sequence, 267–8
  and reality, 265, 268, 270, 276, 283–4
  soundtrack, 267
  storylines, 263
  symbolism, 270, 279, 284, 285, 288n20
  time, 279, 280, 283
  visual references, 266, 273–5, 276, 279, 283, 284
pantomime, 254n12
Pardo Bazán, Emilia: *Los Pazos de Ulloa* [*The House of Ulloa*], 182
Park, Katherine, 51
Partido Popular (PP), 254n8, 258n39
Partido Socialista Obrero Español (PSOE), 258n39
paso doble, 272
Paxton, Robert, 5
Pazos de Ulloa, Los [*The House of Ulloa*], 182
peasants, 3, 49, 120, 138n13
  Romancero marroquí, 42, 44, 49
Pelzer, Peter, 100n36
Pensky, Max, 291n39
Pérez Galdós, Benito, 18n12
Perrault, Charles
  "Bluebeard," 212, 220
  "Little Red Riding Hood," 287n10
Philippines
  colonial status, 87, 91, 150
  siege of Baler, 61, 62–3, 64, 65, 72
  Spain's loss of (1898), 61, 98n25
  women as allegory of, 85
  see also últimos de Filipinas, Los
photography, 140n26, 204
Picasso, Pablo
  Guernica, 37
  Minotauromachia, 279
Picazo, Ángel, 149, 166–7, 168

Plantinga, Carl R., 141, 154, 164, 165
pop culture, 212
Popular Front, 153
Porque te vi llorar, 39n6
Portugal, 150
Prado, Ignacio, 19n19, 24
Preston, Paul, 38, 211
Primer Plano (journal), 67
Primo de Rivera, José Antonio, 4, 23, 142, 240
Primo de Rivera, General Miguel, 62, 175n7
prisoners of war, 258n43
propaganda
 communist, 121
 Delegación Nacional de Prensa y Propaganda, 8–9
 fascist, 43, 143
 Francoist, 8, 10, 81, 101n48, 105–6
 Morocco, 57n2
Propp, Vladimir, 266, 286n4
Pupavac, Vanessa, 257n36
puppet theatre
 Citizen Kane, 129
 Paisà, 139n24
 Surcos, 106, 116, 122–3, 124, 125, *125*, 126, 129, 131–2

¿Qué he hecho yo para merecer esto! 14

Rabal, Francisco, 199n6
Raphael (singer and actor), 235, 241–2
 Balada triste de trompeta ["A Sad Trumpet Ballad"], 224, 226, 231–2, 233–4, 236, 249
Raza, 23–38, *27*
 children, 25, 27–8, 29, 84
 close-up shots, 91–2, *92*, 93, 94
 cross icon, 32, 33, 34, *35*
 death, 8, 29, 30, 33–4, 36
 emotions, 34
 fascist kitsch aesthetics in, 3, 23–4, 29, 35, 173–4
 goals, 38n4
 inserts, 25
 locations, 38n2
 message, 37
 metaphor, 30, 32, 38, 193
 mortuary portrait, 30–1, *31*
 romería, 29
 screenplay, 74
 shadows, 31, 32, 33
 signifiers, 4, 29, 30, 31, 32–3

soundtrack, 149
Soviet influence on, 39nn7, 9
Spanish flag symbolism, 28, 29, 93–4
style, 29, 32, 39n8
tears, 28, 29, 30, 92
themes, 25–6
uplifting kitsch, 34
Reagan, Ronald, 212
regenerationism, 61
religious cinema, 9
Republicans
 in *Balada triste de trompeta*, 209
 flag, 218
 Franco's treatment of, 203, 205, 250
 and memory, 204
 in *Romancero marroquí*, 50
revenge plays, 235, 255n34
Rey, Fernando, 199n3
Richards, Michael: *A Time of Silence*, 138n13
Richardson, Carl, 119
Richardson, Nathan E., 137n6
Riefenstahl, Leni: *Triumph des Willens* [*Triumph of the Will*], 148
Rivel, Charlie, 253
Rivero Franco, Marta, 255n15
Robles, Gil, 152
Rodríguez Tranche, Rafael, 176n17
Román, Antonio
 Raza screenplay, 74
 and *Romancero marroquí*, 45
 and *últimos de Filipinas, Los*, 65–6; *see also* separate entry
Romancero marroquí, 42–57
 children, 55
 colony/metropolis fusion, 50–1
 credits, 47
 criticisms, 45
 death, 8
 dedication to Franco, 50
 dubbing, 42
 emotions, 52
 as fantasy, 46, 48–9
 fascist symbolism, 47
 German release, 58n9
 ideology, 44
 influences, 48
 metaphor, 53, 55
 Morocco's rejection of, 55–6
 musical score, 45, 46
 narrative, 52–3, 55
 natural environment of, 53, *53*
 opening still, *49*, 49–50

Romancero marroquí (cont.)
  peasants, 42, 44, 49
  propaganda, 10
  religious iconography, 42
  representation of Moroccans/Morocco, 46, 50, *51*, 54, 55
  soundtrack, 79
  Spanish release, 45
  time, 7, 46, 52
  voice-over, 45, 47, 49, 50, 54
Romanticism, 17n6
Roots (TV series), 286n8
Rose, Jacqueline, 19n26
Rossellini, Roberto
  Europa 51, 137n5
  Germania Anno Zero, 111
  Paisà, 97n18, 111, 137n5, 138n16, 139n24
  Viaggio in Italia, 107

Sáenz de Heredia, José Luis, 142–3, 162, *163*
  and *Franco, ese hombre*, 141, 150, 154, 155–8, *155*, 168–9, *170*, 173
  and *Raza*, 23, 24
Sáenz de Tejada, Carlos, 39n8, 102
  "Traerán prendidas cinco rosas," 6
Sáinz Rodríguez, Pedro, 141, 177n20
Sánchez Albornoz, Nicolás, 240
Sánchez-Biosca, Vicente, 175n6, 178n26, 201n16
Sánchez Campoy, Rafael *see* Barcones, Enrique Alfonso and Sánchez Campoy, Rafael
Sánchez Mazas, Rafael, 76–7
Sánchez Silva, José, 142
Sánchez Vidal, Agustín, 190
Santiago de Compostela, 30, 46, 201n15
Sarduy, Severo, 20n30, 206
Sargent, John Singer, 3
Saz Campos, Ismael, 17n5
Schivelbusch, Wolfgang: *Railway Journey*, 138n12
Schrader, Paul, 118
Schultze, Norbert, 45
Searchers, The, 174
Second World War, 151, 158–9
siege films, 68–9; *see also últimos de Filipinas, Los*
Sellers, Peter, 172
Semprún, Jorge, 4, 152
Serrano Suñer, Ramón, 9, 159, 167
Seville: Giralda tower, 47

Shakespeare, William: *Hamlet*, 207, 217, 224, 235, 243, 253
Shevel, Oxana, 253n2
Sin un adiós [Without a Goodbye], 233, 257n33
Sindicato Nacional del Espectáculo, 67
"Snow White," 281–2; *see also Blancanieves*
Sontag, Susan
  "Fascinating Fascism," 16n2
  Under the Sign of Saturn, 40n13, 286n3
Sophocles: *Antigone*, 203
Sor Citroën, 14
Sorel, Georges, 17n6
Soviet cinema, 39nn7, 9
space: and time, 65, 69–70, 73, 84
Spanish Civil War
  atrocities, 37
  Balada triste de trompeta as a critique of, 208
  cinema of *see cine de cruzada*
  de-politicization of, 162
  Desfile de la Victoria, 92
  footage, 155–6, 157–8
  Franco's treatment of Republicans, 203
  ideological hegemony, 42
  justification of, 24
  memorial *see* Valley of the Fallen
  siege of Toledo, 97n14
Spanish Empire, 150
Spanish flag, 28, 47, 93–4, 246, 250
Spanish Foreign Legion, 48, 147, 151–2
Spanish transition, 206
Spanish–American War, 25, 28, 60, 61, 67
Spanishness *see Hispanidad*
Stabilization Plan (*Plan de estabilización*), 180
Stalin, Joseph, 151, 152, 153, 158
Steimatsky, Noa, 138n16
Steiner, George, 254n10, 256n26, 259nn48, 49, 260n56
Sternberg, Josef von, 93
Stone, Rob, 117–18
Storey, Robert F.: *Pierrot: A Critical History of a Mask*, 260n55
strikes: miners' (Asturias, 1917), 164, 174n4, 175n10
Surcos [Furrows], 102–36, *110*, *113*, *115*, *119*, *125*, *126*, *130*, *131*, *133*
  bullfighting symbolism, 124
  children, 110–11, 112, 114–15, 120–1
  close-up shots, 124
  as a critique of Francoism, 105

death, 134–6
emotions, 113, 124, 127
female characters, 124
as film noir, 102, 117, 118, 122, 132, 134
García Escudero's support of, 105
Hispanidad, 123, 128–9
ideology, 103, 104
indexical nature of, 132–5, 137n7
influences, 103, 104, 106, 107, 114, 121, 137n5
Madrid, 103, 112, 118, 138n14
masculinity, 117, 119, 120, 121, 122, 128
melodrama, 102
metaphor, 107, 134
misogyny, 106, 116–17, 119, 122, 126, 127, 129
morality, 103–4
musical leitmotif, 112, 113, 121, 122
naturalism, 136n3
neorealism, 102, 103, 104, 105, 109, 111, 113–14, 137nn3, 4
and New Spanish Cinema, 136n2
Oedipal dynamics, 116
origin, 106
patriarchy, 104, 106, 109, 125, 127
premier, 136n1
as propaganda, 105–6
and puppet theatre, 106, 116, 122–3, 124, 125, 126, 129–30, 131–2
rural and urban contrasted, 107–8, 113, 122
script, 106
social class, 137n6
and social truth, 119–20
soundtrack, 121
space, 127–8
style, 105
theme, 104, 114, 117
symbolism, 28–9
Falangist, 6, *49*, 77
Spanish flag, 28, 47, 93–4, 246
Viridiana, 182, 183, 185, 191–2

Tansman, Alan, 8, 36, 40n18, 257nn35, 37
tears, xii–xiii, 1
television, 212, 214, 286n8
temporality, 7, 76–7, 225, 247, 248–9; *see also* time
Teruel, battle of, 163
time
and hauntology, 204
politics of, 46, 50–1, 52
under siege, 65, 69
see also temporality
Times, The (London), 153
Tolentino, Roland, 68
Toro, Guillermo del *see Pan's Labyrinth*
Torrente Ballester, Gonzalo, 106
Torres, Ricardo, 45
tourism, 212
Ministerio de Información y Turismo, 142
"Spain is different" slogan, 3, 13
trains, 107, 108
Tranche, Rafael, 80, 101n48
Trauerspiel, 206, 254n12, 256n26, 260n56
trauma, 286n8
Treglown, Jeremy, 239
Franco's Crypt, 177n24
Tremlett, Giles, 240, 258n43
Triana-Toribio, Nuria, 57n3, 64; *see also* Buse, Peter, Triana-Toribio, Núria and Willis, Andy
Twentieth Century, The (American series), 160

últimos de Filipinas, Los [*Last Stand in the Philippines*], 60–95, *79*, *86*, *90*, *92*
church of Baler, 60, 61, 62, 63, 65, 67, 69, 70, 71–2, *72*, 73, 75, 76, 77–81, 82, 89
close-up shots, 93, 94
context of, 67–8
death, 8
dialogue, 67
double message of, 68
emotions, 83, 84, 85, 89–90
fascist aesthetic, 83–4
fetish, 82, 83, 88
heroism, 91
and *Hispanidad*, 60, 85
identity, 73
influences, 69
kitsch aesthetic, 83–4
melancholia, 75
metaphor, 64, 68, 73
nostalgia, 72, 75, 95n1
plot, 61
political myth, 61
popularity, 11
praise for, 67
release, 96nn10,11
as a siege film, 65–6, 68, 70, 71, 83, 88–9
self-consciousness, 82–3
soundtrack, 79, 89–90
sources, 95n3

últimos de Filipinas, Los (*cont.*)
  temporality, 7, 76–7
  tensions, 96n12
  time and space, 65, 69–70, 73, 84
  voice-over, 70
Unamuno, Miguel de: *La Tía Tula*, 253n1
United States, 68, 212; *see also* American Revolution; New York World Fair; Spanish–American War

Valis, Nöel, 18n12
Valle, Adriano del, 67
Valle Inclán, Ramón del, 207, 229
  Romance de lobos, 182
Valley of the Fallen, 205, 208, 211, 213, 214, 226, 227, 239–40, *239*, 243, 244, 247
Varderi, Alejandro, 18n14, 20n30
Vázquez Montalbán, Manuel, 172
Velo, Carlos, 42, 44–5
Verdiana, St, 181, 201n15, 202n25
Vernant, Jean Pierre, 282
Vertigo, 207, 208, 212, 215, 217, 245
Vieira, Patricia, 176n16
Virgen de la Barca, 26, 30, 32, 179
Viridiana, 179–99, *185*, *186*, *187*, *192*, *194*, *197*, *198*
  as an allegory, 187, 198
  bull motif, 190
  censorship of, 185
  characterization, 186–7
  as a critique of charity, 195–6
  decadence, 182
  desire, 188
  fetishism, 189–90, 192–3
  and Francoist ideology, 186
  Franco's reaction to, 199
  and Leonardo's *The Last Supper*, 183–4
  melancholy, 188–9
  metaphor, 12, 180, 188
  modernity, 182–3, 185, 198
  narrative, 180, 181
  parody, 194

  phallus motif, 190, 196–7, 201n18
  and reality, 266
  sacrilege, 183–4, *184*
  social class, 182, 183
  soundtrack, 184, 191, 197
  suicide, 181, 185, 188, 189, 195
  symbolism, 182, 183, 185, 191–2, 194–5, 197–8
  voyeurism, 190–1
Viscarri, Dionisio, 58n12

war crimes, 243–4
war films, 38n5; *see also cine de cruzada*
Warner, Marina, 264, 265, 286nn5, 6
Webster, Jamieson, 217
Welles, Orson *see Citizen Kane*
Willis, Andy *see* Buse, Peter, Triana-Toribio, Núria and Willis, Andy
Wizard of Oz, The, 169
Wollen, Peter, 78
  Paris Hollywood: Writings on Film, 100n34
women
  abuse of, 213, 216, 225
  as allegory of Philippines, 85
  colonial and Spanish, 88
  and misogyny, 106, 116–17, 119, 122, 126, 127, 129
Wood, Robin, 259n50
Wright, Craig, 270, 289n23
Wright, Sarah: *The Child in Spanish Cinema*, 285n1

Yarza, Alejandro: *Un caníbal en Madrid: la sensibilidad camp y el reciclaje de la historia en el cine de Pedro Almodóvar*, 20n29

Zaragoza, 175n7, 176n16
Zaro, Natividad, 106
Zipes, Jack, 287n16, 292n43
Žižek, Slavoj, 17n7
Zunzunegui, Santos, 100n38, 101n47

EU representative:
Easy Access System Europe
Mustamäe tee 50, 10621 Tallinn, Estonia
Gpsr.requests@easproject.com